Reclaiming Reality

Vincent Bugliosi AND THE Dallas Conspiracy

Gregory Donges

Published by:
Trine Day LLC
PO Box 577
Walterville, OR 97489
1-800-556-2012
www.TrineDay.com
trineday@icloud.com

Library of Congress Control Number: 2021944752

Donges, Gregory S.
Reclaiming Reality—1st ed.
p. cm.
Epub (ISBN-13) 978-1-63424-379-7
Print (ISBN-13) 978-1-63424-378-0
1. Kennedy, John F. -- (John Fitzgerald), -- 1917-1963 -- Assassination 2. Bugliosi, Vincent -- 1934-2015 -- Reclaiming history. 3. Conspiracies -- United States. 4. Oswald, Lee Harvey -- 1939-1963. I. Title

First Edition
10 9 8 7 6 5 4 3 2 1

Printed in the USA
Distribution to the Trade by:
Independent Publishers Group (IPG)
814 North Franklin Street
Chicago, Illinois 60610
312.337.0747
www.ipgbook.com

Contents

Abbreviations

ARRB = Assassination Records Review Board

CD = [Warren] Commission Document

CE = [Warren] Commission Exhibit

DPD = Dallas Police Department

HSCA = House Select Committee on Assassinations; a notation such as 4HSCA35 refers to Volume 4, page 35, of the HSCA Appendix Volumes.

WCT = Warren Commission Testimony. An annotation such as 17H123 indicates volume 17, page 123, of the Warren Commission Hearings and Exhibits.

References to the Warren Report are based on the version of the Warren Report that can be found at maryferrell.org.

References to endnotes refer to such notes on the compact disc that accompanies Mr. Bugliosi's book.

Emphasis (italicized words and phrases) in quoted passages is that of the person or document quoted, except as otherwise noted.

Introduction

I have been an admirer of Vincent Bugliosi (1934-2015) for a long time, not just because of his successful prosecution of the Manson family and other courtroom victories, but also because of all those good books he has written. But when I heard that he had written a book that was essentially an expression of support of the Warren Commission and their Report, I could hardly believe my ears. I was similarly shocked to see him on television, stating that he was absolutely sure that Lee Harvey Oswald was the lone assassin of President Kennedy. Apparently Mr. Bugliosi is unaware of, or has chosen to ignore, the roughly five decades of research establishing that the Warren Report is a colossal hoax, and a cover-up, and that Lee Oswald certainly did not kill President Kennedy (or Officer J.D. Tippit). Dr. James H. Fetzer characterized the Warren Report as "surely the greatest fraud ever perpetrated on the American people."[1] So I obtained a copy of Mr. Bugliosi's book, *Reclaiming History: The Assassination of President John F. Kennedy* from my local library (I certainly wouldn't buy it!), to find out where he went wrong. And I decided that I had to write my own book, to review the facts (as they are known up to the present) and to reclaim the truth, to reclaim reality.

In his introduction, Mr. Bugliosi tells us that over 95 percent of the books on the case are pro-conspiracy and anti-Warren Commission, so, in Bugliosi's view; there is a need for "far more books on the other side to give a much better balance to the debate."[2] This, in itself, is a rather absurd statement. We already have the 880-page Warren Report itself (including footnotes), the accompanying twenty-six volumes of Warren Commission Hearings and Exhibits, the final report of the House Select Committee on Assassinations and its twelve Appendix Volumes (and other background documents), the small handful of books written mostly by people associated with the official investigations, and now Bugliosi's tome, with its 1512 pages of text, along with 950 pages of endnotes (and 170 pages of "source notes") on a compact disc that accompanies his book, all of which support the "Official Story" of the assassination of President Kennedy (although the HSCA concluded that JFK was probably assassinated as a result of a conspiracy). And we nevertheless need far more books? There is a reason why only five percent of the books on the case support the Official Story and that is because the Official Story is hogwash. In any case, it really isn't much of a debate; those of us on the 95 percent side merely point out the weaknesses in and phony nature of the Warren Report and the autopsy materials, the behavior of the key actors, and other aspects of the Official Story about what happened in Dallas in November of 1963. Bugliosi refers to people like Thomas Buchanan, Joachim Joesten, Mark Lane and Harold Weisberg who don't accept the Official Story as "leftist" authors. Bugliosi tells us twice (on pages 353 and 990) that Thomas Buchanan, author of *Who Killed Kennedy?* was an "American Communist expatriate," and reminds us on page 1265 that Buchanan was a "leftist." And Bugliosi quotes from the *Congressional Record* to tell us that Lane had been affiliated with two "cited Communist front" organizations, and that Weisberg had a "known association with agents of the Soviet Union."[3]

Apparently these authors are "leftist" because they do not passively, mindlessly accept the conclusions of the Warren Report, as Mr. Bugliosi has done, nor do they have unlimited respect for and admiration of federal government institutions such as the FBI and CIA. A quick and convenient way of impugning someone's character (and words) during the Cold War was to call someone a communist or communist sympathizer; apparently Mr. Bugliosi is stuck in that era. He states that if the alleged conspirators were so clever, they would have picked a patsy whose marksmanship was beyond question, and they wouldn't have set the patsy up with a nineteen-dollar mail-order rifle.[4] Mr. Bugliosi should have been able to discern that the fingerprints of the Secret Service, the FBI, the CIA, the Pentagon, and certain key individuals were all over the assassination of President Kennedy and the official cover-up. In his stubborn fixation on Oswald and his refusal to consider a conspiracy, Bugliosi was apparently blind to the fact that Oswald's "guilt" was based mainly on a demonstrably false link between the murder weapon, or rather the Mannlicher-Carcano rifle that was displayed to reporters in the Dallas police headquarters and thereby became an official Commission Exhibit, and the carefully and artificially created patsy who conveniently worked in the kill zone, and blind to the fact that the public persona of the supposed lone nut assassin as a "communist defector," promulgated by the Warren Report, was also contrived in order to make the supposed lone nut assassin look even more sinister and unpatriotic.

Bugliosi also believes that the Warren Report must be valid because President Lyndon Johnson would not select a group of reputable people to write a disreputable report (the Warren Report), and he would not be stupid enough to appoint honest men to carry out a dishonest mission.[5] He tells us that it's preposterous that "such distinguished Americans" as the Warren Commissioners, "people of impeccable honor and reputation," would give the killers of President Kennedy a "free pass" in the murder of the president of the United States.[6] This is called specious reasoning – having the ring of truth but actually fallacious. It is like saying, "Mr. Jones couldn't have killed his wife because he surely loved her; he wouldn't have married her otherwise. And he wouldn't kill someone he loved."

Not all of the Warren Commissioners were particularly reputable. Let's start with Commissioner Allen Dulles. David Talbot's 2015 book *The Devil's Chessboard: Allen Dulles, the CIA, and the Rise of America's Secret Government* contains several examples of Dulles' suppressing information coming out of Germany regarding the extermination of European Jews when Dulles was in the OSS (the Office of Strategic Services, forerunner of the CIA). Dulles also helped make it possible for "a number of Europe's most notorious war criminals" to escape justice.[7] He masterminded a successful operation to rescue Nazi SS general Karl Wolff, chief of all SS and Gestapo units in Italy, from a villa in the foothills of the Italian Alps. Tim Weiner referred to Dulles as "a duplicitous man, a chronic adulterer, ruthlessly ambitious. He was not above misleading Congress or even his commander in chief," nor was he above planting stories in the press.[8]

Allen Dulles had little or no experience in investigating assassinations, but plenty of experience in planning them. With his oversight of CIA assassination plots against Fidel Castro, Patrice Lumumba, Rafael Trujillo and Abd al-Karim Qasim, Dulles had already been an accessory to murder. And Dulles had lots of experience in the overthrow of governments (or attempting to do so), including that of Mohammed Mossadegh in Iran in 1953, and that of Jacobo Árbenz Guzmán in Guatemala in 1954. Dulles' Guatemala crew was made up of CIA personnel some of whom would later be allegedly linked to the JFK assassination: Richard Bissell Jr., Tracy Barnes, E. Howard Hunt, David Atlee Phillips and David Morales.[9] In the mid-1950s, Dulles' CIA worked with Winston Churchill's government to try to prevent the re-election of Prime Minister Cheddi Jagan of British Guiana (now Guyana), who had been democratically elected in 1953. (The effort failed.) It is now evident that the CIA worked with Chinese

Nationalists in April 1955 to plant the time bomb that brought down an Air India passenger plane on which Chinese premier Zhou Enlai was scheduled to fly to a conference of nonaligned leaders that was convening at Bandung, Indonesia.[10] Also in 1955, Dulles' CIA tried to overthrow President Syngman Rhee in South Korea and President José Figueres in Costa Rica.

In 1956, Dulles' CIA played a major role in Project OMEGA, intended to overthrow the pro-Nasser government of Syria.[11] The CIA's plans for the overthrow of the Syrian government in 1957 included the assassination of Abdul Hamid Serraj, the longtime chief of the Syrian intelligence service, and the head of the Communist Party.[12] (The coup failed.) There is evidence that in the spring of 1957, Allen and his brother, Secretary of State John Foster Dulles, directed Kermit Roosevelt to work with the British to bring down Egypt's President Gamal Abdel Nasser, who had nationalized the Suez Canal the previous year.[13] In 1957-58, the CIA supported rebel colonels in the Celebes in an unsuccessful attempt to overthrow Indonesian president Sukarno. In 1958, Muslim nationalists and communists revealed that the CIA had rigged Lebanon's presidential elections in favor of the Christian Maronite candidate, Camille Chamoun.[14]

In 1959, the CIA hired 22-year-old Saddam Hussein to assassinate Iraqi Prime Minister General Abd al-Karim Qasim.[15] (Qasim's own countrymen executed him by firing squad on live TV on February 8, 1963.) In Laos in 1959-60, CIA-backed coups toppled the governments of Prince Souvanna Phouma and Phoui Sananikone, and in April 1960, the Agency helped to rig an election for Sananikone's successor, General Phoumi Nosavan. And it is now common knowledge that Dulles' CIA enlisted members of the American Mafia in efforts to assassinate Cuban president Fidel Castro, from 1960 through 1965. In Ecuador, starting in 1960, the CIA infiltrated political organizations of the far left and far right, and would "bomb churches or right-wing organizations and make it appear to be the work of leftists."[16] In August 1960, Allen Dulles sent master chemist Dr. Sidney Gottlieb, head of the CIA's Technical Services Division, to the Democratic Republic of the Congo with lethal toxins for use against Patrice Lumumba, the democratically elected Congolese prime minister. The packet of poisons was passed to Lawrence "Larry" Devlin, the CIA station chief in Leopoldville (now Kinshasa), the Congolese capital. Devlin thought the Lumumba poison scheme was a bad idea, and locked the poisons in his office safe.[17] Nevertheless, according to CIA veteran Ralph McGehee, the Agency worked with the African dissidents who murdered Lumumba on January 17, 1961.[18] In May 1961, shortly after the Bay of Pigs debacle, Allen Dulles sent an all-station cable to CIA personnel that communicated the idea that the Bay of Pigs invasion failed because of Kennedy's failure of nerve.[19] The CIA provided dissidents in the Dominican Republic with three pistols (smuggled into the country via diplomatic pouch, in violation of international protocols) and three carbines in order to facilitate the assassination of Dominican president Rafael Trujillo Molina. Trujillo was assassinated at the end of May, though the Church Committee was unable to determine whether or not the weapons provided by the Agency were those used in the assassination. Also in 1961, the CIA conducted operations to bring down the regime of President José María Velasco Ibarra of Ecuador after he refused to sever diplomatic relations with Cuba. All of these operations were under the leadership of Allen Dulles, though some, like the actions against Mossadegh, Figueres and Árbenz, were apparently approved by President Dwight Eisenhower.

As for John J. McCloy: yes, he had an impressive résumé. He had been assistant secretary of war (1941-45), president of the World Bank (1947-49), and US High Commissioner for West Germany and Military Governor of the American zone (1949-52). McCloy was a partner in Millbank, Tweed, a law firm close to the Rockefellers. McCloy became chairman of the Rockefeller-dominated Chase National Bank in 1953, and in 1955 handled its merger with the Bank of the Manhattan Company, staying on as chairman of the new Chase Manhattan Bank until 1961. McCloy was tied in with the New York legal, financial and banking elite, including Rockefeller interests, Big Oil and the Council on Foreign Relations (he was chairman of the CFR at the time of the assassination). In 1963, McCloy was also chairman of the Ford Foundation and a director of United Fruit, American Telephone & Telegraph, Allied Chemical, Westinghouse Electric and Metropolitan Life. Talbot referred to McCloy, who was President Eisenhower's national security adviser, as "the very personification of the power elite."[20] He was President Kennedy's chief disarmament adviser and negotiator until he left the government in October 1961.

McCloy was responsible, "more than any one individual," for the decision to forcibly remove Japanese-Americans from their homes on the US West Coast and banish them to inland internment camps, according to Kai Bird's biography of McCloy, since President Roosevelt had delegated the matter to him through Secretary of War Henry L. Stimson. As assistant secretary of war, McCloy resisted Jewish pleas to bomb the rail lines leading to the Nazi death camps, falsely claiming that this would require "the diversion of considerable air support." Shortly after President Truman abolished the OSS, in September 1945, McCloy, then assistant secretary of war, defied the president and signed an order saying that "the continuing operations of OSS must be performed in order to preserve them."[21] McCloy did a great deal of work for corporations in Nazi Germany and advised the major German chemical combine I.G. Farben, manufacturer of Zyklon B gas, used by Adolf Hitler's minions in their attempt to kill off the entire Jewish population of Europe. In the early 1950s, as High Commissioner of West Germany, McCloy commuted the death sentences of many convicted Nazi war criminals, and gave early releases to others, including Otto Ambros and Friedrich Flick, notorious users of concentration camp slave labor; I.G. Farben executive Fritz ter Meer; Alfried Krupp and eight members of his board of directors; Baron Ernst von Weizsäker, convicted of complicity in the deportation of some 6,000 Jews from France to Poland in 1942; and Dr. Franz Six, head of Einsatzgruppe B (a mobile killing unit). Though they had been convicted of serious war crimes in the 1945-49 Nuremberg trials, all of these men had been set free by McCloy by 1952. McCloy reduced the sentences of 64 other convicted war criminals in 1951 alone.[22] Of the 15 death sentences handed down at the Nuremberg trials, he carried out only five. Klaus Barbie, the Nazi "butcher of Lyon," was tried by the French and sentenced to death in absentia, but when they asked McCloy to hand him over, he reportedly refused.[23] Instead, the US Army Counterintelligence Corps helped Barbie escape to Bolivia.

The other members of the Warren Commission were Senators Richard Russell (Georgia Democrat) and John Sherman Cooper (Kentucky Republican), and Congressmen (Thomas) Hale Boggs (Louisiana Democrat) and Gerald Ford (Michigan Republican); they will be mentioned from time to time in the following narrative. In the final analysis, whether the commissioners were distinguished or not, reputable or disreputable, is immaterial; the Warren Report is phony, and Mr. Bugliosi's book does not change that.

Because so much has been written on this subject by so many writers, and because I don't want to repeat what others have said, some of the information that follows will be presented in summary form, but with enough background information to support my conclusions. And many points will be familiar to assassination researchers and others, but are included for the sake of completeness.

Mr. Bugliosi assures us that the Warren Commission was devoted to doing a thorough investigation; apparently he is able to read the commissioners' minds retroactively. Numerous writers over the years have pointed out the many shortcomings of the commission's methods and findings, and one of the most effective of those writers was Sylvia Meagher in her book, *Accessories After the Fact*, though Mark Lane was one of the pioneers in this field. I thought that by now most Americans were aware that the Warren Commission never intended to discover the truth about what happened in Dallas on that fateful day, and that the Report they created is mostly fiction. But Mr. Bugliosi takes little notice of, among other things, the inadequate and inappropriate nature of the composition of the commission; it contained no medical doctors, and no experts on forensics or ballistics, even though they were investigating a murder. All of the members were lawyers and were present and former high political figures. All of the members of their formal staff (assistant counsels) were also lawyers. There are reports in the record of President Johnson's badgering Earl Warren, Chief Justice of the United States, into chairing the commission (a gross violation of the constitutional separation of powers), and badgering Sen. Richard Russell into being a member. One point that seems to have gone unnoticed, or at least unmentioned, by other commentators is that President Johnson, as head only of the executive branch, *had no authority* over either man. In an essay, Bertrand Russell pointed out that because of their connection to the government, not one member of the commission would have been permitted under American law to serve on a jury had Oswald faced trial.[24]

Mr. Bugliosi mentions that "the ever-decreasing trust by Americans in their government down through the years started with the Kennedy assassination and the subsequent erroneously perceived notion – fostered by conspiracy theorists – that the government concealed the full truth about the assassination from them."[25] He says that it's the Warren Commission critics, not the Warren Commission, who have distorted the truth and deliberately suppressed the truth from the American people.[25] Our "lies and distortions" have been part of a "wanton and reckless disregard for the facts of the case."[26] Bugliosi apparently underwent a change in his mindset over the last couple of decades. He became involved in a 1975 court proceeding for the reexamination of the firearms evidence in the Robert Kennedy assassination case. Bugliosi was quoted by William Turner and John Christian as telling Judge Robert A. Wenke around that time that Americans "want to know if there is a pernicious force alive in this land which is threatening to destroy our representative form of government by systematically orchestrating the cutting down of Presidents or candidates for President who espouse political philosophies antithetical to theirs."[27]

Mr. Bugliosi tells us that the rest of us see a conspiracy (where there is none) in this case because 1) "Stories of conspiracies ... are simply more appealing to Americans than that of a gunman acting alone..."; 2) "a wide-ranging conspiracy... gives more meaning not only to the president's death but to his life"[28]; and 3) "the instinctive notion that a king cannot be struck down by a peasant."[29] That a head of state or other significant national figure should be killed as a result of a conspiracy is not such a strange concept. As a matter of fact, conspiracies were involved in all of the following assassinations (dates of death are noted for each; I use the term *assassination* to describe the murder of a significant social or political figure for social or political reasons, without any semblance of a proper judicial procedure. And remember, it only takes two to make a conspiracy):

- Pompey the Great (Gnaeus Pompius Magnus), Roman general and statesman (September 28, 48 BC)
- Julius Caesar, Roman general, politician and writer (March 15, 44 BC)
- Marcus Tullius Cicero, Roman orator, statesman and philosopher (December 7, 43 BC)
- Caligula (Gaius Caesar), Roman emperor (January 24, 41 AD)
- Domitian, Roman emperor (September 18, 96)
- Thomas Becket, Archbishop of Canterbury (December 29, 1170)
- Henry Stuart, Lord Darnley, consort of Mary, Queen of Scots (February 10, 1567)
- Albrecht von Wallenstein, Bohemian general (February 25, 1634)
- Czar Peter III of Russia (July 17, 1762)
- Czar Paul I of Russia (March 24, 1801)
- Antonio José de Sucre y Alcalá, president of Bolivia (June 4, 1830)
- Emperor Maximilian of Mexico (June 19, 1864)
- US President Abraham Lincoln (April 15, 1865)
- Czar Alexander II of Russia (March 13, 1881)
- Lord Frederick Cavendish, British Liberal politician (May 6, 1882)
- King Alexander I of Serbia (May 29, 1903)
- King Carlos of Portugal (February 1, 1908)
- Francisco Madero, president of Mexico (February 22, 1913)
- Franz Ferdinand, archduke of Austria (June 28, 1914)
- Grigori Rasputin, Russian mystic (December 30, 1916)

- The Romanovs, Russian ruling dynasty (July 17, 1918)
- Emiliano Zapata, Mexican agrarian revolutionary (April 10, 1919)
- Matthias Erzberger, German political figure (August 26, 1921)
- British Field Marshal Sir Henry Wilson (June 22, 1922)
- Walter Rathenau, German foreign minister (June 24, 1922)
- Michael Collins, Irish revolutionary leader (August 22, 1922)
- Francisco "Pancho" Villa, Mexican bandit and revolutionary leader (July 20, 1923)
- Giacomo Matteotti, Italian socialist politician (June 10, 1924)
- Simon Petlyura, Ukrainian nationalist leader (May 25, 1926)
- Prime Minister Tsuyoshi Inukai of Japan (May 15, 1932)
- Augusto Sandino, Nicaraguan guerrilla fighter (February 21, 1934)
- Engelbert Dollfuss, Austrian chancellor (July 25, 1934)
- King Alexander I of Yugoslavia (October 9, 1934)
- SS Obergruppenführer Reinhard Heydrich, Nazi governor of Bohemia (May 27, 1942)
- Lord Moyne (Walter Edward Guinness), British Minister of State in the Middle East (November 6, 1944)
- Mohandas K. "Mahatma" Gandhi, Indian nationalist leader (January 30, 1948)
- Count Folke Bernadotte, Swedish diplomat (September 17, 1948)
- Lebanese Prime Minister Riad Al Solh (July 17, 1951)
- King Abdullah (Abdullah bin Hussein) of Jordan (July 20, 1951)
- King Faisal II of Iraq (July 14, 1958)
- Solomon Bandaranaike, prime minister of Ceylon (September 26, 1959)
- Patrice Lumumba, prime minister of the Republic of the Congo (January 17, 1961)
- Rafael Trujillo Molina, president of the Dominican Republic (May 30, 1961)
- South Vietnamese leaders Ngo Dinh Diem and Ngo Dinh Nhu (November 2, 1963)
- Malcolm X (Malcolm Little), US Black radical leader (February 21, 1965)
- Pierre Laporte, vice president of Quebec, Canada (October 17, 1970)
- Spanish Prime Minister Luís Carrero Blanco (December 20, 1973)
- Prime Minister Sheikh Mujibur Rahman of Bangladesh (August 15, 1975)

- Lord Louis Mountbatten, former viceroy of India (August 27, 1979)
- Park Chung-hee, president of South Korea (October 26, 1979)
- Archbishop Óscar Romero y Galdámez of El Salvador (March 24, 1980)
- Anastasio Somoza Debayle, former president of Nicaragua (September 17, 1980)
- Ziaur Rachman, president of Bangladesh (May 30, 1981)
- Anwar el-Sadat, president of Egypt (October 6, 1981)
- Benigno Aquino Jr., Philippine politician (August 21, 1983)
- Indira Gandhi, Indian prime minister (October 31, 1984)
- Spanish Vice Admiral Cristóbal Colón de Carvajal y Maroto (February 6, 1986)
- DeKalb County, Georgia (USA), Sheriff-elect Derwin Brown (December 15, 2000)
- Laurent-Désiré Kabila, president of the Democratic Republic of the Congo (January 16, 2001)
- Afghan warlord Ahmed Shah Massoud (September 9, 2001)
- Rehavam Ze'evi, Israeli minister of tourism and former government adviser (October 17, 2001)
- Serbian Prime Minister Zoran Đjinđjić (March 12, 2003)

There are, of course, examples in history of political assassinations being carried out by lone individuals, but the above list seems to indicate that when a significant political figure is assassinated, it is *more likely than not* to involve a conspiracy.

Chapter 1

Dealey Plaza

It turns out that Mr. Bugliosi starts to go wrong on the first page of his Introduction. He starts by telling us how "three shots rang out," and that the three spent cartridges were found in the "sniper's nest" on the sixth floor of the Book Depository provide the most convincing evidence that three and only three shots were fired.[1] As a moment's reflection will indicate, those three shell casings "prove" no such thing. There could obviously have been (and no doubt were) other shooters in Dealey Plaza who used silenced weapons, picking up all their spent casings before leaving their positions. In that case, the finding of three shells in the "sniper's nest" would mean, and does mean, absolutely nothing in terms of the number of shooters or the number of shots fired. On that same first page, Bugliosi also mentions a bullet striking the president in the upper right back and exiting his throat. (Bugliosi again mentions the upper right back entry on page 855 of the main book.) This is the so-called magic bullet, which Bugliosi later describes as entering the back of President Kennedy's neck. The analysis presented below indicates that there were at least three shooters in Dealey Plaza. It now seems probable that two of those shooters used silenced weapons, so that witnesses would only hear three shots, which would cleverly and conveniently coincide with the three empty shells found in the "sniper's nest." Many pages in Mr. Bugliosi's book are engaged in analyzing and discussing "crosstalk" and which police microphones were and were not open in and around Dealey Plaza to prove that there was no fourth shot. He assures us that acoustic evidence of a fourth shot exits only in the minds of conspiracy theorists, not in reality. As I suggest above, acoustic evidence alone proves nothing.

Mr. Bugliosi tells us in his introduction that Oswald was "emotionally unhinged political malcontent" and a "deeply troubled and a restless Marxist" who "hated America."[2] And he hated this country so much that he joined the Civil Air Patrol in junior high school, and joined the US Marine Corps as soon as he was of age to do so. Mr. Bugliosi tells us that "all the evidence points to only Oswald having fired a weapon in Dealey Plaza on November 22, 1963 ..."[3] As will be shown at various points in the following narrative, it is doubtful that anyone was firing from the "sniper's nest" window. Equally disturbing as Bugliosi's tome is the fact that after all these years, others in the print media are still repeating the old lone-nut-assassin story. In 2006, Mark Fuhrman published *A Simple Act of Murder: November 22, 1963,* which repeats the Official Story. Writing in the August 2016 issue of *Vanity Fair* magazine, Sarah Ellison tells us that in 1963, Lee Oswald "bought a rifle he saw advertised in the N.R.A.'s *American Rifleman* magazine and used it to kill President John F. Kennedy."[4] In her 2016 book *Twenty-Six Seconds: A Personal History of the Zapruder Film,* Alexandra Zapruder mentions a brief period during which her grandfather turned off his camera and then turned it back on when he saw the president's limousine giving "ample time for Oswald to have gotten off three shots."[5] The authors of *Dallas 1963* mention Oswald storing his rifle in the Paines' garage and say that he "shot and killed a Dallas policeman."[6] An Associated Press article reprinted in the Longview, Washington, *Daily News* on October 27, 2017, about the release of documents related to the JFK assassination, referred to "assassin Lee Harvey Oswald's trip to Mexico City weeks before the killing..." The following narrative will establish, once and for all, that Lee Oswald did not kill President Kennedy or anyone else in Dallas on November 22, 1963, nor did he make that trip to Mexico City.

The Sixth-Floor Rifle

Mr. Bugliosi spends pages 791-92 trying to destroy the idea that the rifle found in the northwest corner of the sixth floor of the Texas School Book Depository was a German Mauser. In his notes to page 87, he tells us that regardless of what the conspiracy theorists say, there can be no question the rifle found on the sixth floor was a 6.5-millimeter Italian Mannlicher-Carcano. If Bugliosi and the Warren Commission can't convince us that the rifle was a Mannlicher-Carcano, the connection among Oswald, the rifle and the money order Oswald supposedly used to order the rifle is severed and the whole Oswald scenario falls apart. At 12:19 a.m. on Saturday, November 23, Dallas District Attorney Henry Wade told the press that he believed that the rifle was a Mauser; he must have gotten this information from somewhere. The Warren Report lists as "speculation" that the rifle found on the sixth floor of the Book Depository was identified by Deputy Constable Seymour Weitzman as a 7.65 Mauser when, as Sylvia Meagher pointed out, it was a statement of known fact. Weitzman and Dallas County Deputy Sheriffs Eugene Boone and Roger Craig, the three Dallas policeman who discovered the rifle, and even Captain Will Fritz, head of the Dallas Robbery and Homicide Bureau, quickly identified the rifle as a Mauser; nowhere does Bugliosi *or the Warren Report* mention that Boone, Craig and Weitzman subsequently signed affidavits stating that the rifle they found was a Mauser. Roger Craig told Texas researchers that he saw the word *Mauser* stamped on the rifle's receiver.[7] Weitzman's affidavit of November 23, 1963, unequivocally states that it was a 7.65 Mauser bolt action with a 4/13 scope (telescopic sight), and can be found at 24H228. Boone testified that Capt. J. Will Fritz knelt down and looked at the rifle, and said, "It looks like a 7.65 Mauser." In his Supplementary Investigation Report dated November 22, Boone stated that the rifle appeared to be a 7.65 Mauser (and that Officer Whitman was with him when he found the rifle; Whitman did not testify to the commission or its legal staff).[8] Bugliosi nevertheless tells us that none of the police officers "crowding around" the sixth-floor rifle were able to identify it positively. He also states that the rifle found by the policemen "is stamped 'Made Italy,' with a date of 1940 and serial number C2766."[9] None of the aforementioned policemen stated that he saw "Made Italy" stamped on the rifle. Mr. Bugliosi wants us to believe that those words were on that rifle, so he simply made up these "facts" regarding the identification of the rifle.

In a footnote on page 791, Mr. Bugliosi states that it is easy to confuse a Mannlicher-Carcano with a German Mauser. Mark Lane, however, told the commission that a German Mauser is nothing at all like an Italian carbine.[10] The words "MADE ITALY" and "Cal. 6.5" were clearly etched on the barrel of the rifle shown to Lane by the commission. In a report dated June 3, 1964, the FBI acknowledged that there was an inscription on the Mannlicher-Carcano to the effect that it was made in Italy.[11] It would be impossible for a policeman to read that and then swear that it was a 7.65 mm German Mauser. Some bungler tied in with the conspirators planted a German Mauser on the sixth floor of the Book Depository; but later, someone remembered that the Mannlicher-Carcano was the rifle that the conspirators had arranged to link with Oswald, so the Mauser had to become a Carcano.

On page 393 of his endnotes, Bugliosi tells us that "we know" that the Mannlicher-Carcano was found in the sniper's nest, and "we know" that it was the murder weapon. Now that is an odd statement. The policemen who found the rifle stated that it was found between some boxes in the *northwest corner* of the Book Depository, near the stairs, not in the sniper's nest.

Lyndal Shaneyfelt, an FBI photographic expert, told the commission that he was unable to state that the rifle in one of the backyard photos (CE133A, 16H510) was the same weapon identified as CE139, the alleged assassination rifle.[12] Mark Lane showed the commission a photograph of "the murder rifle" from the *New York Times* (December 8, 1963) that was not the rifle being held by the Oswald figure in the backyard photos. (These photos will be discussed in more detail in The Phony Backyard Photos in Chapter 3, below.) The *Times* photo shows a straight stock; a Mannlicher-Carcano has a dip in the top of the stock, behind the firing mechanism, to accommodate one's hand.[13] Lane also told the commission that in the photo of Oswald in the March 2, 1964, issue of *Newsweek* magazine (CE134, 16H510) shows a rifle with almost a straight stock, and no telescopic sight. (Actually, the photo appears too dark to discern whether or not there is a scope on the rifle. It's probably there.) He also testified that the curved line of the stock present in CE339 is absent from every other photo, indicating that the rifle shown in Oswald's hands in Commission Exhibits 334 through 338 (the backyard photos) isn't comparable to the alleged murder weapon as shown to reporters in the Dallas police station. The rifle in the photo on the cover of the February 21, 1964, issue of *Life* magazine, which is also a blowup of one of the backyard photos, also shows no such dip in the stock. The commission nevertheless concluded that the rifle shown in the pictures was the same rifle found on the sixth floor of the Depository on November 22.[14] Bugliosi slavishly reproduces the *Life* magazine cover photo showing Oswald posing with "the rifle he later used to kill President Kennedy and the pistol he used to kill Officer Tippit." This is essentially the same verbiage that *Life* used. Bugliosi says that the rifle found on the sixth floor of the Depository is the same one possessed by the National Archives. He also says that the backyard photos prove that Oswald had "actual possession" of the Carcano, and they are "some of the most damning pieces of evidence against Oswald."[15] It is clear from the above that the rifle in the backyard photos is not a Mannlicher-Carcano. Somehow Mr. Bugliosi didn't notice that.

Will Fritz told assistant commission counsel Joseph Ball, "Some officer told us they thought he was in that building [the Book Depository]." He said that Dallas Police Lt. J.C. Day took pictures of the rifle; "After the pictures had been made, then I ejected a live shell ... Lieutenant Day took that rifle, I believe, to the city hall." Later, Fritz told McCloy, "I let him [he doesn't say who] dust before I ejected a shell."[16]

McCloy: Before Captain Fritz ejected the live cartridge, did you dust the rifle for fingerprints?

> Lt. Day: Not before.
>
> Belin: Did you dust the bolt for fingerprints?
>
> Lt. Day: Yes, sir.
>
> Belin: Before the live round was ejected?
>
> Lt. Day: No, no; the only part that Captain Fritz touched was the round knob. I looked at it through a glass and decided there was not a print there, and it would be safe for him to open the bolt.[17]

So Capt. Fritz said that someone dusted for prints before he handled the rifle, but Lt. Day, the fingerprint man, said that he did *not* dust the rifle before Fritz handled it. One of them was lying (or had a poor memory). And Lt. Day just happened to have a magnifying glass with him?

The Warren Report tells us that after Lt. Day determined that the rifle contained no fingerprints, he held it by the stock while Capt. Fritz ejected a live round by operating the bolt, which is in line with Lt. Day's commission testimony. But Day testified that he "noticed there were traces of two prints visible." The commission record of "Interrogation of Lee Harvey Oswald," unsigned but apparently made by Fritz, states, "After Lt. Day had finished his work with the rifle, I picked it up and found that it had a cartridge in the chamber, which I ejected." Capt. Fritz said that Lt. Day took photos of the rifle.[18] According to a report by R.M. Sims and E.L. Boyd, after police photographer Robert Studebaker, Lt. Day's assistant, and Lt. Day took pictures of the rifle, "Lt. Day then picked up the rifle and dusted it for fingerprints."[19] It could be argued that this is evidence of Dallas police incompetence rather than evidence of conspiracy. More than 90 percent of fingerprints are "latent," and are rarely visible under normal lighting conditions. Latent prints require "development," i.e., special chemical treatment and/or application of an alternative light source, to be usable as evidence. In no forensic or crime scene text I consulted was "looking through a [magnifying] glass" mentioned as a method of discerning latent fingerprints.

On the afternoon of November 22, FBI agents found only one gun dealer in Dallas who ever sold surplus World War II-vintage Mannlicher-Carcano rifles: the H.L. Green Company on Main Street in Dallas. The search indicated that the company hadn't handled a Mannlicher-Carcano with serial number C2766 in the past few years, but the records did identify the importer of such rifles as Crescent Firearms Company of New York.[20] J. Philip Lux, store manager for the H.L Green Company, stated that a Dallas review of records failed to reflect any record of sale of an Italian 6.5 mm rifle with serial no. C2766.[21] Albert C. Yeargan Jr., sporting goods department manager for H.L. Green, also found no record of sale of a 6.5 mm rifle no. C2766.[22]

Parroting the Warren Report, Bugliosi tells us that early on the afternoon of November 22, Dallas FBI agents spread out in Dallas and found only one gun dealer who ever sold Mannlicher-Carcano rifles. That dealer's records identified the importer as Crescent Firearms Company in New York. So Dallas policemen find a *German Mauser* in the Book Depository, and then FBI agents go looking for a gun dealer who sells *Italian Mannlicher-Carcano* rifles. At 10:00 p.m. that day, FBI agents watched employees of the Crescent Firearms Company as they rummaged through their files. Mr. Bugliosi tells us that the records of Crescent Firearms show that C2766 had been wholesaled to Klein's Sporting Goods in Chicago.[23] The Report and Mr. Bugliosi claim that rifle number 2766 had been wholesaled to Klein's Sporting Goods in Chicago, so Chicago FBI agents headed for the home of William Waldman, vice president of Klein's, where they found the coupon that Oswald supposedly used to order the Mannlicher-Carcano. Both sources tell us that shortly after midnight on November 23, FBI agents were working with general operating manager Mitchell Scibor of Klein's, searching for records of Klein's having received a Carcano with serial number C2766. The Warren Report tells us that at 4:00 a.m. on November 23, "the officers of Klein's discovered that a rifle bearing serial number C2766 had been shipped to one A. Hidell" in Dallas.[24]

The Sixth-Floor Window

The Warren Commission found a few people who claimed to have seen a rifle or pipelike object sticking out of the "sniper's nest" window. Like the commission, Mr. Bugliosi hangs part of his tale on witnesses who supposedly saw a shooter in the "sniper's nest" (the southeastern-most window of the sixth floor of the Book Depository.) Fifteen-year-old Amos Euins allegedly told DPD Sgt. David Harkness that he saw a "pipelike object" sticking out of that window (the one "under the ledge") just before the shooting started, but in Euins' affidavit at 24H207 (dated November 22), he doesn't say which floor or which end of the building. Euins' credibility is not great. He told Sgt. Harkness and James Underwood, assistant news director of KRLD-TV and radio, that the man he saw was a "colored man."[25] But in his affidavit for the Sheriff's Department dated November 22, Euins said it was a white man.[26] When David Belin asked Harkness if Euins said whether or not he saw a rifle, Harkness replied, "He couldn't tell."[27] Euins' affidavit however, states, "I saw a man in a window with a gun and I saw him shoot twice."[28] In the Sheriff's office on December 14, 1963, Euins "advised he could not distinguish the features of the individual standing at the window, as he had previously stated, he only saw his hand and a bald spot on his head." Euins later told the commission (i.e., commission assistant counsel Arlen Specter), "I had seen a pipe ... up there in the window ... some kind of pipe ... I seen a bald spot on this man's head ... I could see ... the rifle laying across his hand."[29] How could Euins, standing on the pavement in front of the Depository, possibly see a bald spot on the head of someone way up on the sixth floor of the building? It makes no sense. Bugliosi concedes that Amos Euins' description of the gunman he supposedly saw in the "sniper's nest" was of little value.[30] So much for Euins.

On November 23, 1963, James Worrell Jr. stated that he "looked up and saw the barrel of a rifle sticking out of a window over my head about 5 or 6 stories up. While I was looking at the gun it was fired again," and then he "saw it fire a third time."[31] Robert H. Jackson, a reporter for the *Dallas Times Herald*, said he saw a rifle or what looked like a rifle in the window and as he looked at it, it was drawn slowly back into the window *before* the turn onto Elm; he "saw no one in the window with it." But he also said that the first shot "came from ahead of us, which would be in a northerly direction, northwesterly direction ... from somewhere around the head of the motorcade."[32] Cameraman Malcolm Couch of WFAA-TV stated, "I remember glancing up to window on the far right ... and seeing about a foot of a rifle – being the barrel – brought into the window" on the sixth or seventh floor on the far right of the Book Depository, but he saw no one in that window.[33] Mrs. Earle Cabell, who was in the motorcade, told the commission that she "saw a projection out of one of those windows ... The first or second window of the first group of double windows,"[34] not a "rather long looking projection," as described on page 65 of the Warren Report. These people *may* have seen a rifle or pipelike object in that famous window, but as a moment's reflection will tell you, that does not necessarily implicate Oswald or any other specific person.

When Secret Service agent Clint Hill testified to the Warren Commission on March 9, 1964, he stated that he could see the Depository ahead of him when the motorcade turned north (right) onto Houston Street, but he didn't see anything unusual. He didn't mention seeing a sniper or a rifle in the "sniper's nest."[35] James Underwood heard Jackson's comment about a rifle in the window, but Underwood "looked where he pointed and saw nothing."[36] As soon as he heard the shots, *Dallas Morning News* photographer Tom Dillard took two photos of the east end of the Book Depository. He told the commission twice that he did not see a rifle when he looked up at the building.[37]

One of the photos Studebaker took (reproduced at 21H646) shows the "sniper's nest" window open, but it doesn't appear to be open as much as in the two photos taken by Dillard within seconds of the shooting. Bugliosi says he was unable to resolve this discrepancy.[38] Deputy district court clerk T.E. Moore was standing at the southeast corner of Elm and Houston. In an FBI interview on January 10, 1964, he stated that at the sound of the first shot, he looked up toward the Book Depository, "because the shot sounded like it had come from a high area," but didn't see anything noteworthy there.[39] DPD Officer W.E. Barnett told the commission that he was standing near the intersection of Elm and Houston streets, and that after the second shot was fired, he "looked up at the building [Book Depository] and I saw nothing in the windows."[40] Secret Service agent Forrest Sorrels, in the lead car, stated that at the time of the shooting, he looked toward the Depository and glanced up, but he didn't remember seeing "any object or anything like that in the windows such as a rifle or anything pointing out the windows." He saw no activity and saw no one moving around in the "sniper's nest" window.[41] Associated Press photographer James Altgens was on Elm Street, about 15 feet from Kennedy, when the president was shot in the head. He told the commission that when he heard the first shot, he looked up at the Book Depository and "saw no rifle at any time though I was looking for one."[42] Motorcycle policeman Billy Joe Martin testified that after the first shot, he looked back at the Book Depository but didn't see anything.[43] Willie Mitchell was an inmate at the county jail on Houston Street; he told his attorney Stanley Kaufman that he didn't see anyone in the sniper's nest window. Kaufman reported this to the Warren Commission, and offered to supply them with Mitchell's address (in Dallas), but the commission didn't call Mitchell to testify.[44] Bugliosi mentions the testimony of Robert Jackson and Malcolm Couch about seeing a rifle in the sixth-floor window (though Couch wasn't sure if it was the sixth or seventh floor), but conveniently fails to mention the fact that neither James Underwood nor Tom Dillard nor T.E. Moore nor

W.E. Barnett nor Forrest Sorrels nor James Altgens nor B.J. Martin saw a rifle when they looked up at the "sniper's nest" window, and Bugliosi doesn't mention Willie Mitchell at all.

The enhanced Robert Hughes film shows nothing that looks like a rifle barrel protruding from the "sniper's nest" window; the film only shows what appear to be boxes stacked up in the "sniper's nest." An analysis of the Hughes film by the FBI laboratory and the US Navy Photographic Interpretation Center in 1964 concluded that the film showed no human form in the subject window, and that the "forms recorded in this window can be interpreted as in the same general shapes of boxes, found at and just behind the window in question."[45] Bugliosi mentions that the Itek Corporation studied the Hughes film in 1976 using digital enhancement techniques to determine whether it showed anyone in the southeastern-most window of the sixth floor of the Book Depository. They reported that "motion of an object or person was detected," but the HSCA photographic panel stated in 1978 that "the apparent motion in the window seemed to be random and therefore not likely to be caused by human motion."[46] (The president of Itek in 1963 was Franklin Lindsay, a veteran of the OSS, the CIA, and the Ford Foundation. Itek had CIA links and developed cameras for the U-2 and later the SR-71 spy planes.) Dr. Bob R. Hunt, an aeronautical and electrical engineer who was also associate professor of systems and industrial engineering and optical sciences at the University of Phoenix, assembled a photographic panel to study various photos and films taken in Dealey Plaza on the day of the assassination. He told the HSCA that following their enhancement of the Hughes film and a slide taken by James Powell, Hunt's panel concluded that *there was no one at the sixth-floor "sniper's nest" window at the moment of the assassination.*[47] Nevertheless, according to Mr. Bugliosi, "We know that among other evidence, a gunman was seen in the sixth-floor window..."[48]

Utility clerk Robert Edwards was on the west side of Houston, near the entrance of Elm into the "parkway" (evidently Dealey Plaza) when, before the motorcade came by, he saw a white man in "the corner room" of the sixth floor of the Book Depository with short, light brown hair and wearing a light colored short-sleeve shirt, open at the neck. (He couldn't remember if he could see the man's hands.)[49] This could have been the person who planted the three spent cartridges on the floor near the "sniper's nest" window. In a 1971 unpublished manuscript, Roger Craig wrote that the three shells "looked as though they had been carefully and deliberately placed" near the sniper's nest window. Bugliosi notes that Craig told the Warren Commission that he "didn't look that close" – as though this completely negates Craig's later statement.[50] Maybe the commission changed his testimony, as they did with others who testified before them.

Bugliosi devotes an entire chapter to "Summary of Oswald's Guilt." Among the factors that Bugliosi says demonstrate Oswald's "guilt": 1) Oswald did not bring his lunch on the morning of the assassination; 2) he changed his trousers after returning to his rooming house after the assassination; and 3) Howard Brennan "actually saw" Oswald in the "sniper's nest." On page 305, Bugliosi acknowledges that Brennan was the only eyewitness who claims to have seen Oswald, specifically, in the sixth-floor window, but on page 157, Bugliosi acknowledges that Brennan was unable to pick out Oswald as the man he saw in the "sniper's nest" in a police lineup. On page 143, the Warren Report states that Brennan testified that Oswald, "whom he viewed in a police lineup on the night of the assassination, was the man he saw fire the shots from the sixth-floor window of the Depository Building." But two pages later, the Report states that Brennan "identified Oswald as the person in the lineup who *bore the closest resemblance* to the man in the window but he said he was unable to make a positive identification." (Emphasis added.) And yet on page 250, the Report states that Brennan "made a positive identification of Oswald as being the person at the window." When a document is internally inconsistent, it cannot be considered valid. Forrest Sorrels testified on May 7, 1964, that at the lineup on the evening of November 22, Brennan looked very carefully at each man. Sorrels asked him, "Well, is there anyone there that looks like him [the man in the window]?" Brennan replied, "That second man from the left [indicating Oswald] looks like him, but I cannot positively say." But shortly thereafter, Brennan said, "I am sorry, but I can't do it ... I just can't be positive. I am sorry."[51] Interviewed by FBI agent William G. Brookhart on January 7, 1964, Brennan said only that Oswald "most resembled" the man he had seen on the sixth floor, at a window *near* the southeast corner of the Book Depository; he didn't actually say which window.[52] In Brennan's commission testimony on March 24, 1964, Brennan said that he had lied when he told officers that he couldn't make a positive identification at the lineup; this was, he said, because he was worried about his personal security and that of his family. When Brennan was asked to mark on a photo of the Depository (CE477) the window where he saw the man, he said, "Well, I am confused here.... But I believe this is the sixth floor ... I am confused whether this is the same window." Eschewing a complete sentence, Brennan testified that he told Forrest Sorrels and Capt. Fritz that "Oswald – or the man in the lineup that I identified looking more like a closest resemblance to the man in the window than anyone in the lineup." But minutes later, despite the fact that Brennan had seen Oswald on television before attending the lineup, he told commission assistant counsel David Belin that he could not make a positive identification.[53]

Mr. Brennan said of the man he supposedly saw, "[I]t appeared to me he was standing up and resting against the left window sill ... and taking positive aim and fired his last shot."[54] Unfortunately for Brennan and his credibility, photos taken at the time show that the lower half of the famous window was only half-open, and that there was a stack of three boxes pressed against the window, apparently flush with the inside wall; so the man Brennan allegedly saw could not have been standing *and* firing a rifle. The Warren Report resolved the conflict by stating that the man Brennan saw "most probably ... was either sitting or kneeling."[55] Whoever Brennan saw in the window, if indeed he saw anyone there, was not Oswald. Brennan's Dallas County affidavit of November 22, 1963, states, "He was just sitting [not standing?] there looking down ... he had on light colored clothes, more of a khaki color ... I then saw this man ... taking aim with a high powered rifle."[56] This description does not match the dark trousers Oswald was wearing that day, nor does it match his shirt, which was of a rather dark rust-brown color. (A color photograph of the shirt that Oswald was wearing when arrested appears on page 186 of Robert Groden's book; photographs of the shirt also appear at 21H467-470. Although the photos are not in color, the shirt is obviously quite dark.) Of those who described the clothing of the man allegedly seen in the sixth-floor window, they all described him as wearing a light-colored shirt. In his memoir, Jesse Curry wrote, "Brennan's later testimony [after the lineup] to FBI agents varied from month to month after the assassination."[57] The HSCA didn't bother to interview Brennan, though he was still alive.

It is doubtful that anyone shot from that window at the presidential limousine. At the end of Secret Service man Thomas J. Kelley's testimony, Arlen Specter refers to "a large oak tree which intervened between a point on the sixth floor of the Texas School Book Depository Building and any automobile which would have been driven down the center lane of Elm Street in a westerly direction."[58] And Mr. Bugliosi himself mentions "an oak tree that obscured the sniper's view of the presidential limousine on Elm Street starting at Zapruder frame 166 and continuing on to frame 210."[59]

The Sequence and Source of Shots

What happened in Dealey Plaza can be determined by paying attention to statements of eyewitnesses in the Plaza and Parkland Hospital, and considering a simple diagram. The purpose of this section is to clarify the number and source of shots, the speed of the motorcade through the plaza, and to comment on other suspicious people and activities at that place and time. Because this book is largely a response to Mr. Bugliosi's book, it is necessary to refute some of his statements.

The Warren Report states that only three shots were fired at the limousine. A number of people testified that the heard just three shots, but several others heard more. When he testified on March 10, 1964, James Worrell Jr. told Arlen Specter that he heard four shots "right in succession...While I was running I heard a gun fire two more times."[60] A.J. Millican was standing on the north side of Elm in front of the concrete colonnade. He stated in an affidavit for Sheriff Bill Decker, "Just after the President's car passed, I heard three shots come from up toward Houston and Elm right by the Book Depository Building, and then immediately I heard two more shots come from the arcade [the colonnade] between the Book Store and the Underpass, and then three more shots came from the same direction, only sounded further back."[61] (Millican did not testify to the commission or its legal staff.) Sam Holland, signal supervisor for Union Terminal Railroad, was also on the Triple Underpass. He heard four shots; he stated, "there were definitely four reports."[62] Richard Carr testified at the Shaw trial that he also heard four shots.[63] (Carr did not testify to the commission or its legal staff.)

Sandy Speaker told researcher Jim Marrs that he heard at least five shots from different locations.[64] Jesse Price was on the roof of the Terminal Annex Building. In a statement to the Dallas County Sheriff's Department on November 22, Price said he heard a total of about six shots. He also saw a man wearing a white dress shirt and khaki trousers run toward the passenger cars on the railroad siding after the volley of shots.[65] (Price did not testify to the commission or its legal staff.) Bugliosi says that only one person, Jesse Price, heard six shots.[66] But Bugliosi doesn't tell us that Jean Hill told the Warren Commission that she heard "at least four or five shots, perhaps six ... I know there were more than three."[67] She stated in an FBI interview that she heard four to six shots, and that she believed that they came from just west of the Book Depository.[68] James Fetzer reminds us that his book *Assassination Science* demonstrated that an absolute minimum of six shots were fired. Homer McMahon, who was in charge of the color lab at the National Photographic Interpretation Center, viewed what was apparently the original Zapruder film and reported that after viewing it at least ten times, he concluded that Kennedy was hit six or eight times, from at least three directions.[69]

Bugliosi tells us that "a blanket search of the plaza by law enforcement right after the shooting failed to turn up any evidence of a second gunman,"[70] but the summary of shots provided in this section provides such evidence. Apparently Mr. Bugliosi didn't consider the possibility that the other gunmen may have fled the area immediately after the shooting, nor did he consider the possibility that one of the "tramps" who were picked up in the railroad yards may have been one of the shooters. To prove his point that only three shots were fired, Bugliosi reminds us that "only three empty cartridge cases were found on the floor of the sniper's nest, and no other empty cartridge case was found anywhere else in Dealey Plaza."[71] But in the midst of assuring us that the Warren Report is accurate in its major conclusions, including the point that three and only three shots were fired at the limousine from the sniper's nest by Lee Oswald, Mr. Bugliosi makes the following statement: "It should be noted that the three empty shells found in the sniper's nest don't necessarily prove that three shots were fired from that location ..."[72] This would seem to call into question his and the Report's major conclusion!

In a note on page 486, Mr. Bugliosi tells us that enhancement of certain frames of the Zapruder film, especially frame Z-313, shows that: "Not only were the blood, brain tissue, and skull fragments all blown to the *front* of the president's body, but the five bullet fragments found in the presidential limousine were all to his front." One must wonder if Bugliosi himself believes what he is saying. The Zapruder film shows blood, skull and brain tissue blown all over the trunk of the car, which is why Jacqueline Kennedy started to climb over the trunk to retrieve pieces of her husband's skull immediately after the final, fatal shot. In the same note, Bugliosi tells us that "the president's head moved *forward* at the moment of impact," in distinct opposition to the claim of the crazy conspiracy theorists, that Kennedy's head was being propelled backward (and to the left) by a shot from the front. Never mind that the Zapruder film shows exactly that. Bugliosi claims that Cecil Kirk, a member of the HSCA's photographic panel, told him that his panel concluded that Kennedy's brain tissue was launched so high in front of his body that the motorcycle cops on the left rear of the limousine actually drove into that tissue.[73] How could they, if the ejecta were on the right side of Kennedy's head, as Bugliosi says? In any case, as will be explained below, those motorcycle cops testified that they were hit with considerable force by the cranial ejecta; they did not "drive into" the ejecta.

I have assembled the following on the basis of eyewitness accounts and the Zapruder film:

One shot, probably the first, hit the pavement behind the limousine. Gov. John Connally told the commission that he heard the first shot just after they made the turn onto Elm Street. He said the sound appeared to come from over his right shoulder.[74] DPD motorcycle cop Sgt. Stavis Ellis, who was in charge of the motorcycle escort through Dallas, saw what he believed to be a shot hit the ground across from the Depository on the south side of Elm, shortly after the turn from Houston onto Elm.[75] (Sgt. Ellis did not testify to the commission or its legal staff.) Mark Lane advised the commission that motorcycle policeman James Chaney was quoted in the *Houston Chronicle* on November 24, 1963, as stating that the first shot missed entirely; this was probably the shot seen by Sgt. Ellis.[76] (Chaney did not testify to the commission or its legal staff.) Mrs. Donald Baker told the Warren Commission that between the first and second shots she saw "a shot or something" strike the pavement behind the limousine. She thought it was in the middle of the left-hand lane.[77] But judging from statements quoted herein of other eyewitnesses, this was probably the first shot. Probable source: Dal-Tex Building or Dallas County Records Building.

One shot apparently hit President Kennedy in the back, but did not exit. Kennedy's shirt and jacket reportedly show holes in that location, and the official autopsy photo shows a hole in that location, but we don't know that that was the body of JFK. A June 29, 1966, memorandum from FBI agents James Sibert and Francis O'Neill states that the pathologist could find no point of exit for the bullet that went into the president's back. Two separate FBI reports, in December and January, also stated that there was no point of exit for the bullet that entered Kennedy's back.[78] (Arlen Specter interviewed Sibert and O'Neill, but neither man was called to testify to the full commission.) Robert A. Frazier, special agent assigned to the firearms identification unit of the FBI lab in Washington, told the commission that his examination revealed a small hole in the back of the president's suit coat approximately 5⅜ inches below the top of the collar and 1¾ inches to the right of the middle seam. This is repeated in the HSCA Appendix Volumes.[79] Frazier also saw a hole in the back of the shirt

5¾ inches below the top of the collar and 1⅛ inches to the right of the midline. Both, he said, were round holes consistent with a bullet hole.[80] In his commission testimony, Dr. James Humes confirmed (to Specter) the location of the hole in the president's shirt, as described by Frazier. Humes testified that there was a hole in Kennedy's back approximately six inches below the top of the collar and two inches to the right of the middle seam of the shirt.[81] The Report acknowledges that the suit jacket hole was 5⅜ inches below the top his collar and 1¾ inches to the right of center; and the hole in his shirt was 5¾ inches below the top of the collar and 1⅛ inches to right of the middle of the back of the shirt.[82] Agent O'Neill told the Assassination Records Review Board, "There was a bullet wound in this [*sic*] upper back, the right-hand side." Secret Service agent Glen Bennett stated that he saw a shot hit Kennedy's back "about four inches down from the right shoulder..."[83] (Agent Bennett did not testify to the commission or its legal staff.) Clint Hill told the commission that at Bethesda, after the autopsy, he saw "an opening in the back, about 6 inches below the neckline to the right-hand side of the spinal column."[84] In his written statement at 18H744-5, dated November 30, 1963, agent Hill said he "observed a wound six inches down from the neckline on the back just to the right of the spinal column." The commission suppressed FBI reports dated November 26 and December 9, 1963, and January 13, 1964, all of which asserted "without qualification" that the missile that struck Kennedy's back penetrated only to the length of a finger and did not exit from his body.[85] The January 13, 1964, FBI report stated that the bullet to Kennedy's back penetrated to less than a finger length.[86] Agent Roy Kellerman testified that he heard President Kennedy say, "My God, I am hit."[87] As Mark Lane pointed out in his Orleans Parish Grand Jury testimony, JFK would not have been able to talk after the throat shot (described below), so the back shot was probably the first shot that hit the president.[88] The probable source of this shot: the Dal-Tex or Dallas County Records Building.

One shot hit JFK in the throat from the front. I wondered for years where this shot came from; if it came over the windshield, it would have to have come from some very high elevation near the Triple Underpass at the west end of Dealey Plaza. Finally, Alexandra Zapruder, granddaughter of Abraham Zapruder, was kind enough to publish frame 225 of the Zapruder film in her book (it is also reproduced in the first photographic section of Bugliosi's book). This is the first frame showing President Kennedy after he emerges from behind the large Stemmons Freeway sign. It shows that his hands are already reaching for his throat, and he is facing the grassy knoll, which is the probable source of that shot.

This is the wound that the Warren Report and Mr. Bugliosi want us to believe was an exit wound. The Parkland Hospital medical and nursing personnel saw an entry wound. At a press conference two hours after Kennedy died, Dr. Malcolm Perry described the throat wound as an entrance wound.[89] White House transcript 1327-6 makes it clear that Perry volunteered three times that JFK had an *entry* wound in his throat.[90] Dr. Perry told Arlen Specter, "There was a small wound in the lower anterior [front] third in the midline of the neck ... roughly 5 mm in size or so."[91] He told Dr. Humes that the throat wound was 3-5 mm in diameter, and he told HSCA staff that the throat wound was six to seven millimeters (about a quarter-inch) in diameter.[92] Dr. Ronald Jones said the neck wound was "no greater than a quarter of an inch in greatest diameter."[93] Dr. Paul Peters told the commission that "we saw the wound of entry in the throat ..."[94]

Questioned by Arlen Specter, Dr. Charles Baxter stated that the throat wound was spherical, four to five millimeters in widest diameter and spherical – "a very small wound."[95] Dr. Baxter testified that the throat wound "did not appear to be a jagged wound such as one would expect with a very high velocity rifle bullet ... [it was] an entry, no more than a pinpoint."[96] Dr. Baxter stated that if it were an exit wound, "ordinarily there would have been a rather large wound of exit," which, at four to five mm in widest diameter, the throat wound was not![97] In a 1992 interview, Dr. Baxter stated that his "immediate thought" was that it was an entry wound.[98] Drs. Robert McClelland and Gene Akin testified that it appeared to be an entrance wound.[99] On November 27, 1963, the *New York Times* quoted Dr. Kemp Clark as saying that a bullet struck JFK in the neck, ranged downward in his chest and did not exit. Richard Dudman of the St. Louis *Post-Dispatch* said that when he was at Parkland, the surgeons who attended JFK were in agreement that the throat wound was an entrance wound.[100]

Parkland doctor Charles Carrico's hand-written note of November 22 refers to "one small penetrating wound of anterior neck."[101] Dr. Carrico told the commission that the throat wound was "an even round wound," five by eight millimeters (about a quarter-inch by five-sixteenths of an inch) in size, in the lower third of the neck, between the top of the tie and the Adam's apple. He said this wound was "fairly round, had no jagged edges."[102] In a footnote on page 401, Bugliosi tells us is that this is "consistent with an exit wound of a 6.5 mm bullet," which is absurd. Dr. Charles

Crenshaw, one of the doctors who fought to save the life of the wounded president, saw a small wound in JFK's throat "that was consistent with an entrance wound."[103] (Dr. Crenshaw did not testify to the commission or its legal staff.) Dr. Crenshaw stated in a videotaped interview that the neck wound was one of entrance.[104] Dr. Robert McClelland told the Warren Commission that he saw Dr. Perry make the tracheotomy incision "through a very small, perhaps less than one quarter inch in diameter wound in the neck."[105]

Parkland nurse Margaret Henchliffe saw "a little hole in the middle of his neck ... about as big around as the end of my little finger." It appeared to be "an entrance bullet hole – it looked to me like."[106] Parkland nurse Donna Willie told the Jenkintown, Pennsylvania, *Times-Chronicle*, regarding JFK's throat wound, "I know he was shot from the front."[107] Parkland nurse Diana Bowron also stated that it looked like an entry wound.[108] On page 411, Bugliosi tells us that because the panel of forensic pathologists hired by the HSCA said the throat wound was an exit deficit, it must be so; but he notes in the same paragraph that Dr. Perry enlarged the throat wound, "destroying most of its original configuration." How can the HSCA people describe what kind of wound was originally in the throat, when the original configuration of that wound was enlarged and thus changed at Parkland?

One shot evidently hit the windshield of the limousine. The Warren Report itself states, "The windshield in the Presidential limousine was struck by a bullet fragment on the inside surface of the glass, but was not penetrated."[109] Various witnesses saw a pencil-size bullet hole in the windshield, just left of the center of the windshield. Sgt. Stavis Ellis and former DPD officer H.R. Freeman, also a Dallas motorcycle cop, told a researcher in 1971 that they saw this hole when the limousine was parked at Parkland Hospital; Sgt. Ellis said that the hole was large enough to put a pencil through it.[110] Richard Dudman, correspondent for the St. Louis *Post-Dispatch,* said that he and another man saw a hole "which resembled a bullet hole" in the upper left-hand corner of the windshield of the presidential limousine.[111] In a report published in the *New Republic,* Dudman wrote, "A few of us noticed the [small, round] hole in the windshield when the limousine was standing at the emergency entrance after the President had been carried inside."[112] Frank Cormier, a reporter for the St. Louis *Post Dispatch,* and Dr. Evalea Glanges, then a second-year medical student at UT Southwestern Medical School, next to Parkland Hospital, also saw the hole.[113] Attorney and assassination researcher Douglas Weldon was told by a long-time employee of the Ford Motor Company (who wished to remain anonymous) that he saw a hole in the windshield that was made by a bullet from the front.[114] Secret Service agent Charles Taylor Jr., who was in the limousine when it was driven from Andrews Air Force Base to the White House Garage on the evening of November 22, wrote in his report that he observed "the small hole just left of center from which what appeared to be bullet fragments were removed."[115] Probable source of this bullet: unclear. Weldon believes that the shot to the windshield had to have been fired from the south side of the Triple Underpass near the top of the Stemmons Freeway,[116] though it seems counterintuitive that someone would try to hit a human target with accuracy by shooting through a windshield.

One shot hit Gov. Connally in the upper right back and exited his chest by the right nipple. In his commission testimony, the FBI's Lyndal Shaneyfelt concurred when commissioner McCloy stated, in a discussion of trajectories, that Connally "couldn't have been hit from this [sixth floor] window in the position where he was sitting."[117] Thomas Canning, an engineer from NASA, concluded that the bullet that struck Connally's back was proceeding on a downward trajectory of 25 degrees below horizontal.[118] Given the 25-degree angle given for the Connally back shot, and the fact that he is facing to the right, roughly northwest (or north by northwest) when he grimaces (on the Zapruder film) in reaction to being hit, I believe that the most likely location for the source of that shot was atop the Dallas County Records Building on Houston Street, just south of the Dal-Tex Building. J. Gary Shaw and Larry Harris provide a diagram showing the shot that hit Connally in the back coming from the southwest corner of the Records Building.[119] Josiah Thompson also believed that the bullet that hit Gov. Connally in the back was fired from the Records Building. Bugliosi queries how such a bullet hit Connally where it did without first passing through Kennedy's body. Simple: that bullet was fired from a different, higher location. This will give the reader an idea of how confused Mr. Bugliosi is: In a note to page 287 in his endnotes, Bugliosi says that "we know from the Zapruder film" that Gov. Connally's body was "turned fairly sharply to the right at the moment of impact [of the bullet to his back]." (This is one of the few accurate statements in the book.) If Connally's body was turned sharply to the right, how could the magic bullet enter Kennedy's back (or base of the neck), depart through a little hole in his throat, and then enter Connally's back if that back was then at right angles to Kennedy?

One shot hit Gov. Connally in the right wrist, which was apparently a separate bullet from the one that hit him in the back. Dr. Cyril Wecht told the HSCA that Connally is still holding his Stetson after he was supposedly hit by the same bullet that hit Kennedy, which, he pointed out, would be a physical impossibility given Connally's injuries – his right lung pierced and collapsed, with the distal end of the radius of his right arm comminuted [fragmented] and the radial nerve partially severed.[120] In an interview for the video series *The Men Who Killed Kennedy*, Dr. Wecht noted (on camera) that the Zapruder film shows that Connally's right hand was nowhere near his left thigh when he was hit in the back.

One shot hit the curb in front of James Tague. Mr. Bugliosi had to keep the number of shots to three, so he tells us that the bullet that hit the pavement "went on to strike the south curb on Main Street at the base of the Triple Underpass, propelling a bit of the concrete (or a bullet fragment) into the right cheek of James Tague ..."[121] The concrete thrown up by this bullet did slightly wound Mr. Tague (on his cheek), but it seems doubtful that a bullet that had already hit concrete once would have enough energy to do such damage to the curb in front of Tague (and to Tague). Deputy Sheriff Eddy R. "Buddy" Walthers "found where a bullet had splattered on the top edge of the curb on Main Street ... near the underpass."[122] This was probably the same bullet that hit the concrete near James Tague. Mr. Tague showed Walthers where the bullet that caused a piece of concrete to cut his cheek hit: on the top of the south curb of Main Street, and Bugliosi tells us that from the angle of the mark, it is "obvious" that the bullet came from the direction of the Book Depository. Why is it obvious? Bugliosi tells us that since the bullet fired in the second shot was recovered at Parkland Hospital, the mark on the curb in front of James Tague must have been caused by a fragment from either the first or third shots in Dealey Plaza.[123] L. Fletcher Prouty pointed out many years ago that a line drawn from the curb impact of the bullet that caused the wound on Tague's cheek through an eighteen-inch-diameter circle around Kennedy's head leads to the second floor of the Dal-Tex Building, where an unidentified man was, in fact, seen (and photographed) in a second-floor window behind the fire escape. Thus the probable source of this shot was the Dal-Tex Building. (Prouty was Chief of Special Operations in the Joint Staff, working for the Joint Chiefs of Staff. He stated that his job title was a euphemism for the military support of CIA operations around the world. Bugliosi writes Prouty off as a "zany right-winger.") Mannlicher-Carcano bullets were copper-jacketed; analysis revealed that there was no copper in the segment of curb where the bullet hit.

One shot apparently hit the chrome molding across the inside top of the limousine's windshield. Photos taken after the shooting show a dent in this location, just to the left of the rearview mirror support, that appears to have been made by a bullet. The dent is shown on page 41 of Groden's book and is mentioned in the Warren Report. Robert Frazier found a dent in the chrome strip that goes across the top of the windshield, on the passenger side, on the inside surface, "which had been caused by some projectile," though he said it was more likely caused by a bullet fragment than a bullet traveling at full velocity.[124] Carl Renas, head of security for the Dearborn Division of the Ford Motor Company, drove the death car back to Cincinnati from Washington; he also noticed this dent (and other bullet holes), which he said was clearly "a primary strike" and "not a fragment." The Secret Service told Renas to keep his mouth shut. CE349 in volume 16 of the Hearings and Exhibits is a photograph of the windshield from inside the limousine; it seems to show a bullet strike near the center of the chrome strip at the top of the windshield, just to the right of center. The FBI Protective Research Report of 27 November 1963 noted that "the chrome molding strip above the windshield, inside the car, just right of center, was dented."[125] A letter from James Rowley to Warren Commission Chief Counsel J. Lee Rankin dated January 6, 1964, states that Secret Service agent Morgan Gies believed that the dent in the chrome strip was done before November 22, 1963.[126] The probable source of this shot was the Dal-Tex or Dallas County Records Building.

One shot may have hit Kennedy in the right front of his head. At least one photograph seen by government photographer Joseph O'Donnell within the first week after the assassination showed a right forehead entry.[127] Tom Robinson, the Gawler's Funeral Home mortician who restored Kennedy's head, recalled placing wax into a hole about a quarter-inch across, above the right eye, near the hairline.[128] (Robinson did not testify to the commission or its legal staff.) But we don't know if this was the real Kennedy or the Bethesda make-believe Kennedy.

One shot hit the pavement in front and to the left of the limousine. Royce Skelton, who was standing on top of the Triple Underpass, testified that when the limousine came down closer to the underpass, he saw a bullet hit the cement in the left front of the limousine.[129] So this was late in the shooting sequence. Skelton's co-worker, Austin Miller, was standing next to Skelton, also evidently saw this bullet.[130] Miller stated in an affidavit, "One shot apparently hit the street past the car." His affidavit stated that the bullet hit the pavement in the left or middle lane.[131] Dallas policeman J.W. Foster told the commission that he found a location where a shot had hit concrete near a manhole cover.[132] A photograph on page 70 on Groden's book shows a bullet strike near a manhole cover that appears to line up with the Dallas County Records Building.

NB: One of the shots from behind the limousine was supposed to hit President Kennedy in the back of the head. This would prove a shot from behind, and since Lee Oswald was supposedly firing from the "sniper's nest," this shot would "prove" that Oswald killed the president with a shot to the back of the head. Since none of these bullets hit their mark, and the president was still alive, the plotters had to implement their fall-back position, in the form of a sniper behind the stockade fence on the grassy knoll.

Before the final, fatal shot, limousine driver Will Greer brought the car to a stop, turned around to his right, and apparently looked directly at President Kennedy. This can be seen in the Zapruder film.

One shot, fired from somewhere behind the stockade fence, hit President Kennedy just behind the right ear, blowing off part of his occipital and pushing his head and torso violently back and to the left, and killing him. There may have been a second shot from the knoll. Gordon Arnold was standing in the grassy area in front of the stockade fence. When he was interviewed by Henry Hurt for Hurt's 1985 book *Reasonable Doubt: An Investigation into the Assassination of John F. Kennedy,* he told Hurt about a bullet flying by his left ear and another one flying by him from behind after he hit the ground. In a 1978 re-enactment for Jay Goodwin, photographer for Earl Golz of the *Dallas Morning News,* Arnold placed himself at or very near the southeast corner of the fence. Bugliosi says that photos show that Arnold wasn't on the grassy knoll where he said he was.[133] But Ralph Yarborough, Democratic US Senator from Texas, told Earl Golz in 1978 that he saw someone in Arnold's position drop to the ground after the first shot.

Witnesses also reported that a bullet hit the Stemmons Freeway sign in front of the concrete pergola. This must have been the shot that James "Jim" Hicks, a surveyor from Enid, Oklahoma, reported going over his head into a traffic sign. The sign was removed almost at once by men he assumed to be Dallas police.

As noted above, A.J. Millican heard *five* shots from the area of the colonnade alone. This gives a grand total of around twelve to sixteen shots, not the three shots discussed in the Warren Report (and in Mr. Bugliosi's book). Roy Kellerman told the commission that as he was telling agent

Lawson (via microphone), "We are hit; get us to the hospital immediately," a "flurry of shots" came into the limousine.[134] The shooters were located on the second floor of the Dal-Tex Building, atop (or on an upper floor of) the Dallas County Records Building, and behind the stockade fence on the grassy knoll.

The shots that hit the Elm Street pavement can be found in various places in the Warren Commission Hearings and Exhibits, but they were evidently ignored by the commissioners, since they were never explained in the Report itself.

Re-reading the Warren Report, I discovered another of its false statements: "At about the time he reached the President's automobile, [Secret Service agent Clinton] Hill heard a second shot, approximately 5 seconds after the first, which removed a portion of the President's head."[135] The Zapruder film clearly shows that by the time Hill reaches the limousine, the fatal shot had already hit Kennedy, whose brain and skull tissue, and cranial blood, were scattered over the trunk of the car. Agent Hill ran to the limousine to nudge Mrs. Kennedy back into her seat, because she had partially climbed onto the trunk of the car to gather the fragments of her husband's skull.

Arnold Rowland saw a man holding a high-powered rifle across his chest at the *west* end of the sixth floor at about 12:15 p.m. Rowland testified that he "saw a man standing holding a rifle ... in the west corner of the [Book Depository] building ... both windows were completely open." The man was wearing a light-colored shirt, white or light blue, and standing three to five feet back from the window. The barrel was pointed "in the air toward the ceiling or the wall next to him." He told the FBI agent who was taking his statement that the man was holding the rifle in a port-arms position; but the agent documenting Rowland's statement changed it to parade-rest.[136] Mr. Rowland told his wife Barbara that he saw the rifleman about fifteen minutes before the motorcade came by.[137] Deputy Sheriff Roger Craig testified that Rowland told him that one man had a rifle with a scope; Rowland also told Dallas policeman F.M. Turner that he saw a man in the west window with a scoped rifle.[138] The Warren Report tries to destroy Arnold Rowland's credibility in several paragraphs on pages 251-52. Robert Jackson also saw a man with a rifle on the sixth floor of the *westernmost* part of the Book Depository, though he said the window was only halfway open.[139]

Mr. Bugliosi, quoting Dennis Breo in the *Journal of the American Medical Association,* who is in turn supposedly quoting Dr. Carrico, says that "the four main Parkland doctors who attended to the dying president (Perry, Carrico, Jenkins, and Baxter) now all agree" that the bullets were fired from above and behind by a high-velocity bullet.[140] In fact, nothing in the Warren Commission testimony of Drs. Baxter, Carrico, Perry, or Jenkins mentions a high-velocity rifle bullet fired from above and behind. Dr. Perry stated, "I could not tell whether there was one or two bullets, or from whence they came..."[141]

Smoke Near the Grassy Knoll

Bugliosi goes on at some length in his endnotes attempting to negate the statements of people who said they saw smoke rising from the grassy knoll area.[142] So let us consider the record. The following individuals said that they saw smoke or smelled gunpowder in the grassy knoll area:

DPD Officer Earle Brown was on the Triple Underpass; he told the commission that he smelled gunpowder.[143] Mrs. Donald Baker was standing in front of the Book Depository when the motorcade passed by. She told the commission that she smelled gun smoke after the second shot.[144] Deputy Sheriff A.D. McCurley stated that he "ran over and jumped a fence and a railroad worker stated to me that he believed the smoke from the bullets came from the vicinity of a stockade fence which surrounds the park area."[145] In an affidavit dated November 22, Austin Miller stated, "I saw something which I thought was smoke or steam coming from the group of trees north of Elm off the railroad tracks."[146] (He had no opinion regarding the source of the shots.)

Dealey Plaza eyewitnesses Thomas Murphy and Walter Winborn (the latter was on the Triple Underpass) told author Stewart Galanor in 1966 that they saw smoke under the trees in the knoll area. Winborn told Galanor that he told the FBI about seeing smoke there, but they omitted that from their report.[147] (Winborn had no opinion regarding the source of the shots, but he said they sounded like they all came from the same area. – FBI affidavit, March 19, 1964, 22H833; neither Murphy nor Winborn testified to the commission or its legal staff.)

James Simmons, railroad inspector, and Richard Dodd, Union Terminal foreman, both of whom were atop the Triple Underpass, told Mark Lane that they saw smoke in the knoll area. Simmons "thought he saw exhaust fumes of smoke near the embankment in front of the Texas School Book Depository Building." According to an FBI report of an interview with Simmons dated March 19, 1964, it was Simmons' opinion that the shots came from the direction of the Book Depository.[148] But he told Mark Lane that the last shot appeared to come from the near the picket fence, and that he saw smoke near the fence. (Neither Simmons nor Dodd testified to the commission or its legal staff.) At the Shaw trial, Simmons stated that after he heard the shots, "underneath the trees up on the grassy knoll by the fence I detected what appeared to be a puff of smoke or wisp of smoke."[149]

In an affidavit for the Sheriff's Department, given on the day of the assassination, Sam Holland stated that he saw a puff of smoke that "definitely came from behind the arcade through the trees." Holland stated that after JFK slumped over, "I looked over toward the arcade and trees and saw a puff of smoke come from the trees and I heard *three more shots* from behind the arcade through the trees."[150] (Emphasis added.) This seems to give credence to Gordon Arnold's statement that more than one shot was fired from behind the stockade fence. Holland told the commission that he had "no doubt about seeing that puff of smoke come out from under those trees…" He "looked over toward the arcade and trees and saw a puff of smoke come from the trees and I heard three more shots after the first shot…"[151] He also told Mark Lane that he saw smoke, near the trees, from the third shot.[152] Holland later (1966) told Josiah Thompson that the smoke was from ten to fifteen feet west of the southeast corner of the picket fence. Nolan Potter and Clemon Johnson were atop the Triple Underpass with Sam Holland. Potter "said he recalls seeing smoke in front of the [Book Depository] rising above the trees."[153] According to an FBI interview with Johnson, he said that "white smoke was observed near the pavilion, but he felt that this smoke came from a motorcycle…"[154] (Neither Potter nor Johnson testified to the commission or its legal staff.)

The HSCA noted the observations of Messrs. Miller, Johnson, Holland, Simmons and Potter, and stated, "Based on the statements of these witnesses, if the smoke they reported was in fact the result of gunfire, it would have originated in the area of the top of the grassy knoll."[155]

The Magic Bullet

The following is the genesis of the single-bullet theory and the Warren Commission position: Since Governor Connally appeared to be hit just 2.3 seconds after President Kennedy was hit, and since the lone nut assassin couldn't get off two shots that quickly from a bolt-action rifle, and "knowing" that only three shots were fired, the two men must have been hit by the same bullet. Bugliosi basically repeats the Warren scenario: since the magic bullet went into Kennedy's back and out his throat, the bullet had to go somewhere; and since it wasn't found in the limousine, it must have gone into Connally's back. The bullet that supposedly hit JFK in the back of his neck and the bullet that hit Connally were so close together in time that one person could not have fired both. So Arlen Specter et al. invented the single-bullet or magic bullet theory, i.e., that one bullet hit both men. This theory was essential for the survival of the lone assassin idea. Norman Redlich told Bugliosi that the single-bullet theory was arrived at by him and fellow assistant counsels Arlen Specter, Howard Willens, David Belin and Melvin Eisenberg.[156] Mr. Bugliosi tells us that "because of the alignment of Connally's body vis-à-vis Kennedy's, it was virtually inevitable that a bullet traveling on a downward trajectory and passing on a straight line through soft tissue in Kennedy's body (as both the Warren Commission and HSCA concluded) would go on to strike Connally where it did."[157] Bugliosi reminds us that Robert Frazier told the commission that "because Kennedy and Connally were in direct alignment with each other during those frames from the vantage point of the rifle in the sniper's nest, 'the [bullet] through the president *had* to cause Connally's wound, otherwise it would have struck somewhere else in the car and it did not strike somewhere else. Therefore, it *had* to go through Governor Connally.'"[158] Bugliosi tells us that a test of the single-bullet theory in Dallas on May 24, 1964, "confirmed the theory ... that the alignment of Kennedy's and Connally's bodies to each other in the presidential limousine was such that the bullet that struck Kennedy in his upper right back and exited his throat would have had to go on to hit Connally."[159] Note that the magic-bullet entry has now moved from the back of the neck to the upper right back. Bugliosi parrots Frazier and says that if "the bullet that exited the president's throat did not go on to hit Connally, it would have inevitably gone on to hit the driver or caused some significant penetrating damage to the interior of the car. Yet no such damage was found ... Since the bullet, after exiting Kennedy's throat on a downward trajectory, never struck the interior of the car, *it must have struck someone in the car*. And other than Kennedy, only Connally was hit by a bullet." "It was obvious," says Bugliosi; "The bullet had exited the throat."[160] But the throat wound was an entry wound. The Warren Report states, "[T]he doctors at Parkland agreed that [the throat shot] was an exit wound."[161] On page 105, the Report mentions "the bullet that hit President Kennedy in the back and exited his throat ..." Bugliosi says, "We know from all the medical evidence that the throat wound to the president was an exit wound ..."[162]

The Autopsy Protocol prepared by Bethesda autopsy doctors James Humes and Thornton Boswell describes the back/neck wound as follows: "Situated on the upper right thorax just above the upper border of the scapula there is a 7x4 millimeter oval wound. This wound is measured to be 14 cm [5½ inches] from the tip of the right acromion process and 14 cm. below the tip of the right mastoid process." In his commission testimony, Humes described the acromion as the tip of the shoulder joint. Assuming that the distance between the outer edges of the right and left acromion processes in President Kennedy was about 16 inches, these two 14 cm measurements put the wound in the upper right back, several inches from the base of the neck. Dallas County Medical Examiner Dr. Earl Rose told Bugliosi, correctly, that a point "on the upper right posterior thorax just above the upper border of the scapula" is in the *upper back,* not the lower neck.[163] The thorax is the part of the body enclosed by the ribs; it is not the neck. Interviewed by Jeremy Gunn of the ARRB on February 13, 1996, Dr. Humes stated, "There was a bullet wound in the back above the scapula." This must be the magic bullet, since one bullet missed and one supposedly struck the president in the back of the head, near the external occipital protuberance. So the magic bullet evidently hit first in the upper right back, above the scapula, then traveled across the back and entered the base of the back of the neck, then turned right and exited Kennedy's throat and went on to cause all of Governor Connally's wounds. The death certificate prepared by Admiral George Burkley, President Kennedy's personal physician, dated November 23, 1963, states that the back wound was at the third thoracic vertebra (T3), four to six inches below the point at which the shoulders meet the neck. Dr. John H. Ebersole, assistant chief radiologist at Bethesda, told Dr. David W. Mantik, MD, PhD, that the back wound was at T4. This is the fourth (from the top) thoracic vertebra, not "the base of the neck." (Adm. Burkley did not testify to the commission or its legal staff, though he was the only person to be present at both Parkland and Bethesda on November 22.) In his ARRB testimony, Dr. Boswell stated that the back wound was "certainly not as low as T4 … I would say around T2." This also is not "the base of the neck"; the base of the neck would have been the sixth or seventh *cervical* vertebra (C6 or C7). The autopsy photo showing two gloved hands holding a ruler against the upper back of what is supposedly JFK's body doesn't show a hole in the base of the neck, but it does show what appears to be a small hole about three inches below the neck – where no one saw a bullet hole (in the real Kennedy). Another autopsy photo, also a view from behind, shows one gloved hand at the top of Kennedy's head (where Dr. Humes said there was a large defect), with a "bat wing" of bone hanging out just above the right ear; this photo doesn't show any bullet hole in the base of the neck, either. But then, neither photo is of John Kennedy!

The Warren Report tells us of the "entry near the base of the back of the neck slightly to the right of the spine."[164] In the conclusion to Chapter IV ("The Assassin"), the Report mentions "the shots which struck the President in the back of the neck." This supposed entry wound near the base of the back of the neck was the supposed entry point for the magic bullet.

So it appears that we have *four* posterior wounds in the president's body, officially speaking: one in the base of the back of the neck, one that was four to six inches below the base of the neck (between T2 and T4), one in the upper right back above the scapula, and one (described above under Sequence and Source of Shots and in the Warren Report) 5¾ inches below the top of the president's collar and 1⅛ inches to the right of the midline of his back. But the Warren Report tells us that only three shots were fired: one missed, one (the magic bullet) entered the base of the back of the president's neck, exited the front of the neck, and went on to cause all of Gov. Connally's wounds; and one entered through a small hole in the back of the president's head and exited via the right parietal bone, causing a large wound there (or it exited the right temple, according to the Zapruder film).

Bugliosi notes that FBI agent Elmer Lee Todd was the last in the chain of custody of CE399, the pristine Mannlicher-Carcano bullet that supposedly passed through President Kennedy's neck and cause all of Governor Connally's wounds, and he marked the bullet with his initials "and could therefore positively identify it as the bullet retrieved from the stretcher."[165] That proves only that he received a Mannlicher-Carcano bullet and marked it. Bugliosi says that "we do know that the stretcher bullet was fired from Oswald's rifle to the exclusion of *all* other weapons." He says that the "discovery" of CE399 at Parkland Hospital means "we know that the bullet was fired from Oswald's Carcano rifle."[166] Mr. Bugliosi uses the phrase "we know" quite often, as will be seen, when he really means, "I believe, and I want you to believe, despite all logic, eyewitness testimony and the facts..." Darrell Tomlinson, Parkland chief engineer, told the commission's Arlen Specter that when he pushed a stretcher against a wall to provide a clear area in front of a nearby elevator, "a spent cartridge or bullet rolled out that apparently had been lodged under the edge of a mat."[167] Tomlinson gave the slug to O.P. Wright, chief of security at Parkland Hospital, who gave it to Secret Service agent Richard Johnsen. In a memorandum from agent Johnsen to Secret Service chief James Rowley, dated November 30, 1963, Johnsen states that shortly before leaving Parkland, "Mr. [O.P.] Wright from the security staff came to me with an expended bullet and wished to turn it over to a Secret Service agent... [Wright stated] that the bullet had been found on a stretcher which President Kennedy may have been placed on." (Wright did not testify to the commission or its legal staff.) After returning to Washington, Johnsen turned the bullet over to Chief Rowley, who gave it to an FBI agent.

Bugliosi claims that a copper-jacketed bullet fragment found on the floor on the right side of the driver's seat in the limousine (CE569) "bore enough barrel markings to positively link it to Oswald's rifle through ordinary firearms identification means." What Frazier testified to was that the bullet fragment submitted to him as being found beside the front seat of the limousine was fired from CE139 (the Carcano) to the exclusion of all other rifles.[168] This cannot be accurate; to compare a bullet to the weapon that fired it, one must have a bullet that is whole or nearly so, so that the lands and grooves of the bullet, and the direction of twist, can be compared to a bullet test-fired from the subject weapon. A fragment of a bullet cannot be linked to a single rifle to the exclusion of all others. Of course, another reason why Mr. Frazier's testimony is phony is because the Carcano did not fire any bullets at the limousine!

Among the conclusions of the HSCA Photographic Evidence Panel: "[T]he relative alinement of President Kennedy and Governor Connally within the limousine is consistent with the single bullet theory."[169] Bugliosi says that "the Warren Commission clearly established the single-bullet theory by the testimony of scientists back in 1964"and that when other nonmedical evidence is considered, there can be *no reasonable doubt* that both men were struck with the same, single bullet."[170] It is understandable that Bugliosi adheres to the single-bullet theory, for without it, the lone-nut-assassin concept falls apart.

It isn't particularly difficult to refute the nonsensical single-bullet or "magic bullet" theory:

- After Kennedy is hit and his hands come to his throat, Gov. Connally is seen in the Zapruder film turning around to look at the president. At Z275, Connally has turned nearly a full 180 degrees to look at JFK. Connally isn't hit until Z290 at the earliest; up until then, he is still holding his hat. He is turning back to the front when he shows signs of being hit. So if the two men were hit by the same bullet (and knowing that there were no bullet holes in Kennedy's hands), this means that the magic bullet entered the back of Kennedy's neck, then went out the front of his neck, then paused in the air, then the president's hands went up to his throat, then Connally started to turn back to the front, then the magic bullet hit Connally in the back and wrist. The Warren Report states, "Before the shooting started, Governor Connally had been facing toward the crowd on the right. He started to turn toward the left and suddenly felt a blow on his back."[171] As the Zapruder film shows, Gov. Connally is indeed looking to the right when he emerges from behind the Stemmons Freeway sign, then he turns to face forward, and realizing that Kennedy has been hit, he turns around to look at him, and only then, *after* having turned around thus, does he turn to his left and that is when he is seen reacting to the shot to his back. Furthermore, when Kennedy reacts to the throat shot at Z-225, he is facing the grassy knoll, which is obviously inconsistent with the idea that a bullet fired from the "sniper's nest" window exited the front of the president's neck and went on to hit Gov. Connally, who was in front of Kennedy.

• No bullet went into the back of Kennedy's neck and out the front, because the wound in the throat was an entry wound.

• Any such trajectory, entering Kennedy's back and moving from right to left and exiting his throat, would have to intersect cervical vertebrae, which it did not.[172] Neither the autopsy doctors nor the x-rays indicated any major trauma to the spine.

• The angle of declination of Connally's back wound was too steep to have been caused by a bullet coming from President Kennedy's throat. The Warren Report itself states, "Governor Connally's doctors measured an angle of declination on his body from the entry wound on his back to the exit on the front of his chest at about 25° when he sat erect."[173] Dr. Humes said that his "guesstimate" at the autopsy of the angle of the bullet that hit Connally in the back was 45 to 60 degrees. During the Warren Commission testimony of Gov. Connally at 4H137, Dr. Robert Shaw estimated the angle of the bullet that entered Gov. Connally's back at 25 degrees from the horizontal, but a 1964 FBI analysis came up with an angle of "approximately 35 degrees downward from the horizontal, and approximately 20 degrees from right to left if he was sitting erect and facing forward at the time he was shot" – which, of course, he was not! Both elevations are far too steep to have come from the "sniper's nest," but Bugliosi says this is consistent with Oswald's firing position![174] Furthermore, the angle of a bullet entering someone's body does not depend on how the person is sitting.

• The back shot didn't enter the base of Kennedy's neck; it entered his upper back, and that bullet did not exit. No Parkland doctor saw a small, round entry wound in the back of Kennedy's neck, nor does it appear in Dr. Boswell's official autopsy drawing. Nurse Bowron told Harrison Livingstone in 1993 that she saw a hole in Kennedy's *back* while preparing the body for placement in the coffin. Clint Hill told the commission that when Kennedy's body was at the morgue, he saw "an opening in the back, about 6 inches below the neckline to the right-hand side of the spinal column."[175] Bugliosi embraced the ridiculous "bunched-up shirt and jacket" theory to explain why the holes in JFK's shirt and suit coat don't line up with the concept of a bullet to the base of the back of the neck. FBI agent Sibert remembered one of the doctors, he thought it was Dr. Finck, using a chrome probe to probe the back wound. Dr. Finck said, "There's no exit."[176] Others also said the bullet entered Kennedy's back and didn't exit. Autopsy photographer Floyd Riebe told the ARRB on May 7, 1997, that he saw what looked like a bullet hole in the back that "didn't go very far." (Riebe did not testify to the commission or its legal staff.) Bugliosi tells us of three pathologists rolling the president over on his left side and examining an oval-shaped bullet hole to the right of his spine and just above the right shoulder blade. (What happened to the idea of the entry point being at the base of the back of Kennedy's neck?) Dr. Mantik notes that reports of a bullet lodging in Kennedy's right shoulder appeared in *JAMA* (1/4/64), the *New York Times* (1/26/64), and the *Washington Post* (12/18/63).[177] In the death certificate, Adm. Burkley, the White House physician, noted this wound in the back "at about the location of the third thoracic vertebra." This is five to six inches below the neckline.[178] Interviewing Thomas Kelley of the Secret Service, Specter mentions CE386, which he says is a drawing that was "the basis for the marking of the wound in the back of the President's neck." He adds that "this was made by the autopsy surgeons at Bethesda."[179] Robert Frazier said there was a hole in Kennedy's jacket 5⅜ inches below the top of the collar and 1¾ inches to the right of the midline (both as viewed from the back).[180] The Warren Report notes that Kennedy's shirt contained a hole in the back 5¾ inches below the top of the collar and 1⅛ inches to the right of the middle of the back of the shirt.[181] The Report (p. 91) states that Kennedy's clothing that day "had holes and tears which showed that a missile entered the back of his clothing in the vicinity of his lower neck and exited through the front of his shirt immediately behind his tie...," but on the very next page the Report describes the holes in his coat and shirt 5⅜ inches and 5¾ inches, respectively, below the top of the collar.

• John Connally stated at least three times in public forums that he was absolutely sure that he was hit by a separate bullet than the one that hit Kennedy in the back (or neck). The Warren Commission explained the gap between the Kennedy back shot and the Connally back shot by stating that it was a "delayed reaction." But Gov. Connally himself knew that the magic bullet scenario was false. I counted 1.6 seconds between the throat shot and the shot that hit Gov. Connally. This is the same figure arrived at by Josiah Thompson.[181] Connally told Arlen Specter, "It is not conceivable to me that I could have been hit by the first bullet."[183] In a 1991 CSPAN videotaped interview, Connally stated that after turning around to look at Kennedy, he as in "the process of turning to my left" when he felt the impact of the bullet. There was no "delayed reaction."

• Motorcycle policeman James Chaney, who was riding off the right rear of the limousine, told Officer Marrion Baker that two shots hit Kennedy first, and then the other one hit Connally.[184]

• Any bullet fired from the Book Depository into Kennedy's back would hit at an angle of about twelve degrees from horizontal. Mr. Bugliosi says that the angle of declination of the bullet that hit JFK's back was scientifically determined to be around 20 degrees.[185] But Bugliosi also says, "The bullet that entered the president's body in the upper right part of his back only passed through soft tissue before exiting from his throat."[186] This is Bugliosi's way of explaining why the "exit" wound in the throat is small and circular, rather than large and jagged. On page 414, Bugliosi again says that the doctors were confused about whether the throat wound was a wound of entry of exit because they weren't aware of "the corresponding wound in the president's back." Note that the wound has again moved from the neck to the back. Problem: If the bullet entered the back (which happens to be below the neck) and exited the throat, it would be on an *upward* trajectory, completely inconsistent with a bullet fired from above and behind but consistent with a bullet fired from the rear bumper of the car, or maybe the exhaust pipe. Dr. Finck, head of the Wound Ballistics Pathology Branch of the Armed Forces Institute of Pathology in 1963, told the commission that the angle was "within 45 degrees from the horizontal plane."[187] At the Clay Shaw trial on February 24, 1969, Dr. Finck testified as follows: "[Y]ou will notice that the entry in the back of the neck is higher than the exit in the front of the neck." But later in his testimony, Dr. Finck stated that he saw no exit in the front of the neck[188] Still later in his testimony on that day, Dr. Finck stated, "Photographs 26 and 38 show the wound in the back of the neck higher from the horizontal plane than the wound in the throat."[189] According to Bugliosi, "the physical evidence" is "*absolutely conclusive* that only three shots were fired, and that one of the two shots that hit Kennedy also went on to hit Connally. Hence, Connally was not hit by a separate bullet, which would have established a second gunman and a conspiracy."[190] Note the similarity to the Warren Report, which states: "The bullet that hit President Kennedy in the back and exited through his throat most likely could not have missed both the automobile and its occupants. Since it did not hit the automobile, [firearms expert Robert A.] Frazier testified that it probably struck Governor Connally."[191] Bugliosi also mentions "the *apparent* backward snap of the president's head at the moment of the head shot, and the *alleged* delayed reaction between Kennedy and Connally..."

• Both Dr. Humes and Dr. Finck told Arlen Specter that there were more bullet fragments in Gov. Connally than were missing from CE399; Finck flatly stated that CE399 could not have inflicted the wound on Connally's right wrist.[192] Back in 1967, an article in the *Saturday Evening Post* had already noted that the medical experts found more fragments in Connally's thigh than were missing from "the bullet" (CE399).[193] Dr. Humes told Specter that he did not believe that CE 399 could have gone through JFK's head, and it was "most unlikely" that it could have made the wound in Connally's wrist. He said that was because small bits of metal were found "at various levels" in Connally's wrist, whereas CE399 is basically intact. Based on the fragments shown on the x-rays of JFK's head and on the bullet fragments that had been removed from Connally's wrist, Humes said, "I do not understand how it [CE399] could have possibly have left fragments" of which he had knowledge.[194] Dr. Shaw told the commission that the examination of Gov. Connally's wrist "both by X-ray and at the time of surgery showed some fragments of metal that make it difficult to believe that the same missile could have caused these two wounds. There seems to be more than three grains of metal missing ... I feel that there would be some difficulty in explaining all of the wounds as being inflicted by bullet Exhibit 399 without causing more in the way of loss of substance to the bullet or deformation of the bullet... in the sequence of films [e.g., Zapruder's] I think it is hard to say that the first bullet hit both of these men simultaneously."[195] Ignoring this testimony, the Warren Report states, "All the evidence indicated that the bullet found on the Governor's stretcher could have caused all his wounds."[196]

- Robert Frazier testified that when CE399 was delivered to him for examination within hours of its discovery, the bullet was clean and had no blood or other tissue on it.[197]

Bugliosi notes that Josiah Thompson stated, "Had both victims been hit by the same bullet, we would expect Connally to be manifesting the signs of impact at least *sixteen* frames earlier."[198] Bugliosi says that Thompson is incorrect about the time that Connally first reacts, and says that "subsequent investigations agree that Gov. Connally is shown reacting immediately after emerging from behind the Stemmons sign, at Z222 ..."[199] As the Zapruder film shows, this did not happen. After the president's hands go to his throat, Connally turns around nearly 180 degrees to see what's happening, meanwhile showing absolutely no signs of being hit, and it is only after he is turning back around to face forward that he felt the impact of a bullet (and is seen reacting to that impact). That's what he said in at least two videotaped interviews. Indeed, Bugliosi himself quotes from Connally's statement in the November 25, 1966, edition of *Life* magazine: "They talk about the one-bullet or two-bullet theory, but as far as I am concerned, there is no theory. There is my absolute knowledge ... that one bullet caused the President's first wound, and that an entirely separate shot struck me. It's a certainty. I'll never change my mind."[200] That's exactly what the Zapruder film shows.

Dr. Cyril Wecht submitted the following statement to the HSCA: "The angles at which these two men were hit do not permit a straight line trajectory (or near straight line trajectory) of Commission exhibit 399 (the so-called magic bullet) to be established.... In order to accept the SBT, it is necessary to have the bullet move at different vertical and horizontal angles, a path of flight that has never been experienced or suggested for any bullet known to mankind.... Specifically, there is no way that this bullet [CE399] could have caused all the bone damage to JBC's right fifth rib and right radius, without having sustained more physical deformity."[201] He added, "The vertical and horizontal trajectory of this bullet, 399, under the single-bullet theory, is absolutely unfathomable, indefensible and incredible."[202] The single-bullet theory is thus refuted.

Responding to filmmaker Oliver Stone, Bugliosi says the magic bullet "didn't have to do anything magical at all in midair in order to go on and hit Connally. All it had to do, Oliver, is continue traveling in a straight line."[203] It is not clear how a bullet fired from six stories up could travel in a straight line, parallel to the street, as it passes through the president's neck.

Three of the Warren Commissioners – Boggs, Russell and Cooper – doubted the validity of the single-bullet theory. In a (taped) phone call between Lyndon Johnson and Sen. Russell on September 18, 1964, Russell stated, among other things, that "the commission believes that the same bullet that hit Kennedy hit Connally. Well, I don't believe it!" Johnson replied, "I don't either."

Warren Report Forensics and Ballistics

President Kennedy's wounds move around quite a bit in the Warren Report. Here are the Report's descriptions of the president's wounds, which are scattered over several pages and vary from one point to another. Page 3: After the shot in the "back of the neck," the president "was struck a second time by a bullet which entered the right-rear portion of his head, causing a massive and fatal wound." Page 4: "The autopsy disclosed the large head wound observed at Parkland and the wound in the front of the neck which had been enlarged by the Parkland doctors when they performed the tracheotomy..." The Report has gone wrong already: the autopsy report described a large wound high on the right side of the head, whereas the Parkland doctors saw a wound in the lower right rear of the head. Page 4 also mentions that the autopsy revealed a small wound of entry in the rear of the President's skull. Page 48: "One bullet passed through the President's neck; a subsequent bullet, which was lethal, shattered the right side of his skull." This is false, of course. It is what the Zapruder film seems to show, but the official autopsy photographs show no wound in that location, nor did any of the doctors or nurses at Parkland see a wound in that location. The Warren Report only mentions two Parkland doctors – Charles J. Carrico and William Kemp Clark – who noted the large wound in the *right rear* of the head. On page 54, we read that "Dr. Carrico noted... an extensive wound in the President's head where a sizable portion of the skull was missing." The Report conveniently omits Dr. Carrico's description, in his Warren Commission testimony, of that wound being in the right occipitoparietal area; see "The Phony Autopsy Photos and X-rays," below. Also on page 54, we read that "Dr. Clark ... described a large, gaping wound in the right rear of the head, with substantial damage and exposure of brain tissue..." This is the wound that the doctors and nurses at Parkland Hospital saw, and is obviously at odds with the description on page 48 of the Report.

The Warren Report states, "The autopsy examination revealed two wounds in the President's head. One wound, approximately one-fourth of an inch by five-eighths on an inch (6 by 15 millimeters), was located about an inch (2.5 centimeters) to the right and slightly above the large bony protrusion (external occipital protuberance) which juts out at the center of the lower part of the back of the skull."[204] This wound was, of course, in an area that had been blown out, as described to the commission by Drs. Clark and Carrico. The Report stated, "The small hole in the head was... hidden from view by the large quantity of blood which covered the president's head."[205] The problem, of course, is that nobody at Parkland saw that small hole. Asked (by Arlen Specter) specifically if they saw a smaller wound in the back of Kennedy's head below the massive head wound they described, Drs. Perry, Baxter, Akin, McClelland and Peters, and Nurse Bowron, all said that they did not.[206] The Report states, "The second head wound measured approximately 5 inches (13 centimeters) in its greatest diameter..." The latter passage doesn't say where on the president's head that wound was. (Author's note: 13 centimeters is actually 5.1 inches.) On page 19, it is stated that a bullet entered at the back of Kennedy's neck. On page 87, the word "base" enters the picture: "During the autopsy... another bullet wound was observed near the base of the back of President Kennedy's neck slightly to the right of his spine... The hole was located approximately 5½ inches (14 centimeters) from the tip of the right shoulder joint."[207] These measurements put the alleged wound in the upper right back, somewhat distant from the neck.

Also on page 87, the Report states that Drs. Humes and Boswell concluded "that the [fatal] bullet penetrated the rear of the President's head and exited through a large wound on the right side of his head." In Warren Report Appendices VIII and IX, the fatal head wound has moved to the back of the president's head: in Appendix VIII, pages 517-18, "Medical Reports From Doctors at Parkland Memorial Hospital, Dallas, Tex.," the Report quotes from the autopsy "Summary" signed by Dr. Kemp Clark (CE392): "Two external wounds, one in the lower third of the anterior neck, the other in the occipital region of the skull, were noted... There was a large wound in the *right occipito-parietal region*, from which profuse bleeding was occurring." (Emphasis added.) Back on page 48, it was "the right side of his skull." Appendix IX, page 540, quoting from the Pathology Examination Report, states, "1. There is a large irregular defect of the scalp and skull on the right involving chiefly the parietal bone but extending somewhat into the temporal and occipital regions. In this region there is an actual absence of scalp and bone producing a defect which measures approximately 13 cm. in greatest diameter.... Situated in the posterior scalp approximately 2.5 cm. laterally to the right and slightly above the external occipital protuberance is a lacerated wound measuring 15 x 6 mm. [...] 2. The second wound presumably of entry is a 7 x 4 mm wound in the upper right posterior thorax." This wound is measured to be 14 cm from the tip of the right acromion process and 14 cm below the tip of the right mastoid process. The latter wound, we are told, was caused by "a missile [that] entered the right superior posterior thorax above the scapula and traversed the soft tissues of the supra-scapular and the supra-clavicular portions of the base of the right side of the neck."

According to the Warren Report, an examination of the clothing worn by the president "showed that a missile entered the back of his clothing in the vicinity of his lower neck ..." But in the next paragraph, we are told that Robert Frazier found a hole in Kennedy's suit jacket 5⅜ inches below the top of the collar (and 1¾ inches to the right of the center back seam), and in the paragraph after that, we are told that the shirt contained a hole in the back 5¾ inches below the top of the collar (and 1⅛ inches to the right of the center).[208]

In a memorandum to C.J. Price, the administrator of Parkland Hospital dated November 22, 1963, Dr. Jenkins stated, among other things, "There was a great laceration on the right side of the head (temporal and occipital), causing a great defect in the skull plate so that there was herniation and laceration of great areas of the brain, even to the extent that the cerebellum had protruded from the wound."[209] Dr. Jenkins told the commission in 1964, "I really think part of the cerebellum ... was herniated from the wound." He told the HSCA's Andy Purdy on November 10, 1977, that a segment of occipital or parietal bone was blown out, and that a portion of the cerebellum was hanging out from a hole in the *right rear* of the head.[210] Dr. Perry also saw cerebellum oozing from the head wound.[211] Bugliosi tells us that Dr. Baxter changed his mind regarding the cerebellum after viewing the autopsy photos, expressing the view that what they saw was cerebrum rather than cerebellum; but that's because the autopsy photos are phony. Bugliosi also tells us that Dr. Carrico told him that the Parkland doctors could have been confused about the cerebellum being damaged.[212] The cerebellum is located at the base of the *back* of the brain. If the fatal wound was where the Zapruder seems to show it to be, and where Mr. Bugliosi therefore believed it to be, there would be no cerebellum protruding from the president's head.

Chapter 2

The Patsy

Reading through Mr. Bugliosi's book, it quickly becomes apparent that it is essentially a verbose expansion of the Official Story of the assassination in Dallas as put forth by the Warren Commission and its Report; it is a story with which many readers will be familiar, and it goes like this: After obtaining a hardship discharge from the Marine Corps, an unpatriotic Marxist named Lee Harvey Oswald defected to the Soviet Union, but returned to the US in 1962. Apparently having prescient knowledge that President Kennedy would be riding in a motorcade in an open limousine along Elm Street in the near future, in March 1963 the lone nut ordered a Mannlicher-Carcano rifle through the mail, using an assumed name (Alek Hidell), and on April 10, 1963, he used that rifle in an attempt to kill retired Army General Edwin Walker. Mr. Bugliosi repeats the story that Lee had confessed to wife Marina that he used his rifle in an attempt to murder Gen. Walker.[1] Oswald, the story goes, kept his rifle in a blanket in Ruth Paine's garage. According to the Warren Report, "Ruth and Michael Paine both noticed the rolled-up blanket in the garage during the time that Marina Oswald was living in their home," though the Report concedes that the Paines had no knowledge of a rifle being in the blanket. At some point the lone nut also purchased a .38-caliber revolver through the mail. Oswald had his wife take photographs of him in the back yard of their rented property posing with the firearms that he intended to use in his forthcoming murderous rampage.

Continuing with the Official Story: In late September 1963, Oswald traveled to Mexico City, where he approached the Cuban consulate in an attempt to obtain a visa to Cuba in transit to Russia. The Report stated that Oswald left New Orleans "probably on Continental Trailways Bus No. 5121, departing New Orleans at 12:20 p.m. on September 25..."[2] Albert J. Osborne, using his alias John H. Bowen, took a bus from Nuevo Laredo to Mexico City on September 26, 1963, and the man sitting next to him was Oswald. In his attempt to obtain a Cuban transit visa, Oswald had altercations at the Cuban consulate with Silvia Durán and Eusebio Azcue, the Cuban Consul. Sra. Durán (according to the Report) signed a statement to the effect that Oswald applied for a visa to Cuba in transit to Russia.[3] Oswald returned empty-handed on the second of October. On November 22, 1963, the lone nut Oswald smuggled his rifle (wrapped in a large paper bag) into the Texas School Book Depository, where he worked, and shortly after the limousine carrying President Kennedy, Governor John Connally and their wives entered Dealey Plaza, he fired three shots at the limousine from a window on the sixth floor of the southeast corner of the building; one shot missed; one shot hit JFK at the base of the back of his neck (or the upper or lower right back, depending on which page of the Warren Report one is reading) and went on to wound Gov. Connally in the upper right back and right wrist; and the third, fatal shot entered the back of the president's head near the external occipital protuberance and exited in the upper right parietal area. After shooting the president, Oswald allegedly ran across the sixth floor of the Depository, stashed his rifle among some boxes near the stairs at the northwest corner of the building, then ran down those stairs, went to the vending machine in the second-floor lunchroom, and bought a Coke. After finishing his Coke, Oswald "escaped from the building before the police had sealed off the exits."[4] Following his "flight" from the Book Depository, Oswald returned to his rooming house, retrieved his handgun, and on his way to the Texas Theatre, took a side trip to Tenth Street, and when approached by Officer J.D. Tippit, shot and killed him. Meanwhile, according to the Warren Report, Roy Truly, Book Depository superintendent, "had observed that Lee Harvey Oswald, 1 of 15 men who worked in the warehouse, was missing."[5] He was missing because (after buying a Coca-Cola from the Depository's vending machine and drinking it) he fled the building after committing his dastardly deed. After murdering Officer Tippit, the lone nut discarded his jacket (a light-colored one, according to the Warren Report) under the rear of a car in the parking lot behind a service station on Jefferson Boulevard, where it was found by Dallas Police Captain W.R. Westbrook. The killer of President Kennedy and Officer Tippit then proceeded to the Texas Theatre, where he was arrested. Oswald's palm print was found on the Mannlicher-Carcano, which proves that he handled the weapon, and that fact, combined with the finding of a (pristine) Mannlicher-Carcano bullet at Parkland Hospital, "proves" that Oswald was the assassin of President Kennedy.

The Warren Report tells us that an intact Mannlicher-Carcano bullet was found at Parkland Hospital, and "two of the Commission's firearms experts, Robert Frazier and Joseph D. Nicol, superintendent of the Illinois Bureau of Criminal Identification and Investigation, later confirmed that the bullet [CE399] had been fired in Oswald's Mannlicher-Carcano rifle to the exclusion of all other weapons."[6] Bugliosi repeats this on page 808 of his book, using virtually identical wording; "So we know that Oswald's Carcano was the weapon that murdered the president."[7] Lt. Carl Day of the Dallas police lifted a palm print from the underside of the gun barrel, and that palm print, the story goes, was identified as that of Lee Harvey Oswald.[8] Mr. Bugliosi agrees with all of these points, and repeats them at various places in his book.

The passage of time and many years of research have shown that except for Oswald's hardship discharge and the dates of his time in the Soviet Union, all of the above statements are false, or employ twisted logic. Here is the reality:

1. Lee Oswald was sent to the Soviet Union by an agency of US intelligence. L. Fletcher Prouty told Mark Lane in 1979 that Oswald was "a Marine on a cover assignment," though it is not clear whether he was sent to the Soviet Union by the Central Intelligence Agency (CIA) or the Office of Naval Intelligence.[9]

2. Oswald would have no way of knowing in March 1963 that President Kennedy would be riding in a motorcade in Dallas eight months later.

3. The Warren people did claim to find a mail-order coupon "proving" that Oswald ordered the rifle. The form, money order and envelope used to purchase the Carcano were filled out in handwriting identified as Oswald's, but they could easily have been forged. And even if he really did fill out that coupon, there is no evidence that he picked up the rifle from the post office or used it to shoot at President Kennedy. The Warren Report states, "It is not known whether Oswald's application listed the name A. Hidell as one entitled to receive mail" at his post office box in Dallas, but an FBI investigation revealed that Oswald did *not* indicate on his p.o. box application in Dallas that "A Hidell" or anyone else would receive mail through post office box 2915 (Oswald's p.o. box).[10] The Warren Commission tried to get Mary Bledsoe, who had rented a room to Oswald at 621 North Marsalis in Dallas about six weeks before the assassination, to say that she had seen Oswald with a package approximately the dimensions of a wrapped rifle. She testified that she never saw Oswald in his room with or carrying a long object wrapped in paper or a blanket. After a series of such questions, Ms. Bledsoe said bluntly, "Didn't have anything like that with him."[11] The Report states that the "Oswald" rifle was kept in

Ruth Paine's garage in Irving, and "had been concealed in a blanket." But Mrs. Paine told the commission that she never saw a rifle in her garage, and that she never saw the "assassination" rifle until the police showed it to her in the police station on November 22.[12]

Oswald was at work when he supposedly purchased the money order for the rifle. The post office didn't open until 8:00 A.M.; Oswald's work time sheet shows that he had clocked in by 8:00 that day.[13] Anthony Summers pointed out many years ago that it was never established that it was Oswald who picked up the package containing the rifle at the post office, and no postal worker recalled having given Oswald any such package.[14] It is thus clear that the Mannlicher-Carcano was the weapon that the conspirators intended from the beginning to link to Oswald. Someone – not Oswald – caused a Carcano to be mailed to a post office box in Oswald's name, then someone – again, not Oswald – picked up the rifle and apparently transferred it to the offices of the Dallas police department. Jim Marrs added that no record exists to show that Oswald signed for the handgun that was supposedly shipped to him by Railway Express.[15]

4. The famous backyard photographs are forgeries; they are phony. This will be covered in Chapter 3. Marina Oswald has stated that the photos in evidence are not the ones she took.[16] There is also the absurdity of the idea that someone planning to assassinate a retired general or a US president would have incriminating photos taken of himself, holding the weapons he planned to use in such an act.

5. The evidence shows that Lee Oswald did not shoot at General Walker. The Warren Commission's "evidence" that Oswald tried to kill Gen. Walker: 1) An undated note in Russian, identified as Oswald's writing by an FBI handwriting expert, telling his wife Marina about rent, utility and other bills he had paid and what to do "if I am alive and taken prisoner" (the note didn't mention Walker); 2) the photos of Walker's home found (according to the commission) among Oswald's possessions, which he allegedly showed to Marina; 3) the testimony of firearms identification experts; and 4) Marina's testimony that Lee came home late on April 10 and told her he had shot at Walker.

Mr. Bugliosi, again parroting the Warren Report, says "we know" that Oswald attempted to murder Gen. Walker "because he confessed to his wife that he did." As Mr. Bugliosi well knew, this is what the lawyers call hearsay, and even if it were allowed as testimony in a court of law, it certainly wouldn't be enough to convict Oswald of this shooting. There was also allegedly a record of a conversation that occurred when the de Mohrenschildts were in the Oswalds' apartment on the evening of April 13, 1963; George de Mohrenschildt supposedly asked Lee if he took a shot at Walker, and Oswald "sort of shriveled ... [and] made a peculiar face..." Of course, this proves nothing, and we only have the word of the commission that the conversation occurred at all.

The police concluded that the Walker shot was fired from a fence on an alley, not more than forty yards from Walker's shattered window.[17] (The shot was over Walker's head and to the left of where he was sitting.) The Warren Report gave the distance from the (supposed) sixth-floor rifle in the Book Depository to the back of the president's head when he was struck with the fatal bullet as 265.3 feet.[18] Oswald, the crack marksman, hit JFK, a moving target, from eighty yards, but apparently couldn't hit the stationary Walker from forty yards!

The Warren Report concedes that the Walker bullet was too badly mangled to be identified as to caliber when it was recovered, and "in [Robert] Frazier's opinion could not be identified as having been fired or not fired from that rifle."[19] Frazier merely stated that the mutilated Walker bullet *could have been* fired from a Mannlicher-Carcano rifle. A story in the *Dallas Morning News* on April 11, 1963, by Eddie Hughes indicated that the slug had been identified as a 30.06 caliber. An Associated Press story in the *New York Times* on April 12, 1963, also stated that the Walker bullet was a 30.06, which is inconsistent with any rifle that Oswald allegedly owned.

Marina Oswald has been quoted as saying that Lee told her that he had shot at Walker, but Anthony Summers described her statements about Lee and his alleged rifle as "ludicrously inconsistent." First she said that on the day of the shooting Oswald went to work as usual, but didn't come home until about 11 p.m. But shortly thereafter, she stated that he came home for dinner, then left.[20] Shenon points out that Marina "initially told the FBI that she knew nothing about her husband's attempt to kill Gen. Walker."[21] Marina told the FBI on December 3, 1963, that her husband went to the Walker home on foot, and after shooting at Walker, ran away on foot. She stated that at about midnight on the evening of April 10, Lee came rushing into the house in an agitated state and told her that he had tried to kill Gen. Walker. She said that Lee did not have a rifle with him when he returned to the house. She also stated that Lee told her that he had gone to the location on foot, and after firing the rifle, he ran away and came home on a bus.[22] Marina told the FBI on December 11, 1963, that

Lee did not have his rifle or any other weapon with him when he left their home the night he (supposedly) shot at Gen. Walker.[23] But she also stated (in the same interview) that when she asked her husband what he had done with the rifle, he told her that he had buried it far from the actual spot of the shooting.[24] One must wonder why she would ask him what he had done with a rifle that he did not have with him when he left the house. She said that Lee brought the rifle back home on the Sunday after the assassination attempt on Walker.

Walter Coleman was a teenager who lived next door to General Walker. He saw two men heading for two cars in a nearby church parking lot immediately after the shot at Walker, neither of whom matched Oswald: one had dark bushy hair and the other was described as being around 6 feet one inch tall and 200 pounds.[25] Coleman saw a white male speeding down the church parking driveway in a 1949 or 1950 Ford sedan.[26] An FBI report of an interview with Coleman dated June 4, 1964, states, "Coleman stated he has seen numerous photographs of LEE HARVEY OSWALD and he was shown a photograph of OSWALD... he stated that neither man resembled OSWALD and that he had never seen anyone in or around the WALKER residence before or after April 10, 1963, who resembled LEE HARVEY OSWALD."[27] (Coleman did not testify to the commission or its legal staff.) Gen. Walker himself tried to question Coleman, but Coleman said that he had been told not to talk to "unspecified officials."[28] Interviewed by Vincent Drain of the FBI in December 1963, Dallas police Captain O.A. Jones of the Dallas PD stated that "it is difficult to investigate any type of matter where General Walker is involved since Walker apparently does not know the truth from fiction and leads the police up many blind alleys."[29] (For more information on the Walker shooting incident, see Anthony Summers, *Not In Your Lifetime,* pages 188-97.)

6. HSCA investigators concluded, and the record now indicates, that Oswald never made that trip to Mexico City, nor is it clear how Oswald would have been able to assassinate President Kennedy if he was in Cuba or the Soviet Union. The Warren Report acknowledges, and Mr. Bugliosi concedes, that there is no firm evidence of the means by which Oswald traveled from New Orleans to Houston on the first leg of his supposed Mexico trip.[30] Bugliosi tells us, correctly, that after checking bus, train, and airline schedules and records, the Secret Service and FBI were unable to firmly establish how Oswald got to Houston from New Orleans on that day. Nor is there any documentary evidence of Oswald's presence

on Continental Trailways Bus No. 5121, as stated by the Warren Commission. The driver didn't remember seeing Oswald at any time.[31] Sylvia Meagher pointed out that "not one passenger has turned up who recalled seeing Oswald on Bus No. 5121,"[32] even though that trip took almost 12 hours. Four Continental Trailways ticket agents were interviewed in early 1964, but none could recall selling a ticket to Oswald.[33] The commission believed that on September 25, Oswald probably took the 12:30 p.m. bus out of New Orleans, arriving in Houston at 10:50 p.m. But Mr. Bugliosi concedes that the commission could not come up with any evidence from witnesses or records listing Oswald's name (or any alias of his) of his being on any plane, train, or bus from New Orleans to Houston that day.[34] The FBI checked with Greyhound and Continental Trailways bus drivers of all trips out of New Orleans on September 25, 1963 (the date Oswald allegedly left New Orleans), whose destination could have taken him to Laredo, Texas, and none of them was able to recall any passenger resembling Oswald on their trips.[35] The Report stated that Oswald boarded Bus No. 5133 in Houston and departed at 2:35 a.m. on September 26, but an FBI report states that other than E.P. Hammett, who recalled a man who strongly resembled a photo of Oswald, none of the twelve employees on duty in the Continental Trailways Bus Terminal between the evening of September 25 and 2:30 a.m. on September 26 had any recollection of seeing him.[36] For the period September 24 to September 26, only one ticket was sold from Houston to Laredo, and there were no tickets sold through to Mexico City, according to Ann Lindsey, a Continental Trailways report clerk.[37] An official investigation determined that only three buses departed New Orleans after 8 a.m. on September 25, and arrived in Houston before 2:00 a.m. on September 26. An FBI report states: "The drivers of these busses have failed to identify a photograph of Oswald as a passenger on these busses."[38]

Mr. Osborne/Bowen said the man next to him had a dark complexion and was of Mexican or Puerto Rican descent, and he did not identify photos of Oswald as the man he sat next to. Conveniently, the Warren Commission "attached no credence to his denial that Oswald was beside him on the bus."[39] For whatever reason, they had to put Oswald in Mexico.

Bugliosi says that Silvia Durán "has never wavered" in her belief that it was Oswald who approached her in the Cuban consulate.[40] This is not true. Bugliosi cites page 250 of the HSCA Final Report to support this statement, but that page contains Sra. Durán's statement that the man at the consulate was only five feet six inches tall, and contains that committee's acknowledgement that the description she gave did not match Oswald. It also contains the statement by Eusebio Azcue that the man who applied for an in-transit visa to the Soviet Union was *not* the man who was identified as Lee Harvey Oswald. (It also states that the committee "did ... obtain independent evidence that someone might have posed as Oswald in Mexico in late September and early October 1963." – see below.) Sra. Durán also told the HSCA that the man she encountered at the Cuban consulate had blond hair and blue or green eyes.[41] For some reason, at 3HSCA118 the House Committee has Sra. Durán telling Deputy Chief Counsel Gary Cornwell of the HSCA that the man who came to the consulate was the man she saw on television being killed by Jack Ruby, which is quite inconsistent with her other statements about the man not matching Oswald. In 1979, when Anthony Summers arranged for Sra. Durán to see a TV interview of Oswald made in New Orleans, she stated that "the man on the film is not like the man I saw here in Mexico City."[42]

When Sr. Azcue saw the film of Oswald being killed by Ruby, he was certain that the person in the film was *not* the same man he saw at the Cuban consulate in Mexico City. Shown pictures of Oswald by the HSCA in 1978, Azcue stated that the man in the photos "in no way resembled" the man who had made a scene in his office. Sr. Azcue said the man had blond hair and a deeply lined face; when shown photos of Lee Oswald, he told the committee that the man he saw at the Cuban consulate was *not* Oswald.[43] Comparing Oswald on television to the man at the consulate, Azcue stated, "I did not recognize Oswald.... And the individual I saw in the movie was ... considerably younger, and [had] a fuller face ..." Asked about the hair color, he stated, "He was blond, dark blond."[44] Azcue told Gary Cornwell that the Oswald in the photo looked somewhat heavier.[45] He later told Congressman Christopher Dodd that the man at the consulate was "maybe 35 years of age," and had "a very thin face [and a] very thin straight nose." He said the man at the consulate was definitely different from the Oswald he saw in photographs.[46] Oscar Contreras Lartique, in late 1963 a law student at the National Autonomous University of Mexico, told Anthony Summers that the "Oswald" who approached him and other students for help in getting a visa to Cuba appeared to be over 30 and was at most five feet six inches tall.[47]

After Sra. Durán stated that she had never seen Oswald at the Cuban consulate, "the CIA directed its assets in the police department of Mexico City to arrest her."[48] She was arrested in Mexico City by Mexican police and questioned extensively. She was only released after she signed a statement prepared by the CIA that identified Oswald as the visitor to the Cuban consulate.[49] Following her release, Richard Helms cabled Winston Scott, chief of the Mexico City CIA station, directing him to employ his assets in the Mexican police to arrest her again, and stressing that she must not get the impression that Americans are behind her re-arrest.[50]

A CIA memo states that on October 1, 1963, "Mexico reported that an American male, identified as Lee Oswald, contacted the Soviet Embassy in Mexico City inquiring whether the embassy had received any news concerning a telegram which had been sent to Washington. The American was described as approximately 35 years old, with an athletic build, about six feet tall, with a receding hairline. It is believed that Oswald may be identical to Lee Henry [*sic*] Oswald..."[51] This description isn't a very good fit for Oswald, who was twenty-four years old and at most five feet ten inches tall.

In a five-page preliminary analysis of the assassination, J. Edgar Hoover wrote that he had learned from the CIA that a "sensitive source" reported on October 1, 1963, that a man identified as Lee Oswald had contacted the Soviet embassy in Mexico City. But after seeing photos of the man and listening to a recording of his voice, special agents in the Dallas FBI office who had spoken to Oswald in Dallas were of the opinion that the man wasn't Oswald. Bugliosi ascribes this obvious flaw in his (and the Warren Commission's) Oswald-in-Mexico scenario to the "turmoil and confusion," etc., in the wake of the assassination. Bugliosi assures us that the HSCA, with help from Gordon Shanklin, Dallas FBI special- agent-in-charge (SAIC) managed to correct the "error."[52] Hoover informed President Johnson that the photographic and audio evidence the CIA was using to prove that Oswald visited the Cuban and Soviet embassies, and was urgently trying to visit Cuba, appeared to be falsified by the CIA.[53] In a telephone conversation with Johnson on November 23, 1963, Hoover told the new president that "it appears there was a second person who was at the Soviet embassy down there."[54] At the bottom of a memo on another CIA matter dated January 15, 1964, Hoover made reference to "the false story re Oswald's trip to Mexico" as an example of the CIA's "double-dealing."[55] Nevertheless, Mr. Bugliosi tells us that the "allegation that someone was impersonating Oswald in Mexico City is completely without merit."[56]

Winston Scott reportedly told commission assistant counsel David Slawson in Mexico City that there were no photos of Oswald because, due to lack of funds, photographic coverage was limited by and large to the daylight weekday hours.[57] But CIA man E. Howard Hunt told the HSCA that there was photographic *and* physical surveillance of "Iron Curtain embassies" in Mexico City, including the Cuban consulate and the Soviet embassy.[58] A senior CIA officer who served in Mexico tried to account for the absence of photos of Oswald at the Cuban consulate by claiming that the camera at that site happened to break down during Oswald's alleged visit to Mexico City. But Summers points out that documents now available show that *two* cameras covered the entrances to the Cuban mission on September 27.[59] Bugliosi says that "we know" Oswald went to the Russian embassy in Mexico City, but despite the fact that the CIA had continuous photographic surveillance on both the Cuban and Russian embassies, and despite the fact that, according to Shenon, the CIA's Mexico City station was one of the best-funded and –equipped in the CIA, the Agency was not able to come up with a single photo of Oswald at either of these locations.

The CIA's David Phillips told the HSCA that he didn't believe that Oswald visited the Soviet embassy in Mexico City, and during a debate with Mark Lane, Phillips admitted that there never was a photograph taken of Oswald in that city.[60] During his interrogation, Oswald told Will Fritz that he had not been in Mexico City.[61] Gerry Hemming, described by Lane as a CIA assassin, was a leader of Interpen (the International Penetration Force), a group of anti-Castro guerrillas who, in the early 1960s, trained at No Name Key (in the lower Florida Keys) and later in New Orleans. Hemming told author Noel Twyman that Lee was never in Mexico City.[62] Edwin Lopez and Dan Hardway coauthored the HSCA study of the Mexico City aspect of the case. In 1986, Lopez and Hardway said in a television appearance that they "had no choice but to conclude that Oswald had not visited the embassies."[63] Bugliosi himself cites this in his book, but nevertheless insists that Oswald *did* travel to Mexico City![64]

Regarding Oswald's return from his alleged trip to Mexico City, Bugliosi tells us that "we know" that Oswald was on the 8:30 a.m. bus from Mexico City back to Laredo, but he concedes that Oswald's name doesn't appear on the passenger list for that trip.[65]

Silvia Odio, a member of the anti-Castro group Junta Revolucionaria Cubana (JURE), insisted and would insist for many years to come that it was Oswald who was at the door of her Dallas apartment on Thursday, September 26, or Friday, the 27th, with two other men, when Oswald was supposed to have been in Mexico City. The Warren Report acknowledges that Ms. Odio "was certain that the American who was introduced to her as Leon Oswald was Lee Harvey Oswald."[66]

7. Oswald did not carry a "heavy brown bag" or a "bulky brown paper package" into the Book Depository on the morning of November 22, as the Warren Report states.[67] Buell Wesley Frazier and his sister Linnie Mae Randle both saw the package that Oswald placed in the back seat of Frazier's car, but neither person described the package as long or bulky, nor did Ms. Randle use the term "heavy brown bag"; this is another Warren Commission fabrication, which Bugliosi repeats, telling us that Oswald "placed a long, bulky package" on the rear seat of Frazier's car.[68] And Bugliosi is the man who, throughout his book, continually refers to Oswald's supposedly telling one lie after another, showing his "unmistakable consciousness of guilt." Wesley Frazier has always insisted that the package that Oswald placed in his back seat on the morning of November 22 was not big enough to contain a rifle. Frazier told the Warren Commission that the package that was in the back seat of his car, and that he saw Oswald carry into the Book Depository, was two feet long, give or take a few inches. Wesley Frazier's affidavit of November 22, 1963, states that he saw Oswald enter the back door of the Book Depository at the loading dock with the package under his right armpit.[69] He repeated this in his commission testimony, saying the package was about two feet long, and parallel to Oswald's body, "straight up and down."[70] Ms. Randle told the commission that the package Oswald was carrying was a little over two feet long, and no longer than about 27 inches. When shown the "official" bag (CE364), Ms. Randle said the bag she saw wasn't that long.[71] An FBI report of an interview with Ms. Randle on December 2, 1963, states, "When the proper length of the sack was reached according to Ms. Randle's estimate, it was measured and found to be 27 inches long."[72] The Report stated that Ms. Randle estimated the bag she saw was approximately 28 inches long.[73] The testimony of Randle and Wesley Frazier didn't fit in with the Official Story about Oswald smuggling the three-foot-long Mannlicher-Carcano into the Book Depository, so the commission conveniently concluded that "Frazier and Randle are mistaken as to the length of the bag."[74] The Warren Report concedes that the minimum length of the Carcano broken down is 34.8 inches.[75] This could not fit under Oswald's armpit. In a talk given on September 26, 2014, Frazier stated, "Lee did not take a rifle with him that morning."

Jack Dougherty, order filler at the Depository, told commission assistant counsel Joseph Ball that he saw Oswald when he, Oswald, came into the back door of the Depository at 8:00 A.M. on November 22, and that Oswald had nothing in his hands or arms. Moments after Dougherty made these statements, Ball asked:

Ball: In other words, your memory is definite on that, is it?

Dougherty: Yes, sir.

Ball: In other words, you would say positively he had nothing in his hands?

Dougherty: I would say that – yes, sir.[76]

The Report replaces Dougherty's positive statement with a negative one, but nevertheless concedes that Dougherty "does not remember that Oswald anything in his hands as he entered the door [to the Book Depository]."[77] When commissioner McCloy asked Depository employee Bonnie Ray Williams: "When you saw Oswald that morning was he carrying any package?" Williams replied, "No, sir."[78] But again, Mr. Bugliosi parrots the Warren Report, saying that "we know from all the evidence" that Oswald brought his Mannlicher-Carcano rifle to work with him on the morning of the assassination.[79] The evidence does not show that.

Among the other "evidence" against Oswald cited by Bugliosi to demonstrate Oswald's guilt: his fingerprints and palm print being found at the sniper's nest (Lee worked on the sixth floor of that building, so his fingerprints would be there), his being the only employee of the building to flee the building after the shooting, and the "provable lies" he told during his interrogation.[80]

8. Oswald did not run across the sixth floor of the Book Depository; stash his rifle between some boxes, and then hurry down the stairs at the northeast corner of the building. Victoria Adams told the commission on April 7, 1964, that she was watching the motorcade with Sandra Styles, Elsie Dorman and Dorothy Ann Garner from the third set of double windows from the west end of the building, on the fourth floor of the Book Depository. She thought it took her about one minute to reach the first floor. She testified that upon reaching the first floor and "on the way out to the Houston Street Dock," she encountered Book Depository employee Billy Lovelady and William Shelley, manager of the "miscellaneous department" of the Depository.[81] But when interviewed by the FBI on March 23, 1964, before her commission testimony, Ms. Adams made no mention of encountering Lovelady and Shelley. She stated that after the last shot, she and Ms. Styles ran out of the building via the stairs in the northwest corner of the building and "went in the direction of the railroad where we had observed other people running."[82] Ms. Styles told FBI agents the same story, and stated that neither she nor Ms. Adams saw

or heard anyone else on the stairs at that time. This was at the same time that Oswald was supposedly running down those stairs. (Neither Ms. Styles, Ms. Dorman, nor Ms. Garner testified to the commission or its legal staff.) Commission assistant counsel David Belin asked Ms. Adams if she encountered anyone as she was running down the stairs: "No, sir." Apparently frustrated, he then specifically asked her if she encountered Oswald on the stairs: "No, sir."[83] Belin confirmed that those stairs (in the northwest corner of the building) were the only stairs that led down from the fourth floor.[84] And Roy Truly told the commission that both elevators were on the fifth floor at the time of the shooting, so Oswald would have had to take the stairs if he had shot from the sixth floor.[85] But no one saw Oswald on the back stairs of the Book Depository when he was supposed to have been there.

The Warren Report states the following with regard to Ms. Adams encountering Shelley and Lovelady when she reached the first floor: "If her estimate of time is correct ... she must have run down the stairs ahead of Oswald and would probably have seen or heard him. Actually she noticed no one on the back stairs."[86] And if Ms. Adams and Ms. Styles descended the stairs before the lone nut did, then Shelley, Lovelady, and the two ladies would have seen him rushing past them as he sped from the second floor landing toward the second floor offices. The Warren Report: "If Miss Adams accurately recalled meeting Shelley and Lovelady when she reached the bottom of the stairs, then her estimate of the time when she descended from the fourth floor is incorrect, and she actually came down the stairs several minutes after Oswald and after Truly and Baker as well." This scenario makes no sense either, for it supposes that the lone nut assassin, who was supposedly at a window two floors above Ms. Adams and her co-workers and at the other end of the building, had time to run across the sixth floor to the northwest corner of the building, remove two or three shims from beneath the telescopic sight (see the discussion of the Mannlicher-Carcano, below), stash the rifle behind some boxes, then continue to the stairs, all *before* Ms. Adams reached those same stairs, even though she was much closer to the stairs than the lone nut was.

The Report states, correctly, that Lovelady and Shelley testified that they went out into the street right after Gloria Calverly ran up to them and told them that the president had been shot.[87] (Ms. Calverly did not testify to the commission or its legal staff.) Lovelady testified that he had been watching the motorcade from the front steps of the Depository with Sarah Stanton when the shots rang out. (Ms. Stanton did not testify to the commission or its legal staff.) After being approached by Ms. Calverly, the two men ran down Elm Street all the way to the railroad tracks. Lovelady testified that he stayed around the railroad tracks for a minute to a minute and a half, then went back up Elm Street and re-entered the Depository from the back.[88] Shelley told the commission on April 7, 1964, that, "We walked on down to the first railroad track there on the dead-end street and stood there and watched them searching the cars down there in the parking lots for a little while...." He stayed on Elm a minute or two, and then returned to the shipping room. He didn't remember if he saw Victoria Adams on the first floor when he got there.[89] Given the statements of Shelley and Lovelady that they headed down Elm Street when the shooting stopped, it is difficult to understand how Ms. Adams could have encountered the two men when she reached the foot of the stairs on the first floor. Lovelady said that he encountered a woman who *may* have been Victoria Adams; he didn't say anything about seeing her at the base of the stairs.[90]

Bonnie Ray Williams' affidavit states that he, Hank (evidently Harold Norman) and Junior Jarman (James Jarman Jr.) were on the fifth floor watching the motorcade. After the last shot, they ran to the west end of the building. Williams told the commission that the three of them stood at the west window for a while, then "ran down to the fourth floor, and came on down." He said that he didn't see Oswald at all during that period.[91] Williams stated, "I did not see anyone come down from the sixth floor via the stairs."[92] Commissioner Joseph Ball referenced an FBI report saying that Williams told agents on November 23 that he went to the sixth floor at noon and only stayed there three minutes. But Williams told Ball that he didn't remember telling agents that he only stayed three minutes; he told Ball that he left the sixth floor at 12:15 or 12:20 p.m.[93] Eddie Piper, a janitor at the Book Depository, told the commission about seeing Roy Truly and a police officer (presumably Marrion Baker) running up the stairs after the shooting. Joseph Ball asked Piper, "Had anybody come down the steps before they went up the steps?" Piper replied, "No, sir."[94]

It will be noted below that two or three shims had to be added to the telescopic sight of the Mannlicher-Carcano in order for it to accurately view the limousine in the kill zone, so that means that the lone nut took the time to remove those shims before he stashed the rifle behind some boxes on his way down the stairs. Ridiculous.

9. Lee Oswald was not mysteriously missing from the Book Depository in the minutes after the assassination. Roy Truly told the commis-

sion that he told Deputy Police Chief George Lumpkin, "We have a man here that's missing."[95] (Lumpkin did not testify to the commission or its legal staff.) In his FBI affidavit, Roy Truly stated, "We made a quick examination of the roof area and then I returned to the first floor area and started to account for the location of each of my employees. I was not able to locate Oswald."[96] He told the commission that about fifteen or twenty minutes after the shooting, "I noticed some of my boys were over in the west corner of the shipping department … I noticed that Lee Oswald was not among these boys."[97] That's because Oswald was on the second floor drinking a Coke. When Joseph Ball asked Truly if he made a check of his employees, Truly replied, "No, no, not complete. No, I just saw the group of employees over there on the floor and I noticed this boy [presumably Oswald] wasn't with them."[98] Junior Jarman pointed out to the commission that Book Depository employee Charles Givens was also missing "when we started to line up to show our identification."[99] Givens, in fact, had a police record; at one point, Inspector J. Herbert Sawyer put out a call via police dispatch to have *him* picked up.[100] Bugliosi also mentions the "missing employee named Oswald," though he concedes Givens was also missing. (The Warren Report doesn't mention Givens' departure from the Depository.) Bugliosi incorrectly states that Oswald was the only employee to leave the Book Depository Building right after the shooting in Dealey Plaza, "showing he was in a very big hurry."[101] On the contrary: the fact that Oswald left the building after the shooting does not show that he was in a hurry, nor was he the only employee to leave at that time, nor did he leave the Depository right after the shooting. Bugliosi says that we crazy conspiracy theorists "proceed to assume, again without any evidence, that Oswald became aware of this [assassination] conspiracy at the time of the shooting in Dealey Plaza, and believed that he was being set up to take the fall for the assassination, and *this* is why he fled the Book Depository Building."[102] I don't know of any conspiracy theorist who assumes those things; and it is Mr. Bugliosi who repeatedly states that Oswald fled the Book Depository. And incidentally, before he "fled" the Depository, Oswald went to the vending machine on the second floor of the building, bought a soda, and proceeded to drink it while perambulating the second floor.

Mr. Bugliosi tells us that about 1:30 p.m., police officers were conducting a roll call outside of Supervisor William Shelley's office at the Book Depository, "collecting the names and addresses of the building's employees."[103] Bugliosi apparently got this from the testimony of Officer Gerald

Hill, who told the commission that shortly after Oswald was in custody, Capt. Fritz told detectives Guy Rose and R.S. Stovall to "go out to some address on Fifth Street" and pick up someone named Oswald. When Hill asked Fritz why he wanted this done, Fritz told him, erroneously, that Oswald hadn't been present for a roll call of the employees. (This story is repeated in the Warren Report.) In a talk given by Wesley Frazier on September 26, 2014, he does mention a roll call, but he made no mention of this in his testimony to the Warren Commission fifty years before. He told the commission that some police officers came in and "talked to all of us. They asked us to show our proper identification, and then they had us write our name down and who to get in touch with if they wanted to see us." Then they "told us all that was there could go ahead and go home."[104] Eddie Piper testified that a police detective "lined us all up and told us to give our name and address and just to go home."[105] Roy Lewis stated in his affidavit, "Following the assassination, all employees were dismissed from work."[106] Mr. Shelley didn't mention any afternoon roll call in his Warren Commission testimony.[107] Oswald's absence is discussed by Roy Truly in volume 3, pages 238-39, and in volume 7, pages 382-85 of the Hearings and Exhibits; there is no mention of a roll call.

George O'Toole in *The Assassination Tapes* points out that apart from the very shaky evidence that Oswald killed Kennedy, there is nothing in the Warren Commission's reconstruction of Lee's movements during the ninety minutes between the assassination and his arrest in the Texas Theatre to suggest that he "had just committed the crime of the century."[108] Bugliosi tries to refute this by saying, among other things, that "only Oswald" left the Book Depository after the shooting and was unaccounted for.[109] This is not true. Mary Hollies and Jane Berry were Scott, Foresman and Company employees who worked in the Book Depository. They both stated that they and the other Scott, Foresman employees were dismissed after the assassination.[110] Volume 22 of the Hearings and Exhibits (at CE1381) contains FBI affidavits made by people who worked in the Book Depository. Reading through these affidavits, I counted 62 people who left the building before the normal end of the working day. It could be said that these people were also "missing." None of these employees mentioned any roll call. Apparently there was none.

In a footnote on page 959, Bugliosi refers to Oswald's "immediately fleeing the Book Depository Building" as an indication of his guilt. He later reminds us that flight, in the criminal law, "is always considered circumstantial evidence of a consciousness of guilt."[111] The fact that Oswald left the Depository after the shooting does not show consciousness of guilt, nor was it "flight."

10. The bullet found at Parkland Hospital was not a Mannlicher-Carcano bullet, and the Mannlicher-Carcano bullet presented as "evidence" could not have inflicted all of the wounds that the Warren Commission and Mr. Bugliosi say that it inflicted. During Joseph Nicol's commission testimony, assistant counsel Eisenberg stated that Commission Exhibits 567 and 569 (photos of deformed bullets) were found in the "front portion" of the limousine, but neither Nicol nor Robert Frazier mentions bullet fragments on the driver's seat in his commission testimony. If the magic bullet that supposedly hit Kennedy and Connally ended up in pristine condition, and the fatal bullet (according to Bugliosi and the Warren Report) blew out the *side* of Kennedy's head, how could there have been bullet fragments in the driver's seat or "front portion" of the limousine?

As noted above in the section on The Magic Bullet, a nearly pristine Mannlicher-Carcano bullet was supposedly found at Parkland Hospital, labeled by the Warren Commission as Commission Exhibit 399. After receiving the bullet from Parkland chief engineer Darrell Tomlinson, security chief O.P. Wright gave it to Secret Service agent Richard Johnsen. But when shown CE399 by FBI agent Elmer Lee Todd, Johnsen said he couldn't identify it as the bullet he got from Wright. Wright said it "looked like" the slug found at Parkland. Secret Service chief James Rowley couldn't identify CE399 as the bullet he got from Johnsen.[112] When FBI agent Bardwell Odum showed CE399 to Tomlinson and Wright on June 24, 1964, both said it was *not* the bullet they had given to agent Johnsen on November 23, 1963.[113] That's because CE399 was not the bullet that Darrell Tomlinson found. In a 1966 interview with Josiah Thompson, Wright and Tomlinson picked a spitzer (pointed-tip) bullet shape, rather than a round nose shape similar to CE399, as the bullet they found that day.[114]

11. There is no firm evidence that Oswald's palm print was found on the Mannlicher-Carcano – or was it a Mauser? What Lt. Day actually testified to was that he saw "traces of a palm print near the firing end of the barrel about three inches under the woodstock ... on the bottom side of the barrel ... [and] when I took the wood stock loose ... I tried lifting them, the prints, with scotch tape in the usual manner. A faint palm print came off."[115] Before the days of deoxyribonucleic acid (DNA) analysis, there was no way that a trace of a palm print could be linked to any specific individual. But inasmuch as the rifle found in the Depository was evident-

ly a German Mauser, it appears that the "faint palm print" must have come from *that* rifle! Of course, Mr. Bugliosi says the palm print proves that Lee was in possession of the rifle.[116]

Bugliosi makes almost his entire case based on the concept that the palm print found on the Carcano was Oswald's; but the palm print "evidence" is rather shaky. (The rest of his case is that Oswald once ordered a Mannlicher-Carcano, and a Mannlicher-Carcano bullet was found on a stretcher at Parkland Hospital.) Lt. Day testified that the fingerprint traces on the trigger housing were only "traces" and "unclear," so that he could not positively identify them. He told Bugliosi more recently (according to Bugliosi) that the general pattern of the two fingerprint traces he had seen on the trigger housing "were the same as Oswald's, but the ridges just were not clear enough for me to say they were his."[117] Lt. Day refused to sign a statement verifying that he lifted the palm print. An FBI memo states that Day "would rather elaborate orally on the lifting of the palm print ... rather than to make a written signed statement."[118] Regarding the three fragmentary prints on the rifle, FBI fingerprint expert Sebastion Latona testified that "the indications were that the pattern types ... were consistent with the pattern types which were on the hands of Lee Harvey Oswald."[119] So we went from a trace of a palm print to "consistent with ... Lee Harvey Oswald." No palm print could be detected when the rifle reached FBI headquarters. Latona testified that the FBI failed to make an identification of a fingerprint or palm print on the rifle, but received a "lift" from Dallas supposedly obtained by Lt. Day, and "the palm print which appears on the lift was identified by me as the right palm print of Lee Harvey Oswald."[120] Latona didn't confirm that the palm print had been lifted from the rifle; he merely identified the lifted print as Oswald's.[121] Summers points out that even if the palm print were authentic, it would only prove that Oswald had handled the rifle at some time.[122]

Bugliosi says that the fact that Oswald handled the rifle was "evidenced by his right palm print being found on it." Bugliosi also says that Warren Commission and HSCA firearms experts had no difficulty linking two bullet fragments to "Oswald's rifle to the exclusion of all other weapons."[123]

Bugliosi notes that in 1993, PBS' *Frontline* asked Vincent J. Scalice, who had been the HSCA's fingerprint expert, to compare the latent prints in Dallas police crime-lab detective Rusty Livingston's photographs with fingerprints of Oswald's. Scalice only examined two Dallas police photos (from five negatives Lt. Day had taken from the Carcano's trigger housing) showing latent prints on the Carcano trigger housing for the HSCA in 1978, but in 1993, three more such photos were produced by Lt. Day because he and Livingston had managed to "squirrel them away." Scalice had agreed with the FBI and the Warren Commission that the first two photos weren't clear enough to make an identification. But in 1993, according to Bugliosi, after viewing all five photographs, Scalice was miraculously able to determine that the prints were Oswald's.[124] Latona told the commission that he saw faint ridge formations on the trigger guard on the left side of the rifle, but "the latent prints which were there were of no value."[125] The director of the Miller Funeral Home told Jim Marrs that the FBI fingerprinted Oswald's corpse; at one point an FBI agent also carried the Oswald rifle to the funeral home, as well as a camera and a crime lab kit.[126]

12. Oswald did not shoot Officer J.D. Tippit to death; this will be covered under "The Tippit Murder," below.

Bugliosi wants us to believe that Oswald was a crack shot, and tells us at least five times (on pages xxviii, 494, 496, 549 and 1388 of the main book) that he qualified as a sharpshooter, scoring a 212, while in the Marines, but that was back in December of 1956, seven years before the assassination. Bugliosi only mentions once (on page 562) that on the firing range in the spring of 1959, Oswald's score dropped to 191, barely qualifying him as a marksman (the lowest ranking).

Bugliosi tells us that after being exposed to the evidence, "I have become satisfied beyond *all* doubt that Lee Harvey Oswald killed President Kennedy, and beyond all *reasonable* doubt that he acted alone."[127] The facts say otherwise.

The Three Points

1. Oswald was nowhere near the sixth floor of the Book Depository at the time of the assassination. Junior Jarman stated that he quit for lunch about 11:55 A.M., washed up, got his sandwich and went to the second-floor lounge for a soda pop. He said that after he got his soda pop in the lounge, he went back down to the window where he and Oswald had been talking; but he said that he didn't have lunch with Oswald. It isn't clear whether Jarman went to the lounge before or after he ate his sandwich, but it does seem to indicate that he was at a window on the second floor talking with Lee sometime between 12:00 and 12:20 P.M. Jarman stated in an affidavit, "At about 11:45 A.M. all of the employees who were on the sixth floor came downstairs..."[128] Eddie Piper testified that he saw Oswald at noon on the first floor.[129] Billy Lovelady's affidavit states, "Our

lunch period is from 12 to 12:45 p.m. All of us left the sixth floor to see the President."[130]

Bonnie Ray Williams stated in his FBI affidavit of March 19, 1964, that he last saw Oswald at about 11:40 a.m. on the sixth floor on the east side of the building.[131] Williams ate lunch on the sixth floor of the building that day, between 12:00 noon and about 12:20; *he saw nobody else there.*[132] Bugliosi distorts this somewhat by saying on pages 30 and 31 that Williams saw nobody on the sixth floor *at 12:06*. Williams got a soda from the machine, then went back up to the sixth floor to eat his lunch. Joseph Ball asked, "Did anyone go back?" Williams replied, "Nobody came back up. So I just left." He said that he didn't see anyone else up there that day, and didn't see anyone in the southeast corner of the building.[133] Ball asked him if, during the shooting, he heard "anything upstairs at all?" Williams replied, "No, sir, I didn't hear anything."[134] Williams' affidavit is at 24H229, dated November 22, 1963; it quotes him as saying that the shots "sounded like they came from just above us." In his commission testimony, he only said "it sound like it was right in the building, the second and third shot."[135] Williams' testimony seems to indicate that Oswald left the sixth floor some time between 11:40 and noon, and did not return.

Bugliosi says that Charles Givens was startled to see Oswald on the sixth floor at noon.[136] In his testimony to the commission on April 8, 1964, Givens stated that he took the elevator down from the sixth floor of the Depository at about 11:45 a.m., but realizing that he left his jacket and cigarettes up there, he immediately took the east elevator back up to the sixth floor and went to the southwest corner of the building to pick up his jacket and cigarettes. He saw Oswald, clipboard in hand, walking from the southeast corner of the building to the elevator; Givens reached the first floor about 11:55.[137] But in an affidavit given by Givens on the day of the assassination, he stated that he worked on the sixth floor until about 11:30, went to lunch at noon, then went to the parking lot at Record and Elm. He made no mention of returning to the sixth floor at 11:45 or 11:55, or at any other time.[138] So Givens was not startled to see Oswald on the sixth floor at noon, since he never said that he saw Oswald on the sixth floor at noon (or that he was startled). Sylvia Meagher pointed out that because of all the cartons and the structural columns (36 in all) on the sixth floor, it would be physically impossible for Givens to have seen Oswald as he testified he did.[139] She concluded that Givens' testimony was fabricated.

Carolyn Arnold, secretary to the Book Depository's vice president, told author Anthony Summers in 1978 that she saw Oswald in the second-floor lunchroom at about 12:15, but "it may have been slightly later," and that he appeared to be having lunch.[140] Ms. Arnold similarly told the FBI that she believed she caught a fleeting glimpse of Oswald standing in the hallway on the first floor of the Depository, between the front door and the double doors leading to the warehouse, a few minutes before 12:15 p.m. on November 22.[141] (As you might expect, Ms. Arnold was not called to testify to the commission or to its legal staff.) The motorcade was due in Dealey Plaza in just ten minutes (at 12:25), though it was running five minutes late; so a lone nut assassin would not be on the first floor of the Depository if his target was due to enter the plaza in just ten minutes. When Will Fritz asked Oswald what he was doing in the lunchroom, he said he was having his lunch.[142]

Mr. Bugliosi does not hesitate to call Lee Oswald a liar when the latter's words do not comport with the Official Story, but the present narrative points out several demonstrably false statements by Bugliosi. Here is another example: pages 213 through 218 of *Reclaiming History* feature a supposed dialogue between Capt. Fritz and Oswald during Oswald's interrogation by Fritz. But inasmuch as few if any notes were taken at this time, and the interrogation was not recorded, most (if not all) of this dialogue appears to be made up. Bugliosi's book also contains dialogues between Lee and wife Marina which also appear to be fabricated.

Mrs. Robert Reid, a clerical supervisor at the Book Depository, was standing next to the street with Roy Truly and Ochus Campbell (vice president of the Book Depository) in front of the main entrance to the Book Depository.[143] Mrs. Reid told the commission that after hearing three shots, she "looked up in the windows and saw three colored boys." She didn't mention anything about seeing a rifle or a sniper in the "sniper's nest." She stated, "I ran into the building... I ran up to our office [on the second floor]... I kept walking and I looked up and Oswald was coming in the back door of the office... I didn't pay any attention to what he said because I had no thoughts of anything of him having any connection with it all because he was very calm. He had gotten a Coke and was holding it in his hands..."[144] The Report states, "As she approached her desk, she saw Oswald. He was walking into the office from the back hallway, carrying a full bottle of Coca-Cola in his hand, presumably purchased after the encounter with Baker and Truly."[145] This is an obvious distortion of what Mrs. Reid said; she didn't say "a full bottle." Bugliosi repeats the distortion by stating that Oswald "cuts through the office from the lunchroom, a full bottle of Coke in his hand."[146] Bugliosi quotes the Warren Report, rather than what Mrs. Reid actually said, which clearly shows that he is more interested in supporting the Report and the Official Story than in accurately reporting witness testimony. (I haven't found any reference to a full Coke bottle in anyone's testimony.) Mrs. Reid testified that with David Belin she timed at two minutes the interval between the last shot and when she saw Oswald.[147] Thus the Report says it took two minutes (and they supposedly timed it) for Mrs. Reid to make it from the sidewalk in front of the Depository to the second floor offices. Again parroting the Report, Mr. Bugliosi says that Mrs. Reid saw Oswald on the second floor of the Book Depository walking toward the front stairway leading out of the building two minutes after the last shot was fired.[148] When Depository employee Geneva Hine mentioned Mrs. Reid's coming back into the Depository, commission assistant counsel Joseph Ball lied and told her, "Mrs. Reid told us she came in alone and when she came in she didn't see anybody there."[149]

From the top of the second floor stairs to where Mrs. Reid encountered Oswald was about 70 feet. The building that serves as the center of county government in my county also has a series of steps leading to the main door and the first floor of the building, and another set of steps near that entrance leading to the second floor, as is the case with the Texas School Book Depository. Starting at the sidewalk one day, at a quick walk (recall that Mrs. Reid said that she *ran* up the stairs), I ascended to the second floor; it took me about 34 seconds.

In his March 25, 1964, testimony, Patrolman Marrion Baker told the commission that after the shooting he "ran straight to" the Book Depository. After pausing briefly, he entered the building and he and Roy Truly went to the southeast corner of the building, then went to the northwest corner. He then saw Truly push the button for the elevator. Truly hollered twice for the elevator but it didn't come down, so Baker said, "Let's take the stairs." Baker got to the second floor (behind Truly); he went through one door and saw Oswald through a second door, about twenty feet away, walking away from him in the lunchroom. Baker ran over to him and hollered, "Come here."[150] It is now fairly well known that Officer Baker testified that when he encountered Oswald on the second floor, Lee didn't appear to be out of breath, as if he had been running, but was instead calm and collected; he "didn't seem to be excited or overly afraid," according to Baker.[151] Similarly, Roy Truly told the commission that when he and Oswald were encountered by Officer Baker, "I didn't see him [Oswald] panting like he had been running or anything."[152] Bugliosi acknowledges these statements, but still wants us to believe that Oswald had just run across the sixth floor of the Depository and had also run down four flights of stairs and had proceeded quickly to the second-floor lunchroom.[153] Bugliosi mentions timed tests showing that Oswald could have run down the stairs from the sixth floor to the second floor in as little as 74 seconds, well within the 90 seconds that the Warren Commission estimated that it took Officer Baker to reach the second floor (after the shooting stopped); but he wouldn't have had time to descend from the sixth floor *and* buy a soft drink from the vending machine *and* start to drink it.[154]

Roy Truly testified that Oswald had nothing in either hand when he and Baker encountered Oswald on the second floor, and the Report states that when encountered by Baker, Oswald had nothing in his hands.[155] Officer Baker's testimony of March 25, 1964, makes no mention of what Oswald did or did not have in his hands.[156] But in a September 23, 1964, handwritten statement that Officer Baker gave to the FBI, he wrote, "I saw a man [evidently Oswald] standing in the lunchroom drinking a coke." Baker subsequently crossed out the words 'drinking a coke' and placed his initials above the words crossed out.[157] (Note that Baker now has Oswald standing in the lunch room, rather than walking through a door, as he previously testified.) Apparently Baker belatedly realized that to have Oswald drinking a Coke would not fit in with the Official Story, i.e., that Oswald had just run down from the sixth floor and hadn't yet purchased his Coke. It would appear that Oswald was already drinking or had finished the soda that Mrs. Reid had seen him with when Officer Baker encountered him.

The following figures are based on the scaled diagram of the second floor of the Book Depository on page 150 of the Warren Report, and assume that there are ten feet between floors. Diagonally across sixth floor of Book Depository: 125 feet; four flights of stairs (from the sixth to the second floor, measured at an angle): 56 feet; from stairs to Coke machine: 46 feet; from Coke machine to where Oswald was seen by Mrs. Reid: 55 feet, for a total of 282 feet. From the top of the stairs (on the second floor) at the front of the Book Depository to the point where Mrs. Reid encountered Oswald is about 70 feet. The average person walks at about 3.1 miles per hour. Combining these figures and doing some simple calculations, and assuming that Mrs. Reid was walking at an "average" pace after she reached the top of the stairs, it would have taken her about 16 seconds for her to get from the top of the stairs to the point where the Report says she encountered Oswald. Adding these sixteen seconds to the thirty-four seconds it would have taken her to get to the top of the stairs gives a total of 50 seconds. This means that if we are to believe the Warren Report, we must believe that Oswald covered 282 feet – nearly the length of a football field – and had time to remove two or three shims from beneath the rifle's tele-sight, hide the rifle on the sixth floor, descend four flights of stairs, buy a soda from the second-floor vending machine, *and* walk from the vending machine to the point where he was seen by Mrs. Reid, all in the roughly 50 seconds that it would have taken Mrs. Reid to move from the sidewalk in front of the Book Depository to the point where she saw Oswald entering the second-floor offices. An FBI investigation found that walking at a brisk pace from the sixth-floor "sniper's nest" and descending from that floor via the stairs, it would have taken Oswald one minute, forty-five seconds to reach the front door of the Book Depository.[158]

The Report states that within about one minute after encountering with Baker and Truly, Oswald was seen passing through the second-floor offices with a full bottle of Coke; this refers to Mrs. Reid's encounter with Oswald. The Report also states that Mrs. Reid "probably" met Oswald at about 12:32, approximately 30 to 45 seconds after the lunchroom encounter with Baker and Truly.[159] As stated above, the Report wants us to believe that the soda that Mrs. Reid saw Oswald holding was purchased *after* the encounter with Officer Baker and Roy Truly. But Baker entered the building about 90 seconds after the shooting stopped, whereas by my calculations Mrs. Reid encountered Oswald just 50 seconds after she ran into the building. So Oswald must have purchased the soda a few minutes *before* the shooting started.

The Report states that during a re-enactment, it took one minute and eighteen seconds to get from the "sniper's nest" window to the second floor lunchroom at a normal walking pace, and at a fast walk, one minute 14 seconds.[160] That is more than twice as long as it would have taken Mrs. Reid to go from in front of the Book Depository to the point where she encountered Oswald.

So, in contrast to what the phony Warren Report wants us to believe, here is what must surely be the actual sequence of events (let us assume that the first shot was fired at the president at 12:30:00, and the shooting lasted eight seconds):

12:00 – Eddie Piper sees Oswald on the first floor; Oswald heads for the second-floor lunchroom to have lunch.

Between 12:00 and 12:20 – Bonnie Ray Williams eats lunch on the sixth floor; he sees no one else there.

Between 12:15 and 12:20 – Carolyn Arnold sees Oswald in second-floor lunchroom.

12:25 – Oswald finishes his lunch and buys a Coke.

12:30:00 – First shot at President Kennedy.

12:30:08 – Last shot; Mrs. Reid runs into Book Depository.

12:30:08 - 12:31:08 – Victoria Adams and Sandra Styles leave the fourth-floor window and descend the stairs at the northwest corner of the fourth floor of the Book Depository; they do not see Oswald on the stairs.

12:30:58 – Mrs. Reid encounters Oswald in second-floor offices carrying a Coke.

Between 12:31:15 and 12:31:30 (by Officer Baker's own testimony) – Baker and Roy Truly encounter Oswald in second-floor lunchroom.

(Officer Baker did "trial runs" – reenactments - after the assassination, and these resulted in his time estimates of between 75 and 90 seconds from the time he heard the first shots until he encountered Oswald in the second floor lunchroom.)[161] But William Shelley said that he saw Truly and Baker enter the Depository three or four minutes after the last shot was fired.[162] This would put the two men in the building at 12:33 or 12:34, and would have given Oswald enough time to finish his soda, which would explain why Baker and Truly testified that he had nothing in his hands when they encountered him, assuming the two men were testifying truthfully (and assuming their testimony wasn't changed).

The source of my eight-second figure is as follows: Viewing the Zapruder film on YouTube, I timed the interval between the first and last shots at about six seconds. But knowing that frames have been removed from that film, the actual interval is probably more like eight seconds. And the Final Report of the HSCA states, "The committee found from its acoustical analysis that approximately 8.3 seconds elapsed from the first shot to the fatal head shot."[163]

Among the HSCA conclusions: "There is an apparent rearranging of boxes [in the sixth floor "sniper's nest" window of the Book Depository] within two minutes after the last shot was fired at President Kennedy."[164] This was based on Dr. Bob R. Hunt's testimony to the committee, in which he compared photos of the sixth-floor window taken by James Powell of Army Intelligence and Tom Dillard at that time. He concluded that between the Dillard photo, taken a few seconds after the last shot was fired, and the Powell photo, taken one or two minutes after the last shot was fired, "you get the distinct impression there is some sort of motion or a change of the object within the window," and that "somebody or something moved boxes around in that room during the taking of those two pictures."[165] This would have been about the time that Officer Marrion Baker was ascending the stairs on his way to the sixth floor.

Will Fritz stated in a report that Oswald told Bonnie Ray Williams that he ate lunch with "some of the colored boys who worked with him. One of them was called 'Junior' and the other was a little short man whose name he did not know."[166] Similarly, Mr. Bugliosi concedes that "there are no credible reports that anyone saw Oswald on the sixth floor during the thirty-five minute period between 11:55 a.m. and the time of the shooting at 12:30 p.m." Mr. Bugliosi is nevertheless certain that he was on that floor during that time, "preparing his murderous deed." He tells us that conspiracy theorists cite a handful of witnesses who said they saw Oswald on the first and second floors between 12:00 and 12:30.[167] One would not have to be a conspiracy theorist to know that Oswald was seen on those floors within that time frame, because that's what happened. What Mr. Bugliosi does not tell us is how Oswald could be on the first or second floor of the Book Depository while he was at the "sniper's window" firing at the president. The police, according to Bugliosi, "can place Oswald on the sixth floor of the Depository a few minutes before the shooting…"[168] This obviously contradicts Bugliosi's statement regarding "no credible reports" quoted above. Furthermore, no policeman offered any testimony definitively placing Oswald on the sixth floor at that time. Jesse Curry, Dallas chief of police at the time, wrote in his memoir, "We don't have any proof that Oswald fired the rifle, and never did. We never were able to put Oswald in that window with a gun in his hands."

2. The fatal bullet was fired from the right front of the limousine. Bugliosi tells us on page 380 of his book that the HSCA's conclusion of a fourth shot being fired from the grassy knoll, and that there was therefore a conspiracy, was wrong. He then proceeds to tell us on that page and, by my count, eight more times (on pages 393, 427, 846, 858, and 864 of the main book, and on pages 331-32, 494 and 505 of his endnotes) that all of the physical (medical and scientific) evidence shows beyond all doubt that the two shots that hit the president, including the fatal one, were fired from the "sniper's nest" on the sixth floor of the Book Depository, and that there is no evidence of any shots being fired from the grassy knoll. And Mr. Bugliosi reminds us that this is the same conclusion that was reached by all of the forensic pathologists who examined either Kennedy's body or the x-rays and close-up photos of his wounds.[169] His logic: The alleged conspirators would never have gunmen of theirs firing from different directions, because witnesses would notice the "two separate gunmen," and that would indicated a conspiracy. Actually, witnesses and

evidence *did* indicate gunfire from different directions, and, hence, there *was* a conspiracy. And there were three gunmen firing from different directions, not two. Bugliosi is simply parroting the Warren Report, which states four times, by my count, that there was no credible evidence that the shots were fired from the railroad bridge over the Triple Underpass, the nearby railroad yards or any place other than the Book Depository.[170] Bugliosi also tells us that he believes the HSCA story that Kennedy's rearward head snap at the end of the shooting sequence was the result of a "neuromuscular reaction."[171] This is contradicted by the phenomena described in the paragraph above and by Figure 1 herein (page 228), which is based on eyewitness testimony and the Zapruder film; the heavy black dashed line bisects the angle formed by the widest dispersal of the president's cranial blood and tissue (from B.J. Martin's motorcycle to the windshield of the follow-up car), and shows the source of that shot. All of the physical, video (e.g., the Zapruder film) and eyewitness testimony indicates that there is no possibility that the fatal shot came from anywhere other than the right front.

Bugliosi cites as a "fact" that although many people ran to the grassy knoll after the shooting to investigate, no witness saw any human, with or without a rifle, running or walking away from (or standing behind) the stockade fence after the shots rang out.[172] For one thing, in the immediate aftermath of the shooting, a gunman behind the stockade fence would not still be standing there with a firearm in his hand, waiting to be arrested, while the civilians and policeman stormed the area. Furthermore, as is well known, there *were* suspicious-looking people behind the fence in that area: the three "tramps" found in a railroad car; see The Phony Tramps in Dealey Plaza, below. And a deaf-mute named Virgil "Ed" Hoffman, from his vantage point near the Triple Underpass, saw two men, one wearing a dark business suit and the other dressed like a railroad worker and carrying a soft brown bag (similar to a traditional railroad brakeman's tool bag), behind the stockade fence. Hoffman saw that the "businessman" had a rifle and fired it over the fence as the limousine passed him, and immediately afterward, he ran down to the west end of the fence and handed off the rifle to the "train man." The "businessman" then ran north past the parked cars and into the railroad yards, and disappeared. Meanwhile, the "train man" knelt down behind a railroad switch box, disassembled the weapon, placed it in the brown bag, then walked or ran north into the railroad yards in the general direction of Lee Bowers' tower. He ran behind a train, "right around the caboose," and disappeared.[173] Mr. Hoffman has told his story more than once, on camera, and it is difficult to think of any reason why he would invent this story. (Hoffman did not testify to the commission or its legal staff.)

Billy Harper told the FBI, according to their report, that he found a skull fragment "approximately 25 feet south of the spot where President Kennedy was shot."[174] The Harper fragment is about 7 centimeters (two and three-quarters inches) wide by about 5.5 cm (about two and three-sixteenths inches) high, very close to the size of the wound that the Parkland doctors saw in the back of the president's head. Harper took the fragment to his uncle, Dr. Jack C. Harper, who took it to Methodist Hospital, where it was photographed and manually examined by the chief pathologist, Dr. A.B. Cairns. Dr. Cairns told the FBI that the fragment "looked like it came from the occipital region of the skull."[175] The fragment must have been from JFK because it had "relatively fresh blood" on it.[176] In his HSCA deposition on March 11, 1978, Dr. Ebersole recalled a large piece of occipital bone being brought to the morgue during the autopsy.[177] This is obviously quite inconsistent with the small entry hole in the back of the president's head as described in the autopsy report and the Warren Report.

In his endnotes, Bugliosi notes that the HSCA asked Dr. J. Lawrence Angel, curator of physical anthropology at the Smithsonian Institution, to "identify and anatomically situate the two large skull fragments (not among the three found inside the presidential limousine) recovered after the assassination."[178] Dr. Angel's memo of October 24, 1977, states that the fragment(s) came mainly "from the upper middle third of the right parietal bone." It should be noted that Dr. Angel, as he states in his memo, based his findings at least partly on autopsy x-rays and photos in the National Archives, which, as we know, are phony. Looking at the sketch Dr. Angel provided on the last page of his memo, it is clear that he started with the "autopsy Kennedy" – a skull showing a large defect in the upper right area. He then tried to fit the Harper fragment into the back part of the opening, and the other skull fragment (where did that come from?) in the front. This is obviously in conflict with Dr. Cairns' conclusions, which Mr. Bugliosi himself acknowledges in his endnotes! Dr. Mantik notes that no fewer than three Dallas pathologists examined the Harper fragment and identified the site of origin as the occiput. He opines that Dr. Angel was probably misled by the faulty HSCA diagram that showed no hole in the back of the skull.[179] The idea that the fragment was parietal bone, for Mr. Bugliosi, is confirmed by the fact that "the high-contrast photo of

Zapruder frame 313 ... clearly shows that all the brain matter and skull fragments from the president's head are going in a forward direction."[180] Actually, that Z-frame doesn't show that at all; it shows the trunk of the car covered with pieces of the president's brain and skull, some spray going straight up, as well as the Blob, rolling around on the *side* of the president's head, at the right *temporal* and *sphenoid* bones, not from the upper right *parietal* bone.

Motorcycle policeman Bobby Hargis was riding with Officer B.J. Martin at the left rear of the limousine, Hargis being closest to the car. Martin testified that they were both sprayed with blood and brain matter.[181] Bugliosi says that Hargis testified that the shots might have been from the Book Depository.[182] This is a conveniently incomplete characterization. What Hargis said was, "Well, at the time it sounded like the shots were *right next to me*," though he added, "I had a feeling that it might have been from the Texas Book Depository and these two places was [*sic*] the primary place that could have been shot from." (Emphasis added.) Hargis told the commission, "I was spattered with blood and brain, and kind of a bloody water."[183] Martin, riding to the left of Hargis, found blood stains on his helmet and what looked like pieces of flesh. He also told the commission that there was "blood and matter" on the left shoulder of his uniform and on his windshield.[184] Neither Martin nor Hargis is even mentioned in the Warren Report. Dealey Plaza eyewitness Jim Hicks told the Orleans Parish Grand Jury in 1968 that he saw "the blood and all that going to [the] back."[185] It seems not only odd, but absolutely mind-boggling, that Mr. Bugliosi, like the Warren Commission, could completely discount all of this testimony.

The "Harper fragment" (the piece of the president's occipital bone) blown off to the left rear of the limousine, as well as the movement, as clearly shown in the Zapruder film (and something the plotters couldn't realistically alter), of the president's head and torso being rapidly and violently pushed to the left rear by the impact of a bullet from the right front; the large number of people who heard shots coming from the grassy knoll or near the concrete colonnade; the motorcycle policemen to the left rear of the limousine and the windshield of the follow-up car (and its driver) all being sprayed with cranial blood and tissue; the people who saw or smelled smoke in the knoll area; the many policemen and civilians who rushed to the area behind the stockade fence immediately after the shooting – all of this is "evidence" that shots came from an area or areas to the west of the Book Depository.

Dr. Crenshaw's 1992 book *JFK: Conspiracy of Silence* is in Mr. Bugliosi's Bibliography, so one would assume that he has read that book. But he must have missed the following statement of Crenshaw's: "There is absolutely no doubt in my mind that the bullet that killed President Kennedy was shot from the grassy knoll area."[186] Bugliosi tries to downplay Dr. Crenshaw's role, but Dr. Kenneth Salyer testified that Dr. Crenshaw was in the emergency room when President Kennedy was being attended to.[187] Dr. Baxter also said that Dr. Crenshaw was there.[188] Dr. Robert McClelland said in 1988, "We all know the fatal shot came from the grassy knoll... There was somebody on the grassy knoll who shot at the President and blew his head off."[189] Professor Mark Weiss of the Department of Computer Science at Queens College at the City University of New York analyzed the acoustics of Dealey Plaza and told the HSCA that the probability was "95 percent or better" that a shot was fired from the grassy knoll.[190] In January 1967, *Ramparts* published the results of a study for the magazine by Dr. R.A.J. Riddle, assistant professor of physics at the University of California at Los Angeles. After studying the relevant segment of the Zapruder film, he applied the law of conservation of momentum and concluded that the fatal shot came from the front and right of the car.

Mr. Bugliosi says the shot to the head was descending at a 16-degree angle below horizontal and from a point 29 degrees to the right of true north from the president, and the HSCA estimated that the earlier shot to Kennedy's back "was descending at an angle of 21 degrees below horizontal," i.e., moving from right to left, which, we are told, was "again consistent with Oswald's perch above and to the right rear of the presidential limousine." Mr. Bugliosi's book is replete with phrases such as "The HSCA later found..." (p. 490) and "The HSCA determined..." (p. 491). Again, one does not evaluate the accuracy of a document by quoting that document. And if all of the conclusions of the HSCA (and the Warren Report) are accurate, why was it necessary for Mr. Bugliosi to write his book?

Bugliosi says the test on Oswald's hands "showed a positive reaction, indicating, *though not conclusively*, he had recently fired a weapon."[191] (Emphasis added.) That statement represents more Bugliosi distorted logic (and wording); if the test "inconclusively indicated" (two terms that seem to contradict each other) that Oswald had recently fired a weapon, it really only means that Oswald *could have* fired a gun. But later, Mr. Bugliosi tells us that Dallas police performed a paraffin test on Oswald's hands at the time of his interrogation, "and the results were positive, indicating the presence of nitrates from gunpowder residue on his hands."[192] This is another false statement. The Warren Report does state on page 560 that the paraffin test results were positive for Oswald's hands, but on the very next page, the Report states that the paraffin test "is completely unreliable in determining either whether a person has recently fired a weapon or whether he has not." Any nitrate residue on Oswald's hands could have been picked up from the books he was handling in the Depository. Lt. J.C. Day and W.E. Barnes, a sergeant in the Crime Scene Search section of the DPD Identification Bureau, reported to the commission that the paraffin test on Oswald's right cheek was negative.[193] In a footnote on page 165, Bugliosi concedes that no nitrate residue was found on Oswald's right cheek. And the Warren Report (p. 560) itself states, "The cast of the right cheek showed no reaction."

Mr. Bugliosi quotes from page 71 of the Warren Report, stating, "When the shots were fired, many people near the Depository believed that the shots came from the railroad bridge over the Triple Underpass or from the area to the west of the Depository." Mr. Bugliosi references this passage as evidence of the Warren Commission's objectivity. The fact is that the commission ignored those people, since their statements conflicted with the Official Story.

3. The Mannlicher-Carcano could not have been the murder weapon. FBI firearms expert Robert Frazier told the commission, "We found ... that the gun could not be sighted-in merely by changing the screws.... When we fired on November 27th, the shots were landing high and to the right."[194] Ronald Simmons, chief of the Infantry Weapons Evaluation Branch of the Ballistics Research Laboratory of the Department of the Army, said that the people who ran the machine-rest tests with the Mannlicher-Carcano "could not sight the weapon in using the telescope.... We did adjust the telescopic sight by the addition of two shims." Commission assistant counsel Melvin Eisenberg had three shims in evidence.[195] At 17H259, CE576-78, there are photographs of "Three shims inserted under the mount of the C2766 rifle during tests performed on the rifle." In other words, the "murder weapon" couldn't be sighted to focus accurately on anyone in the presidential limousine. (Were there three shims or two?) After the FBI tested the Carcano, a letter from Hoover to J. Lee Rankin, dated March 26, 1964, stated that "the telescopic sight could not be properly aligned with the target since the sight reached the limit of its adjustment before reaching accurate alignment."[196] Bugliosi offers no refutation of this FBI statement, but says that

"the FBI found the scope to be defective," and that Arlen Specter, co-author of the single-bullet theory, "believes that the scope ... may very well have become misaligned when Oswald dropped it in haste onto the sixth floor of the Depository Building during his quick getaway."[197] It is not clear how Mr. Bugliosi knew what Mr. Specter believed, but in any case, no one reported finding any shims on the sixth floor of the Book Depository. Bugliosi says it is likely that Oswald used the iron sights on the rifle, in preference to the telescopic sight.[198]

Robert Frazier testified that the rifle allegedly owned by Oswald "showed the effects of wear and corrosion.... It is a surplus weapon." But the Warren Report tells us that Frazier described the rifle as accurate.[199] Despite hearing much testimony about the cheap, crude, unreliable nature of the Carcano, the Report states that according to Ronald Simmons, "the assassination rifle was an accurate weapon... as accurate as current military rifles..." Naturally, Mr. Bugliosi agrees, telling us that the Mannlicher-Carcano was just as accurate as the M-14, the American military rifle being used at the time.[200] The Report also stated that according to the Italian Armed Force Intelligence Service, the "Oswald" rifle was the only rifle of its type bearing serial number C2766.[201] In fact, the commission already had in its hands a twenty-two-page report from J. Edgar Hoover, dated April 30, 1964, that stated that "the same serial number appears on weapons manufactured by more than one concern [factory]. Some bear a letter prefix and some do not."[202] Mark Lane told the commission that Oswald would supposedly use not only an inferior rifle but the only one in the world that could be traced to him, "which rifle he is going to leave behind as a calling card after the assassination is complete."[203] An essay by Dr. Gary L. Aguilar and Kathy Cunningham states that it was Senator James O. Eastland (Mississippi Democrat) who bought the Mannlicher-Carcano from Klein's Sporting Goods, though they do not provide a reference or other supporting documentation.[204]

The Tippit Murder

According to the Warren Report, Oswald arrived at his rooming house "at approximately 1 P.M. and left a few minutes later." The Report states: "If Oswald left his rooming house after 1 P.M. and walked at a brisk pace, he would have reached 10th and Patton shortly after 1:15 P.M."[205] And Tippit's murder "was recorded on the police radio tape at about 1:16 P.M."[206] The following sections describe the problems with the Official Story with regard to the Tippit murder.

1. The Timing Was Wrong. Earlene Roberts, the housekeeper at Oswald's rooming house, said he came in at 1:00 "or a little after."[207] She also testified that Oswald stayed in his room not more than three or four minutes, and "a moment" after he left, she saw him standing on the curb at the bus stop just to the right (on the corner of Fifth Street and North Beckley Avenue, and on the same side of the street as her rooming house, which was the third house from the corner).[208] When he came into the house, a Dallas police car stopped in front of the house and honked, "just kind of tit-tit," and then "eased on."[209] The cop car honked right after Lee entered the rooming house. How could the cops possibly know that Oswald would be at the rooming house at 1:00? It is apparent that he left the area of the rooming house at about 1:04. About 30 minutes later, Mrs. Roberts said, three Dallas policemen came to the house looking for Oswald, and while they were searching his room, two FBI agents came in. The police and agents took everything in the room that belonged to Lee.[210]

Messrs. Wood and Bugliosi give the time of Oswald's arrest at around 1:50 P.M.[211] If Mrs. Roberts' timing is correct, the search of Oswald's room occurred before he had even been arrested, which again indicates foreknowledge of Oswald's status as a patsy. Jesse Curry told the commission that someone, "apparently a citizen," came on the police radio and said, "Somebody shot a police officer at 404 Tenth Street." Curry said this was about 1:15 P.M., and at 1:19 the dispatcher said, "The subject is running west on Jefferson from the location."[212] Since it would take some time to get to the police radio after the shooting, Tippit was obviously killed before 1:15.

Helen Markham, a waitress in downtown Dallas, was near the corner of Tenth Street and Patton, on her way to catch her usual 1:15 bus for work, when Tippit was killed. Mrs. Markham testified that the Tippit shooting was about six or seven minutes after one o'clock.[213] Her affidavit of November 22 states that it was approximately 1:06 when she saw Tippit's squad car stop and a "young man" approach the passenger side of the car.[214] She also told Mark Lane that it was approximately 1:06 when the killing occurred.[215] Similarly, the Warren Report states that she put the time of the slaying at "just after 1:06 P.M." The Report nevertheless concluded that the time of the shooting "has been established at approximately 1:15 or 1:16 P.M., on the basis of a call to police headquarters on Tippit's car radio by another witness to the assassination, Domingo Benavides."[216] In his affidavit of December 2, 1963, T.F. Bowley stated, "I saw a police officer lying next to the left front wheel. I stopped my car and got out to go to the scene. I looked at my watch and it said 1:10 p.m. Several people were at the scene."[217] (Bowley's first name isn't given in the affidavit; and he did not testify to the commission or its legal staff. Neither the Warren Report Index nor its Witness List [Appendix V] mentions the Bowley affidavit; the Report doesn't mention Bowley at all.) Two witnesses stated that Tippit was killed no later than 1:12. When Deputy Sheriff Roger Craig, who was at the Book Depository at the time, heard the report of Tippit's death on the radio, his watch read 1:06 p.m.[218] Given Mrs. Markham's statements and the fact that Tippit was already down when Mr. Bowley arrived at the scene, it seems clear that Tippit was shot between 1:06 and 1:08 p.m. Cab driver William Scoggins testified that he was eating lunch in his cab at 1:20 when the shooting started,[219] but this is inconsistent with the times given by other witnesses; and the fact that that time is given in his testimony doesn't necessarily mean that he actually said that.

Dallas Sheriff Jim Bowles told Bugliosi that the 1:08 P.M. call from Tippit most likely pertained to Oswald (call to channel 1 police dispatcher).[220] An FBI report by agent Robert P. Gemberling of May 15, 1964, states, in pertinent part: "[I]t is apparent that he [Oswald] could not have been there [at the Tippit murder scene] because he could not have covered the ten blocks from his rooming house in six minutes. [Joachim] JOESTEN tried it several times and his fastest time was ten minutes and he is a bigger man than Oswald with a longer stride and, therefore, could walk faster than OSWALD ... OSWALD was probably at the bus stop for one minute. This leaves him just five minutes to walk the ten blocks to where officer TIPPIT was killed."[221] Sylvia Meagher pointed out that the commission itself estimated Oswald's other walks at one minute per block. "At that rate, Oswald would have required 18 minutes to walk from his rooming house to the spot where Tippit was shot ... Oswald did not have time to reach the Tippit scene on foot even if the shooting took place at 1:15 P.M ..."[222] Ms. Meagher noted that commission assistant counsel David Belin re-enacted the walk, stopwatch in hand, in 17 minutes, 45 seconds.

Mr. Bugliosi even knows what people are thinking; he tells us that at 2:17 P.M. on November 22, it's already "pretty clear to the officers in Homicide and Robbery" that the man arrested for the murder of Tippit is "most likely" responsible for the assassination of the president.[223]

The commission didn't explain why it took "Oswald" twelve or thirteen minutes to cover the nine-tenths of a mile between his rooming house and the Tippit murder scene (using the commission's 1:16 p.m. figure), while taking some 25 minutes to go from there to the theater – a distance of only six-tenths of a mile. It was shown above that Officer Tippit was probably shot between 1:06 and 1:08 p.m. But the commission, evidently realizing that Oswald could not reach the Tippit murder scene by that time, simply moved the time of Tippit's murder to "about 1:16 p.m." on page 157 of the Warren Report, or "approximately 1:15 or 1:16 p.m." on page 651 (Appendix XII).

2. The Description Didn't Match. During Mrs. Markham's commission testimony, a tape was played that recorded her talking over the phone with Mark Lane. She is heard telling Lane that Tippit's killer was short and on the heavy side, and that his hair was a little bit bushy; she admitted that it was her voice on the tape at that point.[224] Mrs. Markham told *Dallas Morning News* journalist Hugh Aynesworth that the man who shot Tippit was short and stocky, and had bushy hair. Nowhere in the Warren Report does this description by Mrs. Markham of Tippit's killer's hair being "a little bit bushy" appear. Officer Gerald Hill told the commission that after Tippit's body had been removed from the scene of his murder, the first man who approached him told him that Tippit's killer had brown *bushy* hair.[225]

William A. Smith testified that he "saw Oswald," but he also stated that the man he saw on television – the real Oswald – had lighter hair than the man he saw running from the Tippit scene. The man's hair was "brownish-black. It was dark."[226] Domingo Benavides testified that the killer's skin was a little bit darker than average and a little bit ruddier than average, and that the hairline at the back "sort of went square instead of tapered off, and he looked like he needed a haircut for about two weeks."[227] Benavides said that the killer's hair was a little bit curlier than David Belin's. Photographs of Belin's hair indicate that it was much like Oswald's – quite straight. Nowhere in the Warren Report does this description by Benavides of Tippit's killer appear. The skin color doesn't match Oswald, and videotape of him in custody clearly shows that he had fairly short, straight hair, and the hairline in the back is neatly tapered, as if he had had a very recent haircut. Benavides also testified that the killer was around five feet eleven inches tall.[228] Oswald was known to be no taller than five feet ten inches.

3. The Clothing Didn't Match. Patrolman J.M. Poe broadcast a description over the police radio (1:22 p.m.) of the Tippit suspect; it included: "thirties, five feet eight inches, black hair, slender built, wearing white

shirt and black slacks."[229] When Poe was interviewed by the commission's Joseph Ball, Ball noted that the radio log transcript says, "White male, 30s, black hair, slender built, wearing white shirt, black slacks." Poe remembered giving Officer C.T. Walker that description.[230] The Warren Report tells us that according to Patrolman Poe, the description of Tippit's killer wearing a white shirt and white jacket came from Helen Markham and Barbara Davis.[231] The description actually originated with Patrolman R.W. Walker; the police transcript from Patrolman Walker to dispatch reads: "He's a white male, about 30, five feet eight inches ... wearing a white jacket, white shirt and dark slacks."[232] (Patrolman R.W. Walker did not testify to the commission or its legal staff.) Between 1:33 and 1:40 p.m., Patrolman Howell W. Summers called in a description from an "eyeball witness" that included "five feet eleven inches, 165, black wavy hair... wearing a light gray Eisenhower-type jacket, dark trousers and a white shirt, apparently armed with a .32, dark finish, automatic pistol, last seen running on the north side of the street from Patton to Jefferson ..."[233] (Patrolman Summers did not testify to the commission or its legal staff.) Jesse Curry told the commission that at 1:22 p.m., the police dispatcher broadcast a description of the fleeing killer: white jacket, white shirt, dark trousers.[234] Ted Callaway, manager of Dootch Motors in Oak Cliff, said that he couldn't see the killer's shirt, but according to Detective James Leavelle's report (page 2), Callaway told him that the killer's shirt was light in color.[235] So the Report references various reports about the killer's white shirt, and concedes (on page 159) that Oswald was wearing a brown shirt when arrested, the commission's scribes see no conflict there, and assure us that Oswald was Tippit's killer! (Warren Reynolds, the witness who was shot in the head after telling the FBI that he couldn't identify Oswald as the fleeing killer, wasn't asked about the shirt color of the running man he saw.)

The Warren Report states that a Mrs. Brock, the wife of a mechanic who worked at a gas station on Jefferson Boulevard, saw a white male wearing *light clothing* walk past her at a fast pace with his hands in his pockets, and that she identified a picture of Oswald as being the same person.[236] The Report, based on an interview of Mrs. Brock, states that she identified Oswald from a photo that was shown to her. But the Report doesn't mention that she described the killer as being about 30 years old (Oswald was 24) and was wearing *light-colored* clothing.[237] Barbara Davis testified that Tippit's killer wore a *light colored* shirt.[238] Helen Markham told the commission that the killer wore a *light shirt* and dark trousers. When shown

CE150 (the shirt Oswald had on when arrested), Mrs. Markham said that the killer had on a "lighter looking shirt than that."[239] William Scoggins said that the Tippit killer had on a light (but not white) shirt. He said he picked Oswald out of the police lineup, but also said that he saw Oswald's photo in the morning newspaper before he went to the lineup.[240]

Sam Guinyard worked at Harris Motor Company on East Jefferson, a block or two from the Tippit murder scene. He said the killer wore a brown shirt, black trousers and a light gray jacket.[241] Domingo Benavides testified that the shirt was dark in color.[242] But all the other Tippit area witnesses listed above who expressed a viewpoint as to the shirt color of the Tippit killer stated that he was wearing a white or light-colored shirt or (as in the case of Mary Brock) light-colored clothing.

When Oswald was arrested, he was wearing a rust-colored shirt. Officer Baker said that Oswald was wearing a "brown-type shirt" or jacket (he wasn't sure which) at the police department. Julia Postal also testified that when she saw Oswald in the theater, he had a brown shirt on.[243] Johnny Brewer, manager of Hardy's Downtown Shoe Store, said the man later identified as Oswald had on a brown sport shirt with the shirttail out, was light-complected, and didn't have a jacket on.[244] Elmer Boyd said that at the lineup, Oswald was wearing a brown long-sleeved shirt and dark slacks.[245]

The Report states, "Oswald's jacket was found along the path of flight taken by the gunman as he fled from the scene of the killing" It states that the jacket found in a parking lot behind the service station at the northeast corner of Crawford Street and E. Jefferson Boulevard (CE162) belonged to Oswald, and that wife Marina identified it as such.[246] The jacket brandished by the commission as being the one discarded by Oswald as he supposedly fled from the Tippit scene carried inside a laundry mark "30 030" and a dry-cleaning tag "B9738," but Marina Oswald stated in an FBI interview on April 1, 1964, that she couldn't recall that her husband ever sent either of his jackets to any laundry or cleaners anywhere.[247] Earlene Roberts' affidavit states, "It was a dark shirt he had on," and she told the commission that Oswald was wearing a *dark* jacket when he left the rooming house, and that the jacket was darker than CE162.[248] Thomas Hutson testified that he had heard that another policeman had picked up a *white* jacket behind some parked cars.[249] The commissioners showed a jacket owned by Oswald (CE162) to witnesses who had been in the area of the Tippit murder and asked them if it looked like the one worn by the fleeing killer. William A. Smith said that CE162 "looks like what [the killer] had on."[250] But several other witnesses said it did *not* look like the jacket worn by the fleeing killer. When the light gray zipper jacket supposedly discarded by Oswald (CE162) was shown to Mrs. Markham, she said it did *not* look like the one she saw on Tippit's killer. She told the commission that the killer's jacket was darker than the jacket shown to her by Joseph Ball.[251] She described the killer's jacket as grayish tan, and that the "Oswald" jacket, CE162, was darker than the killer's jacket.[252] Mrs. Markham told Mark Lane that it was a light gray jacket.[253] Benavides described the killer's jacket as a light-weight light beige jacket.[254] Wesley Frazier testified that Oswald had with him a light gray "wool-looking" jacket on November 22, and it was *not* one of the two jackets that commission staff showed him.[255] Officer Poe testified that one of the Davis girls (he didn't say which one) gave him the same description that Mrs. Markham had given – that the killer was wearing a *white* jacket.[256] Mr. Scoggins said the killer's jacket was a little darker than CE162, the jacket shown to him by David Belin.[257] Barbara Davis said the killer wore "a dark coat... it looked sort of rough. Like more of a sporting jacket." When shown CE162, she testified that it looked nothing like the jacket worn by the man who ran across her lawn.[258] Virginia Davis testified that Tippit's killer had light brown hair, and was wearing a light tan jacket and black trousers.[259] The commission's obvious motive in all this is to show that the jacket found in the service station parking lot was Oswald's, and therefore Oswald was the man who ran from the Tippit murder scene, and therefore Oswald was Tippit's killer. But it clearly was not Oswald's jacket.

The Warren Report says that Harold Russell identified Oswald as Tippit's killer. The FBI report of an interview with Russell (dated 1/22/64) states that he was *not* a witness to the actual shooting of Tippit (he and Pat Patterson headed for the intersection of Tenth and Patton after hearing gunshots), but goes on to say that Russell identified a photo of Oswald as being identical with the man he had observed "at the scene of the shooting" of Tippit – another false statement.[260]

Mr. Bugliosi has Mrs. Markham saying only, "The second one," and "Number 2." And later, he tells us that she "identified Oswald in a lineup," which is a blatant distortion of what she actually said, and conveniently omits the much more telling part of her testimony.[261] Questioned by assistant counsel Joseph Ball, Mrs. Markham stated several times that she didn't recognize anyone in the police lineup, e.g., "I didn't know nobody.... No. I had never seen none of them, none of these men." But after prompting by Mr. Ball regarding "a number two man," she eventually is quoted as saying, "Number two is the one I picked.... Number two was the man I saw shoot the policeman."[262] This, of course, was a complete contradiction of what she had said minutes before. And this assumes that the transcript was accurate. The Warren Report falsely states that in her commission testimony, Mrs. Markham "confirmed her identification" of Oswald, but "even in the absence of Mrs. Markham's testimony, there is ample evidence to identify Oswald as the killer of Tippit."[263]

Let us review. **Tippit killer**: white or off-white shirt, light-colored or white jacket, somewhat ruddy complexion that was a little darker than average, wavy or bushy hair squared-off in back. **Lee Oswald**: rust-colored shirt, dark jacket, smooth (and light) skin, straight hair neatly tapered in back.

4. There Was Confusion With Bullets and Casings. The shells ejected at the scene were inconsistent with the revolver that Oswald allegedly had on his person when he was arrested, and there was no evidence that that revolver was fired that day. Describing the gun that was supposedly found on Oswald, Sgt. Gerald Hill later described to Warren Commission assistant counsel David Belin a revolver with six live rounds in its chambers. The problem is that shells were found at the Tippit scene, and revolvers don't eject shells. Robert Groden notes that according to the police radio report, the shells found at the Tippit scene were from an automatic pistol and "could not have been fired from Oswald's gun."[264] Sgt. Hill radioed to the dispatcher that the shells at the scene indicated that the suspect was armed with an automatic .38 rather than a pistol.[265] Marrs points out that Officer Poe stated in an FBI report that he marked the shell casings found at the Tippit murder scene with his initials, but he couldn't find his initials on the casings shown to him later, suggesting that shell casings from "Oswald's" revolver were substituted for the ones marked by Poe.[266] Bugliosi says Summers' and Hill's radio transmissions regarding a semi-automatic pistol regarding the Tippit scene were "simply routine errors."[267] FBI firearms expert Cortlandt Cunningham told the commission that it was not possible from an examination of the bullets found in Tippit's body to determine whether or not they had been fired from the "Oswald" revolver; he merely stated that one of the bullets could have been fired from that revolver. This testimony is reflected in the Warren Report.[268] Bugliosi quotes the Report as saying that Cunningham declared that the Oswald revolver fired the four empty cartridge cases found near the scene of the Tippit shooting to the exclusion of all other weapons. But the Report also states,

"Consecutive bullets fired from the revolver by the FBI experts could not be identified as having been fired from that revolver."[269] Dr. Monty C. Lutz of the HSCA firearms panel told the committee that microscopic examination and comparison of bullets recovered from Tippit's body failed to identify the "Oswald" revolver as the one that fired those bullets. Similarly, the panel "concluded that the CD 602 through CD 605 bullets could not be conclusively identified or eliminated as having been fired from the CE 143 revolver."[270] This point is conceded by Mr. Bugliosi.[271] Repeating the Report's finding, he also concedes that the barrel of Oswald's revolver was too large for the bullets. Furthermore, two different brands of bullets were taken from Tippit's body; one was a Remington-Peters lead bullet and three were copper-jacketed and made by Winchester-Western. Since people do not usually mix bullets in the same gun, this seems to indicate that *two* gunmen did the shooting.[272] It is probably worth mentioning that Earlene Roberts told the commission that she never saw a gun in Lee's room, and she didn't see a pistol or revolver in Oswald's belt when he left the rooming house.[273]

In a letter to Robert Blakey, Dr. Cyril Wecht, a member of the HSCA forensic pathology panel, indicated that he was "disgusted and appalled at the manner in which this entire matter has been handled." He wrote that he planned to continue his criticisms of the Warren Report and "and all the subsequent sycophantic reports that have followed under the imprimatur of the Federal Government."[274]

5. No One Saw Oswald Running. Jim Marrs noted that the Warren Commission couldn't find anyone who had seen a man walking or running between Oswald's rooming house and the Tippit murder scene, and Sylvia Meagher similarly pointed out that no one ever came forward who saw Oswald walking or running from the rooming house to the Tippit murder scene.[275]

6. Other Points: The commission describes as "speculation" or "rumor" that an unidentified woman who was also a witness to the Tippit murder was interviewed by the FBI and "alleged to have stated that she saw two men involved in the shooting and that they ran off in opposite directions afterwards." The commission denied that they or the FBI had any knowledge of such a woman.[276] But she did exist; her name was Acquilla Clemons and according to Groden and other sources, she was admonished by the FBI and Dallas police to keep her mouth shut.[277] Ms. Clemons told Mark Lane that she saw *two* men standing near Tippit's car

moments before one of them shot Tippit. She also told him that the gunman was short and "kind of heavy." In a YouTube interview, Ms. Clemons said that neither man she saw resembled Oswald. (Ms. Clemons did not testify to the commission or its legal staff, nor is she named in the Warren Report. A partial transcript of an interview with her can be found at Anthony Summers, *Not in Your Lifetime,* page 105).

The Report states, "At least 12 persons saw the man with the revolver in the vicinity of the Tippit crime scene at or immediately after the shooting."[278] But of all the witnesses to the Tippit murder listed by the Report, only Barbara Davis, Ted Callaway, William Scoggins and Helen Markham testified to the full commission. In fact, Barbara Davis, Mr. Callaway and Mrs. Markham were questioned only by Joseph Ball and Allen Dulles, and Mr. Scoggins was questioned only by Dulles and David Belin.

There is a video on YouTube of an interview with Jack Tatum, a sometime medical technician at Baylor Hospital. He stated that he was driving north on Denver Street and turned left on Tenth Street when he saw Tippit's killer, whom he identified as Oswald. After the shooting, according to Tatum, the man started a "slow run" toward him, and Tatum watched in his rear-view mirror as the man continued down the street. Since Tatum was driving west, this would mean that the killer was running in an easterly direction, *away* from the Texas Theatre, just the opposite of what the other witnesses saw. In his affidavit of November 23, 1963, for example, Scoggins said the killer ran west after the shooting.[279] William A. Smith also said that the killer ran west.[280] Barbara and Virginia Davis[281] both testified that the killer was moving south on Patton, toward Jefferson (i.e., westerly from the murder scene), which is also what the Warren Report itself states.[282] One must therefore have doubts about Mr. Tatum's credibility.

7. The Whole Official Scenario Was Ludicrous. The brief honks of the police car's horn right after Oswald returned to his rooming house were obviously his signal to head to the Texas Theatre, since that is where Oswald (the real one) is next seen forty to forty-five minutes later. This was all choreographed in advance: the cops had to time everything so that Oswald would arrive at the theater around the same time that the angry, boisterous crowd would magically materialize outside the theater; see The Shills Outside the Texas Theatre in the following chapter. If Lee was walking, he would obviously take the most direct route to the theater, by going south on Beckley to E. Jefferson Boulevard, then west to the theater. To believe the Official Story, one must believe that instead of taking the

most direct route to the theater, Oswald suddenly remembered that he wanted to kill a policeman, and yet *having no way of knowing whether or not there would happen to be a policeman on Tenth Street at the time*, ran down and around several residential streets looking for a policeman to kill. And if he really was the president's assassin, he would have kept his head down and kept on walking (or would have taken off running) when he saw Tippit's police car approaching. But instead, he ambles over to the driver's window and engages in a conversation with Tippit. Joachim Joesten asks, "Can we imagine Oswald, if he truly was the assassin of the President, placing his elbows on the window of a police car to start a conversation?"[283] Bugliosi says the Tippit killing, which shows that Oswald was in flight from some awful deed, confirms his guilt for the murder of JFK.[284] Actually, the Tippit killing shows neither of those things.

Lee Oswald did not kill President Kennedy or Officer J.D. Tippit, nor did he shed his jacket behind a service station on Jefferson Boulevard.

Something relating to Officer J.D. Tippit's assignment in Dallas that day was also related to the assassination and necessitated his murder by one of the thugs tied in with the plotters. Lee Oswald did not fit the description of Tippit's killer, but the fact that Tippit was tied in somehow with the plotters made it convenient to assign his murder to Oswald as well. Robert Morrow's story that Tippit was killed for failing to kill Oswald as the latter "resisted arrest" is plausible. A likely scenario: With Officer Tippit nearby, Oswald was directed to head for the theater, and on the way, Tippit was to intercept Oswald and shoot him while he was "resisting arrest." When Tippit failed to do this, one of the conspirators caught up with him on Tenth Street and killed him as a punishment for this failure and to keep him quiet. Naturally, pinning the Tippit murder on Oswald would further the notion that Lee was a violent psychopath who was capable of killing the president. According to Harrison Livingstone, based on a deathbed interview with the widow of sometime Dallas policeman Roscoe White, White himself shot Tippit after the latter refused to drive Oswald to the Redbird Airport.[285] Roscoe's son Ricky claims that his father's diary stated that two shots were fired by Roscoe, that Mauser rifles were used in the assassination of the president, and that the diary stated, "I killed an officer at 10th and Patton."[286]

Chapter 3

Indications of Conspiracy

Those of us who believe there was a conspiracy are, according to Mr. Bugliosi, "conspiracy loonies," liars, etc. He tells us that conspiracy theorists are also "unhinged," and the various conspiracy theories are "utterly vapid and bankrupt." He also tells us that there is no credible evidence that anyone conspired with Oswald to kill Kennedy.[1] Maybe that's because Oswald didn't kill Kennedy. Mr. Bugliosi tells us that "after more than four decades of searching by the conspiracy theorists, they haven't been able to come up with one speck of credible evidence that some *other* person killed Kennedy, which is additional circumstantial evidence of Oswald's guilt."[2] Bugliosi says that all the evidence shows that the bullet to the president's head came from the vicinity of the "sniper's nest" window, and the physical evidence – Oswald's ownership of the murder weapon, his finger and palm prints, etc. – proves that Oswald fired the rifle, and there is no evidence that the fatal bullet was fired from a lower floor in the Book Depository or from the Dal-Tex Building.[3] I am at a loss to understand what would motivate Mr. Bugliosi to churn out this nonsense, and it really is unfortunate that he would spoil a lifetime of good work (and good books) by ending his publishing career with such a mess of a book.

Mr. Bugliosi devotes an entire chapter to "Conclusion of No Conspiracy," attempting to prove a negative, usually a dubious venture. He gives 32 reasons to back up his "conclusion," but his logic is again rather lame; for example, there was no conspiracy because the conspirators couldn't keep a secret for so many years. Several of his other paragraphs in the chapter *start* with the conclusion that the Warren Report is correct, that Oswald was the lone nut assassin, and there is no credible evidence that the military-industrial complex or an organ of government such as the CIA or the FBI conspired with Oswald, that it would be reckless and irrational for any such group to conspire to kill the president, and that it couldn't be a conspiracy involving a group such as these because they wouldn't have picked an inexperienced hit man like Oswald for the job. In response to Bugliosi's "someone would have talked" concept, one could point out that Jack Ruby, Johnny Roselli, and CIA agents David Phillips, David Morales and E. Howard Hunt *did* talk before their deaths.

Jesse Ventura and his co-authors counted each of several mysterious deaths as an indication of conspiracy, whereas I lump them all together as a single indication of conspiracy. But I nevertheless came up with thirty-two indications thereof, and even then I may have missed one or two.

Here is my list, roughly in chronological order:

1. Actions of Richard Case Nagell

On September 20, 1963, Nagell walked into the State National Bank in El Paso, Texas, and fired two shots into the ceiling, then went outside the bank, sat on the curb and waited to be arrested.[4] He stated that he wanted to be arrested. Bugliosi says that in order to establish an alibi for himself, Nagell "decided to commit a bank robbery in El Paso and get caught so he would be in custody at the time Kennedy was killed." Bugliosi calls this Nagell's "bizarre tale." In fact, as indicated above, Nagell didn't rob that bank – another distortion of the truth from Mr. Bugliosi, who also incorrectly states that after firing the two shots, Nagell got into his car and started to pull out. (Nagell is only mentioned in Bugliosi's endnotes [pp. 698-99]. He tells us that Nagell has a long history of mental illness.)

Nagell later said that he had stumbled into "a domestic-formulated and domestic-sponsored conspiracy" to assassinate President Kennedy, and wanted to be elsewhere, even if that meant being in prison. At his arraignment in 1963 on the bank charge in El Paso, Nagell shouted out to the local press that the FBI was in some manner responsible for the JFK assassination.[5] He was sentenced to ten years, but an appellate court overturned his conviction after five years on the grounds that there was no evidence of intent to rob.[6] The executor of Nagell's estate later confirmed that the idea was for Nagell to get himself picked up and protected. According to an FBI report of Nagell's questioning, Nagell said he got arrested "to keep anyone from following me."[7] Gerry Hemming told author Twyman that Nagell was "strictly" under James Angleton's control.

Nagell ostensibly left US Army Intelligence (where he occasionally performed intelligence services on behalf of the CIA and acted as a confidential informant for the FBI) in 1959, but from August 1962 until his arrest in September 1963, he was intermittently employed by the CIA as an "informant and/or investigator," and as an intelligence courier and "cut-out," according to a report of the Defense Department's Military Intelligence Department. According to Nagell, a plot to assassinate President Kennedy was being discussed among some Cuban exiles in the spring of 1963. He claimed to have a tape recording of a meeting that he attended sometime between August 23 and 27 of that year, where the subject under discussion was the assassination of JFK in the latter part of September; there was also talk of killing his brother Robert and possibly other "highly placed officials" of the American government.

2. Arrangement of the Motorcade

Jesse Curry confirmed in his book *JFK Assassination File* that the final motorcade route was settled on November 18, 1963, at a meeting between representatives of the Police Department and the Secret Service. James Fetzer rightly describes the sequence of vehicles in the motorcade as "completely absurd. A proper motorcade would have the lower-ranking dignitaries early on"; and the press car should have been in front of the presidential limousine, so members of the press could film the president and the motorcade. In this motorcade, according to Fetzer, the first press car was six cars behind the presidential limousine, and Admiral Burkley, the president's personal physician, was in the very last car.[8] Bugliosi says the first press car was four cars back from the presidential limousine, and the first camera car was five cars back. These statements appear to be false. Cameraman Malcolm Couch told the commission that he was in the fifth or sixth car back from the lead car, and newsman James Underwood testified that the car he was in was the sixth or seventh car behind the presidential limousine.[9] The press usually rode on a flatbed truck directly in front of the presidential limousine.[10] This altered sequence of cars in the motorcade obviously prevented the press from filming the assassination.

L. Fletcher Prouty noted in his essay "The Guns of Dallas" that never before in the history of the Secret Service had they allowed the president and the vice president to be in close proximity in the same city and the same procession.[11]

3. Behavior of the Secret Service

They failed to pass on information regarding threats to President Kennedy's life. Secret Service agent Gerald Behn told the HSCA that the Protective Research Service (PRS) of the Secret Service, whose job it is to gather and evaluate information on people and groups who are thought to present some potential danger to the president and make sure it is usefully disseminated, did not forward on to the agents responsible for Kennedy's Dallas trip information it had on threats to the president's life for his November 2, 1963, trip to Chicago, his November 18, 1963, trip to Miami, or the Joseph Milteer threat, recorded on November 9 by government informant Willie Somersett, during which Milteer told Somersett that JFK's assassination was "in the working." The HSCA found that although Miami Police intelligence officers met with Secret Service agents on November 12 and provided a transcript of the Milteer recording, the Milteer threat was ignored by Secret Service personnel in planning the trip to Dallas.[12] In a YouTube interview, retired FBI agent Don Adams stated that Milteer's threat should have stopped the motorcade.

Several Secret Service agents assigned to the president's detail went drinking the night before the Dallas motorcade until the wee small hours of November 22. Bugliosi notes that four of the Secret Service agents assigned to the motorcade route had beer and mixed drinks at the Fort Worth Press Club the night before the motorcade, the last one leaving at 2:00 a.m. "Seven agents then proceeded to the Cellar Coffee House in Fort Worth, which served no intoxicating beverages," according to Mr. Bugliosi.[13] The Report states, "There is no indication that any of the agents who visited the Cellar Coffee House had any intoxicating drink at that establishment."[14] In his memoir, agent Gerald S. Blaine tells us that the Cellar didn't serve alcohol, "so after a couple of glasses of fruit juice, the group [of Secret Service agents] returned to the hotel."[15] Agent Blaine stayed until 5:10 a.m. Imagine going to a joint like the Cellar and staying until the wee small hours to drink fruit juice! Cellar owner Pat Kirkwood told a reporter, "Those guys were bombed. They were drinking pure Everclear," which is grain alcohol that is available in two strengths: 75.5% and 95% alcohol.[16] (Kirkwood did not testify to the commission or its legal staff. Bugliosi doesn't even mention Kirkwood in his book.) Even Clint Hill, the only Secret Service man to try to save anyone's life in Dealey Plaza, admitted to the Warren Commission that he had a Scotch and soda at the Fort Worth Press Club and then went to another club, where he remained until he returned to his hotel at 2:45 a.m. on November 22. According to Blaine, the "other club" was the Cellar Coffee House. Agents Dave Grant, Andy Berger, Dick Johnsen and Ernie Olsson were also at the Cellar. Agents Glen Bennett, Paul Burns, Donald Lawton and Jack Ready stayed until 3:00 A.M. or a little later, and Agent Paul Landis Jr. didn't leave until 5:00 A.M. These were all violations of Secret Service regulations for agents on protective detail. Such late-night drinking would also leave those agents short of sleep, probably hung over, and less likely to react quickly to shots fired at the motorcade than would otherwise be the case.

The Secret Service ordered the removal of all four front motorcycle escorts. Agent Will Greer told the commission, "We usually do have them [motorcycles] on the two front fenders and two rear fenders, and some probably preceding that..."[17] Dallas motorcycle policeman B.J. Martin told the commission, "They instructed us...that we were to ride to the rear, to the rear of the car, about the rear bumper."[18] He didn't say who "they" were. Jesse Curry testified that in the planning of the motorcade, "we had more motorcycles lined up to be with the President's car, but the Secret Service didn't want that many...we wanted four on each side and they asked us to drop out some of them and back down the motorcade... which we did." He testified that it was Secret Service agent Winston Lawson, the White House advance agent for the Dallas trip, who wanted the motorcycles to stay at the rear fender of the limousine.[19] When queried by the commission about the motorcycle escorts, Lawson testified that it was his understanding that President Kennedy didn't like a lot of motorcycles surrounding his car. But he also acknowledged that there were no orders given by or on behalf of the president with respect to the locations of the motorcycles attached to the limousine.[20] Former agents Sam Kinney and Art Godfrey confirmed that Kennedy never gave direct or implicit instructions to remove those motorcycles.[21] In *Survivor's Guilt: The Secret Service and the Failure to Protect the President,* Vincent Palamara clarified that JFK never interfered with Secret Service protocols. A report of a meeting on the evening of November 21, attended by upper-echelon Dallas police personnel and a couple of Secret Service agents, states that when DPD Captain Perdue Lawrence said that there would be four motorcycles on either side immediately to the rear of the president's vehicle, Secret Service agent Lawson said that that was too many, that he thought that two on either side would be sufficient.[22]

Agent Lawson testified that seeing that the weather was clear, he told his fellow agents forty-five minutes to an hour before Kennedy was scheduled to arrive in Dallas to leave the bubble top off of the presidential limousine.[23] So it was agent Lawson who made these two decisions to reduce the security around the president – unless, of course, he was following orders from a higher authority. The Warren Report nevertheless states, "Rigorous security precautions had been arranged at Love Field with the local law enforcement authorities by Agents Sorrels and Lawson."[24] In his memoir, Secret Service agent Blaine tells us that the "four police motorcycles escorting the president's limousine were strategically placed, according to the White House Advance Manual…"[25] For some reason, Blaine doesn't mention agent Lawson's removal of the front motorcycle escorts.

The Secret Service driver of the limousine, Will Greer, made a roughly 120-degree turn onto Elm Street. Secret Service regulations call for a maximum 90-degree turn during a presidential motorcade. Agent Greer drove the limousine very slowly through Dealey Plaza, no doubt to provide an easier target for the shooters. When L. Fletcher Prouty was in Mexico City preparing for President Eisenhower's visit to that city, he was told by a Secret Service agent that according to the Secret Service manual, the president's car must maintain a speed of forty-four miles per hour until clear of any danger zones.[26] Secret Service agent Sam Kinney said the motorcade was going three to five miles per hour at the time of the first shot.[27] Motorcycle cop B.J. Martin testified that the motorcade was going four to five miles per hour when it turned onto Elm Street, and did not pick up speed on Elm.[28] The Warren Report gives the speed as 11 miles per hour along Elm Street.[29] But we don't know which version of the Zapruder film the Report's writers were using for their calculations. Lyndal Shaneyfelt calculated through analysis of that film that the average speed of the motorcade limousine through Dealey Plaza (from Zapruder frames 161 to 313) was 11.2 miles per hour.[30] But inasmuch as frames have been removed from that film, the limousine would appear to move faster than it did in reality.

As James Fetzer has pointed out, there was no protective military presence, there was no coverage of open windows, and agents were not riding on the presidential limousine, as they should have been. And when the shooting started, neither agent Roy Kellerman, sitting next to Greer, nor any agent in the follow-up car (directly behind the presidential limousine), took any action to shield the president from the gunfire. Secret Service agents are required to take immediate action to shield a president who comes under fire; that is why they are there. As soon as the bullets started flying, Kellerman should have rushed to the president, thrown him down and covered the president's body with his own, as regulations require. Kellerman instead remained calm – and seated. (In the vice president's car, agent Youngblood, sitting on the front passenger side in front of Lyndon Johnson, immediately vaulted over the front seat of the car and threw himself over Johnson.) Sen. Yarborough stated that "all of the Secret Service men seemed to me to respond very slowly, with no more than a puzzled look ... I am amazed by the lack of instantaneous response by the Secret Service, when the rifle fire began."[31] Jacqueline Kennedy reportedly fumed to friends later about agent Greer's reactions, which she described as "geriatric." According to the Warren Report, "Special Agent [John] Ready, on the right front running board of the Presidential follow-up car, heard noises that sounded like firecrackers and ran toward the President's limousine. But he was immediately called back by Special Agent Emory Roberts ..."[32] Agent Roberts ordered the agents not to move. In his statement for the commission, agent Ready stated that when he heard noises that sounded like firecrackers – obviously the gunshots – he left the follow-up car but was "re-called" by agent Emory Roberts.[33] Agent Ready did not testify to the commission or its legal staff, but he did write a memorandum to Chief Rowley that stated: "After SA [Clint] Hill got on [the] rear step of the President's car, it appeared that SA John Ready was about to follow and go for the right step, however, I told him not to jump, as we had picked up speed, and I was afraid he could not make it."[34] So Ready didn't actually leave the follow-up car (and the motorcade had not picked up speed). This is obviously at odds with the Report's version, which has Ready running toward the limousine as soon as the shots ring out. The Zapruder film does not show agent Ready's alleged run, but there is videotape showing a Secret Service agent trotting along with the presidential limousine at some point (apparently before the motorcade turned onto Elm Street), near its right rear fender, until he is called back to the follow-up car by a fellow agent. The agent stops, and looking perplexed, he raises his hands, then obeys the order.[35] Earlier along the motorcade route, agent Floyd Boring told agents not to get on the presidential limousine, and agent Don Lawton was running alongside the limousine with his hand behind President Kennedy when someone pulled him back from the car.[36]

Secret Service regulations require a car carrying a president to speed up and make evasive moves to throw off the aim of a sniper.[37] Instead, the Secret Service driver of the presidential limousine brought the car to a brief halt as the final shots were fired. (Apparently it didn't occur to Mr. Bugliosi to question why that stop doesn't appear in the Zapruder film.) The Warren Report, in its "Speculations and Rumors" section, states, "The Presidential car did not stop or almost come to a complete halt after the firing of the first shot or any other shots. William Greer testified that he accelerated the car after what was probably the second shot. Motion pictures of the scene show that the car slowed down momentarily after the shot that struck the President in the head and then speeded up rapidly."[38] So the car did not "almost come to a complete halt," but it "slowed down momentarily." Greer should have sped the car up immediately and driven out of Dealey Plaza. Greer testified that when he saw Gov. Connally start to fall, "I realized there was something wrong. I tramped on the accelerator...Just as soon as I turned my head back from the second shot right away I accelerated right then."[39] This is clearly false, as eyewitnesses and films of the event indicate. Kenny O'Donnell told the commission that the motorcade accelerated right about the time that Clint Hill grabbed onto the back of the limousine, *a few seconds after the last shot,* which doesn't agree with Greer's testimony.[40] What is equally appalling is that the Report cites Greer's testimony as "evidence," though he is obviously trying to show himself in a positive light and minimize his culpability. A film taken by Marie Muchmore shows the limousine's brake lights on for nine frames just before it takes off for Parkland Hospital. (The Muchmore film was reportedly bought by UPI, and according to Groden, while in their possession the film was damaged at the frame that showed the moment of the fatal head shot.) Bill Newman also saw the car's taillights coming on.[41]

The following Dealey Plaza witnesses stated that the car slowed and "almost" came to a stop at some point during the shooting sequence: Charles Brehm, civilian eyewitness (22H837-38, FBI affidavit, 11/25/63); Bo Byers, Houston Chronicle reporter (Palamara, "59 Witnesses: Delay on Elm Street," in Fetzer, 2000:120); Ochus V. Campbell, civilian eyewitness (22H845); Rose Clark, civilian eyewitness (24H533); Mrs. Herman (Billie P.) Clay (22H641); D.V. Harkness, Dallas policeman (6H309); Peggy Hawkins, civilian eyewitness (Fred T. Newcomb and Perry Adams, *Murder from Within,* unpublished MS, 1974, p. 97) Jean Hill, civilian eyewitness (6H209, 24H212); Sam Holland, civilian eyewitness (taped interview with Holland, April 1965, cited by V. Palamara in Fetzer, 2000, p. 124); Harry Holmes, postal inspector (7H291); Douglas Jackson, DPD motorcycle officer, riding outboard at the right rear of the death car (Newcomb and Adams, op. cit., p. 71, quoted in Fetzer, 2000, p. 121); Secret Service agent Sam Kinney, who stated that driver Greer's foot "must have come off the accelerator." (Palamara in Fetzer, 2000, p. 122); motorcycle policeman B.J. Martin (Shaw trial, p. 49 of testimony); Mary Moorman, civilian eyewitness (FBI interview, 11/23/63, 22H838); John Ready, Secret Service (18H750); James Simmons (Shaw trial testimony, February 15, 1969); Merriman Smith, UPI White House reporter (UPI story, 11/23/63); Marilyn Willis, civilian eyewitness (FBI report dated

6/19/64; Harold Weisberg, *Photographic Whitewash*, p. 179). Senator Yarborough stated in an affidavit, "When the noise of the shot was heard, the motorcade slowed to what seemed to me a complete stop (though it could have been a near stop)." (7H440) (Neither Ms. Hawkins, Ms. Moorman, Ms. Willis, nor Mrs. Clay, nor Messrs. Brehm, Byers, Jackson, nor Kinney, nor Sen. Yarborough, testified to the commission or its legal staff.)

Vincent Palamara counted 59 witnesses who stated that the limousine came to a halt or almost to a stop as the final shots were being fired, but by my count (based on Palamara's list), about a dozen of those didn't use that phraseology, merely saying that the car accelerated suddenly after those shots were fired. Bugliosi concedes that some 48 eyewitnesses testified that the limousine either "slowed," came "almost came to a halt," or "stopped completely" as the final shots rang out. But he also says that the only reference he could find in the Warren Commission volumes to the slowing of the limousine after the head shot was the testimony of Dallas motorcycle policeman Bobby Hargis, who was riding inboard at the left rear of the limousine.[42] I found a few more. The following witnesses all said that the limousine (or the motorcade) came to a stop at some point during the shooting sequence in Dealey Plaza: **Robert Baskin**, *Dallas Morning News* reporter (*Dallas Morning News*, 11/23/63, p. 2); **Hugh Betzner**, civilian eyewitness (statement, 19H467; affidavit, 24H7); **David Broden**, reporter (*Washington Evening Star*, 11/23/63, p. 8); **Earle V. Brown**, Dallas policeman (6H233); **Peggy Burney**, civilian eyewitness (*Dallas Times Herald*, 11/24/63, quoted by Palamara in Fetzer,2000, p. 124); **Henry Burroughs**, AP photographer (letter, Burroughs to Palamara, dated 10/14/98); **Mrs. Earle Cabell**, civilian eyewitness (7H487); **James Chaney**, Dallas motorcycle policeman, riding inboard at the right rear of the death car (2H44, 3H266); **Bob Clark**, ABC reporter (WFAA-ABC, 11/22/63, quoted in Fetzer, 2000, p.120); **James Courson**, Dallas motorcycle policeman (Quoted in Fetzer, ibid.); **J. W. Foster**, Dallas policeman (CD897, pp. 20-1; Newcomb and Adams, op. cit., p. 97, quoted in Fetzer, 2000, p.121); **Bobby Hargis** (6H294; *Dallas Times Herald*, 11/22/63, p. A19); **D.V. Harkness**, Dallas policeman (6H309); **Billy Lovelady**, civilian eyewitness (FBI affidavit, 3/19/64, 22H662); **Robert MacNeil**, reporter (Ira David Wood III, "22 November 1963: A Chronology," in Fetzer, 2000, pp. 40, 120, from MacNeil's book, *The Way We Were, 1963: The Year Kennedy Was Shot*, 1988, p. 193); **Billy Joe Martin**, Dallas motorcycle policeman riding outboard at the left rear of the limousine

(Newcomb and Adams, op. cit., p. 71, quoted in Fetzer, 2000, pp. 121, 341); **Bill Newman**, civilian eyewitness (Bill Sloan, *Breaking the Silence*, p. 169); **Joe Henry Rich**, Texas Highway Patrolman (Newcomb and Adams, op. cit., p. 71, Palamara in Fetzer, 2000, p.121); **Alan Smith**, civilian eyewitness (Newcomb and Adams, op. cit., p. 71, who cite the *Chicago Tribune*, 11/23/63, p. 9); **Malcolm Summers**, civilian eyewitness; **L.R. Terry**, civilian eyewitness (Marrs, 1998, p. 26); **Roy Truly**, civilian eyewitness (3H221); **Phil Willis**, civilian eyewitness (7H497); and **Mary Woodward**, *Dallas Morning News* reporter (2H43). Both Roy Truly and Officer James Chaney stated that during the shooting, the limousine pulled to the left and stopped. (3H266; 3H221) More such eyewitnesses can be found at Palamara, "59 Witnesses: Delay on Elm Street," in Fetzer, 2000, pp. 119-27. The United Press International (1964, *Four Days*) and *Newsweek* (December 2, 1963, p. 2) both mentioned that the limousine came to a halt during the shooting. (Neither Messrs. Baskin, Broden, Burroughs, Clark, Courson, MacNeil, Newman, Rich, Smith, Summers, nor Terry, nor Ms. Burney, testified to the commission or its legal staff.)

Bugliosi doesn't deal with the limousine halt discrepancy in the Zapruder film. He states that the film (which he considers to be a completely accurate record of the assassination) shows the car slowing, but not stopping, and therefore it did not stop – which means, of course, that all of the eyewitnesses cited in the above paragraph are simply wrong! Bugliosi tries to justify the slowing of the limousine as follows: "Secret Service agent Greer slows the presidential limousine to a crawl as the crowds press in."[43] This is evidently an attempt by Bugliosi to make the Secret Service appear less culpable. But it is false. Secret Service agent Emory Roberts stated, "The crowd was very sparse, in fact only a few people were along the motorcade route at the time of the shooting... After this turn [onto Elm Street], there was essentially no crowd."[44] In a memorandum to "Chief" (presumably Rowley), dated November 29, 1963, from SAIC Rufus W. Youngblood, who was in the vice president's car, Youngblood stated that after the left turn onto Elm "the sidewalk crowds were beginning to diminish in size." Secret Service agent William McIntyre said in a statement that after the turn onto Elm Street, "there was essentially no crowd..."[45] (McIntyre did not testify to the commission or its legal staff.) Secret Service agent Forrest Sorrels testified that the crowd "had begun to thin out after we made the turn on Elm Street there."[46] Will Greer testified that "when we got around on Houston Street, the crowds thinned out quite a lot ... there wasn't [sic] too many people on Elm Street – a few scattered people at that point." He said the same thing in his report.[47] Secret Service agent Clint Hill said the crowd was already "thinning out considerably" as the motorcade reached the end of Main Street and turned onto Houston Secret.[48] Secret Service agent Roy Kellerman told the commission that after they turned onto Elm, "the crowds just diminished."[49] Governor Connally stated that after the turn onto Elm street, "We could look ahead and see that the crowd was beginning to thin along the banks, just east, I guess[,] of the overpass."[50] Jacqueline Kennedy told the commission that after the motorcade "really slowly" turned the corner (presumably onto Elm Street), "there were very few people."[51] Lady Bird Johnson stated that as they entered Dealey Plaza, the "crowds began to get thinner and I remember we were some five minutes behind schedule."[52] Robert Jackson, a *Dallas Times Herald* photographer in the motorcade, told the commission, "The crowd thinned out as we got down near the intersection of Main and Houston."[53] Still photographs and video taken at the time, including the Zapruder film, also show that the "crowds" were not "pressing in." The Warren Report itself states that the crowd "thinned abruptly along Elm Street."[54] Thus Mr. Bugliosi's statement about the crowds pressing in doesn't even accord with the Warren Report, which he so trusts and admires.

Agent Blaine, in his memoir, tries to justify Greer's slowing of the limousine by saying that Greer thought that he heard a firecracker or that he might have blown a tire, so he "tapped on the brake to see how the car would respond."[55] This convenient explanation is phony on two counts: First, there had already been several shots fired when Greer slowed (or stopped) the car. Second, if Greer merely wanted to "see how the car would respond," there would be no point in turning around and looking straight at President Kennedy just before the fatal shot was fired, unless he thought that the president was going to tell him if the car had in fact blown a tire. On page 215 of his memoir, Blaine describes agent Hill as practically flying off the Secret Service follow-up car after seeing Kennedy react to the first shot, when in fact, as the Zapruder film shows, Hill does nothing in reaction to the throat shot, and it isn't until after the fatal shot has been fired that Hill runs to the back of the limousine to push Mrs. Kennedy back into her seat.

Secret Service agents put pressure on certain key individuals to change their views. In a 1977 HSCA interview, graduate student James Gochenaur quoted Secret Service agent Elmer Moore as admitting that he, Moore, was in charge of the Dallas doctors' testimony in the case, and that he pressured Dr. Perry to change his original statement that the wound in Kennedy's throat was an entry wound.[56] Gochenaur testified to the Church Committee that Moore told him this. Gochenaur said that Moore went on at some length in a rant against Kennedy, saying that he was "a pinko who was selling us out to the communists."[57] Mark Lane told the commission that Richard Dudman, a Washington correspondent for the St. Louis *Post-Dispatch,* stated that the Parkland doctors were never questioned by the FBI or Secret Service about the "vital evidence," but that after the autopsy, two Secret Service agents, armed with the autopsy report, went to Parkland to convince the doctors there that they were all in error "at the outset."[58] According to Bertrand Russell, two Secret Service agents spent three hours with the Parkland doctors and persuaded them that they were all misinformed: the entrance wound in the President's throat had been an exit wound.[59]

The Secret Service changed the statement of at least one Dealey Plaza eyewitness. Bugliosi quotes Harold Norman as "knowing" that the shots came from above him and James Jarman; Norman supposedly said to Jarman, "I could hear the action of the bolt and the cartridges hitting the floor."[60] Joseph Ball quoted from a Secret Service report of an interview with Norman, quoting Norman as saying that he knew the shots came from directly above him. Norman told Ball that he didn't make that statement.[61]

Secret Service agents prematurely destroyed key evidence. Physical evidence such as blood and brain tissue was washed from the limousine at Parkland even before the president had been pronounced dead. DPD motorcycle policeman Sgt. Stavis Ellis and DPD officer James Courson saw a Secret Service man grab the camera of a young boy who had filmed the President's limousine at Parkland Hospital, and remove and expose the film.[62] Dr. Mantik says that several people witnessed this incident.[63] (Courson did not testify to the commission or its legal staff.) Both White House photographer Robert Knudsen and Secret Service agent James K. Fox told of the Secret Service destroying autopsy films. Knudsen told his family that he had photographed the autopsy, though no one recalls his presence there.[64]

Secret Service agents forcibly removed the president's body from Dallas in the face of vigorous objections from Dallas County Medical Examiner Dr. Earl Rose and in violation of Texas law. Agent Roy Kellerman and other Secret Service men, Gen. Godfrey McHugh, and JFK aides Kenny O'Donnell, Dave Powers and Lawrence F. "Larry" O'Brien bullied their way past Dr. Rose with JFK's body and prevented a Texas autopsy. O'Donnell stated in an affidavit for the commission that Mrs. Kennedy "said she would not leave here without her husband.... So, therefore, it was our determination that the President should be taken from the hospital." O'Donnell admitted that he was among those who "pushed them all aside."[65] In an interview, Dr. McClelland, one of the surgeons who fought to save the president's life at Parkland Hospital, stated that one Secret Service man picked up "the pathologist" (apparently Dr. Rose) and set him against the wall. Regarding Kennedy's body, Adm. Burkley told Dr. Earl Rose, "We are removing it!" He added, "You can waive your local laws," or "there should be some consideration in an event like this."[66] For a long time, I believed that the reason for this forcible removal of the president's body was so that people in Washington could control the autopsy and ensure that such autopsy would support the Official Story; but this, I have come to believe, is only partly true. I can see now that the purpose could well have been to switch the body with that of the second Kennedy, with the back of the latter's head intact.

Secret Service agent Clint Hill changed his story (and Mr. Bugliosi prevaricated). In his written statement of November 30, 1963, Hill stated, "As I lay over the top of the back seat, I noticed a portion of the President's head *on the right-rear side* was missing and he was bleeding profusely."[67] (Emphasis added.) In Hill's 2013 book (with Lisa McCubbin), *Five Days in November* (New York: Gallery Books, 2013), page 103, Hill says the fatal bullet spewed blood, brain matter and bone fragments onto him. But on page 234, he changed his tune, stating, "In reaction to the first shot, President Kennedy's head was turned toward Mrs. Kennedy in such a way that when the third bullet pierced the back of his skull, it exited out the *right* side of his head [emphasis added]." This is quite different from his commission testimony and is clearly false, and is shown to be false in the Zapruder film; the film does *not* show Kennedy's head turning to the left, toward his wife, in reaction to the first shot (to the throat). If the bullet exited the right side of Kennedy's head, it could not have spewed the cranial ejecta onto him. Apparently Mr. Hill is trying to express his support for the Official Story as well as defend the phony blob on the side of Kennedy's head in the film and the rather bizarre diagram shown in the Hearings and Exhibits at 16H984 (CE388), labeled as the "Schematic drawing made at Bethesda Naval Hospital of what Cmdr. James J. Humes observed." We are not told who drew the diagram, which shows the path of a projectile entering at a low point at the back of Kennedy's head and exiting the *top*. This would put the shooter in the trunk of the limousine. There is also the problem that none of the Parkland doctors or nurses saw a wound in the side of the president's head. But near the end of his book, Mr. Hill reassures the reader that Oswald was in fact the assassin. He does not, however, tell us how a bullet fired from the "sniper's nest" on the sixth floor of the Book Depository could cause Kennedy's cranial matter to be thrown back and to the left, onto the limousine's trunk (and onto Hill). At 2H139, Hill is telling the commission that he saw Kennedy put his hands to his throat as he, Hill, was leaving the follow-up car, but the Zapruder film shows that he didn't leave the follow-up car until he saw Jackie Kennedy climb onto the trunk of the limousine to gather her husband's cranial matter. Agent Hill wrote in his foreword to Blaine's book, "I would be very pleased if the results of the Warren Commission and its investigation would be accepted as the final word."

In his endnotes, Mr. Bugliosi tells us that Clint Hill "never mentioned seeing anything like brain matter or part of a skull behind the president" when Jacqueline Kennedy climbed onto the trunk.[68] Not so. Mr. Bugliosi had easy access to Mr. Hill's commission testimony, the same as anyone else, so it is difficult to understand why he would make this obviously false statement. In his commission testimony (to Arlen Specter), Hill stated, "The right rear portion of his [Kennedy's] head was missing. It was lying in the rear seat of the car. His brain was exposed. There was blood and bits of brain all over the entire rear portion of the car. Mrs. Kennedy was completely covered with blood.... There was ... one large gaping wound in the right rear portion of the head."[69] But agent Hill also testified that he never had the impression that there was a shot that originated from the front of the limousine.[70] If there was blood and bits of brain on the rear portion of the car, one wonders how that shot could have come from anywhere but the front.

In a letter dated April 29, 1964, from Mark Lane to the commission's J. Lee Rankin, Lane stated that he had secured information proving that a story widely circulated throughout the United States on February 10, 1964, alleging that an eyewitness (a janitor) actually saw Oswald pull the trigger was planted by an agent of the Secret Service.[71] This eyewitness story is mentioned in Appendix XII of the Warren Report under "Other Rumors and Speculations," where it is stated that the commission concluded that the alleged eyewitness story had no foundation in fact.

Yet despite all this, Bugliosi assures us that "there is absolutely no evidence that the Secret Service was involved in the assassination." He concedes that mistakes were made, but "these failures almost assuredly did not contribute to what ultimately happened...." Bugliosi asks what motive the Secret Service would have had to be involved in the assassination.[72] That can be answered easily: their cooperation was essential in providing an easy target for the hit; and they no doubt had their orders.

Secret Service chief James Rowley told the Warren Commission that there was no official reprimand or disciplinary action taken against the Dallas agents. During Rowley's appearance before the commission, Earl Warren berated him over the fact that so many members of the president's Secret Service detail went out drinking until the wee small hours of the morning of November 22. Rowley told Warren, "I don't think that these people should be blamed for the tragedy."[73] That wasn't the point. They violated Secret Service rules regarding the consumption of alcohol while in travel status, and should have at least have been disciplined for that. When J. Lee Rankin asked Rowley if anything had been done to reprimand the drinking agents, Rowley replied, "They were interviewed by the inspector at the time ... I think they recognize the seriousness of their acts." Regarding the actions and behavior of his agents in Dealey Plaza that day, Rowley told the commission that their conduct "had no bearing on the assassination." How about driving the presidential limousine at one-fourth the regulation speed for motorcades and removing the front motorcycle escorts (among other things)? Rowley stated that his agents "performed their duties from the time they departed in the follow-up car from Love Field until the point of the tragedy in a most satisfactory manner. There was nothing deficient in their actions or their alertness."[74] He had already acknowledged that the drinking at the Press Club was a violation of chapter 1, section 10, of the Secret Service Manual. So to all you Secret Service agents out there: If you flagrantly violate regulations with regard to presidential protection before and during motorcades, you had better watch out; you might be interviewed! Rowley continued to serve in the Johnson administration. The HSCA conveniently found "no evidence of Secret Service complicity in the assassination."[75]

4. Multiple Shooters in Dealey Plaza

Several people stated that the second two shots were very close together. Secret Service agent Glen Bennett testified that after a shot hit JFK in the back, a "second shot followed immediately..."[76] Secret Service agent Will Greer testified that "the last two [shots] seemed to be just simultaneously, one behind the other..."[77] In a memorandum to Gerald A. Behn, who was chief of the president's Secret Service detail, dated November 30, 1963, agent George W. Hickey Jr. stated that the second shot "appeared to me completely different in sound than the first report and [the two shots] were in such rapid succession there seemed to be practically no time element between them."[78] (Hickey did not testify to the commission or its legal staff.) Secret Service agent Clint Hill said that the second shot he heard "had almost a double sound..."[79] Secret Service agent Winston G. Lawson testified that he heard one report, then a pause, then two more reports closer together.[80] James Crawford testified that the second shot was "followed very quickly by the third one."[81] Roger Craig said there were not more than two seconds between the second and third shots; he testified at the Shaw trial that the second and third shots were very close together.[82] Thomas Atkins, an official White House photographer who photographed the motorcade (but did not testify to the commission or its legal staff), also said that the last two shots were clustered together.[83] Patricia Donaldson heard two shots in rapid succession less than a second apart.[84] (Ms. Donaldson did not testify to the commission or its legal staff.) Dallas County Deputy Sheriff Jack Faulkner was standing outside the sheriff's offices on Houston Street; he also said that the second and third shots were in rapid succession.[85] Motorcycle policeman Clyde Haygood told the commission, "The last two were closer than the first. In other words, it was the first, and then a pause, and then the other two were real close."[86] Sam Holland testified that he heard four shots, and that the third and fourth shots were close together.[87] Robert Jackson said that the second and third shots were "very close together."[88] James Jarman Jr. said the third shot was fired right behind the second.[89] Billy Lovelady said that the second two shots were close together.[90] Luke Mooney said that the "second and third shot was [*sic*] pretty close together."[91] Mrs. Lillian Mooneyham told the FBI that the second and third shots were closer together than the first and second.[92] William Shelley heard one firecracker sound and a slight pause, and then "two more a little bit closer together."[93] Ruth Smith told the FBI that she heard a shot, then a pause, then two more fairly close together.[94] John Solon said that he heard, "First shot; pause two shots..."[95] Pearl Springer heard two shots close together after the first shot.[96] At the JFK assassination symposium in Dallas on November 17, 1991, Malcolm Summers stated that "the second and third shots came so close together that there's no way one man could be doing it."[97] Deputy Constable Seymour Weitzman testified that the second two shots seemed to be simultaneous.[98] Bonnie Ray Williams testified that the second and third shots were closer together than the first and second; he "remembered three shots, because there was a pause between the first two shots. There was [*sic*] two real quick."[99] Joe Molina said the second and third shots were closer together than the first and second.[100] Linda Willis, daughter of Phillip Willis, told the commission, "I heard one [shot], then there was a little bit of time, and then there were two real fast bullets together."[101] (Neither Willis testified to the commission or its legal staff.) Mary E. Woodward told Walt Brown that the last two shots were almost simultaneous.[102] (Ms. Woodward did not testify to the commission or its legal staff.) Edward Shields told the commission that he "heard one shot and then a pause... and then two shots [one] right behind the other.[103] Dallas Mayor Earle Cabell told the commission that he was three or four cars behind the presidential limousine. He said the second and third shots "were in a rather rapid succession."[104] Lady Bird Johnson said that she heard "two more shots in rapid succession."[105] Sen. Yarborough stated that "there seemed to be a long time between the first and second shots, a much shorter time between the second and third shots..."[106] The Warren Report concedes that several witnesses recalled that the second and third shots were bunched together.[107] Since a bolt-action rifle could not operate that quickly, this is clear and incontrovertible evidence of at least two shooters. Neither the Ivy League-educated doctors of jurisprudence on the commission nor those on the commission's legal staff were able to draw this obvious conclusion.

Steven Wilson thought there was a greater space of time between the second and third shots than between the first and second, but this is the only witness I have found who said this.[108]

An Ernest Mentesana film reportedly shows Dallas policeman removing a rifle with no sling and no scope from the roof of the Book Depository.[109] (Mentesana did not testify to the commission or its legal staff.) According to a Secret Service document, Frank Ellsworth of the Bureau of Alcohol, Tobacco and Firearms confirmed that the Mannlicher-Carcano was found by a DPD detective not on the same floor as the cartridges but on the fourth or fifth floor of the Book Depository.[110] (Ellsworth did not testify to the commission or its legal staff.)

Mark Weiss, electrical engineer and professor in the Department of Computer Science at the City University of New York, and former vice president for acoustical research at the Federal Scientific Corporation, told the HSCA that his analysis indicated that there was at least a 95 percent probability that a shot was fired from the grassy knoll. Congressman

Louis Stokes (Ohio Democrat), HSCA chairman, told Weiss: "[I]f the committee accepts your testimony, the committee then, in effect, accepts the fact that on that particular day in 1963 when the President was assassinated, there were two shooters in Dealey Plaza."[111]

The summary of shots provided in Chapter 1 of this book also provides clear evidence of multiple shooters in Dealey Plaza.

5. The Phony Tramps in Dealey Plaza

It was apparently between 1:00 and 2:00 P.M. on the day of the assassination that Sam Holland saw a train making an unauthorized departure from behind the Book Depository, ordered it stopped, and called the police. DPD Sgt. D.V. Harkness found three men in one of the train cars; he and other officers then arrested the men and walked them through the Plaza to the police department.[112] Their images are captured in a series of seven photographs taken that day. Though under arrest, they are not handcuffed. All three "tramps" had obviously shaved that morning. Their clothing wasn't dirty, just wrinkled; and the soles and heels of their shoes were in excellent shape. It's all part of the charade. It has been said that one of the "cops" accompanying the tramps resembles Grayston Lynch, a Texas CIA agent. The DPD arrest records of the three tramps, discovered in 1992 by Dallas Municipal Archives and Records Center journalist Mary La Fontaine, gave their names as Harold Doyle, John F. Gedney, and Gus W. Abrams.[113] In his section on "Other Assassins," Bugliosi accepts these identifications as immutable truth.

The tramp who walks in front of the other two in Dealey Plaza looks to be in his thirties; he has dark hair with a receding hairline and has become known as the **Oswald tramp**; the HSCA refers to him as tramp A. In their book *The Man on the Grassy Knoll*, John R. Craig and Philip A. Rogers identify him as Charles F. Rogers; Houston police forensic artist Lois Gibson also identified him thus. The authors of *The Man on the Grassy Knoll* tell us that Christine Anderson, who saw Charles Rogers a few months before his parents were murdered, recognized him as the 'Oswald' tramp, but comparing the photos of Rogers in the aforementioned book and on the Internet with photos of the Oswald tramp, it can be seen that the chin of the Oswald tramp is significantly more protrudent than that of Charles Rogers. The Oswald tramp could be Rogers after some plastic surgery in the chin area, but otherwise I would only rate the probability of the Oswald tram being Charles Rogers at about sixty to seventy percent. French journalist William Reymond has stated that the Oswald tramp was a French mercenary named Max, known for his marksmanship. Reymond also stated that French intelligence sources told him that the Oswald tramp fired one of the head shots and was the primary shooter. According to Allard Lowenstein, an attorney and sometime member of the US House of Representatives, the Oswald tramp was someone known as "Frenchy," a French-Canadian. Comparison photos of Charles Rogers and the Oswald tramp can be found at jfkmurdersolved.com and in *The Man on the Grassy Knoll.*

The tallest of the three has become known as the **tall tramp**; the HSCA refers to him as tramp B. Jim Marrs stated in his book that contract killer Charles V. Harrelson was the tall tramp; he stated that Harrelson was connected to Jack Ruby through Russell D. Mathews; an associate of Florida Mob boss Santos Trafficante.[114] Lois Gibson also identified Harrelson as the tall tramp. On the day he was arrested in 1980 for the assassination of US District Judge John H. Wood Jr., Harrelson confessed to killing JFK, but he later recanted that statement. To me, the identification of Harrelson as tramp B is not quite convincing. Photos of the tall tramp compared to photographs of Harrelson can be found on the internet and in other sources, including Fetzer, *Murder in Dealey Plaza,* p. 64. In *Coup d'état in America,* Canfield and Weberman say that the tall tramp is Daniel L. Carswell, which is the name given for an electrical engineer who was one of the US citizens arrested by the Castro regime in September 1960 for being part of a spy ring that tapped the telephones of the Havana office of Hsinhua, the Communist Chinese news agency. He would have been about 45 at the time of the assassination (the tall tramp appears younger than that). Gerry Hemming told a researcher that when "Carswell" was arrested in Cuba, the CIA tried frantically to break him out, because he was their "number one stone cold killer" who had the proverbial "license to kill" and knew about every assassination plot the CIA had going at the time. Canfield and Weberman also provide evidence that Harold Doyle was not one of the tramps.[115] William Reymond stated that the tall tramp, like the Oswald tramp, was French.

The shortest and apparently oldest of the three has become known as the **oldman tramp**; the HSCA refers to him as tramp C. He appears to be E. Howard Hunt, a full-time employee of the CIA at the time. At the 1991 Kennedy assassination symposium in Dallas, Lois Gibson identified Chauncey Holt, a career con man who claimed to be working for the CIA at the time, as the oldman tramp. But Holt is not tramp C; a comparison of his photo with that of the old man tramp shows that the distance from the base of the nose to the top of the upper lip is greater in Holt than in that tramp. The internet has a photo of Holt purportedly taken in 1963; he looks nothing like the old man tramp. Howard Hunt naturally denied being in Dallas on November 22. He told the HSCA that he was with Tracy Barnes in the new Domestic Operations Division of the Plans Directorate at the time of the assassination. The Hunts' housekeeper, Mary Trayner, submitted an affidavit saying that Hunt and his wife were at home in Maryland on November 22. Lisa Hunt, Howard Hunt's daughter, said that her father was at home with the family in the afternoon and evening of November 22. The second story: Hunt stated that he and his wife heard about the assassination on the car radio while they were downtown in Washington, D.C. Hunt testified in court that he was out shopping for Chinese food with his wife on November 22, 1963. Confronted with the discrepancy by Robert Olsen of the Rockefeller Commission, Hunt suggested over the phone on March 7, 1975, that Ms. Trayner was simply in error. E. Howard Hunt's son Howard Saint John Hunt describes his father's alibi as "just the biggest load of crap in the world." His mother told him that his father was on a business trip to Dallas. During the *Hunt v. Liberty Lobby* trial, it was established that Hunt was in Dallas on November 22, "acting as one of the paymasters for the conspiracy."[116] St. John Hunt told *Rolling Stone* magazine (April 5, 2007) that when he saw the old man tramp, his reaction was, "It looks like my dad. There's nobody that has all those same facial features." He remembered that he and other fifth-graders were sent home on November 22, "and I remember going home. I have no recollection of him being there." Joseph J. Trento, staff correspondent at the Wilmington, Delaware, *News Journal,* tells of having been invited to lunch by James Angleton at the ArmyNavy Club, and that during that lunch, Angleton asked Trento, "Did you know Howard Hunt was in Dallas on the day of the assassination?" Angleton told Trento that "some very odd things were going on that were out of our control." There are side-by-side photographs of Hunt and the old man tramp on the internet; the similarity is clear. (Hunt later spent 33 months in prison as a result of his part in the Watergate break-in.)

The HSCA noted that Thomas Vallee, Frank Sturgis, Fred Lee Chrisman and Daniel Carswell have been suggested as likely tramp candidates, but concluded that Vallee, Carswell, Sturgis and Howard Hunt were not the men with whom they were being compared.[117] The Rockefeller Commission concluded that Hunt and Sturgis were not two of the tramps, but this cannot be considered a completely unbiased source. Bugliosi notes that *Rolling Stone* magazine commissioned the Institute of Forensic Sciences in Oakland, California, "to make a comparison of the tramp photos with those of Hunt and Sturgis, and the institute concluded Hunt and Sturgis were not the tramps."[118] But I wouldn't take their word for it. (Some photographs of the tramps can be found at 6HSCA267-73.)

6. Phony Secret Service agents in Dealey Plaza

Bugliosi spends several pages in his Secret Service Agents on the Grassy Knoll chapter assuring us that witnesses saw nobody in the area behind the picket fence, but he begins the chapter by telling us that Seymour Weitzman testified that when he ran into the parking lot in the railroad yards behind the fence, he encountered "other officers, Secret Service as well." Weitzman, Sgt. D.V. Harkness[119] and Patrolman Joe M. Smith[120] all encountered men behind the stockade fence who identified themselves as Secret Service agents, though the commission acknowledged that there were no Secret Service agents on the ground in Dealey Plaza at the time of the assassination until agent Forrest Sorrels returned to Elm Street and entered the Book Depository at 12:50 or 12:55 p.m.[121] Weitzman told the Warren Commission that he encountered "Secret Service in the railroad yards."[122]

Officer Harkness told the commission on April 9, 1964, that when he went to the back of the Depository, "There were some Secret Service agents there. I didn't get them identified. They told me they were Secret Service."[123] Bugliosi tells us that in a report on his 1978 interview with Harkness, an HSCA investigator wrote that Harkness "told me that there was quite a bit of confusion and he would have to say that he may have assumed that the men were Secret Service."[124] But Harkness was quite specific in 1964: "They told me they were Secret Service." It is quite doubtful that his memory improved after the passage of fourteen years.

When Patrolman Smith was in the parking lot west of the Book Depository, he encountered a man who "showed me that he was a Secret Service agent."[125] In an interview with HSCA investigators on February 8, 1978, Patrolman Smith again stated that the man he encountered *told* him he was a Secret Service agent but Bugliosi explains this away by saying that Smith may have only *assumed* that the badge was a Secret Service badge.[126] Bugliosi repeats this in his endnotes, saying that Smith told the Warren Commission in 1964 that he only *believed* the man was Secret Service.[127] This is false, as is shown by his testimony quoted above. Mr. Bugliosi informs us that HSCA investigators got Joe Smith and D.V. Harkness to say that "Weitzman didn't know who the man was." HSCA investigators Leodis C. Matthews and Harold Rose got Harkness to say that he "may have assumed that the men were Secret Service."[128]

Gordon Arnold told Jim Marrs that when he went behind the picket fence, he encountered a man who showed him a badge and told him that he was with the Secret Service (and didn't want Arnold in the area).[129] Mr. Arnold told Earl Golz of the *Dallas Morning News* the same thing in 1978, adding that the man told Arnold that he "didn't want anybody up there."

Bugliosi scoffs at the stories of Secret Service agents (fake or otherwise) in Dealey Plaza and quotes the HSCA statement that "because the Dallas Police Department had numerous plainclothes detectives on duty in the Dealey Plaza area, the Committee considered it possible that they were mistaken for Secret Service agents."[130] One does not get to the truth about an official document by quoting that document.

Retired Army Lt. Col. Robert E. Jones was commanding officer of the 112th Military Intelligence Region that encompassed Texas in 1963. He told the HSCA that the Department of Defense Intelligence had eight to twelve military intelligence personnel in plainclothes assigned to Dallas to provide supplemental security for JFK's visit. "He indicated that these agents had identification credentials and if questioned, would most likely have stated that they were on detail with the Secret Service." But the Department of Defense reported that its files showed no record indicating any DoD Protective Services in Dallas.[131]

The presence of phony Secret Service agents in Dealey Plaza as well as three people disguised as tramps in the railroad yards behind the picket fence should make it clear that we are looking at an elaborate charade, a kind of malevolent kabuki play, and a clear picture of conspiracy.

7. Behavior of J. Edgar Hoover and others in the Justice Department

The FBI received – and ignored – five separate and distinct threats to President Kennedy's life: from Carlos Marcello, from Santos Trafficante, from Garry Trapnell (August 1963), from Richard Case Nagell on September 17, 1963, and from Joseph Milteer in early November 1963.

Prior to the arrival of JFK's casket at Andrews AFB, Dr. Robert Livingston telephoned Bethesda and eventually reached Dr. Humes. Dr. Livingston was the Scientific Director for the National Institute for Mental Health and the National Institute of Neurological Diseases and Blindness (two of the National Institutes of Health). He told Humes about reports describing the small wound in the President's neck, stressing that it would have to be a wound of entrance, and emphasizing the importance of carefully tracing the path of the projectile. Their conversation was interrupted briefly, and when Humes returned to the phone, he told Dr. Livingston, "I can't talk with you any longer. The FBI won't let me."[132]

On the day of the assassination, J. Edgar Hoover stated that Oswald was the assassin and that he had acted alone, before any investigation had begun. Nicholas Katzenbach was assistant attorney general at the time. On Sunday afternoon, November 24, Hoover telephoned Lyndon Johnson aide Walter Jenkins and said, "The thing I am most concerned about, and so is Mr. Katzenbach, is having something issued so we can convince the public that Oswald is the real assassin."[133] Bugliosi explains this away by suggesting that since Hoover believed Oswald was guilty, he merely "wanted to help make sure a vulnerable and severely traumatized American public, susceptible to rumors and speculation, also became convinced of this reality."[134] What Hoover "believed" wasn't necessary a reality; and how could Oswald's "guilt" by a "reality" just two days after the assassination, before any serious investigating had been done?

On November 25, Katzenbach wrote the famous memo to Bill Moyers, President Kennedy's press assistant, stating, in part, that "the public must be satisfied that Oswald was the assassin; that he did not have confederates who are still at large; that the evidence was such that he would have been convicted at trial."[135] Katzenbach stated the need to cut off speculation about Oswald's motivation and the need to "head off speculation or congressional hearings of the wrong sort." The memo was sent before the Warren Commission was formed. According to *Newsweek* magazine, Hoover and Katzenbach "feared that an unfettered investigation of the assassination would lead in dangerous directions."[136] To show that Katzenbach's motives were pure, Mr. Bugliosi points out that further down in his memo, Katzenbach states that it is "important that all the facts" surrounding the assassination be made public.[137] Presumably, this is to happen after speculation is cut off.

Hoover opposed the creation of any public commission to study the JFK assassination and, once it was established, did not want the Warren Commission to conduct an exhaustive investigation. According to William C. Sullivan, sometime head of the FBI's Domestic Intelligence Division (not to be confused with William H. Sullivan, a career Foreign Service officer who held a number of ambassadorships in the 1960s and

1970s), Hoover ordered that that information be leaked to United Press International (UPI) to "blunt the drive for an independent investigation."[138] On December 3, two days *before* the Warren Commission held its first meeting, UPI carried a story on its national wire stating that the FBI report "now nearly ready for the White House will indicate that Lee Harvey Oswald was the lone and unaided assassin of President Kennedy, government sources said today."

Long before the commission issued its report, the FBI started leaking information on its initial report on Oswald to the press.[139] As early as December 3, 1963, someone was leaking to the Associated Press and other news outlets that the FBI was close to completing an "exhaustive report" that would conclude that Oswald, without accomplices, had fired three shots at the presidential limousine, two of which hit Kennedy and one that hit Connally. The consensus among several commissioners was that the "someone" was Hoover and the FBI. It was an apparent effort "to cement public opinion around the idea that there had been no conspiracy that the FBI might have been able to find."[140] The Bureau failed to turn over to the Warren Commission important ballistic evidence pertaining to the assassination. This failing was disclosed in January 1975, by Hale Boggs' son, Hale Jr. "Even after the passage of the JFK Records Act in 1992," Anthony Summers adds, "the FBI continued to resist full disclosure."[141]

According to commissioner Boggs, Hoover "lied his eyes out to the Commission – on Oswald, on Ruby, on their friends, the bullets, the gun, you name it."[142] For example, when asked by the Warren Commission why Oswald didn't simply shoot at the limousine as it approached the Book Depository, Hoover lied and said, ""The reason for that is, I think, the fact there were some trees between his window on sixth floor and the cars as they turned and went through the park [Dealey Plaza]."[143] As photographs taken at the time show, there were no trees between those two points.

James Tague wrote that "every piece of evidence that I have been able to obtain in the last 40 years points directly to J. Edgar Hoover ... as being responsible for trying to cover up that one shot fired during the assassination of President Kennedy went astray and hit the curb in front of me, spraying debris into my face."[144]

The substance of an FBI report on some men engaging in mock target practice on the grassy knoll two days before the assassination was not mentioned in the FBI's investigation of the assassination.

Gordon Shanklin, FBI agent-in-charge in Dallas, was quoted in the *New York Times* (November 25, 1963) as saying that the "paraffin" (dermal nitrate) administered to Oswald was positive for his hands *and cheek*, which would indicate that he had fired a weapon recently. The report of the paraffin test, obtained by Mark Lane in January 1964, indicates that no nitrates were found on the cast of the right side of Oswald's face.[145] The Warren Report acknowledges that this cast showed no reaction. If Shanklin was quoted accurately, he clearly lied about this important issue.[146] (See also Behavior of the Dallas Police, below.) Shanklin was also the man who released the three "tramps." In April 1964, Shanklin asked Jean Hill to sign a statement repudiating her earlier one about seeing Jack Ruby in Dealey Plaza moments after the assassination. She refused.[147]

Peter Dale Scott states, "In February 1964, when Mark Lane was planning to present the case for a grassy-knoll assassin before a public meeting at Town Hall in New York, the FBI tried unsuccessfully to prevent the meeting from taking place."[148] On the morning of April 29, 1964, Lane was accosted by two special agents of the FBI who demanded to know if he had documents from the FBI files in his possession. They told him that they had "confidential information" indicating that he had illegally secured such documents. Lane reported this in a letter to the commission that same day.[149] He later told the commission, "I don't expect to be accosted in front of my house by agents of the police, Federal, State or local authorities. Those are the actions not of a democratic society, but of a police state..."[150] Shenon states that through the winter and spring of 1964, "Lane was trailed by the FBI almost everywhere he went in the United States."[151] The FBI apparently also monitored the public appearances of Marina Oswald. Bugliosi reports in his endnotes that the FBI wiretapped Marina's telephone conversations and monitored her activities during the year after the assassination (if not longer).[152] These underhanded actions were no doubt based on the fact that Mark Lane and Marina Oswald were opposing the Official Story. Apparently the commissioners were somewhat obsessed with Lane; his phones were tapped and his offices bugged by the FBI, and when Arlen Specter was taking Jean Hill's testimony, he wanted her to tell him "all the things you told Mark Lane."[153] The commission also asked the FBI to monitor Lane's public appearances in this country, "which the bureau proceeded to do."[154] After the publishing house of Holt, Rinehart and Winston agreed to publish Lane's book *Rush to Judgment* in 1966, Hoover deputy Dick Derocher called a Holt executive to the FBI office in Manhattan and told him that he should not publish Lane's book.[155]

Arnold Rowland thought he saw a man with a high-powered rifle with scope standing twelve to fifteen feet back from a window on the second floor from the top (fifth floor) at the extreme *west* end of the Depository.[156] When Rowland told FBI agents who were questioning him at home about seeing a "Negro" man at a window at the southwest corner of the Book Depository, they told him it didn't have any bearing on the case, and to "forget it."[157]

FBI agents warned Parkland Hospital engineer Darrell Tomlinson to keep quiet about his observations at Parkland Hospital. Milton Klein, owner of Klein's Sporting Goods, whence the Mannlicher-Carcano was ordered by "Alek Hidell," told Mark Lane that FBI agents had ordered him not to discuss the case. Aguto Marcelli, a correspondent for the Italian publication *L'Europeo*, tried to talk to Klein, but Klein told Marcelli, "The FBI warned me to keep my trap shut."[158] (Klein did not testify to the commission or its legal staff.) The FBI also forwarded to Congressman Boggs a file that contained derogatory information about commission critics.

A report dated November 22, 1963, from Lt. Jack Revill to Capt. W.P. Gannaway states that when Revill met FBI agent James Hosty in the basement of the Dallas Police Department on November 22, Hosty told him that the Bureau "had information that this subject [Oswald] was capable of committing the assassination of President Kennedy."[159] Lt. Revill similarly told the commission that at about 3:00 p.m. on the day of the assassination, after he and Detective V.J. Brian had just completed their search of the Book Depository, they entered the police basement, where they encountered Agent Hosty, who "made the statement that Lee Oswald killed the president, and that Oswald was a Communist."[160]

As stated above, the supposed Oswald jacket found a few blocks from the Tippit murder scene bore a laundry tag with the number B 9738. The FBI did not bother to trace the tag (and the commission didn't ask the FBI to trace it), presumably because it would have pointed away from Oswald's being the fleeing man and thus being Officer Tippit's killer.

The FBI prevented a representative of the American Civil Liberties Union from visiting Oswald at the police station on the day after the assassination.[161] Immediately after the assassination, Marina Oswald was incarcerated by the Secret Service and held essentially incommunicado. Several days after the "protective custody" began, a reporter sought an interview with her, and she expressed a desire to meet with the reporter. The FBI intervened and prevented the interview.[162]

Journalist and TV personality Dorothy Kilgallen had been telling friends that she was going to "break the real story" of the assassination. She had also met with Jack Ruby, though accounts differ as to how much time she actually spent with him. According to an article by Liz Smith in the *Daily News* ("The Kilgallen Story: A New Page," December 15, 1976), in 1964, several weeks before the Warren Report was released, Ms. Kilgallen prematurely published Jack Ruby's testimony to the Warren Commission. The FBI began investigating her; they tapped her telephones and placed her under surveillance. Ms. Smith's article stated that the FBI had "voluminous" material on her, and the CIA had about twenty pages on her. (See also *The Suspicious Deaths*, below.)

Jean Hill told Mark Lane that Mary Moorman took a photo a brief moment before the first shot was fired; FBI agents took the film from her and she never saw it again.[163] Ms. Moorman said that she gave one photo to two Secret Service agents and one to "Bureau Agents."[164] In a letter to the HSCA, Robert Groden stated that Ms. Moorman took three consecutive photographs, and the first and third of the three show evidence of retouching. He also stated that after the FBI confiscated the first Moorman print, it lost the sixth floor, "which was there originally in the photograph," as well as the eastern end of the Book Depository and the "assassin's" window.[165]

As discussed in Chapter 2, above, Parkland Hospital security Chief O.P. Wright told Josiah Thompson that the bullet he gave to the Secret Service man, apparently agent Richard Johnsen, was a spitzer bullet. Wright apparently mentioned the name of Darrell Tomlinson, who found the bullet, to the Secret Service man, because on the night following the assassination, Tomlinson received a phone call from the FBI warning him not to talk about his discovery. After Ed Hoffman's second visit to the FBI (June 1967), an agent told him to keep quiet about what he had seen, or "you might get killed."[166] Hoffman said the FBI later tried to pay him not to talk about what he saw.[167] Hoffman said the same thing (via sign language) in a videotaped interview. Richard Carr had seen a heavy-set man on the sixth floor of the Book Depository minutes before the shooting. FBI agents came to his home and threatened him into silence after he stated that the man he saw on the sixth floor of the Depository wasn't the man he saw identified on television as Lee Oswald. One agent told him, "If you didn't see Lee Harvey Oswald in the School Book Depository, then you didn't see anything." Carr also testified at the Clay Shaw trial about the FBI telling him to keep his mouth shut.[168] After William Crowe Jr., an entertainer at Jack Ruby's Carousel Club, told the Associated Press on November 25, 1963, that he was positive that he had seen Oswald in the Carousel about a week before the assassination, Crowe was contacted by FBI agents, who told him to check out of his Dallas hotel and go into hiding.[169] The *New York Times* (December 6, 1963) stated, "Most private citizens who had cooperated with newsmen reporting the crime have refused to give further help after being interviewed by agents of the Federal Bureau of Investigation."

Dealey Plaza eyewitness Steven F. Wilson was visited repeatedly by FBI agents after telling one on March 25, 1964, that the shots came from the west end of the Book Depository or from the colonnade.[170] (Wilson didn't testify to the commission or its legal staff.) Paul Groody, owner of the funeral home to which Oswald's body was taken, said that FBI agents put ink on Oswald's hands and put them on the rifle. The FBI told him to shut up. On the way to meet disc jockey Alex Jones to discuss the case, a truck ran Groody off the road.[171]

It has been reported that Acquilla Clemons saw *two* men (in addition to Tippit) at the Tippit murder scene. Phillip Nelson says that Hoover ordered the Special Agent in Charge of the Dallas FBI office (apparently Gordon Shanklin) not to permit his agents to question Ms. Clemons or Mr. and Mrs. Wright, "a fact later revealed when the FBI memo from Hoover to Gordon Shanklin was noted in Michael Kurtz's book, *Crime of the Century*."[172] Frank Wright claimed to have seen Tippit's killer drive away from the scene in an old grey coupe.[173] (Mr. Wright, like Ms. Clemons, did not testify to the commission or its legal staff.)

In their 1992 book *Yes, Americans, a Conspiracy Murdered JFK!* (San Marino, CA: Bureau of International Affairs, 1992), Stanley and Ethel Marks list 60 witnesses who accused FBI agents of distorting their statements given to those agents, with references to Warren Commission volumes. Among those whose statements were distorted by the FBI were Carolyn Arnold, Nelson Delgado, Orest Peña, Jack Dougherty, Alfred Hodge, B.M. Patterson, Richard Saunders, James Simmons, Bonnie Ray Williams, Harold Norman and Loran Hall. When Carolyn Arnold saw the FBI report of her comments, she claimed that what she told them was quite different from their report of her comments.[174] Nelson Delgado, who served with Oswald in the Marines, reported that he was interviewed repeatedly by FBI agents; "they weren't satisfied with my testimony of him [Oswald] not being an expert shot" Delgado said one of the FBI men who interviewed him "kept badgering me ... he kept staring at me."[175] Delgado also testified that FBI agents misrepresented some of his statements and omitted others; for example, an FBI report states that Oswald discussed socialism with Delgado in Spanish, but Delgado told the commission that he did not.[176] Orest Peña, owner of a New Orleans bar, testified that FBI agent Warren De Brueys came to his bar and tried to intimidate him. According to Peña, De Brueys told him "not to talk to him anymore because what he could do is get me in trouble."[177] During his commission testimony, Peña denied that he had made the statements attributed to him by the FBI agents who interviewed him a month earlier.[178] An FBI agent named Kreutzer reported that Book Depository employee Harold Norman told him that after he heard a shot, Norman stuck his head out of the window and looked up toward the roof. Norman told the commission's Joseph Ball that he didn't remember saying that; he told Ball that he never put his head out of the window.[179] FBI agents Alfred C. Ellington and James W. Anderton quoted Dougherty as saying that he heard a loud explosion that sounded like a rifle shot coming from the next floor above him. Dougherty told assistant counsel Ball that he didn't tell them that.[180]

Kennedy aides knew that the shots were coming from the knoll area, but the FBI dissuaded them from saying so. Over dinner in 1968, Kennedy aide Kenny O'Donnell told Thomas "Tip" O'Neill Jr., erstwhile Speaker of the House of Representatives, that he was sure that he had heard two shots that came from behind the fence on the grassy knoll. After the FBI told him it couldn't have happened that way, "I testified the way they wanted me to."[181] Kennedy aide Dave Powers also told Tip O'Neill that the FBI persuaded him to change his testimony that the shots came from the grassy knoll. Powers told WCAP radio producer Woody Woodland that he knew that the shots came from behind the fence on the knoll; but "we were told not to [testify to that fact] by the FBI."[182]

One day in mid-September 1963, Mrs. Fenella Farrington was at the Mexican consulate in New Orleans to see about getting her family automobile returned from Mexico. At the consulate she encountered a young man (accompanied by a woman with a scarf tied around her head) who caused something of a stir when he asked the desk clerk about taking "firearms or a gun into Mexico." Four days after the assassination, the FBI located Mrs. Farrington in Washington, D.C. The agent who telephoned her told her that Oswald was the young man at the consulate, and insisted, despite her repeated denials, that she had seen Oswald in Mexico City, even before the scene at the consulate. Mark Lane later interviewed Mrs. Farrington at Garrison's request, and showed her 17 photos of various people; she stated that two of them could have been the man she saw. She picked out a picture of Lee Oswald and one of Kerry Thornley, a "Marine buddy" of Oswald's.[183] Thornley was the only man who was at El Toro

Air Force Base with Oswald who testified that Lee had Marxist leanings, although Thornley hadn't even lived on the same side of the base as Oswald. There is an artist's rendering of Thornley's face on page 465 of the Fensterwald and Ewing book *Assassination of JFK: Coincidence or Conspiracy?*; he seems to bear a strong resemblance to Oswald.

In a January 27, 1964, memorandum, Washington, D.C., FBI agent Thomas Lenihan wrote that the Minox camera found among Oswald's effects should be listed as a Minox light meter, though both Dallas detective Guy F. Rose and William Alexander identified it as a camera. The FBI later created its own inventory, which listed a Minox light meter, rather than a camera. Rose stated that the FBI tried to get him to change the records. On January 31, 1964, the FBI said the camera belonged to Michael Paine.[184]

Warren Commission general counsel J. Lee Rankin found it unusual that the FBI was insisting that Oswald was the lone assassin without having investigated leads in Mexico and Russia.[185] Rankin told Earl Warren, "They [the FBI] have decided that it is Oswald who committed the assassination, they have decided that no one else was involved."[186] Secret Service Inspector General Thomas J. Kelley distrusted Hoover and believed he was involved in covering up the truth about the assassination of President Kennedy. Gerry Hemming told Twyman that Hoover was the person who put the whole assassination plot together.[132]

The Justice Department never bothered to analyze the Charles Bronson film of the assassination, as it was urged to do by the House Select Committee on Assassinations.

At the very least, the FBI is guilty of obstruction of justice. This obstruction took several forms, including confiscating evidence, falsifying evidence, attempting to silence witnesses by warnings and other forms of intimidation, distorting the statements of witnesses, and withholding ballistic evidence from the Warren Commission, as noted above. There are those of us who believe that the FBI should be solving crimes, rather than committing them.

8. Behavior of Dallas Police

Dallas policemen M.N. McDonald, E.I. Cunningham, K.E. Lyons and Paul Bentley affixed their names to an arrest report dated November 22, at 1:40 p.m., which states, "This man shot and killed President Kennedy and Police Officer J.D. Tippit. He also shot and wounded Governor Connally."[188] It's the early afternoon on the day of the assassination, and the Dallas police, before any forensic or other evidence has been collected, have already solved these two murders! (Neither Cunningham nor Lyons testified to the commission or its legal staff.)

The many failings of the Dallas Police Department have been described in some detail in other publications, especially in Sylvia Meagher's *Accessories After the Fact.* It is not always clear if they behaved (or failed to act) as they did out of mere incompetence, or as a manifestation of their role in a conspiracy, which would include knowing that Oswald was the designated patsy. I will let the reader decide.

The Dallas police who entered the parking lot behind the stockade fence didn't bother to look inside the cars parked there, and, as Groden points out, they allowed bystanders to come and go freely.[189] And despite clear indications that shots may have been fired from behind the stockade fence, from which point they could assume that an assassin may have fled, they set up no roadblocks in the immediate aftermath of the shooting.

In an interview with HSCA investigators on September 26, 1978, off-duty Dallas police patrolman Tom Tilson stated that immediately after the shooting, he saw a man running from Dealey Plaza and slipping and sliding down the embankment on the north side of Elm Street west of the Triple Underpass. The man appeared to throw something onto the back seat of a nearby car, then got into the car and drove off at a high rate of speed. Patrolman Tilson knew Jack Ruby, and said the man looked enough like Ruby to be his twin. Tilson followed the car, got the license number, and called it in to the DPD Homicide office the same afternoon. Tilson never heard back from the Dallas police; apparently they weren't interested in identifying someone who may have been carrying the murder weapon away from the scene of a presidential assassination. But knowing that patrolman Tilson was himself a Dallas policeman, one must wonder why *he* didn't simply look up the license number when he came back on duty.

The Warren Report acknowledges that "Patrol cars bearing at least 15 officers converged on the Texas Theatre."[190] Contemporaneous accounts noted that ten squad cars and a media crew showed up at the theater for the arrest of Oswald. Why send fifteen cops to investigate someone going into a movie theater without paying?

Dallas police did not bring Oswald in front of a magistrate immediately, as required by Texas state law. The Dallas police and DA repeatedly announced Lee's guilt, in violation of the rights of the accused, and before he had even been arraigned.

The Sixth Amendment to the US Constitution states: "In all criminal prosecutions, the accused shall enjoy the right ... to be informed of the nature and cause of the accusation... and to have the Assistance of Counsel for his defense." When, at the Friday midnight press conference, a member of the press asked Oswald if he had killed the president, he replied, "No, I haven't been charged with that. In fact, no one has said that to me yet." The Dallas cops have the man they think killed the president, and yet they haven't gotten around to telling him about it? Oswald repeatedly asked for someone to come forward and represent him, but his requests were ignored by the Dallas police. Captain Fritz told the commission, "I told him [Oswald] he certainly could have an attorney any time he wanted it."[191] He testified that before he questioned Oswald, he "told him that any evidence that he gave me would be used against him," and Oswald, according to Fritz, replied that "he didn't want a lawyer." Later in his testimony, Fritz said that Oswald didn't want "the local attorneys"; he wanted New York attorney John Abt.[192] When David Belin asked DPD Sergeant W.E. Barnes if Oswald asked for an attorney to be present, Barnes said, "He didn't request one." But moments later, Barnes said that when he asked Oswald to sign the fingerprint card, Oswald said he wouldn't sign anything until he talked to an attorney.[193] Of course, Oswald never got a lawyer.

Dallas police falsified Julia Ann Mercer's affidavit. Ms. Mercer claimed that in the late morning of November 22, while driving westward on Elm Street past the Book Depository, she saw the passenger of a Ford pickup truck illegally parked near the grassy knoll remove what appeared to be a rifle case from the truck's bed and carry it up the hill that "forms part of the [triple] overpass"; she later identified the driver as Jack Ruby. Her affidavit states that the truck had the words "air conditioning" on the side, but she denied having made this statement. Ms. Mercer told Jim Garrison that her testimony, as given to the Dallas sheriff's office and the FBI, had been completely altered. She also told Garrison and the HSCA that her "notarized" signature on her Dallas sheriff's office affidavit was not her signature.[194] (Ms. Mercer did not testify to the commission or its legal staff.)

The FBI evidently, and for whatever reason, falsified at least one item of photographic evidence in the case. There is a photo in the record of Gen. Walker's residence with a 1957 Chevrolet parked in the driveway; in the photo, the area where the license plate would be has been torn out. After viewing the photo, Detective R.S. Stovall "surmised that OSWALD had ... taken the license plate number area out of the photograph to keep anyone from identifying the owner of that vehicle."[195] Detective Guy Rose also said that the section that would normally show the license plate was torn out of the photograph when it was discovered.[196] They both had to be lying, because Dallas Police Chief Jesse Curry's 1969 book *JFK Assassination File* contains a photograph of Chief Curry's desk, with Oswald's possessions spread out on it, including the Walker residence photo showing the Chevrolet. It shows the license plate area intact. Bugliosi says that Oswald took the photo of the back of Walker's house, showing the 1957 Chevrolet, and that it was "likely" that the hole around the license plate "was accidentally torn out by someone..."[197] This is another Bugliosi absurdity. One does not "accidentally" tear a small area out of the middle of a photograph. (The altered photo is reproduced on page 124 of Groden's book, among other places.)

In Jesse Curry's commission affidavit of August 10, 1964, he stated, "The first time Mrs. Markham was shown Oswald, she positively identified him as the slayer of the officer."[198] This was false, as indicated above under the discussion of the Tippit murder.

Mark Lane stated in his Grand Jury testimony that he tried to contact Domingo Benavides, whose pickup truck was across the street from the Tippit murder scene, but the Dallas police intervened and told Benavides that he had better not speak with Lane.[199]

When chief counsel J. Lee Rankin asked Chief Curry if he knew of any Dallas police records showed that the weapon that was purportedly used in the assassination was a Mauser, he replied, "No, sir, not to my knowledge."[200] His police department already had police affidavits stating that it was a Mauser.

A report by Dallas police lieutenant T.L. Baker states that Cecil McWatters was among those who identified Oswald as the man seen running from the Tippit murder scene. McWatters was a bus driver and was not a witness to the Tippit murder or its aftermath.[201]

Brushing aside death threats against Oswald, the Dallas police relaxed security around Oswald just enough to provide for his murder by Jack Ruby. At 2:30 a.m. on November 24, there came that anonymous call to City Hall: a man's voice saying, "...tonight, tomorrow morning or tomorrow night we are going to kill the man who killed the president.... We will be there and we will kill him."[202] Dallas police communications officer Billy Grammer received one of the telephone threats on Oswald's life; he later recognized the voice as that of Jack Ruby. Captain Fritz testified that "I have always felt that [it] was Ruby who made that call." This has been seen, and probably was, an effort on Ruby's part to motivate the police to increase the security around Oswald, thereby making it more difficult for Ruby to carry out his assignment to silence him. At 10:20 a.m. on November 24, according to Bugliosi, Fritz and Curry discussed the threats on Oswald's life, but no effort was made to bolster the security around him.[203] FBI special agent Melton Newsom called Sgt. Perry McCoy at the DPD about 12:30 a.m. on November 24 to tell him that Oswald was going to be killed. Newsom called Capt. William Frazier three hours later and said he had received a threat that a large group of men were going to try to kill Lee sometime that day.[204] (Agent Newsom did not testify to the commission or its legal staff.) Shenon states that both the Dallas PD and the FBI had received "scores of phone threats against Oswald's life in the hours before his death."[205]

Captain O.A. Jones instructed his men to "form a line on each side of the passageway leading from the jail office to the ramp and parking area so that Oswald and his escorts will have a protective lane to pass through on their way to the armored car once they emerge from the jail office." Photos taken at the time show that this did not happen; the "protective lane" was a hodgepodge of cops and civilians, including one civilian in a fedora who was packing a .38-cal. revolver. And there was no armored car. Chief Curry said that he discussed with Assistant Chief Charles Batchelor "the threats we had had" before Oswald's transfer. Curry told the commission that he had heard of the threats that had been made against Oswald, but he nevertheless wanted the press to witness Oswald's transfer. He stated, "[W]e were trying in the police department to let the press have an opportunity to observe the proceedings as they were ... I saw no particular harm in allowing the media to observe the prisoner."[206] In an FBI affidavit dated December 10, 1963, Lt. George Butler stated that Curry was too level-headed to have attempted to transfer Oswald to County Jail with all the news media present and in the way it was handled when Oswald was shot. Butler felt that Curry must have been pressured and ordered to bring Lee out under those circumstances, but he did not know by whom.[207] But the chief told the commission that he told the reporters, "I believe if you are back here by 10 o'clock you will be back in time to observe anything you care to observe." Curry might well have added: "So if anybody wants to ambush and kill the man we think killed the president, that would be your best chance."

Once Oswald and his police escorts reached the basement, the cops only had to keep their prisoner alive for the few seconds it would have taken to get him from the building to the waiting car. Detective Leavelle noted that the unmarked car that was to transport Oswald was not where it was supposed to be. Leavelle told the commission, "The captain should have known that the car was not in the position it should be, and I was surprised when I walked to the door and the car was not in the spot it should have been.... In fact, if the car had been sitting where we were told it was going to be, see, it would have been sitting directly upon the spot where Ruby was standing when he fired the shot."[208] If the car had been where it was supposed to be, it would only have been about fifteen feet from the basement exit door to the passenger side door; the Dallas police couldn't keep Oswald alive for the three or four seconds it would have taken to cover those fifteen feet. Why didn't they simply fit the prisoner with a bullet-proof vest?

In an FBI interview dated November 29, 1963, Dallas attorney Travis Kirk stated that he believed that it was "entirely possible and probable" that Will Fritz had deliberately arranged to have Oswald shot in order to close the case.[209] Philip Shenon quotes Senator Russell, a member of the Warren Commission, as saying, after the commission wrapped up, "It appeared to me that the Dallas police department was determined to let Oswald be executed without a trial."[210] In his essay entitled, "Amazing Facts about the Kennedy Assassination," Donald E. Wilkes Jr. asserts that just before Oswald was shot by Ruby, Will Fritz "suddenly speeded up and began to walk ahead so fast that he became separated from Oswald by several feet, thereby leaving Oswald no longer protected from the front."[211] Video taken at the time shows no police personnel in front of Oswald.

Jesse Curry told the commission that "they did seal off this building and also that they had checked all the employees of the Building and found out that there was one missing, I think this is when they suspected him of being involved in the fatal shooting of the President..."[213] But there is no logical connection between someone leaving the Book Depository after the shooting and his being guilty of shooting the president. This seems to indicate that Curry knew that Oswald was the designated patsy. And as stated above, Lee was not the only person who was missing.

Two hours after the assassination, Buell Wesley Frazier was at Pioneer Medical Center in Arlington, visiting a sick relative, when he says that he was approached by Dallas detectives Guy Rose and R.S. Stovall, who called him out to the nurses' station, put him up against a wall, handcuffed him and told him that he was being arrested for being involved in the assassination of President Kennedy. They took him to a Dallas police station, where various cops took turns interrogating him. He was also photographed and fingerprinted. Meanwhile, Dallas police went to Frazier's home and confiscated his .303 British Enfield rifle and a shotgun, apparently with no search warrant, and searched his car. Eventually, Capt. Will Fritz entered the room where Frazier was being interrogated, presented him with a written confession stating that he, Frazier, was involved in the assassination, and demanded that he sign it. He refused. Frazier also reported that Fritz at one point took a swing at him, which Frazier blocked. They didn't let him go until the wee hours of Saturday morning, November 23.[213]

9. Behavior of Dallas District Attorney Henry Wade

Mr. Bugliosi tells us of a meeting at 11 p.m. on the day of the assassination, in the Homicide and Robbery Bureau, involving DA Henry Wade, Assistant DA Bill Alexander, FBI agent Jim Bookhout and Capt. Fritz: "At Wade's request, Fritz begins to outline the considerable amount of evidence the Dallas Police Department has impressively gathered so far – the gun, the witnesses, the arrest, and the fingerprints…"[214] According to Mr. Bugliosi and the Warren Report, however, it wasn't until 4:00 a.m. on Saturday, November 23, during a visit of FBI agents to Klein's Sporting Goods in Chicago that Mitchell Scibor, general operating manager of Klein's, found through microfilm records that a Mannlicher-Carcano with scope was mailed to A. Hidell at a post office box in Dallas.[215] A rifle had been found, but as yet no link to Oswald, and no incriminating fingerprints; and an arrest is no indication of guilt. At a 12:30 a.m. press conference on Saturday, November 23, Wade told reporters, "We are still working on the evidence. This has been a joint effort by the Secret Service, the Federal Bureau of Investigation, the Dallas Police Department, the Dallas Sheriff's office, my office, and Capt. Will Fritz has been in charge of it." But no more than five minutes later, he told reporters that there was "definitely" sufficient evidence to convict Oswald of the assassination of President Kennedy.[216] This was before any tests had been done on 1) Oswald's hands or cheek, or 2) the rifle found in the Book Depository. The rifle was on its way to the FBI crime lab in Washington, D.C., at the time. At the same press conference, Wade said he didn't know if it was one man or an organized plot, and stated that Oswald had been charged with killing both Officer Tippit and the president."[217] Justice of the Peace David Johnston stated that Oswald had *not* been charged with killing JFK and hadn't been told of such a charge. At another press conference on "Sunday P.M." on November 24, Wade falsely stated, "The paraffin tests showed that [Oswald] had recently fired a gun." (The Warren Report itself was critical of Wade, stating that he "might have influenced prospective jurors by his mistaken statement that the paraffin test showed that Oswald had fired a gun.") Wade also stated, "I would say…there's no question that he was the killer of President Kennedy," and that witnesses put Oswald on the sixth floor at 12 o'clock and shortly thereafter.[218] It is not clear who these witnesses were; the Book Depository employees who worked on the sixth floor had obviously not yet testified to any official body, and as noted in Chapter 2 above, Bonnie Ray Williams was on the sixth floor between 12:00 and 12:20 and saw no one else there, Junior Jarman said all of the sixth floor employees went downstairs at 11:45, and Eddie Piper said that he saw Oswald on the *first* floor at noon. And even if Oswald had been on the sixth floor at noon "and shortly thereafter," that would prove absolutely nothing in terms of his (supposedly) firing a rifle at the presidential limousine. So this statement about "witnesses" from DA Wade is just another slanderous and mendacious effort to make Oswald look guilty. Wade had also conveniently forgotten about something in the law called the presumption of innocence.

On the day Oswald died, Wade stated at a press conference that Oswald went from a bus to a taxicab driven by Darrell Click. Lane investigated this and discovered that there had never been a taxi driver named Darrell Click in the history of Dallas.[219]

The *New York Times* published an interview with Wade in which he stated that Tippit was killed a block or two from Oswald's rooming house. In fact, Tippit was killed ten blocks away from the rooming house.[220] Wade said that he had uncovered a map in Oswald's room that showed that he had planned the shooting just as it took place. But Wade later (on November 27) announced that there never was an Oswald map showing the motorcade route.[221]

When Secret Service agents and Kennedy aides were in a confrontation with Dr. Rose, trying forcefully to remove JFK's body from Dallas and avoid a Texas autopsy, someone got the idea of looking for a local Justice of the Peace to settle the dispute (see Behavior of the Secret Service, above). They finally located Judge Theron Ward, from Dallas County Precinct 3, who was unable to do so. At some point, DA Wade told Judge Ward that he had no objection whatever to the removal of Kennedy's body from Dallas, in violation of Texas law. According to William Manchester, Wade had told Dr. Rose to "step aside and let the Secret Service handle everything."[222]

10. Confiscation of Assassination Films

Several people took video and still photographs of the assassination. Beverly Oliver's film of the assassination was confiscated; this will be covered in more detail under The Doctored Zapruder Film, below. At the courthouse, men whom Jean Hill assumed were Secret Service "were interested that day in those pictures; they got them all from us."[223] John Wiseman, a Dallas County deputy sheriff, confiscated witness Mary Ann Moorman's Polaroid camera photo taken moments after the hit that shows the "Oswald" window.[224] (Wiseman did not testify to the commission or its legal staff.)

Orville Nix' film of the assassination was also confiscated. Nix' original film "disappeared in 1978 after it was returned to UPI by the [House] Assassinations Committee."[225] Bugliosi says that Orville Nix "received his film back [from the FBI] on December 4, 1963."[226] When Nix got his film back from the government, he noticed that there were frames missing. The Nix film indeed seems to have been doctored; the limousine stop is not shown. Twyman developed information showing that Nix' film was altered to make it more or less match the Zapruder film; for example, it shows a continuous speed of 9.4 mph.[227]

At some point, a policeman demanded Gordon Arnold's camera, pulled out the film, and returned the camera to Arnold.[228] Deputy Sheriff Eugene Boone confiscated the photos that Hugh W. Betzner Jr. had taken of the assassination. But Boone claimed that after developing Betzner's film, his camera and film were returned to him.[229] DPD Sgt. Stavis Ellis and Officer James Courson saw a Secret Service man grab the camera of a young boy who had filmed the President's limousine at Parkland Hospital, and remove and expose the film.[230] Dr. Mantik says that several people witnessed this incident.[231] See also "The Doctored Zapruder Film," below. Confiscation of film and still photographs is scarcely mentioned in Bugliosi's book.

The Fifth Amendment to the US Constitution states that no person shall be "deprived of life, liberty, or property, without due process of law; nor shall private property be taken for public use, without just compensation."

11. Actions of the Central Intelligence Agency

Richard Helms was the CIA's Deputy Director for Plans (DDP, the clandestine operations or "dirty tricks") Department at the time of the assassination. He was also liaison between the Warren Commission and the CIA.[232] He helped protect the CIA during the Warren Commission investigation by not telling the commission about the Agency's Castro assassination plots; and he had advance knowledge of the president's assassination, according to Gerry Hemming. Helms didn't respond to the commission's memorandum requesting CIA information on Jack Ruby until the Warren Report was being typeset. Helms falsely claimed that a photo was taken of Oswald in front of the Soviet Embassy in Mexico City on October 4, 1963 (the photo, which is reproduced in Dick Russell's book, is obviously not of Lee). Helms, who was a good friend of Howard Hunt, reportedly initialed a 1966 memo about keeping the importance of Hunt's presence in Dallas on November 22 a secret, and stated that a cover story providing Hunt an alibi "ought to be considered." As noted above in the context of Oswald's alleged visit to Mexico City, it was Helms who ordered the second arrest of Silvia Durán; he probably ordered the first arrest as well.

The Senate Select Committee on Intelligence discovered that the CIA had withheld significant evidence from the Warren Commission.[233]

Rolando Otero said that his training led him to believe that between thirty and thirty-five CIA operatives were in Dallas on November 22, including the actual hit team. "Otero said he understood that most of the final planning and coordination took place at meetings in the Dallas YMCA Building," and he gave Gaeton Fonzi the names of five Miami men who, according to Otero's source ("Ten-One"), were involved in the plot.[234]

On October 1, 1964, a letter from the CIA, signed by Richard Helms, sent to commission general counsel J. Lee Rankin included a copy of a Gestapo document dated November 8, 1937, branding commission critic Joachim Joesten as unpatriotic because he fled Hitler's Germany to warn the people of Denmark to arm against the Nazis![235] Attached to the CIA letter was another letter, on Gestapo letterhead and dated "Berlin, 8 November 1937," stating that Joesten was a leftist and had "seriously transgressed against his duty to remain faithful to his people and State by his anti-German conduct in foreign countries." The Gestapo ordered that Joesten's German citizenship be revoked and that his possessions be confiscated. The CIA letter repeated the Gestapo charges. The Agency sent copies of their transmittal to the FBI, the Department of State and the Immigration and Naturalization Service. So here we have the CIA using a Gestapo document to discredit a Warren Commission critic by claiming that he opposed the Nazis – presumably to demonstrate that he was a leftist (and therefore not credible).[236]

Richard Helms was very worried about Jim Garrison's investigation of the assassination, according to Victor Marchetti, who spent fourteen years with the Agency, the last three of which were as a staff assistant to Helms.[237] Marchetti recalls attending several high-level meetings during which Helms expressed alarm over Garrison's conspiracy charge against Clay Shaw; Marchetti said that Helms identified Shaw as a CIA "contact" and David Ferrie as a contract agent at the time of the Kennedy assassination. Helms warned that these ties had to be kept secret and that Shaw would "receive all the help the CIA could give him." At Helms' daily staff meetings during the Shaw trial, Marchetti recalls Helms asking questions like, "Are we giving them all the help they need?"[238] The HSCA found that Helms sent in agents in an attempt to sabotage Garrison's case and planted agents on Garrison's staff.[239] Helms finally admitted in 1979 that Clay Shaw had Agency connections; he testified in a *Liberty Lobby* case that Shaw was "one of the part-time contacts of the Domestic Contacts division."[240]

On April 1, 1967, in the midst of Garrison's investigation, the CIA circulated a dispatch to "Chiefs, Certain Stations and Bases" (Document 1035-950, "Concerning Criticism of the Warren Report"), whose express purpose was "to provide material for countering and discrediting the claims of the conspiracy theorists, so as to inhibit the circulation of such claims in other countries." The key recommendations were (1) to refrain from initiating discussion of "the assassination question" where it was not already taking place; (2) point out to "liaison and friendly elite contacts... that the Warren Commission made as thorough an investigation as humanly possible," that "further speculative discussion only plays into the hands of the opposition," and that "parts of the conspiracy talk appear to be deliberately generated by Communist propagandists"; and (3) "employ propaganda assets to answer and refute the attacks of the critics." The document suggested that arguments such as the following should be employed: "No significant evidence has emerged which the Commission did not consider...the make-up of the Commission and its staff was an excellent safeguard against over-commitment to any one theory," and "the FBI conducted 25,000 interviews and re-interviews," etc. (FBI interview reports are found in volumes 20 through 26 of the Warren Commission Hearings and Exhibits. I counted about 1420 FBI interviews.) Regarding the suspicious deaths that have been pointed out by various authors, "the individuals concerned have for the most part died of natural causes..." The document suggested additional strategies for downgrading the arguments and credibility of commission critics.[241]

Item 4c of Document 1035-950 states, "Conspiracy on the large scale often suggested would be impossible to conceal in the United States..." Compare this to the following assertion in Bugliosi's "Conclusion of No Conspiracy" chapter: "[W]e all know from our own experience in life that it is almost impossible to keep a secret,"[242] and with so much incompetence in all levels of government, and with it being so difficult for any group of people to keep a secret, no group of conspirators would have been able to keep the assassination conspiracy secret for all these years. It might not be too difficult to keep the secret if failure to do so would likely result in a series of convictions for first degree murder and conspiracy to commit first degree murder, with sentences of life in prison and/or the death penalty. Item 4e of CIA document 1035-960 states that, "Oswald would not have been any sensible person's choice for a co-conspirator." In the same "No Conspiracy" chapter, Bugliosi tells us that to believe that a group of conspirators like the CIA or the Mob would entrust the biggest murder in American history to Oswald, "a highly unreliable, highly disturbed, and emotionally unhinged political fanatic" is "too preposterous a notion for any rational person to harbor in his or her mind for more than a millisecond."[243] Bugliosi also states that the CIA would have paid Oswald, but he only had (according to the Warren Commission) $183 to his name when he was arrested. All of Bugliosi's assertions are based on the false idea that Oswald killed President Kennedy. We unhinged leftists don't believe that the CIA or the Mob paid Oswald to kill Kennedy; we believe – we *know* – that Oswald did *not* kill Kennedy.

James Angleton was head of CIA counterintelligence at the time of the assassination. In a memo to J. Edgar Hoover dated January 13, 1969, Angleton noted that Bernard Fensterwald Jr. was setting up a Washington-based committee to investigate assassinations, and asked Hoover to run some kind of vaguely defined identification check on Fensterwald and three other Warren Commission critics associated with him.[244] In 1972, when Fensterwald was investigating possible CIA complicity in the assassination of President Kennedy, he and the group he headed, the Committee to Investigate Assassinations, were placed under surveillance by a Washington D.C. police intelligence unit that reported its findings to the Agency.[245]

The CIA appears to have done all it could to obstruct the House Select Committee on Assassinations investigation, using the techniques of procrastination and an "inability to find" what was requested. Summers noted that senior HSCA staff "ended their probe still stymied by CIA procrastination and evasiveness." Gaeton Fonzi wrote that David Phillips had committed perjury before the HSCA.[246] Phillips was the CIA's chief of Cuban operations in November 1963, supervised early efforts to counter the Fair Play for Cuba Committee, and eventually rose to be chief of the Western Hemisphere Division at CIA. Lane says that Phillips "admitted that he had led a CIA effort that tried to destroy the reputations and livelihoods of those who sought the truth about the assassination in order to protect the agency [CIA]."[247] When Robert Blakey was chief counsel for the HSCA, his staff investigators were trying to obtain key documents from the CIA. But they found that they were being stonewalled by George Joannides, who had been brought out of retirement to serve as liaison between the Agency and the committee.[248] (In 1963, Joannides was chief of the Psychological Warfare branch of the CIA's JM/WAVE station in Miami. In that role he was case officer for the Directorio Revolucionario Estudiantil, or DRE, a group of young, militant, anti-Castro Cuban exiles created by the CIA.) Blakey believed that the CIA's failure to cooperate with the HSCA amounted to obstruction of justice.[249]

During the deliberations of the HSCA, someone opened the committee's safe without permission and looked at a photo of the back of JFK's head before hastily returning it to the photo album. Fingerprints revealed the culprit to be Regis Blahut, who was a CIA agent on assignment to the HSCA. According to Summers and the sources he references, Blahut was assigned to protecting secret CIA documents temporarily in the custody of the committee.[250] Blahut opened the (unlocked) HSCA safe and examined the photos. Blahut "had at first denied removing the photos from the safe but then, after failing a polygraph test, admitted he had and said he had an innocent explanation, which he would not give, adding that 'there's other things that are involved that are detrimental to other things.'" Bugliosi says the photos were only in disarray, and that nothing had been taken.[251] Summers says a folder had been removed, and one photo of the dead president's head ripped out of its cover.[252]

It was indicated above that CIA agent E. Howard Hunt was in Dealey Plaza at the time of the assassination, dressed as a tramp. On August 14, 1978, *The Spotlight*, a weekly newspaper associated with Liberty Lobby, Inc., published an article by Victor Marchetti ("CIA to Admit Hunt Involvement in Kennedy Slaying"), who predicted that in upcoming HSCA hearings the CIA would admit that Hunt was involved in the conspiracy to kill JFK. Hunt, the Watergate ex-con, sued the paper for defamation and won. Liberty Lobby and Mark Lane appealed the case to the US Court of Appeals for the Eleventh District, and at the second trial, Marita Lorenz testified that two days before the assassination, she drove from Miami with Frank Sturgis, a CIA contract agent (Sturgis' status as a CIA contract agent was confirmed to Mark Lane by Richard Helms); Gerry Hemming; brothers Guillermo and Ignacio Novo; and Pedro Diaz Lanz for the purpose of transporting firearms to Dallas, and that there were two cars in the caravan. Diaz Lanz was the former chief of the Cuban Air Force. According to John Judge, Diaz Lanz was smuggled out of Cuba by the CIA's David Morales (of whom more later). Lane says that Ms. Lorenz' testimony indicated that the Novo brothers were involved in the assassination on behalf of the CIA. She also stated that on November 21, she saw Hunt give an envelope full of money to Sturgis in a motel, and about 45 minutes after Hunt left, Jack Ruby came to the door. Ms. Lorenz testified that Sturgis later told her, "We killed the president that day." (The jury found for Liberty Lobby.) The HSCA claimed that in 1978, Hemming, Diaz Lanz and Sturgis all denied Ms. Lorenz' allegations, but Gerry Hemming later told Mark Lane that everything Ms. Lorenz had stated was true, except that there were three cars in the caravan, not two.[253]

Ray Cline was head of the CIA's Directorate of Intelligence when President Kennedy was assassinated. After a September 1977 debate on Latin America at the University of Southern California between "former or present high-ranking CIA officers and those who were critical of their actions," Cline and Mark Lane came face to face in a hallway, and Lane asked him about the CIA's policy toward the Dominican Republic. Cline started to respond, then interrupted himself and shouted, "I know who you are. You're the Kennedy writer. You're the most disgusting of the lot. I'm going, we're going, to get you."[254] If the CIA was *not* involved in the assassination, surely Mr. Cline would have said something like, "I understand you're investigating the assassination. Feel free to share your findings with us, in case we missed anything. We want to find out who really killed President Kennedy as much as you do."

12. Circumstances of Oswald's Arrest

Motorcycle cop Thomas Hutson told the commission that "as we were proceeding west on East Jefferson, the radio dispatcher said that a suspect had just entered the Texas Theatre."[255] DPD Detective Bob Carroll stated that "we were in the 300 block of East Jefferson when the call came out on the radio that a suspect had been seen going into the Texas Theatre."[256] Calvin Owens said that "some of my men yelled to me that they had a suspect in the Texas Theatre..."[257] The Warren Report states that at 1:45 p.m., the police radio stated, "Have information a suspect just went in the Texas Theatre on West Jefferson."[258] At this point, the police had no evidence whatsoever that this "suspect" had any connection to the murder of Officer Tippit or President Kennedy. This is further evidence of a conspiracy and a pre-arranged patsy.

As note above, a minute or two after Oswald returned to his rooming house on the afternoon of November 22, a Dallas police car stopped briefly in front of the rooming house, then sounded the horn twice and drove off.[259] It is interesting to note that the same Dallas police department that had two of its men drive by Oswald's rooming house a half-hour after the assassination and give him the signal to head for the Texas Theatre was the same department that miraculously "solved" the crime and found the "assassin" at that theater within an hour and a half of the assassination and barely fifty minutes after giving him the signal to go there! Captain Westbrook testified that "a patrolman hollered 'It's just come over the radio that they've got a suspicious person in the Texas Theatre.'"[260] Ten squad cars and a media crew converged on the Texas Theatre; but how did the media crew know that the "suspect" would be there? Officer McDonald told the commission that when he arrived at the theater, there were several police cars at the scene and three or four officers standing outside with shotguns guarding the rear exits, and three other officers at the rear door.[261] The Dallas police entered the Texas Theatre with guns drawn – to apprehend someone who walked in without paying. McDonald told the *Dallas Morning News* that a man sitting near the front of the theater "tipped" him that the man he wanted was sitting in the third row from the rear.[262]

CD1107 is an FBI report dated May 15, 1964, that contains a translation from the French of an article by Joachim Joesten, pages 583-84, which reads, in pertinent part:

> The *New York Times* quotes District Attorney WADE as saying that when approached in the Texas Theater OSWALD had tried to hold a gun against the head of patrolman MC DONALD. The gun was snapped but did not fire. Mr. WADE repeated this statement. The press quoted MC DONALD as saying he rammed his hand into the top of the man's trousers and grabbed his revolver.' According to newspaper reports FBI firearms experts found the firing pin of the gun reportedly taken from OSWALD so bent that it could not strike the 'cap of the bullet.'
>
> It, therefore, appears more probable that the pursuing officers who began the search after TIPPIT was killed actually found the killer and killed him or otherwise disposed of him, took his gun

> and forced it into OSWALD'S hand after they found him after bending the firing pin on the pistol. This was done to insure that OSWALD could not shoot someone after the gun was forced into his hand.

In the same vein, author Stanley Marks concluded that the Dallas police had "Oswald's" revolver in their possession *before* Oswald's arrest and before the murder of Tippit; "Which, in turn, implies that Officer Tippit was primed to be murdered with the knowledge of some Dallas policemen."[263]

13. The Shills Outside the Texas Theatre

Julia Postal, the box office attendant at the Texas Theatre, told the commission that as the policemen were removing Oswald from the theater, she saw outside "a live mob scene ... they started screaming profuse [*sic*] language and – 'Kill the so-and-so,' and trying to get to him."[264] Warren "Butch" Burroughs, who operated the theater concession stand, said that when Oswald was taken out of the theater, "there was a mob of people out there – more people than I have ever seen before..."[265] Detective Bob Carroll told the commission that "there was quite a crowd out there outside the theater [as they brought Oswald out] and it was pretty noisy and several people were hollering, you know, 'Kill him,' or 'Let us have him, and we'll kill him.'"[266] In a letter to Chief Curry dated December 3, 1963, Detective E.E. Taylor stated that when he and the other policemen left the theater, "there was a large crowd of people gathered outside. The people were shouting 'kill him' and 'let us kill him.'"[267] (Detective Taylor did not testify to the commission or its legal staff.) Officer Gerald L. Hill told the commission that as Oswald was being taken out of the theater, "there were shouts at this time from the crowd of, 'That is him. We ought to kill him. String him up. Hang him.'" He estimated the crowd to be about two hundred. (Officer Hill also said that "as we walked into the lobby there was a man shooting movies.... He was from channel 8...")[268] DPD Officer C.T. Walker told the commission, "People out there were hollering, 'Kill the S.O.B. ... Let us have him. We want him.'"[269] On page 156 in volume 20 of the Hearings and Exhibits, there is a photo of Oswald being subdued in the theater; why did someone happen to be there with a camera?

Similarly, Mr. Bugliosi, on page 106, explains the presence of all those vociferous people outside the Texas Theatre by telling us that word had spread among the crowd that the police had cornered the president's killer. This, again, is something that Bugliosi simply made up. FBI agents did not "discover" the money order for a Mannlicher-Carcano rifle that was sent to "A. Hidell" until 4:00 A.M. on the day *after* the assassination. Neither the money order nor the magic bullet (supposedly linking the bullet to the rifle and the rifle to Oswald) had been found yet and there was absolutely no evidence linking Oswald to the murder of President Kennedy. Even the police communications themselves didn't mention that the man who entered the theater without paying was a suspect in Kennedy's murder. Oswald wasn't charged with that crime (if he was charged at all) until several hours later. Noah Webster defines "shill" as "one who works as a decoy, as in a confidence game, by posing as a customer or innocent bystander." No doubt the shills outside the theater were arranged in advance by an agency of US intelligence, in order to draw attention to their patsy, Oswald. The crowd would have to be brought together by someone in order for "word" to "spread" among them. There is no other explanation for one or two hundred people magically appearing in front of the Texas Theatre in the few minutes it took to locate and arrest Oswald.

14. Jack Ruby's Murder of Oswald

Mr. Bugliosi believed that Jack Ruby's murder of Oswald was a spontaneous act, and since Ruby didn't know exactly when Oswald would be transferred, it was just a coincidence that Ruby arrived in the basement at the same time that Oswald did. Bugliosi calculated that Ruby had been in the basement less than a minute before Oswald appeared.[270] Bugliosi says that Ruby's murder of Oswald cannot have been a planned event, because Ruby wouldn't have cut it so close; if he had been delayed a minute or two at the Western Union office, where he had stopped shortly before entering the Dallas police basement, he would be too late to kill Oswald. "Ruby's killing Oswald," says Bugliosi, "was exactly as he said it was, a spontaneous decision on his part that was not pursuant to any conspiracy involving others."[271] Then why was he packing heat? Why did he make that phone call – "we are going to kill the man who killed the president" - ? Detective James Leavelle told Jim Marrs that Capt. Fritz gave him the order to move Oswald after conferring with FBI and Secret Service officials. Marrs points out that "Most serious researchers now understand ... that Oswald was transferred only after Ruby was in a position to shoot him."[272] Garnett Hallmark worked for Allright Auto Parts and was general manager of the Dallas operation. He testified that knew Ruby, and heard him say that he planned to be at the scene of the Oswald transfer. He heard Ruby on the phone on November 23 with Ken Dowe of Dallas radio station KLIF. Ruby closed the conversation with, "You know I'll be there."[273] Frederic Rheinstein of NBC News saw Ruby around his sound truck before lunch on November 23. Later in the afternoon he saw Ruby go into DA Wade's office, probably before 5 p.m.[274] Warren Richey saw a man he came to believe was Ruby at around 8:00 a.m. on November 24 on the sidewalk next to the city court building. He saw him again around 10:00 a.m. "I think they told us it would be about 10 o'clock" that they would bring Oswald out. He said it was "an hour or better" between the last time he saw Ruby and the time Lee was shot.[275] John A. Smith saw Ruby at around 8:15 a.m.[276] Mr. Bugliosi tells us that the commission "concluded that its investigation of Ruby did not produce 'any grounds for believing that Ruby's killing of Oswald was part of a conspiracy.'"[277] Again, Mr. Bugliosi simply repeats the conclusions of the commission. Jack Anderson quoted Johnny Roselli as saying that Ruby was ordered to eliminate Oswald, based on concerns that he would crack and disclose information that might lead to the "underworld conspirators."[278]

Bugliosi says if Ruby had help from a Dallas policeman regarding the timing of Oswald's transfer, Ruby would have ratted him out after learning he was being sentenced to death. And he wouldn't leave his favorite dog Sheba in his car if he knew he was going to be taken into custody and not be able to come back to the car.[279] Bugliosi's arguments contain a certain logic, but there is substantial evidence on the other side, that Ruby killed Oswald on someone's orders. On the polygraph (June 18, 1964), Ruby indicated that he first decided to kill Oswald on Sunday morning.[280]

Officer Billy Grammer knew Ruby and recognized his voice and pointed out in an interview that Ruby's call – "We are going to kill the man who killed the president" – shows his plan to do that; it was not a spontaneous act. (Grammer did not testify to the commission or its legal staff, and isn't mentioned in the Warren Report.) The HSCA itself found that "Ruby's shooting of Oswald was not a spontaneous act, in that it involved at least some premeditation."[281] Don Ray Archer, one of the Auto Theft detectives, told British television in 1988 about how Ruby became calm after hearing that Lee had died; "I would say his life depended on him getting Oswald."[282]

On the morning of November 24, George Senator, Ruby's roommate, called Dallas attorney Jim Martin and asked him to represent Ruby – shortly *before* Ruby shot Oswald. This is according to Seth Kantor, a reporter for Scripps-Howard. According to Mr. Bugliosi, Ruby initially told Will Fritz that he "felt terribly sorry" for Jackie Kennedy and didn't want to see her have to come back to Dallas for a trial.[283] Bugliosi says that if Jack Ruby killed Oswald for the Mafia, he would have killed him on Friday night to prevent further interrogation of Oswald. The fact that he didn't do so is "virtually conclusive evidence that he didn't kill Oswald for anyone but himself..." Furthermore, according to Bugliosi, Ruby "never once suggested that he killed Oswald for someone else."[284] That is not accurate (see Statements of Jack Ruby, below). James Wilcott wrote, "Among the close circle of friends with which I discussed all this openly, there was no doubt that Ruby was paid by CIA to do away with Oswald, and Oswald was a patsy."[285]

15. The Phony Backyard Photos

Let us review: The Warren Report tells us, in Appendix X, that two photos, allegedly taken by Marina Oswald, were found among Oswald's possessions in Ruth Paine's garage. Groden reports that the third photo was found in the possession of Geneva Dees, the widow of DPD officer Roscoe White. One shows "Oswald" with a rifle in his left hand and pamphlets in his right (directly under his chin), one shows the man holding a rifle in his right hand and what looks someone else's left arm (and empty hand); and one shows a rifle in his left hand and pamphlets in his right, this time holding the pamphlets to the right of his head. In all three photos, the figure has a handgun holstered on his right hip. One does not have to be an expert in photography to see that these photos are forgeries with Oswald's head on someone else's body, which is exactly what the real Oswald told his interrogators in the offices of the Dallas PD. In Capt. Fritz' report of the Oswald interrogation, he states that Oswald told him that the backyard photo he was shown had been made by someone superimposing his face on someone else's body and that the other part of the photo was not him at all.[286] First, there are three photos, but the head is exactly the same on all three. Second, the shadows under the nose, which indicate a sun directly above, don't match the shadows of his body behind him, which indicate a sun low in the sky. Furthermore, the shadow under Oswald's nose is the same in all three photos. In 1966, *London Times* photographers tried to duplicate the shadows that appear on the Oswald photos, but were unable to do so.[287] Third, the real Oswald's chin is rather pointed, while the chin in the photos is rounded. Close-ups of the head photo on page 171 of Groden's book show a horizontal line just below the man's lower lip, which was probably the seam where the Oswald head was attached to someone else's body. Fourth, FBI firearms expert Lyndal Shaneyfelt testified that the sling in the backyard photos appeared to be a different sling than "is presently on the rifle."[288] Oops! The rifle being held aloft by the Dallas police has a sling that is dark and there is no slack in it. The sling in the backyard photos is very light in color and has much slack in it. (When shown a photograph of the sling that was attached to the rifle "found on the sixth floor of the Texas School Book Depository building on November 22," Marina Oswald told the FBI that she did not recognize the sling.[289] Fifth, the "Oswald" in the photos is wearing a watch on his left wrist, but all witnesses have stated that Oswald didn't own and didn't wear a watch. And neither the shirt nor the watch worn by the Oswald figure in the photos was found among Oswald's possessions.

Jim Marrs reported that two Dallas commercial photographic processors who examined and processed assassination-related photographs for the Dallas police and the FBI said they saw an FBI agent with a color transparency of one of the backyard pictures on November 22, which was the day *before* the police said they found the photographs.[290]

The British Broadcasting Corporation invited Detective Superintendent Malcolm Thompson, who ran the Police Forensic Science Laboratory Identification Bureau at Britain's Scotland Yard for twenty-five years, to examine the backyard photos. The HSCA volumes include a transcript of the BBC broadcast. Thompson stated that "one can only conclude that Oswald's head has been stuck onto a chin, not being Oswald's chin." He also noted that the lower lip in the photo was thicker than Oswald's. "[O]ne comes to the conclusion," he stated, "that it is the same picture used for both faces ... and there has been retouching done in the chin area which is what [one] would expect if my conclusion is correct, that this face has been added on to the chin." He also found retouching in other areas of the photos. He stated outright that the photos were "a fake." He also told the HSCA that the two backyard photos he examined were fakes.[291] (Close-up photos of the "Oswald" head in the backyard photos are at 2HSCA332.) Thompson wrote to Congressman Richardson Preyer, chairman of the HSCA, to say that one of the backyard photos was a montage of three different photographs: "[T]he shadows are so exact that there is no doubt in my mind, it is either a common negative used to produce the two prints or two successive negatives with the camera on a tripod and neither camera or tripod moved in any way between the two exposures.... The body shadows don't relate to the other shadows in the picture ... one sees the gun at an angle to the body which does not relate to the angle of the shadow." He also stated that the arm in one photo looks as if it has been stuck to the body.[292]

The HSCA noted that a photographic analyst for the Canadian Department of Defense (apparently referring to Major John Pickard) also reached the conclusion that the backyard photos were composites.[293] The HSCA acknowledged that both Thompson and Pickard concluded that the backyard photos were fakes.[294] Nevertheless, under "Alleged Gunmen in Dealey Plaza" in volume 6 in the HSCA Appendix Volumes, and again in the Final Report, we are told that the Photographic Evidence Panel of the HSCA found "no evidence of fakery" in the backyard photos![295] But this is evidence of fakery in the House committee's report, which is clearly just a warmed-over version of the Warren Report. The HSCA panel concluded that the horizontal line in the chin, which appears to be where the head was attached to the body, was the edge of a water spot! Bugliosi said it would be "absurd" for anyone to join a head to a chin at that point, rather than follow some natural line in the photo.[296] Bugliosi also says the plotters wouldn't have bothered to make three fake photos, "tripling the chances that the fakery would be detected…"[297] This is more specious reasoning from Mr. B. They *are* fake photos, and the fakery was detected!

Jack White, vice president of Witherspoon and Associates, an advertising and public relations firm, had done "extensive work in all areas of reproduction, including photographic, mechanical, printing, and the graphic arts," according to the HSCA. He told the committee in 1978 that two of the heads in the backyard photos were identical in height and width, "with the exception of the lip area, which shows strong signs of retouching." Mr. White also noted the difference in the chins and the fact that one face tilts four degrees from another face, and the nose shadow should have moved, but doesn't. He also said that "all three bodies are slightly different lengths than each other if you make the heads the same size." Further, "I do believe the heads on A and B are the person called Lee Harvey Oswald, down to a point right below the lips.… In my opinion, the bodies have been superimposed on the background.… Well, just as Oswald said, I think they are fakes." Mr. White also observed that the alleged assassination rifle looks different in many of the photos taken of it that weekend.[298] White compared three of the alleged assassination rifles as shown in various photos, lined them up one beneath the other as shown on 2HSCA342 (Exhibit F-396), and found them to be different lengths. His conclusion: "It is my opinion that we have been shown by the authorities more than one gun as being the assassination weapon."[299] (Mark Lane told the Warren Commission way back in 1964 that the photo in the December 8, 1963, issue of the *New York Times* doesn't match the rifle being held by Oswald in various photographs.[300]) Members of the HSCA's photographic panel explained away most of these anomalies by pointing out White's lack of formal training in photography. I don't have any such training, and I can see these obvious problems with the photos! Nevertheless, in response to the "speculation" that "the rifle picture" of Oswald (actually there were three pictures) was doctored, the Warren Report falsely states, "Experts ... state that the picture was not a composite."[301]

Mr. Bugliosi asserts that when Oswald was shown a backyard photograph of himself holding the Mannlicher-Carcano rifle, "he lied and said it was not he holding the rifle, that someone had superimposed his face on someone else's body."[302] Because Bugliosi has accepted those rather sloppy forgeries as authentic, for him that means that Oswald was lying when he pointed out that the photos were forgeries!

Mr. Bugliosi reminds us on pages 795 and 1386 that the backyard photos of Oswald are genuine because the HSCA concluded that they were genuine, that there was no evidence of fakery in them, and that the rifle in the photos was identical to the rifle found on the sixth floor of the Book Depository on November 22, 1963. One does not draw conclusions as to the validity of a document by quoting from that document. Bugliosi says that when Oswald denied holding the rifle (in the backyard photos) and even owning a rifle, these were two "blatant lies that showed an unmistakable consciousness of guilt."

Lyndal Shaneyfelt, the FBI's photographic expert, was "reasonable certain" that the backyard photos of Oswald "were not composites, and that Oswald's face had not been pasted on someone else's body," but he also stated, "I cannot entirely eliminate an extremely expert composite."[303] The HSCA stated that Shaneyfelt "did not find enough peculiarities to state categorically that the rifles were identical." The committee nevertheless found that the rifle in the backyard photographs "is probably the rifle found in the Texas School Book Depository."[304] As I noted earlier, the rifle featured in the backyard photo of Oswald on the cover of *Life* magazine (February 21, 1964) doesn't match the rifle being displayed to reporters in the Dallas police offices shortly after the assassination. The rifle in that photo has a light-colored strap and the stock is straight, top and bottom, from the butt end to the area of the scope and trigger mechanism, without the notch for the shooter's trigger hand shown in the rifle that was waved in front of reporters in the Dallas police offices. And the official Mannlicher-Carcano (the commission exhibit) has a very dark-colored strap.

Marina Oswald told author Harrison Livingstone and Larry Howard of the JFK Assassination Information Center in Dallas that the backyard photos in evidence were not the photos she took.[305]

16. The Phony Rifle Bag

As is widely known, numerous Dallas policemen converged at the southeast corner of the sixth floor of the Book Depository in the minutes after the assassination. But how would they know to go to that building (and that floor), and not the Dal-Tex Building or the Dallas County Records Building, both of which were behind the presidential limousine? Deputy Sheriff Luke Mooney told the commission that he went directly to the sixth floor and headed to the southeast corner, but he didn't know why. He was joined there by Officers Bill Vickery, Sam Webster and A.D. McCurley.[306] (None of these three policemen testified to the commission or its legal staff.)

The Warren Report states that a long paper bag was found alongside the southeast window on the sixth floor.[307] Similarly, Mr. Bugliosi tells us that the paper bag was found in the sniper's nest in the southeast corner of the sixth floor, parallel to a box on the floor, about six inches from the south wall.[308] Captain Will Fritz, Officers Eugene Boone, and Gerald Hill, Deputy Constable Seymour Weitzman, and Deputy Sheriffs Roger Craig and Luke Mooney were on the sixth floor of the Book Depository in the hour after the assassination. They all testified to the Warren Commission, but none of them mentions a bag that is large enough to contain a rifle. Detective V.J. Brian testified that he, Lt. Jack Revill, and Detectives O.J. Tarver and Roy W. Westphal searched the Depository "for a couple of hours." (Neither Tarver nor Westphal testified to the commission or its legal staff.) Detective Brian told the commission that "we didn't find anything."[309] Deputy Craig stated that he saw a small paper bag, "the kind that you carry your lunch in," but made no mention of a large bag, though he was specifically asked.[310] Deputy Mooney stated that after he found the three cartridges, he stayed on the sixth floor fifteen or twenty minutes longer. He also said that he saw a paper bag, about eight to ten inches long; "just a regular paper bag," but he never mentioned seeing the large bag that is described in the Warren Report.[311] In the report of Dallas policemen Richard Sims and Elmer Boyd, who were also on the sixth floor, there is no mention of a large paper bag.[312] Detective J.B. Hicks testified that he did *not* see a paper sack on the sixth floor or in the items that were taken from the Book Depository.[313] An FBI report of an interview with Lt. Day dated November 30, 1963, says that Lt. Day "stated he found the paper bag."[314] But in his commission testimony, Lt. Day said that "a homemade sack, brown paper with 3-inch tape" *was found* in the southeast corner of the building "near where the slugs were found." The bag was "between the pipe and the wall and folded over."[315] An FBI report dated March 11, 1964, quotes police photographer Robert Studebaker, Lt. Day's assistant, as saying that *he* found the "homemade sack," which (he said) was lying in the sixteen-inch space between a cardboard box (containing books) and the south wall, and it was folded double. But Studebaker told the commission that the bag was in a storage room [?] in the southeast corner of the sixth floor, east of "the three boxes"; he said that the bag was 3½ to 4 feet long, and about eight inches wide. (How could it be that long if it was doubled?) He had a 4 by 5 Speed Graflex camera with him, but said he didn't take a photograph of the large bag before he picked it up, which is why this bag isn't depicted in any of the photos of the sniper's nest. So he picked up the big bag, and *then* took photographs? That doesn't make much sense. Studebaker testified that he picked up the large bag and dusted it. At first he said that there were just smudges on it, but a minute later he said that he found a partial print.[316] Dallas policeman E.D. Brewer was also on the sixth floor. He saw a paper lunch sack and a "relatively long" paper sack to the left (east) of the window at the southeast corner.[317] Detective L.D. Montgomery said he saw a paper sack "that looked like the rifle was wrapped in." He testified that Studebaker picked up the large sack. During Montgomery's commission testimony, assistant counsel Joseph Ball asked Montgomery, "Where was the paper sack?" *before* Montgomery mentioned a paper sack.[318] In a report, Montgomery stated that he found "a long brown paper sack looking item that looked homemade."[319] Detective Marvin Johnson said he saw a long narrow paper bag; he said that Montgomery (not Studebaker) picked it up and unfolded it. He said it was a *fairly small package* that had been folded and refolded.[320] Marvin Johnson's affidavit states that in the course of "our search, we found ... a long sack made of heavy wrapping paper."[321] It is interesting to consider the fact that of all the police personnel who searched the sixth floor that day, only Day, Brewer, Studebaker, Montgomery and Johnson saw the alleged large paper bag, and Johnson described it as a "fairly small package." When Marina Oswald was shown the paper bag "found near the window from which the assassination shots were fired," to use the FBI wording, she said that she had never seen the bag or one like it.[322] The Warren Report concedes that: "Neither Ruth Paine nor Marina Oswald saw the paper bag or the paper and tape out of which the bag was constructed."[323] And Mr. Bugliosi concedes that the FBI was unable to make a positive match between the fibers found inside the paper bag found in the Book Depository and the blanket in Ruth Paine's garage.[324]

The Report says that FBI fingerprint expert Sebastion Latona identified a fingerprint and palm print on the bag as belonging to Oswald.[325] During Latona's testimony, he was given a brown paper bag that assistant commission counsel Melvin Eisenberg said was found on the sixth floor of the Book Depository, near the easternmost window. Latona said he examined it the same day he received it. He said he dusted it with black fingerprint powder, and stated, "There was nothing visible in the way of latent prints on there at that particular time." But a few minutes later, Latona testified that he found a fingerprint and a palm print of Oswald's on a paper bag.[326] Lt. Day told the commission that after the bag was dusted with magnetic fingerprint powder, no legible prints were found on the outside of the bag.[327]

According to an FBI report dated November 30, 1963, the paper used in packing books at the Book Depository was found to have the same observable characteristics as the brown paper bag "shaped like a gun case" found in the Depository. Similarly, the Warren Report states, "It has been demonstrated that the paper and tape from which the bag was made came from the shipping room of the Texas School Book Depository..." But researcher J. Gary Shaw found in the National Archives the apparently original FBI report, also dated November 30, which states that the paper from the roll in the Depository "was found not to be identical with the paper gun case found at the scene of the shooting." Both documents were written by FBI agent Vincent Drain. On December 6, 1963, the FBI sent an airtel to Dallas with replacement pages "to replace page 129 of reference report." (The FBI statement at the top of this paragraph regarding the bag's having "the same observable characteristics" is found on page 129 of Commission Document 5.)

It appears that the "rifle bag" was another plant, or a prop, like the three Mannlicher-Carcano shells and the rifle found on the sixth floor of the Depository, and the pristine Mannlicher-Carcano bullet supposedly found at Parkland Hospital. The bag, if it ever existed, was probably created in some obscure technical office of the CIA, designed to bolster the Official Story that the assassination rifle was smuggled into the Book Depository, and to further incriminate Oswald.

17. The Casket Switch

It has been well-documented that the president's body left Dallas in a fancy, expensive bronze casket and arrived at the Bethesda morgue in a cheap gray shipping casket ... or a substitute corpse arrived in the gray shipping casket. Newsreel footage showed a gray ambulance removing a bronze casket from *Air Force One*. Paul O'Connor, laboratory technologist at Bethesda, told David Lifton that President Kennedy's body arrived in a cheap gray metal casket at 8:00 p.m., and that he helped lift the body from the zippered gray body bag inside. O'Connor was certain that the shipping casket that came into the morgue wasn't the casket that went on *Air Force One*.[328] (O'Connor did not testify to the commission or its legal staff.) Bugliosi implies that O'Connor was the only one who saw a cheap shipping casket.[329] This is inaccurate. Autopsy technician James Jenkins told William Law that Kennedy's body arrived in a "plain coffin."[330] Autopsy photographer Floyd Riebe and x-ray technician Edward Reed both saw the body arrive in a metal shipping casket; Reed said it was a "typical" aluminum or steel military casket. (Reed did not testify to the commission or its legal staff.) Riebe told the ARRB that he saw a "kind of a gunmetal gray, a dull finish ... a very plain, inexpensive type casket." Bill Sloan reports that Hugh Huggins, Robert Kennedy's representative at the autopsy, says that he arrived at Bethesda "just in time to see two caskets, one plain gray and one ornate bronze, unloaded from two different ambulances, and that "Jack's body was in the plain casket..."[331]

In an ARRB telephone interview on February 14, 1997, Petty Officer Dennis David, who was chief of the day for the medical school at the time, said that he received what he understood to be the body of Kennedy in a simple gray shipping casket that was delivered at the morgue loading dock (the rear entrance of the Bethesda morgue) by men in suits from a black Cadillac hearse between 6:40 and 6:45 p.m. on November 22, and he was adamant that this occurred prior to the arrival of the motorcade from Andrews Air Force Base carrying Mrs. Kennedy and the Dallas coffin.[332] Dr. Humes told the ARRB in 1996 that the president's body arrived in a "good-looking" wooden casket. (He also repeated his story that he saw "a large defect in the right parietal area" – more evidence that either the right parietal area of the president's cranium was cut open before his body reached Bethesda, or Dr. Humes et al. were not autopsying President Kennedy.) So we have one John Kennedy arriving in a cheap gray shipping casket via a black Cadillac hearse, and another John Kennedy arriving in a fancy wooden or bronze casket via a gray ambulance.

On October 28, 1997, Petty Officer David recalled that Kennedy's body arrived before the Andrews motorcade, and well before the Dallas casket first entered the morgue at about 7:17 p.m. About a half-hour later, he saw a gray ambulance (in the motor cavalcade) drive up outside the front of Bethesda Tower and saw Jacqueline Kennedy, Robert McNamara, and several others enter the lobby from the motorcade and go directly to the seventeenth-floor suite on an elevator. He saw Mrs. Kennedy arrive in the gray ambulance (containing the bronze Dallas casket) at the front of Bethesda approximately fifteen to thirty minutes *after* he helped unload the shipping casket at the morgue loading dock.[333] (Petty Officer David did not testify to the commission or its legal staff.)

Layton Ledbetter (chief of the day for the Medical Center command), Lt. Richard Lipsey (an aide to Army Major General Philip C. Wehle), Petty Officer Donald Rebentisch, Army Sgt. James Felder, Paul O'Connor and several members of the Casket Team recalled a black 'decoy' ambulance.[334] X-ray technician Jerrol Custer said, "There was a casket brought in the back by a black Cadillac ambulance. Plus, there was a casket that Jacqueline Kennedy had in her entourage, too." He said that he left for an hour, and saw the second casket when he returned. (Custer did not testify to the commission or its legal staff) James Jenkins told Harrison Livingstone that there was "definitely" an "ornate type casket already in the laboratory when the President came in."[335] A report by Marine Corps Sgt. Roger E. Boyagian, NCO In Charge of the Marine Corps Barracks Security Detail at the Bethesda Morgue on November 22nd and 23rd, indicates that the cheap metal casket arrived at Bethesda at 6:40 or 6:45 p.m., before the arrival of Mrs. Kennedy and the Dallas casket at Andrews AFB.[336] Douglas Horne says, "The Boyagian report is proof and validation of [David] Lifton's basic hypothesis, which is that the President's body was intercepted after it left Parkland hospital, and that wounds were altered prior to the official start time of the autopsy at 8:15 p.m."[337]

Floyd Riebe said that the president's body was in a "rubberized-type body bag," with a zipper down the center. David Lifton quoted Riebe and Captain John Stover, commanding officer of the Medical School at Bethesda, as telling him that there was a body bag. Petty Officer Rebentisch also said the body came into the morgue in a body bag, which was in a plain gray metal shipping casket.[338] (Capt. Stover did not testify to the commission or its legal staff.) Jerrol Custer and Ed Reed also said the body was zipped inside a body bag.[339] Paul O'Connor "said the body had arrived at about 8 p.m. and was wrapped in a body bag, the head in a sheet."[340] James Metzler, a third-class corpsman who was in the autopsy room briefly, said there was no body bag.[341] (Metzler did not testify to the commission or its legal staff.) Bugliosi claims that John Stringer, the official autopsy photographer, and FBI man James Sibert told him that there was no body bag, just sheets, and that Dr. Humes said the same thing in 1992.[342]

18. The Alterations to or Substitution of the Body

In his Warren Commission testimony, Dr. Humes described President Kennedy as "an extremely well-developed, muscular young man with a very well-developed set of muscles in his thoraco [*sic*] and shoulder girdle."[343] However, James Jenkins said of JFK on the autopsy table, "He was thin. He was a small man."[344] Paul O'Connor said that the body looked "emaciated as hell. He didn't look like a healthy human being."[345] According to the autopsy report, the real John Kennedy was six feet one-half-inch tall, and he was a "muscular, well-developed male weighing approximately 170 pounds."

From the Boyajian report indicating that the cheap shipping casket arrived at the Bethesda morgue shortly after 6:35 p.m., Horne concludes that the bronze casket was empty when FBI men Sibert and O'Neill ushered it into the morgue at 7:17 p.m., and that the president's body was intercepted after it left Parkland Hospital, and that wounds were altered prior to the official start time of the autopsy at 8:15 p.m. I believe that these strange phenomena do not necessarily prove that the Dallas casket was empty when it arrived at the Bethesda morgue, and that another explanation is possible – namely, that the Dallas casket contained the president's body, and that the shipping casket contained a Kennedy look-alike that exhibited head wounds that would fit in with the Official Story. This would also explain why the Humes-Boswell-Finck autopsy report is completely inconsistent with what the Parkland doctors and nurses saw. And some Kennedy aides stated unequivocally that the bronze Dallas casket never left their sight from the time it left Dallas until it arrived at Bethesda. Dr. Humes told the commission that the body was received at 7:35 p.m., but we don't know if this was the Kennedy in the cheap shipping casket or the Kennedy in the fancy bronze casket – if, indeed, there was a body in the bronze casket.

Dr. Humes stated that he didn't know if the photos that the autopsists had made would be available to the commission, so "to assist in making our testimony more understandable to the commission members, we decided to have made ... schematic drawings, of the situation as we saw it ..." He said the drawings were made under the supervision of him and Dr.

Boswell by a Mr. H.A. Rydberg, a medical illustrator at the Naval Medical School.[346] (Rydberg did not testify to the commission or its legal staff.)

19. Shenanigans at the Autopsy

The Comedy of Errors: Dr. Boswell called the autopsy a three-ring circus. He also said that the Secret Service agents were "running around like chickens with their heads off."[347] In his 1989 book *Unnatural Death: Confessions of a Medical Examiner*, Dr. Michael Baden wrote, "Where bungled autopsies are concerned, President Kennedy's is the exemplar."[348] At the Shaw trial, when Dr. Finck was asked if the Kennedy autopsy was a complete one under the definition used by the American Board of Pathology, he replied, "No ... because to my recollection we based our autopsy report on the 24th of November on the information received from people at the scene. We based it on our gross autopsy findings..."[349] (Which was it?) When asked about his statement that three shots were heard, Dr. Finck replied, "At the time we wrote this we had this information obtained from people who had been at the scene to the best of my recollection."[350] Dr. Cyril Wecht described the Bethesda autopsy as "extremely superficial and sloppy, inept, incomplete, incompetent in many respects..."[351] Dr. Wecht called the autopsy "a military endeavor, not a scientific undertaking." He refused to go along with the majority on the HSCA forensic pathology panel when they concluded that "one, and only one, bullet struck the president's head from behind."[352] Dr. Wecht also disagreed with the HSCA forensic pathology panel's conclusion that one bullet had caused all of Gov. Connally's wounds.[353]

In its 1978 critique of the president's autopsy, the HSCA's forensic pathology panel concluded that the Bethesda autopsy was incomplete and inaccurate in a number of areas, and that the three pathologists who performed the postmortem examination committed a number of procedural errors resulting in an incomplete autopsy, including their failure to confer with Parkland Hospital doctors prior to the autopsy; their failure to examine the president's clothing, which would have provided them clues about the direction of the shots (the clothing wasn't available to them); their failure to determine the precise exit point of the bullet that caused the head wound; their failure to properly examine and section the brain; their failure to dissect the back and neck; their failure to determine the angles of the bullet tracks through the body relative to the body axis; their failure to have proper photographs taken, and so forth.[354] One example: Page 3 of the Pathological Examination Report signed by Humes, Boswell and

Finck, stated: "Situated on the upper right posterior thorax just above the upper border of the scapula there is a 7 x 14 millimeter oval wound. This wound is measured to be 14 cm. from the tip of the right acromion process and 14 cm. below the tip of the right mastoid process." The medical panel of the HSCA stated that the reference points used to document the location of Kennedy's back wound – the mastoid process and the acromion – were movable points and should not have been used.[355] Even Mr. Bugliosi states, "The one phase of the Kennedy investigation that most experts agree was decidedly botched was the autopsy..."[356] Nevertheless, Mr. Bugliosi again parrots the Warren Report, telling us that "despite the insistent and strident claims by conspiracy theorists that the fatal wound to the president's head was fired [*sic*] from his right front, *all* of the medical and scientific evidence proves not just beyond a reasonable doubt but beyond all doubt that it was fired from his rear, and the wound to the backside of the president's head was an entrance wound."[357]

Jerrol Custer saw a Navy chief, "the gentleman who committed suicide, supposedly," taking movies with a movie camera. This seems to confirm that William Bruce Pitzer, head of the audio-visual unit at Bethesda, was present at the autopsy and was taking those movies, though Pitzer was a lieutenant commander. Custer also stated that he was ordered to tear a page out of the duty log; "I gave it to Ebersole and he destroyed it." John Stringer wasn't allowed to develop his own film. Stringer recalled that at one point a federal agent took a camera from Floyd Riebe and exposed the film.[358] (Stringer did not testify to the commission or its legal staff.)

The body of an Army or Air Force major (Jenkins was told it was an Air Force major) came into the morgue in an ornate casket between 3:30 and 6:30 p.m. on November 22, and it sat in a casket on a pop-up cart in the cold room. The duty (hospital) corpsman told James Jenkins not to log in the major's body, and said that he himself (the corpsman) had been told not to log the body in.[359]

Nobody Knew Who Was In Charge: In his HSCA testimony, Dr. Humes told Dr. Baden that he walked out onto the loading dock and, seeing a crowd out there, asked who was in charge, and it was then that he heard Gen. Wehle, the commanding officer of the US Military District of Washington, D.C., say, "I am." During Dr. Finck's commission testimony, there was no mention of who was in charge of the autopsy. But Dr. Finck testified at the Shaw trial on February 24, 1969, that several people were in charge of the autopsy. He also stated at that trial that when Dr. Humes asked "Who is in charge here?" Dr. Finck heard an Army general say, "I am."[360] Humes told the ARRB on February 13, 1996, that the Army general referred to by Dr. Finck was Gen. Wehle. Dr. Finck also mentioned that there were admirals in the autopsy room.[361] Bugliosi quotes Dr. Humes as telling the *Journal of the American Medical Association* in May 1992 that *he* was in charge "from start to finish and there was no interference – zero..."[362] But Dr. Humes told Dr. Baden, in the HSCA context, that "we were being urged to expedite this examination [autopsy] as quickly as possible."[363] Humes implied that Dr. Burkley was the source of this pressure. At first, Burkley tried to argue that a full autopsy was unnecessary. Sibert and O'Neill prepared a memo on November 26, 1963, documenting Dr. Burkley's objection to a complete autopsy.[364] Dr. Boswell and John Stringer recalled Dr. Burkley's repeated attempts to limit the scope of the autopsy.[365] The HSCA states that Captain David Osborne, Bethesda Hospital's chief of surgery, "stated at the beginning of the autopsy there was tremendous pressure to perform a 'quick post' and to leave the hospital." He also "stated in committee interview that Dr. Humes was successful in resisting pressure to perform an incomplete autopsy and that no one issued any orders limiting it."[366] Dr. Mantik notes that several witnesses described Dr. Burkley as having controlled the autopsy.[367] Dr. Burkley ordered Dr. Humes, who was officially in charge of the autopsy, not to track the path of the bullet wounds through JFK's body, and authorized Humes to destroy the original notes made of the autopsy. Dr. Burkley also admitted that he doctored the autopsy report. Horne's Appendix 73 in Volume 1 of *Inside the Assassination Records Review Board* describes Dr. Burkley's perjury in the latter's affidavit for the HSCA on November 28, 1978; Burkley stated that the wounds he observed at Parkland Hospital appeared the same as those he observed at Bethesda, and that he directed Dr. Humes to perform a complete autopsy. In his ARRB deposition, Humes suggested that he was writing the autopsy report for Dr. Burkley.[368] Dr. Finck was told not to dissect the track of the bullet wound "that you have described to me today," but he couldn't remember by whom. At the Shaw trial, Dr. Finck was asked twice why he didn't remove or dissect the organs of the neck. Finck replied, "As I recall I was told not to, but I don't remember by whom."[369]

Conflicting Accounts Regarding the Brain: The Parkland doctors reported that about a quarter to a third of the president's brain was missing. Dr. McClelland told the commission that "probably a third or so, at least, of the brain tissue, posterior cerebral tissue and some of the cerebellar tissue had been blasted out."[370] But at Bethesda, Paul O'Connor and Jerrol Custer told researchers that the brain had been removed before the body arrived; O'Connor said the brain was 90 percent gone, and Custer told Livingstone that there "definitely was no brain."[371] FBI man Francis O'Neill told the ARRB in 1997 that more than half of the brain was missing.[372] In his ARRB interview, Dr. Boswell stated that one-third of the brain was missing. Floyd Riebe told ARRB counsel that when the brain was removed, "it was less than half a brain there."[373] James Jenkins told Livingstone that "probably a fourth of the brain was lost."[374] Dr. Peters told the ARRB that there was "obviously quite a bit of brain missing." Dr. Humes told the *Journal of the American Medical Association* that the upper two-thirds of the right cerebrum were missing, but Tom Robinson, the mortician, told the ARRB that the missing part of the brain was in the back.[375]

There is a notation in the Supplementary Autopsy Report that has Drs. Humes, Finck and Boswell stating that the president's brain weight was 1500 grams. This is at the upper limit of normal human brain weight, and the notation is especially odd considering that a quarter to a third of the brain had been blown away in Dallas! There are also reports of the brain stem having been severed before Kennedy's body arrived at the Bethesda morgue.[376] If the president's body went directly from Dallas to Bethesda, who cut the brain loose from the spinal cord before the body arrived at Bethesda?

Douglas Horne demonstrated convincingly that there were two brain examinations; the first, from which Dr. Finck was excluded, involved the real brain, with severely damaged cerebral and cerebellar tissue, and the second involved a substitute brain. The first brain could not be allowed to remain in evidence, because it showed the effects of the actual fatal head wound and was inconsistent with the Official Story.[377]

20. The Phony Autopsy Report

First, the fatal head wound (the real one): Parkland doctors Gene Akin (6H61-2); Charles Crenshaw; Charles Carrico (3H36; 6H6; 17H2; 7HSCA268); William Kemp Clark (6H20, 29; 17H2-3); Richard Dulany; John Ebersole (see below); Ronald Jones (6H53); Robert Karnei (Livingstone, *High Treason 2*, p. 182); Robert McClelland (see below); Malcolm Perry (3H372; 6H9; 7HSCA295, 302); and Paul Peters (6H71); autopsy photographer Floyd Riebe and other Bethesda staff as indicated below; Secret Service agents Clint Hill, Emory Roberts and Sam Kinney; autopsy photographer John Stringer; Parkland nurses Audrey Bell, Diane

Bowron, Patricia Hutton and Doris Nelson, as well as Aubrey Rike, the Dallas ambulance driver, all said that the fatal head wound was in the back or right rear portion of the skull; these people saw no other head wound.

Nurse Bell stated that she saw "a massive wound at the back of his head ... a gaping hole ... three or four inches" with "brain and fluids dripping out."[378] (Nurse Bell did not testify to the commission or its legal staff.) Nurse Bowron told the commission that she saw the condition of the president's head when he was being wheeled into Trauma Room One; she "just saw one large hole" in the back of his head, and no other wounds on his body. She stated, "The back of his head ... was very bad." When Arlen Specter asked Nurse Bowron, "Did you see a small bullet hole beneath that one large hole," she replied, "No, sir."[379] Nurse Nelson, supervising nurse of the emergency room, was not asked by Specter to describe the size or location of the fatal head wound, but she told Harrison Livingstone, "The back of his head was blown away.... He was shot from the side and it blew the back of his head off." She said, "There was no hair back there.... It was blown away ... his brains were fallen down on the stretcher." Nurse Hutton, who was present during the resuscitation effort, said in a statement to Parkland Hospital administrator Charles Price that the president was "bleeding profusely from a wound on the back of his head.... A doctor asked me to place a pressure dressing on the head wound. This was of no use, however, because of the massive opening on the back of his head."[380] (Nurse Hutton did not testify to the commission or its legal staff.)

Secret Service agent Clint Hill stated in an affidavit on November 30, 1963, "I noticed a portion of the president's head on the right rear was missing.... Part of his brain was gone. I saw a part of his skull with hair on it lying in the seat." He saw "one large gaping wound in the right rear portion of the head." In his written statement dated November 30, 1963, agent Hill stated that he observed, at the Bethesda morgue, "a wound about six inches down from the neckline on the back just to the right of the spinal column." He further stated that in addition to the wound he saw in the president's back, he "observed another wound on the right rear portion of the skull."[381] Agent Emory Roberts Emory Roberts stated, "I saw what appeared to be a small explosion on the right side of the President's head."[382] Secret Service agent Kellerman told the commission that the right rear portion of the head was "removed."[383] Secret Service special agent Sam Kinney was the driver of the follow-up car. In interviews with Vincent Palamara between 1992 and 1994, Kinney stated, among other things, that the fatal wound was "in the back of the head ... I had brain matter all over my windshield and left arm.... It was the right rear part of his head, because that's the part I saw blow out."[384] This is corroborated by Secret Service agent Gerald Blaine, who describes agent Kinney feeling the blood from Kennedy's head spraying over the top of his windshield. The statements of agents Kinney and Blaine are further corroboration for the fatal shot having come from the right front; agent Blaine himself describes a fist-size hole "clearly visible" in the back of Kennedy's head.[385]

Dr. John Ebersole, Bethesda radiologist, told Dr. Mantik in 1992 that he saw a big single beveled wound in the back of the head. In his HSCA deposition, Ebersole recalled that the back of JFK's head was missing.[386] Ed Reed said the head wound "was very large and located in the right hemisphere in the occipital region."[387] James Metzler also stated that the wound was in the back of the head.[388] John Stringer told David Lifton in a taped interview that when he helped lift the president's body out of the coffin at Bethesda, he saw that the main damage was in the *back*, in the occipital area. When interviewed by Mark Flanagan for the HSCA, lab technician Jan "Nick" Rudnicki stated that the back right quadrant of the head was missing.[389] (Rudnicki did not testify to the commission or its legal staff.) Joe Hagen of Gawler's Funeral Home said that the wound in the back of the head was so big that "we had to replace just all of that area with plaster of Paris."[390] In a January 12, 1977, HSCA staff report of an interview with mortician Tom Robinson, he described a round defect in the rear of the head the size of a small orange.

Three or four days after the autopsy, Lt. Cmdr. William Pitzer had a 16-millimeter black and white film of the autopsy and some slides. Dennis David remembered a slide that showed a "huge gaping hole" in the back of Kennedy's head. He also saw a round or oval wound, about one-quarter-inch by three-eighths of an inch in diameter in the right front temporal area of the head, about three inches forward of the right ear, just below the hairline, which he interpreted as a bullet wound. The top of the head looked intact. Pitzer never said he was at the autopsy, but Mr. David assumed he had been there. Government photographer Joseph O'Donnell told ARRB counsel Jeremy Gunn that he remembered seeing an autopsy photograph of a gaping wound in the back of Kennedy's head that was big enough to put a fist through.[391]

Bugliosi says that the reason why Parkland doctors failed to find an entrance wound in the rear of the president's head was that, as they testified, they never turned his body over.[392] This is very misleading, maybe deliberately so. Whether they turned his body over or not, the doctors and nurses were quite clear on what they did see: a baseball-size hole in the *back* of Kennedy's head.

Dr. McClelland told the commission that "the right posterior portion of the skull had been extremely blasted..."[393] In an interview with Dr. McClelland on YouTube, the doctor stated that the head wound was "probably five inches in diameter"; he told Drs. Perry and Baxter that the right side of the back of the head was "essentially gone." Dr. McClelland told Bugliosi over the phone that the president had "a massive hole to the back of his head." After Bugliosi tried to lead Dr. McClelland away from this conclusion, the doctor iterated that the fatal bullet "exited in the occipital region" of Kennedy's head, "leaving a hole so big I could put my fist in it."[394] And that is exactly what Dr. McClelland's 1966 drawing of the fatal wound shows (reproduced on p. 81 of Groden's book and on p. 180 of *Murder in Dealey Plaza*). During their telephone chat, Bugliosi asked Dr. McClelland how the fatal wound could be in the right rear if in the Zapruder film, "the explosion is clearly to the right frontal portion of the president's head with a large amount of brain matter spraying out, and the back of his head appears to be completely intact?"[395] Incredible! Mr. Bugliosi believes the doctored Zapruder film rather than the Parkland doctors and nurses. Bugliosi also failed to notice that in the official autopsy "blank stare" photo, apparently showing a supine Kennedy, the area where the famous film seems to show a wound (in the right temple) is *completely intact.*

Dr. Clark told the commission that cerebral *and cerebellar* tissue was damaged and exposed.[396] But Mr. Bugliosi was not to be discouraged by the observations of eyewitnesses. He informs us that because the autopsy report doesn't say anything about part of the cerebellum being missing, and because Dr. Michael Baden of the House Assassinations Committee told Bugliosi that the cerebellum was intact (according to the autopsy x-rays and photos), any doctors at Parkland who said they saw damage to the cerebellum were simply wrong![397]

Doctors Boswell and Finck were adamant from the beginning that there was an entrance wound low in the back of Kennedy's head.[398] This is the Kennedy of the Official Story. Finck told the commission that the fatal bullet "entered the back of the head and went out on the right side of his skull, producing a large wound, the greatest dimension of which was approximately 13 centimeters." He said that the wound of entrance was "fairly small."[399] At the Shaw trial on February 24, 1969, Dr. Finck stated that he saw a wound at the side of the back of the head, slightly above the external occipital protuberance and one inch to its right. He also said that he saw a wound 13 centimeters in diameter "occupying the right side and the top of the head of the President."[400] On that day he said that he saw a small wound on the right side in the back of the neck. He said the throat wound was consistent with its having been a point of exit, and that a bullet entered at the back of the neck and exited through the front of the neck, and the former wound was higher than the latter. Dr. Humes told the commission that the small wound in the back of the head "was in a portion of the skull which had remained intact."[401] This, of course, was the area that the Parkland doctors knew had been blown away. Dr. Humes told the commission three times that the posterior wound was in the low neck, but his own autopsy report stated that wound was in the upper right back. In Volume 7 of the HSCA Appendix Volumes, we find that as a result of phone calls to Dr. Perry at Parkland Hospital on the morning of November 23, "Dr. Humes concluded that the missile which had entered the upper back had traversed the body and exited in the anterior portion of the neck."[402] So now the entry point has moved from the low neck to the upper back. The bullet was magic indeed; it went from a point near the top of a tall building to the rear, hit the low neck or upper back, and then its path changed to a horizontal or slightly upward trajectory such that it exited the front of the president's neck!

Dr. Humes also mentioned two lesions that neither the doctors nor the nurses at Parkland ever mentioned: one laceration 2.5 centimeters to the right of the midline of the skull, and another of the corpus callosum (the body of fibers that connects the two hemispheres of the brain to each other).[403] This is another indication that Dr. Humes was not working on John Kennedy. Humes told Arlen Specter that in addition to the hole about six inches below the collar and two inches to the right of the midline, there was another "deficit" just below the collar, high in the back of the coat.[404] The president's blood-stained shirt is shown on page 78 of Groden's book; it shows no hole "just below the collar."

Dr. Gary Aguilar pointed out that the autopsy report "contradicts *both* JFK's photographs and X-rays. It describes the skull defect as a continuous, bony right parietal-temporal-occipital defect."[405]

Bugliosi tells us, "*All* pathologists who examined the evidence in this case for four national commissions ... reached the same conclusion: that the two wounds to the back side of the president's body (i.e., the upper back and back of the head) were *entrance*, not exit wounds, and that both exited toward the front of the body."[406] What happened to the magic bullet that entered the base of the back of the president's neck? On page 246 of his endnotes, Bugliosi states that neither Dr. Perry nor Dr. Carrico saw any wound to the back of JFK's head, but on pages 403-4 of the main book, he notes the observations of doctors Perry, Carrico, Clark, Akin and Zedelitz in their descriptions of the fatal wound being in the right occipital-parietal area (the lower right rear of the head). Bugliosi nevertheless tells us that "lay observations ... have to yield to hard, scientific evidence." The Parkland doctors and nurses are lay people? Bugliosi also misquotes Dr. Carrico as saying the wound was in the "right posterior parietal area," when in fact the doctor told the commission that the wound was in the right occipital-parietal region.[407] Bugliosi concedes in a footnote on page 409 that FBI agent Francis O'Neill's 1997 drawing for the ARRB shows the exit wound encompassing the right rear quadrant of the head.[408]

Mr. Bugliosi states, "A significant minority of Parkland doctors saw the exit wound essentially, or close to, where the autopsy and X-rays showed it to be."[409] This is another false and misleading statement; again, the pattern is clear: Bugliosi will grasp at every available straw to bolster the Warren Report's conclusions regarding Kennedy's head wounds. Bugliosi's "significant minority" are doctors Baxter (6H41, 44), Grossman, Clark (6H29, 17H2), Giesecke (6H74), Jenkins (17H15), Salyer (6H81) and Seldin (letter to V. Palamara). Let's take them one by one: **Dr. Charles Baxter** described "a large gaping wound in the skull...the right side of his head had been blown off." Dr. Baxter described the wound as in the temporal and parietal area. Douglas Horne reported in an ARRB memo that on being shown the Ida Cox drawing of the autopsy image of the back of the president's head, showing it intact, **Dr. Robert Grossman** stated that it was completely incorrect. Dr. Grossman "drew on a diagram of a human skull a defect square in the occiput that coincided with his clear recollection of the size and location of a defect in the back of JFK's skull."[410] (Dr. Grossman did not testify to the commission or its legal staff.) Bugliosi managed to find an article by Ben Bradlee in the *Boston Globe* (June 21, 1981, p. A23) wherein **Dr. William Kemp Clark** supposedly states that the fatal wound was "in the parietal area above the right ear."[411] In fact, Dr. Clark told the commission that the fatal wound was "in the right occipital-parietal region of the president's skull," and in his Summary (of what he observed when President Kennedy was brought into Parkland), he again describes a large wound in the right occipital-parietal region. **Dr. Adolph Giesecke** described it as "a very large cranial wound ... on the left-hand side of the head ... this is just my memory of it." His memory could have used improvement; no one else at Parkland (and no one at Bethesda) saw a large wound on the left side of Kennedy's head. In a letter to Parkland Administrator J.C. Price, dated November 22, 1963, (reproduced on p. 218 of Fetzer, 2000), **Dr. Marion Jenkins** described the wound as temporal and occipital, and stated that "cerebellum had protruded from the wound." Dr. Jenkins wasn't precise about the location of the head wound in his later commission testimony, but he did testify that "part of the cerebellum ... was herniated from the wound."[412] The cerebellum is at the base of the *back* of the brain. And Dr. Jenkins told the HSCA's Andy Purdy that "a segment of occipital or temporal bone" had blown out, and he mentioned a hole in the "right-rear of the head."[413] (The back of the temporal bone touches the occipital, so this characterization is also consistent with a defect in the lower right rear of the head.) **Dr. Kenneth Salyer** testified that the head wound was "a wound of his right temporal region"; he didn't specify in which part of the temporal bone he saw this wound.[414] But asked to show with his right hand where the fatal wound was, Dr. Salyer indicated an area behind and slightly above the right ear, and not where the autopsy photos and x-rays showed the fatal wound to be (see photo at Groden, p. 87, and in Fetzer, 2000, p. 174). Dr. Salyer told Dr. Aguilar on October 18, 1993, that JFK's head wound definitely extended behind JFK's ear.[415] Bugliosi quotes from a letter from Dr. Donald Seldin, chairman of the Department of Medicine at Parkland, to Vincent Palamara dated August 27, 1998, stating that "the entire frontal, parietal and temporal bones were shattered."[416] Clearly, only Drs. Baxter and Seldin stated that the major wound was at or near where the autopsy photos and x-rays showed it to be. That is quite a significant minority, indeed: two people. Bugliosi states in some places that the fatal wound was where the Zapruder film shows it to be (in front of the right ear), but in others states that the wound was where Dr. Humes and the autopsy report say that it was – in the upper right parietal bone. Apparently Mr. Bugliosi has no problem in describing the fatal wound being in two different places, nor with the fact that the gross destruction described by Dr. Seldin is completely inconsistent with the official autopsy photographs. Of course, the statements of Bugliosi's "significant minority" do not change the fact that the fatal wound was in the lower right rear of the president's head!

It isn't that complicated (but apparently too complicated for Mr. Bugliosi to comprehend): A large, gaping wound in the lower right rear of the president's head was inconsistent with the Official Story, as put forth in the Warren Report, that a lone nut assassin fired from an elevated position to the rear, and that the fatal bullet that he fired entered the back of the president's head through a small hole and exited on the side of his head. So the either the autopsy doctors had to generate a phony autopsy report, or they had to be given a corpse to autopsy that wasn't President Kennedy and had to write an autopsy report based on that other corpse (which autopsy report would also be phony). Mr. Bugliosi quotes from page 6 of the Pathological Examination Report at 16H983, signed by Humes, Boswell and Finck, which says in part, "It is our opinion that the deceased died as a result of two perforating gunshot wounds inflicted by high-velocity projectiles fired by a person or persons unknown. The projectiles were fired from a point behind and somewhat above the level of the deceased... The fatal missile entered the skull above and to the right of the external occipital protuberance.... A portion of the projectile made its exit through the parietal bone on the right, carrying with it portions of cerebrum, skull and scalp... The other missile entered the right superior posterior thorax above the scapula and traversed the soft tissues of the supra-scapular and supra-clavicular portions of the base of the right side of the neck."[417] At first I thought I was confused, because the trajectory of the "other missile" didn't seem to make sense; but I consulted my local county coroner, and he confirmed that the trajectory Humes describes is one that is *horizontal*, and from Kennedy's *right* (from "above the scapula" to the back of the neck). This supposed wound obviously could not have resulted from a shot from an elevated location to the rear – another nail in the coffin of the Magic Bullet theory, which holds that a bullet hit the back of Kennedy's neck, exited his throat and went on to cause all of Gov. Connally's wounds. (Halfway through his commission testimony, Dr. Humes again states that he "identified a wound in the low posterior of the neck of the President." He stated that this wound was parallel to the long dimension of the body, 4 mm wide and 7 mm long.[418]) Humes went on vaguely to describe an oval wound in the "low neck ... just above the upper border of the scapula, and measured 7 by 4 millimeters, with its long axis roughly parallel to the long axis of vertical column."[419]

Dr. Humes' explanation for the fact that the holes in Kennedy's clothing didn't line up with his "low neck" wound: it was because the president was "extremely well-developed," and because CE396 shows him "with his [right] hand raised, his elbow bent.... I believe this action would further accentuate the elevation of the coat and shirt with respect to the back of the President." In other words, his clothing was so bunched up that the holes in Kennedy's shirt and jacket and the supposed hole in his "low neck" all aligned with each other! It is all nonsense, of course. Humes also said that the wound in the front of the neck was physically lower than the point of entry "posteriorly." That prompted Commissioner John McCloy to ask: "If, contrary to the evidence we have here, that anterior wound was the wound of entry, the shot must have come from below the President to have followed that path." Humes: "That course, that is correct, sir."[420] It could be mentioned here that no one else saw a wound at the base of the back of Kennedy's neck, nor does the official autopsy photo of the back of the dead president's head show such a wound. The posterior view on the Autopsy Descriptive Sheet prepared by Dr. Boswell, reproduced herein as Figure 2 (page 229), shows no such wound! Either Dr. Humes was lying his eyes out (possibly on orders from above) or he performed his autopsy on someone other than John Kennedy. Before the ARRB, Humes testified that there was "a bullet wound in the back above the scapula." That would be several inches to the right of the neck.

Dr. Humes stated that "we concluded that the large defect in the upper right side of the skull ... would represent a wound of exit."[421] In a videotaped interview, Dr. Humes described an "exit wound," pointing to the top of his head, to the right. No one else seems to have seen a wound in this area, nor does such a wound appear even in the doctored Zapruder film. Humes told the commission that he recalled seeing "a photograph showing the massive head wound with the large defect," though he didn't say where the defect was.[422] He also stated, "The second wound was found in the right posterior portion of the scalp. This wound was situated approximately 2.5 centimeters to the right, and slightly above the external occipital protuberance.... The third obvious wound ... was a huge defect over the right side of the skull.... This wound measured approximately 13 centimeters in greatest diameter..."[423] The official autopsy report, signed by Humes, Boswell and Finck, describes "a large irregular defect of the scalp and skull on the right involving chiefly the parietal bone but extending somewhat into the temporal and occipital regions," and that the defect "measures approximately 13 cm. in greatest diameter."[424] The autopsy report (p. 4) also describes another wound: "Situated in the posterior scalp approximately 2.5 cm, laterally to the right [of?] and slightly above the external occipital protuberance is a lacerated wound measuring 15 by 6 mm. In the underlying bone is a corresponding wound through the skull which exhibits beveling of the margins of the bone when viewed from the inner aspect of the skull." (A 15x6-millimeter wound is about nine-sixteenths of an inch by a quarter-inch.) This is the Bethesda (or third) Kennedy.

Bugliosi says that "we know" from the autopsy x-rays and photographs that doctors Carrico, Clark, Akin and Salyer were wrong in placing the exit wound in the right rear of the president's head, but in the same sentence, Bugliosi states that "the exit wound, though mostly to the right front of the president's head, did extend into the occipital region," referencing CE387, 16H980, the Pathological Examination Report.[425] This is another misleading statement from Mr. Bugliosi, apparently intended to validate the apparent wound in front of the president's ear, as shown on the doctored Zapruder film; the autopsy report to which Bugliosi refers (at 16H978-83) does not use the phrase "right front." Furthermore, the right front of the head is the temporal and sphenoid bones, which are quite distant from the occipital. Bugliosi tells us that he believes the Zapruder film, but that film doesn't show any wound in the occipital region!

At the Shaw trial, Dr. Finck said the first shot went into the back of Kennedy's neck. He said that when he arrived at the morgue he "found the wound of entry in the back of the neck, no corresponding exit."[426] If there was no corresponding exit, how did this magic bullet go on to cause all of Gov. Connally's wounds? Later in his testimony, Dr. Finck parroted Dr. Humes' description of the fatal head wound, but he refuted the finding of the HSCA's medical panel; he said the fatal wound was "approximately one inch to the right and slightly above external occipital protuberance, and it was definitely not four inches or 100 millimeters above it..."[427] Dr. Finck was asked four times why he didn't remove the organs of the neck and trace the track of the wound. His first answer: "I had the cause of death." But shortly later, he said, "As I recall I was told not to, but I don't remember by whom."

21. The Phony Autopsy Photos and X-rays

One can get to the truth about what did and didn't happen in Dealey Plaza, and about the fakery in the official autopsy photos, by paying attention to what the Parkland Hospital doctors and nurses observed, and by the use of a couple of simple diagrams created for this volume.

Mr. Bugliosi goes on at some length to assure us that the HSCA, with all their experts, concluded that all the autopsy photographs and x-rays depict President Kennedy and no one else, and that the autopsy photos and x-rays were authenticated by the Photographic Evidence Panel of the HSCA in 1978, which panel also concluded that the photos and x-rays had not been altered in any manner.[428] Again, Bugliosi is telling us that the official reports should be accepted because they are the official reports, and what was observed by the Parkland doctors and nurses, and several other eyewitnesses, should be ignored. He reassures us that "the autopsy photographs and X-rays do locate the wound precisely, though … not where the autopsy reports says."[429] How would he know "precisely" where the wound was? And isn't that statement an acknowledgment that the autopsy report is phony?

Bugliosi tells us of an "immense" hole in the side of the president's head, "five inches in its greatest diameter."[430] "The opinion of all the pathologists who either conducted the autopsy or examined closely photographs and X-rays of the president's head and wounds was unanimous … the [fatal] bullet proceeded in an essentially straight and forward path" and exploded out of the right side of the president's head.[431] The official autopsy photograph shows no such massive hole in the side of the head. The doctors supposedly (according to Mr. Bugliosi) found a small, oval hole in the back of the scalp, and a "corresponding but larger hole in the bone beneath the scalp." The doctors, says Mr. Bugliosi, recognize this as an entrance wound. And the big wound in the side of the head is "presumably the result of the bullet exiting the head …"[432] Alas, Mr. Bugliosi does not explain how a bullet moving along a "straight and forward path" could enter the back of someone's head, then make a right turn and go out the side.

Many Parkland witnesses described severe damage to the right cerebellum, but the brain photos in the National Archives show no damage whatsoever to that area.[433] Dr. Perry said later, "The 'official' autopsy photos do not depict the same wounds I saw in Trauma Room One at Parkland. The wounds I saw were wounds of entrance, and thus they could not have come from the rifle of Lee Harvey Oswald."[434] Floyd Riebe claimed that the photographs in the National Archives are "phony and not the photographs we took."[435] FBI men Sibert and O'Neill said the autopsy photos of the back of the head were not what they recalled. When shown an official photo of the "wound of entrance in the right posterior occipital region," Sibert said, "I don't have a recollection of it being that intact … I don't remember seeing anything that was like this photo."[436] When FBI agent O'Neill viewed the Archives brain photographs during his ARRB deposition, "he said that the photos he was viewing could not be President Kennedy's brain because when he viewed the removed brain at the autopsy, the damage was so great that more than half of it was missing. He described the brain photos in the Archives as depicting a 'virtually intact' brain."[437]

The official autopsy photo of the President's back is also phony. Nurse Diane Bowron told Harrison Livingstone that the official photo allegedly showing the President's back "is not the President's back." She wrote on the photo that he sent her, "THIS IS NOT THE BACK I SAW."[438]

Several of the autopsy photos clearly were not taken in the Bethesda morgue; Paul O'Connor was adamant that they were not taken there; he described the autopsy photos and x-rays to Livingstone as "totally wrong."[439] The autopsy photograph of the left side of the head of the alleged Kennedy, reproduced herein as Figure 3 (page 230), shows a comparison, both at the same scale, of the real John Kennedy (top) to the fake Kennedy. The latter photograph shows a stirrup under the head of the dead president. FBI agents Sibert and O'Neill told the ARRB that they didn't recall the metal stirrup under the head, nor did Dr. Humes himself recall the stirrup under the head.[440] Dr. Mantik reports that the autopsy technicians, the FBI note takers, the photographers and the embalmers recall a block or chock under the head, rather than a stirrup. Earl McDonald, medical photographer at Bethesda from 1972 to 1980, told the ARRB that he never saw the metal stirrup used as it appears in the autopsy photos.[441] Paul O'Connor told Noel Twyman that the metal head rest shown in the photo was not in use at the Bethesda autopsy room. Nobody at the 1991 assassination symposium in Dallas recalled the metal brace under the head shown in the photos. In fact, nobody at Bethesda recalled the metal brace that is shown supporting the head in the supine profile photo. "They said it was never used."[442] The lower photo in Figure 3 is clearly not of John Kennedy's head. The obvious conclusion is that a Kennedy look-alike was photographed in some location other than the Bethesda morgue, and published as an official autopsy photograph of John Kennedy. Bugliosi tells us that in the autopsy photo of the left side of Kennedy's head as he is lying on his back (the one showing the head in a metal stirrup), only the throat wound is visible, but it is clear that the back wound "was definitely *above* the exit wound in the throat."[443] How can he make this statement if the back wound is not visible in the photo? In any case it is physically impossible for a back wound to be above a wound in the throat. Bugliosi's statement is absurd.

Mr. Bugliosi mentions the "terribly gruesome" autopsy photos in Groden's book that "clearly show that the president's thick hair, drenched in blood, is all going in the direction of the rear..."[444] Apparently Mr. B. didn't notice that those photos don't show the large parietal wound on the upper right side of the head described by Dr. Humes in his autopsy report. In fact, the "blank stare" photo to which Bugliosi refers shows a man whose hair is almost black; John Kennedy's hair was reddish-brown. Nor did Mr. Bugliosi notice that the area where the Zapruder film shows a wound (in the right temple) with brain tissue supposedly bubbling out (the Blob) is smooth and undamaged in the autopsy photos – more evidence that the film has been doctored. But we don't know that the photos are of Kennedy. The official autopsy photos can be viewed online, in Harrison Livingstone's *High Treason 2,* and in Groden's book, among other sources.

Dr. Crenshaw stated on the ABC newsmagazine *20/20* in 1992 that the size of the tracheotomy incision in the autopsy photographs was at least twice as large as the small, neat incision that he observed at Parkland Hospital on the day of the assassination. And Dr. Humes told the ARRB that when he received the body, there was "a gaping defect that was obviously a tracheotomy incision in the anterior neck."[445] Dr. Ebersole recalled a tracheotomy incision that was neatly sutured "by a surgeon" when the body was received at Bethesda.[446] The "blank stare" photo shows no such suturing. These points provide further evidence that the "Kennedy" shown in the supine "blank stare" autopsy photo is not Kennedy.

White House photographer and former Navy chief Robert Knudsen told his family that he had photographed the autopsy, and had been involved in developing autopsy pictures. He also stated that the photos in evidence included some that were altered.[447] He stated that four or five of the autopsy photos shown to him by the HSCA did not represent the wounds he saw or photographed at the autopsy.[448] Knudsen told the ARRB that the photos of the back of the head looked to have been doctored, and that the brain photos did not match his recollection.[449] The ARRB uncovered evidence that the autopsy photos of Kennedy's brain are not of his brain.

The HSCA wrote that because "all of those interviewed who attended the autopsy corroborated the general location of the wounds as depicted in the [autopsy] photographs ... it appears more probable that the observations of the Parkland doctors are incorrect."[450] Because the autopsy photographs don't agree with the Official Story, they're simply wrong! Similarly, Dr. Baden told Bugliosi that all the Parkland doctors were wrong, essentially because their statements didn't agree with the autopsy photos and x-rays.[451]

In his autobiography, Billie Sol Estes stated that the alterations were to a Kennedy look-alike, and that the alterationist was James M. Liggett, a Dallas mortician. Estes says that Liggett was assigned to acquire a body that matched Kennedy, and to make sure that the body matched the first descriptions at Parkland. Liggett, according to Estes, performed surgery on a plane from Dallas to Washington; there were two bodies at Bethesda, and "at least ten pictures were taken of each body...The autopsy report and photographs were immediately sent to the White House," which controlled the evidence sent to the Warren Commission and the National Archives.[452]

Saundra Spencer was an E-6 photographer's mate first class who, in November 1963, was in charge of the White House photo lab, a small room in the Naval Photographic Center at Anacostia, Maryland. In a June 5, 1997, deposition to the ARRB, she stated that on the morning of November 24, a Secret Service agent gave her four or five color film holders that he wanted developed. He told her they were autopsy pictures from Bethesda. She said these photos were quite different from the official autopsy photos shown to her by Jeremy Gunn. The neck wound she saw was circular and about the size of a person's thumb and substantially smaller than the wound shown in the official autopsy photographs, and the head wound was a "large, gaping gash" in the center of the back of the head, about 2 to 2½ inches wide, three to four inches above the hairline. She processed the color autopsy film brought to her by Secret Service agent James Fox and Robert Knudsen.[453] She didn't identify a single one of the official autopsy photos as being among those she processed on November 23. She told the ARRB that when books on the assassination came out with autopsy pictures, "they were not the ones that I had worked on." One photo she saw showed a wound at the back of the head, "a hole, inch, two inches in diameter at the back of the skull ... where the brim of a hat would hit." She said the face was different, and *the eyes and the mouth were closed.* "Again, none of the heavy damage that shows in these photographs were [*sic*] visible in the photographs that we did." She said that the wound she saw in the back of the head wasn't in the photos she was shown. The photos showed measuring devices that she didn't recall. She told Gunn that there was "no similarity" between the photos she developed and the official autopsy photos in the current inventory. "[T]he only thing I can think of is that a second set of autopsy pictures was shot for public release if necessary."[454] She was being shown colored images, both transparencies and prints, which are in the National Archives. Mr. Bugliosi tucks this information away in his endnotes, rather than the book itself.[455] His response to Ms. Spencer's statements: "We know she's wrong," because her statements are out of line with the observations of the autopsy doctors and the official autopsy photos and x-rays.[456]

Parkland doctors Gene Akin, Fouad Bashour, Charles Baxter, Charles Crenshaw, Richard Dulany, Adolphe Giesecke, Robert Grossman, Jackie Hunt, Marion Jenkins, Ronald Jones, Robert Karnei, Robert McClelland, and Paul Peters, and Parkland nurses Margaret Henchliffe and Doris Nelson, all told Harrison Livingstone that the official photos of the back of the head were inaccurate or completely wrong.

Virtually all the Parkland doctors and nurses who described the fatal head wound said that it was about three inches in diameter, and roughly circular. Dr. Carrico stated, "I would estimate [it] to be about 5 to 7 cm in size, more or less circular, with avulsions [forcible separations] of the calvarium and scalp tissue."[457] The official autopsy photo of the back of the head, however, shows it to be completely intact. This is irrefutable evidence that the autopsy photos of the back of the head are phony.

The HSCA said the autopsy attendees saw what was depicted in the autopsy photos.[458] This statement is difficult to understand, given that the descriptions of the head wound given by the autopsy doctors don't match the autopsy photos!

Autopsy photographer Floyd Riebe told the ARRB on May 7, 1997, that the "right side in the back [of Kennedy's head] was gone; just a big gaping hole with fragments of scalp and bone hanging in it ... the occipital." Riebe told David Lifton in a taped interview described a "big hole" in the occipital region of the head. Riebe said he took several four-by-five shots of the head with its gaping hole, though Stringer didn't remember Riebe taking any pictures. FBI agent Francis O'Neill was at the back of Bethesda at around 7:05 p.m. He told the ARRB on September 12, 1997, that Kennedy's eyes were open, and there was a massive wound in the *back* of the head. FBI agent Sibert told the ARRB on September 11, 1997, "Well, there was a massive wound ... right back in this part of the head" (in the cowlick area).[459] Hidden away on page 245 of Mr. Bugliosi's endnotes is his observation that in 1981, the *Boston Globe* interviewed many of the Parkland doctors and nurses who saw the president's head wound, and reported that five doctors and three nurses said that the Ida Cox tracing of autopsy photograph number 42 "does not show the wound as they recall it," and that they "recalled seeing a large wound in the right rear of Kennedy's head." Ida Cox was the HSCA's medical illustrator. Her drawing of the head was based on the official photo of the back of the head, and shows a small circular hole in the cowlick area. The drawing was made under the direction of Dr. Michael Baden.[460] Dr. Mantik points out that no Parkland doctor recognized the official autopsy photo of the rear of the skull as authentic.[461]

When shown autopsy photos of Kennedy's skull by ARRB counsel Gunn, Sibert and O'Neill both stated that the photos disagreed with what they saw at the autopsy. Sibert stated, "I don't recall anything like this at all during the autopsy... the wound was much more pronounced."[462] They testified that JFK's fatal skull wound "looked nothing at all like the photographs that showed the backside of JFK's skull and scalp intact," and John Stringer told the ARRB that the photos of the brain in the official inventory are not those that he took at the time.[463] Stringer told Gunn that Captain Stover, commanding officer of the US Naval Medical School and Stringer's superior, ordered him to sign a document stating that all the photos he took were present in the official inventory, though Stringer knew that the statement was false.[464]

The supine "blank stare" autopsy photo (reproduced in Groden, p. 183, and Fetzer, 2000, p. 274) shows the right side of Kennedy's head completely intact, which is completely at odds with the Zapruder film, which shows the Blob escaping from a supposed wound in the president's right temple. FBI agent James Sibert told the ARRB that there was no damage to the president's head forward of the right ear. Apparently Mr. Bugliosi didn't notice any discrepancy there.

Bugliosi ridicules David Lifton's findings, but the fact that the alleged thirteen-centimeter-long wound on the upper right side of JFK's head, described by Dr. Humes et al., wasn't seen at Parkland supports Lifton's thesis that either the body was altered between Parkland and Bethesda, or the Bethesda doctors were not autopsying John Kennedy. The third option is that Humes was simply lying. Bugliosi also ridicules the idea put forth by Lifton regarding surgery on President Kennedy's head before his body reached Bethesda, calling Lifton's scenario "insane," though Bugliosi quotes from a report by Sibert and O'Neill that stated that there had been "surgery of the head area, namely in the top of the skull." The HSCA refers to that report, but states, "no surgery of the head area was known to have been performed."[465] In their ARRB interviews, Sibert and O'Neill insisted that Humes had asked about surgery to the head.[466] Bugliosi tells us that even before the ARRB hired Douglas P. Horne to be the board's chief analyst for military records, Horne already believed in Lifton's "crazy theory" that Kennedy's body was stolen and his wounds altered before his autopsy.[467]

Jerrol Custer has stated that the x-rays in evidence are not the ones he took that night, and he told reporter Sylvia Chase that he didn't see the wound depicted on the official x-rays. The lateral autopsy x-ray of Kennedy's skull, reproduced in Bugliosi's book and other publications, shows a large deficit in the right front of the skull that doesn't match where Dr. Humes said it was (or showed where it was, on videotape), nor does it match the wound that the Parkland doctors saw, though it "sort of" matches the doctored Zapruder film.

Dr. McClelland of Parkland Hospital also denied the authenticity of the x-rays. After he reviewed the set of autopsy x-rays at the National Archives in 1989, Dr. McClelland told the television program *Inside Edition* that the official x-rays don't show the same injuries to the president's head that he saw in the emergency room in 1963, and that those x-rays are even inconsistent with each other. "I don't understand that, unless there has been some attempt to cover up the nature of the wound."[468] Another anomaly: Dr. Mantik made his own detailed studies of the autopsy skull x-rays and found that they show virtually no brain tissue in a fist-size area at the front of the skull, just where the photographs show nearly intact brain.[469]

A 6.5 mm object, possibly but not necessarily metallic, was added to the frontal x-ray, and that object, being identical to the caliber of the Mannlicher-Carcano, was then used to tie Oswald to the assassination.[470] In a conversation with Dr. Mantik in December 1992, Dr. Ebersole told him that he did not see any big bullet fragments on the skull x-ray. Doctors Humes, Boswell and Finck denied seeing the 6.5 mm object at the autopsy, nor do any other Bethesda witnesses recall any discussion of such an object.[471] Questioned by Jeremy Gunn about a 6.5 mm fragment, Humes stated that he didn't remember anything of that size. Regarding that fragment, Dr. Boswell told Gunn that "we did not find one that large."[472] Dr. Mantik also discovered that the lateral cranial x-ray was fabricated by imposing a patch over the massive defect in the back of the head.[473] Dr. Ebersole told Dr. Mantik in December 1992 that "eyewitness evidence suggests that the x-rays were altered promptly after the assassination,"[474] and in 1993 Mantik found that the x-rays of Kennedy's head were composites.

22. The Doctored Zapruder Film

The Secret Service agent who couriered the (apparently) original Zapruder film to the CIA's National Photographic Interpretation Center in Suitland, Maryland, told the ARRB that "the film had been developed by Kodak at Rochester, NY., contrary to the existing documentary record, which indicates that the film and three copies were processed in Dallas, TX, instead." The NPIC was created by President Eisenhower in the 1950s, as a sub-element of the CIA, and is one of the most sophisticated photo laboratories in the world. In a telephone interview with the ARRB's Dave Montague and Douglas Horne, Homer McMahon, manager of the NPIC color lab, stated that the Zapruder film was developed at Kodak headquarters (Hawkeye Works) in Rochester, New York, and that he was sure that "we had the original film." The ARRB found that the film was delivered from Hawkeye Works to Kodak's research and development laboratory by a Secret Service courier. McMahon stated in a telephone interview that a Secret Service agent whom he identified as "Bill Smith" delivered the film to him at the NPIC.[475] Smith said that he picked up the film from Zapruder, had it flown to Rochester, New York, for developing, then couriered it to Washington for NPIC analysis. But Bugliosi says it was "well established that the original film was developed at Kodak *in Dallas,* not Rochester, and that two copies were given to Secret Service agent Forrest V. Sorrels in Dallas, one of which ... made its way to the NPIC for analysis."[476]

On the evening of November 24, Bill Smith arrived at the NPIC with a second version of the film. Smith told McMahon that the subject matter was to be treated "above top secret" and said that not even his supervisor was allowed to participate or even to know what he had worked on. McMahon and Morgan Bennett "Ben" Hunter were brought in to handle the altered film (Dino Brugioni, chief of information at NPIC, wasn't notified). When interviewed by ARRB staff on June 17, 1997, Ben Hunter recalled that a Captain Sands delivered the Zapruder film to him and McMahon. Capt. Sands also directed that Hunter and McMahon not talk about their work with anyone, not even anyone else at NPIC.[477] Hunter told Douglas Horne on June 26, 1997, that he believed that Capt. Sands was a high-ranking employee in the NPIC's management structure.[478] In an interview with the ARRB later in 1997 (on August 14), McMahon recalled that Capt. Sands was a Navy captain who was one of the duty officers at the NPIC. At the same meeting, Hunter said he didn't recall the name "Bill Smith," but he did recall that a Secret Service agent delivered the film to the NPIC, and it was a Secret Service agent who told him not to discuss the work with anyone.[479] McMahon's opinion was that President Kennedy was shot six to eight times from at least three directions, but Secret Service man Smith's opinion was that there were three shots from the Book Depository.[480] Hunter and McMahon told the ARRB that "about eight shots" were fired at the limousine. Interviewed by Janney in 2011, Brugioni stated, on being shown the one and only frame showing the fatal head shot, that one or more frames were missing that would have shown the spray (of blood, and skull and brain tissue, presumably) shooting up three or four feet above the president's head.[481]

In 1997, McMahon and Hunter told the ARRB that they received, worked on and analyzed the Zapruder film, but that they only did enlargement (forty times original size) of selected still frames. Hunter stated that the NPIC didn't have the capability to reproduce the film as a motion picture.[482] Bugliosi insists that the original film was never out of the physical possession of Zapruder and *Life* magazine "during the period when the alteration supposedly took place."[483]

According to Dino Brugioni, the film went to Chicago, and was then brought to Washington, D.C., at 10 p.m. on Saturday, November 23, by two Secret Service agents; they had just gotten off an airplane. Brugioni believed that this was the original film. He prepared briefing boards. The film showed up again at his building late Sunday night, well after dark (Brugioni wasn't shown the film). A new work crew was called in; they also made briefing boards. Horne says this was the altered film. The prints from the second event, of which Homer McMahon was in charge, are identical to the film we know today. The Secret Service men who brought it to him said it was developed at Hawkeye Works. The Secret Service agents left NPIC at 3:00 a.m. on November 24 and clearly went to Hawkeye. Horne calculated that there was a period of twelve to fourteen hours to work on the film. It probably came back at nine or ten p.m. on Sunday night, after which the second event took place.

CIA item 450, released under the Freedom of Information Act, is a group of documents that indicate that the Zapruder film was at the NPIC possibly on the evening of November 22, 1963, and certainly within days of the assassination. Pincher and Schaeffer concluded that the crucial editing of the film was performed within an approximate five-hour time period between the assassination itself and the debut of the film to the news media the following morning in Zapruder's dress shop. They calculated that the film arrived at Andrews AFB about 9:30 p.m. EST and was in the hands of the NPIC not long after 10:00 EST. This calculation coincides with David Lifton's report that the film was in the possession of the CIA on the evening of November 22.[484]

When Lifton viewed a high-quality copy of the film in Time-Life's Los Angeles office, he noticed that the rear of JFK's head appeared to have been blacked out; he also noticed splices in the film.[485] Page 44 of *Life* magazine's October 2, 1964, issue is a full-page photograph showing Kennedy's occipital blacked out. Bugliosi refers to David Lifton's claim that the conspirators blacked out the back of the president's head to conceal the large exit wound, and painted on what looked like a large exit wound to the right front of the head, as an "absolutely incredible allegation."[486] But a close look at the relevant frames of the film supports Lifton: there is a blacked-out area at the back of the head that appears on the same frames as the Blob. A close look at the film indicates that the blacking out is perhaps most obvious at frame 328. (Mr. Zapruder was not called to testify to the full commission; he testified only to Arlen Specter.) How the Blob could have been and probably was added to the film and the real fatal head wound blacked out are described in Harrison Livingstone's *Killing Kennedy and the Hoax of the Century*, pages 160-62. Mrs. Connally heard Jacqueline Kennedy say, "They have killed my husband. I have his brains in my hand."[487] The film, however, shows the *right* side of Kennedy's head being blown out. If that happened, how could she have her husband's brains in her hand, since she was sitting on his left?

The Zapruder film, says Mr. Bugliosi, "proves conclusively, and beyond all doubt, where the exit wound was ... the large, gaping exit wound was to the *right front* of the president's head. *The back of his head shows no such large wound and clearly is completely intact*."[488] Mr. Bugliosi doesn't attempt to explain why the frames he references (Z313 and Z328) show an obviously blacked-out area at the back of the president's head (exactly where the Parkland medical and nursing staff saw a large, gaping wound), or why no fragments of skull escape from this alleged wound, or why the official autopsy photographs show no wound in the side of the head, or why, if the wound was in the right side of the head, the trunk of the limousine is covered with fragments of Kennedy's skull and brain.

Bugliosi references a 1976 Itek Corporation analysis of one Zapruder frame (313) which states that "the explosion of the bullet impact radiated matter in all directions." He also quotes Cecil Kirk, his photo expert at the London trial, saying the brain tissue was launched high and "*all* to the front" of the president's body, and the cops drove into it.[489] At eleven or twelve miles an hour? Hardly. (Mr. Kirk was also a member of the HSCA photographic panel.) The film doesn't show any brain matter moving in a forward direction, much less in "all directions." And since the Zapruder film has had frames removed, analyzing a single frame is not going to be particularly revealing. Bugliosi's problem is that he ignores eyewitness testimony and the observations of the Parkland doctors and nurses, and instead considers the Zapruder film, the autopsy and the Warren Report itself to be absolutely accurate and unquestionable Revealed Truth.

The Zapruder film has been used to support many of the conclusions of the Warren Report. The film, however, has been extensively reworked and cannot be considered to be an accurate record of the assassination. Fetzer states, correctly, that the Zapruder film "has been extensively edited using highly sophisticated techniques."[490] The available evidence indicates that the film was reworked at the National Photo Interpretation Center. Here is a summary of some of the main problems with the film:

1. Several frames have been cut out near the beginning of the film. Mr. Zapruder told CBS News that he started filming when the President's limousine turned onto Elm Street; an FBI document also states that Zapruder "stated that he first picked up the motorcade as it made the turn on to Elm Street from Houston Street."[491] Similarly, after CBS' Dan Rather watched what was apparently an earlier version of the film on the day after the assassination, he described seeing the car turning from Houston Street onto Elm Street. The current version of the film, however, shows some of the motorcade's advance motorcycles turning left onto Elm street, after which the limousine suddenly appears on Elm Street (at Z-133), roughly even with the west end of the Book Depository. The purpose of splicing the film at that point was probably to ensure that there was no photographic record of the sharp turn onto Elm Street, a turn that was in violation of Secret Service procedures.

2. Frames 155 and 156 are missing, according to Model and Groden, *JFK: The Case for Conspiracy*, page 141, and Fetzer, *Assassination Science*, page 344. In viewing the enhanced version of the film, "Image of an Assassination," I noticed that the film jumps at this point (around Z-160), indicating a splice and the removal (or addition) of frames.

3. The film jumps again at about frame 190, just as the President's car is going behind the Stemmons Freeway sign, indicating another splice. Dr. Mantik noted that from Z-194 to Z-195, the motorcade occupants appear unchanged, but both the background and foreground are very fuzzy in Z-195 – "quite different from Z-194." He said the most likely explanation is that these frames are composites.[492]

4. Daryll Weatherly found that in the frames from 196 to 206, the vehicles and occupants are blurred in the odd-numbered frames, but the even-numbered frames have, "for the most part, sharp images of the motorcade figures ... I am convinced that the sequence of frames from 194 to 207 contains some composite scenes, and that the corresponding frames of the original Zapruder film were both different in their content and greater in number."[493]

5. Harold Weisberg pointed out shortly after the Warren Report was published that frames 208-211 were missing from the sequence published in Volume 18 of the Hearings and Exhibits, and that published frames 207 and 212 had visible splices running through them.[494] These were apparently the frames damaged by *Life* magazine. *Life* asserted that frames 208-

212, capturing the time interval during which *Life* said that JFK had turned to face the Depository, had inadvertently been destroyed while in the magazine's possession, necessitating a splice at that juncture.[495] Calvin McCamy was a physicist and a member of the HSCA's photographic evidence panel. At one point in his questioning by HSCA counsel Michael Goldsmith, Goldsmith told McCamy that the original Zapruder film was missing four frames (208 through 211), and that they were spliced out when Time-Life had possession of the film. McCamy stated that Robert Groden obtained the missing frames.[496]

6. In Z-212, the posts on the Stemmons Freeway sign are blurred, but holes in the masonry wall in the background are not. Model and Groden noted that on the top half of that frame, there is a tree on the right, but on the bottom half, the tree is in the middle.[497] And in some frames, the white spot on the grass behind the limousine is two to three times wider than it should be.

7. When I viewed the enhanced version of the film, I noticed that the film jumps at about frame 215, and the limousine seems to lurch forward as the car is emerging from behind the freeway sign. This would indicate that there is a splice at this point, and frames have been removed.

8. In Z-295 through Z-304, the limousine suddenly slows from 12 to 8 mph, a deceleration of about .37g, and yet the car's occupants don't seem to be affected by this. This half-second slowing could be a remnant of what was originally a much longer, more noticeable deceleration. This, along with the fact that the blurring in 302 does not appear in 303, shows that the car was stopped or nearly stopped in 303, and that a block of frames was removed between 302 and 303. Dr. Roderick Ryan, a leading technical expert on motion picture film, also believes the film shows the limo moving in Z-302, but standing still in Z-303. He says the limousine could not have decelerated from 11 mph to a complete stop in one-eighteenth of a second. Daryll Weatherly noted similar anomalies in the sequence 308 to 311. Weatherly stated, "I think a number of frames have been removed from the fatal shot sequence."[498]

9. Several people seem to move faster than is humanly possible from frame to frame; for example, Hugh Betzner's movements in frames 144-153, the too-rapid shifting of feet of a woman who is the thirteenth person east of the Stemmons sign in frames 153-155, Linda Willis' movements in frames 155-161, Linda and Rosemary Willis' movements in frames 161-180, the changes in position of Charles Brehm's son in frames 277-286 (the lad emerges from behind his father in .55 seconds [ten frames

at 18.3 frames per second]), and Gov. Connally's turning in frames 312-321. Limousine driver Will Greer looks back at Connally and Kennedy, and then to the front, in two frames (Z-291 and Z-292), which computes to one-tenth of a second, and yet his head is not blurred. The speed of the head turn alone is humanly impossible.[499] Other anomalies noticed by various researchers include the movement of Jacqueline Kennedy's right arm between frames 327 and 328, JFK's head motions in frames 321-336, and the movement of Malcolm Summers' left leg between frames 353 and 355 (Summers' left leg goes from being extended in Z-353 to being bent backward in Z-354, one-eighteen of a second later. But in Z356, the left foot seems to be on the ground). All of these anomalies indicate excised frames.[500]

10. Many people saw the limousine stop just before or just after the fatal head shot, as discussed above under Behavior of the Secret Service. The official version of the Zapruder film shows the car moving at a fairly constant speed; the limousine stop has been edited out of the film. As stated above, Mr. Bugliosi is certain that the limousine does not come to a partial or full stop just before the head shot because this is not in the film; but he also concedes that some forty-eight eyewitnesses said it did.[501]

11. The lower right rear of JFK's head was blown away by the fatal shot; this is what all of the Dallas witnesses both in Dealey Plaza and at Parkland hospital said they saw. But the Zapruder film shows only the *right* side of his head, in front of the ear, puffing out (supposedly from the impact of a bullet). The wound shown in the film is just above and to the front of the President's ear. But *there was no wound in this area; no one in Dallas saw a wound there*; Dr. Paul Peters (one of the Parkland Hospital doctors), when shown color blowups made from the Zapruder film frames depicting the fatal shot, wrote in a letter to Wallace Milam dated April 14, 1980, "The wound you marked… I never saw and I don't think there was such a wound."

When the fatal shot hits JFK, the film shows a bubble of tissue (which has become known as the Blob) at the right side of his head, above the ear.' The Blob, by my count, lasts from Z-318 to Z-370, nearly three full seconds; it's still there, bouncing around in front of Kennedy's ear, when his torso has slumped to the left and his head is nearly horizontal, and it is still there as Jacqueline Kennedy is starting to climb out onto the trunk of the limousine. This is nonsensical; it defies the laws of physics and gravity (and human anatomy). This is proof that what is shown on the film is anatomically impossible, and that the Blob was painted in or otherwise added artificially. Livingstone asserted that "there is no medical or physical way to explain what is seen in the film other than to postulate that the Blob is drawn onto the film to make it appear that a shot from behind has removed part of his face."[502]

But Bugliosi found Richard W. Burgess of the Department of Classical Studies at the University of Ottawa who said it would be difficult, if not impossible, to create the Blob and make it look credible. He said, according to Bugliosi, that "it would have been impossible for anyone to have been able to maintain perfect registration of the wound on the head. Without perfect registration the wound would move around on the head, as if it weren't attached."[503] Except that it *does* move around somewhat on the head. Difficult or impossible as it may be, the Blob is nevertheless fake, and has been artificially added. How do we know this? Let me count the ways: First, the number of frames, and therefore the amount of time during which the Blob rolls around on Kennedy's head. Second, no bone (skull) tissue escapes from the make-believe wound; the brain is fairly firm and wouldn't puff out of a small opening (it must have been small, since no bone blows out) like a red water balloon. (Apparently the forgers wanted us to believe that there was no skull in that part of JFK's head.) Third, we know from Parkland doctors and nurses that the fatal wound was in the *back* of the President's head. Even the autopsy doctors said the wound was in the temporal-parietal area, not in the temporal-sphenoid area, which the Zapruder film seems to show. Fourth, a bullet entering the back of the president's head, or anyone else's head, wouldn't execute a right turn and exit the side, obviously. Fifth, the "blank stare" autopsy photo, showing the supine president, shows that part of his head completely intact, though it is doubtful that the corpse in the photo is John Kennedy. After viewing slides of the film at the National Archives on June 23, 1994, Dr. Mantik became convinced that the Blob is "an unnatural add-on to the film." Furthermore, those who take a careful look at the Zapruder film will notice, at frames Z-272 through Z-317, a tennis ball-size red "tumor" growing on the president's lower right cheek just before the fatal head shot. (An enlarged Z-frame showing this tumor can be seen on the cover of Galanor's book and in various places in Groden's book.) This could well be where some of the photographic people at the NPIC spilled some of the fluid they intended to use to create the Blob. Roderick Ryan told Twyman, "it looks as if the blobs have been painted in."[504]

The film shows the cranial tissue on the trunk of the car, which is what Mrs. Kennedy is trying to gather up. There would obviously be no such debris on the trunk if debris were ejected from the *right* side of JFK's head, nor would that amount of debris have resulted from the "official" tiny hole in the back of the head that Dr. Humes' autopsy report and the Warren Report describe. Navy autopsy photographer Saundra Spencer saw photos taken shortly after the autopsy. She remembered no damage to the right side of Kennedy's head.[505] Bugliosi evidently didn't see any inconsistency between the Blob on the side of the president's head, apparently showing an exit wound there, and Mrs. Kennedy crawling onto the trunk of the limousine to retrieve pieces of her husband's brain and skull, indicating such ejecta going in that direction, the exact *opposite* of the exit wound shown in the (doctored) film.

12. Abraham Zapruder's business partner Erwin Schwartz says that he viewed the film several times during the weekend after the hit, and he "insists that he saw blood and brains come out the back of JFK's head."[506] Dealey Plaza surveyor Chester Breneman, who assisted *Life* magazine and the Secret Service with motorcade reconstructions and had been furnished color enlargements of all Z-frames to work from, wrote in a letter that on three frames after a frontal entry shot, "we saw blobs leaving the back of the President's head and disappearing on the fourth frame"; the large blobs of blood and brain matter were "flying from Kennedy's head to the *rear* of the car."[507] These blobs cannot now be seen on the Zapruder film. Mr. Breneman also noted that all the frame numbers had been changed.[508]

13. Newcomb and Adams noted that the bloody halo appears for only one frame (frame 313); they stated that the halo "was manufactured on the film in the area around the President's head in frame 313."[509]

14. Noel Twyman found that from Z-315 to Z-317, driver Will Greer's head turns about 105 degrees in one frame, or one-eighteenth of a second, which is humanly impossible.[510] Greer is seen reacting to Gov. Connally being hit, so that he, Greer, would know when to bring the limousine to a stop to facilitate the final, fatal shot to Kennedy, which arrives at about frame 317.

15. Twyman also discovered that frame 317 was misnumbered; what is numbered as frame 317 is actually frame 308.

16. In the photo taken by Altgens, motorcycle officer Chaney seems to be abreast of the limo, looking directly into the face of JFK; no Zapruder slide can be found that shows this.[511]

17. The film jumps again at about frames 375-385, indicating another splice.

18. One researcher claimed that when the limousine passes behind the lamppost, first Connally and then Kennedy can be seen through the

lamppost. (This is in the Kurtis A&E film.) Weatherly explains that "the film was stretch-framed by taking parts of one frame and combining it [*sic*] with part of another to make a slow-motion film. We don't see this in the slides in the Archives ..."[512]

19. Michael Parks discovered that some of the frames have been reversed (e.g., Z-331 and Z-332) and that others have been removed (Z-341 and Z-350).[513]

20. Dr. Mantik reports that in his ARRB deposition, government photographer Joseph O'Donnell "recalled showing the Zapruder film to Jackie Kennedy, who said that she never wanted to see it again. O'Donnell interpreted this to mean that he was to remove the headshot images," so he removed about ten feet of the film! O'Donnell told the ARRB about a very obvious halo around Kennedy's head after the fatal head shot that he no longer sees in the film.[514]

21. A 2010 article by Alen J. Salerian entitled "President Kennedy's death: A poison arrow-assisted homicide" at elsevier.com makes the following points (among others) about the film: Frames 223 and 230 show Governor Connally turning 180 degrees sideways in less than four-tenths of a second (at 18 frames per second). "Frames 344-354 violate physical laws where a man slowly falls down from mid air to a squatting position ... These frames are consistent with the reversal of the frames."

Mr. Zapruder himself was reportedly "troubled by several things he distinctly remembered seeing no longer being in the film, such as certain movements by Kennedy and Connally he could not find."[515]

Dr. Mantik tells us that William Reymond, Rich Della Rosa and Scott Myers all claimed to have seen a Zapruder film that is different from the extant one. Reymond and Myers both described specific motorcade events that are not seen in the extant film, such as the 120-degree turn from Houston onto Elm.[516]

Bugliosi asks: "How would the conspirators know they only had to secure Zapruder's film and didn't have to seize the films of these other people?"[517] In his endnotes, from information taken from an HSCA document, he gives the names of 13 people (and an unnamed woman in a blue dress), in addition to Mr. Zapruder, who took motion picture film "at or around the time of the shooting," and another 15 people (plus the "Babushka Lady") who were taking still photos at that time.[518] One wonders if Mr. Bugliosi noticed that of the 13 people who took motion picture film, only *two* – Malcolm Couch and James Underwood – testified to the commission; or of the 15 named people who took still photographs, only *three* – James Altgens, Thomas Dillard and Phillip Willis – testified. One also wonders why most of these films and still photographs have never seen the light of day. And here again, Mr. Bugliosi is bending the truth a bit. Neither Couch nor Underwood filmed the assassination. Mr. Couch told the commission that he picked up his camera and took motion picture film *after* the final shot, when he photographed some people on his left and right; he then ran back up Elm Street to the Book Depository and took "some sweeping pictures of the crowd standing around."[519] Mr. Underwood, a *Dallas Morning News* photographer, told the commission that just before the car he was riding in reached the corner of Elm and Houston, something in his camera broke. He got ahold of a camera from a colleague *after* the shooting and took "some films," apparently around the grassy knoll area.[520] Mr. Dillard testified that he took photographs of the fifth and sixth floor windows on the east end of the Depository in reaction to hearing Robert Jackson exclaiming, "There's a rifle up there!" When asked by Joseph Ball if he saw anything in those windows, Dillard stated that other than two men in windows below the "sniper's nest" window, he saw nothing.[521]

Mr. Bugliosi scoffs at the idea that frames are missing from the Zapruder film, and says that there is "no rhyme or reason" to allegations that the film has been altered.[522] In fact, Bugliosi says the conspirators couldn't have altered the film, because they would also have to alter all the other films that were taken in Dealey Plaza that day. For Mr. Bugliosi, this is "proof" that the Zapruder film was not altered – another display of twisted logic. Actually, they would only have to confiscate and/or alter the films that contradicted the Official Story. If they did not do that, it was probably because those other films didn't show a clear refutation of the single-bullet theory, as the Zapruder film would have if it hadn't been altered. And several of them *were* confiscated. The "Babushka Lady" to whom Bugliosi refers is probably Beverly Oliver; he did not include her name among those who filmed the assassination. (Ms. Oliver did not testify to the commission or its legal staff.) According to Robert Groden, two men went to see Ms. Oliver at the Colony Club where she worked, and confiscated her film of the assassination. In a "photo line-up," she identified a photograph of FBI agent Regis Kennedy as being the person who confiscated her camera and film the day after the assassination. She never saw her film again.[523] Mr. Bugliosi says that if there were one thing that the conspirators would have altered, they would have altered it to make it look like Kennedy's head had been violently thrust forward. But they couldn't change the direction of Kennedy's head movement in the Zapruder film because that would have shown his head going from a slumped-down position next to Jackie's shoulder to a more erect position, which would have looked too unnatural. Bugliosi mentions "the gruesome frame showing the president's head exploding in blood and brain tissue."[524] In fact, this cloud of exploding tissue continued for several more frames.

Dino Brugioni was the NPIC duty officer on Saturday, November 23, and Sunday, November 24. Brugioni said he saw a completely different head explosion from the now-current film.[525] Brugioni saw portions of Kennedy's skull "fly into the air" on the film's first showing. He saw brain matter exploding above the president's head to a height of three or four feet. He saw more than just one frame (313) with the mist above Kennedy's head; he said that the bloody mist above the president's head went on for several frames, and that he couldn't imagine that it would only appear on one frame. He also said that he never saw the same Zapruder film after that day, and that the briefing boards (in the National Archives) are not the ones he assembled. The Secret Service wanted a list of everyone who was involved in the printing of the film, and Brugioni complied.

23. The Threats and Gag Orders

In addition to the threats and gag orders mentioned in previous sections, we have the following:

- Right after the shooting, Mrs. Jean Hill saw a man wearing a brown coat and a hat running from the scene; in her testimony she was not specific about where he ran, nor did her interrogator ask her specifically, but he was apparently running up the steps just east of the stockade fence on the grassy knoll. She testified that an FBI or Secret Service man told her not to mention the running man she saw.[526]

- As noted above in the discussion of the shot at Gen. Walker, eyewitness Walter Coleman stated that he had been told not to talk to "unspecified officials."[527]

- Federal agents took Dealey Plaza witness Howard Brennan away for about three weeks and evidently scared the hell out of him. Sandy Speaker, Brennan's supervisor, was also threatened into silence.

- Book Depository superintendent Roy Truly was threatened by federal authorities and remained fearful until his death.[528]

• Dr. Humes told Charles Kramer, an attorney, that he was not permitted to discuss the autopsy.[529] At the 1969 Shaw trial, Dr. Finck stated that Admiral Kenney, who happened to be Surgeon General of the Navy, "told us not to discuss the case without coordination with the Attorney General [Robert Kennedy]."[530] When Dr. Finck was asked on the second day of his testimony for the name of the person who said the people in the morgue were not to discuss the autopsy findings, he replied, "Well, there were several people in charge, there were several Admirals," and he again gave the name of Admiral Kenney.[531]

• Mark Lane reported in an interview that Dr. Perry told a *Newsweek* magazine reporter that he was "not permitted to discuss the case. I'm only permitted to say the wound in the throat is an exit wound..."[532] In an interview on YouTube, Dr. McClelland related that someone approached Dr. Perry and told him that he "shouldn't say anything, to keep his mouth shut." When the ARRB interviewed Parkland nurse Audrey Bell, operating room nurse supervisor, she said that Dr. Perry complained to her the day after the assassination that people from Bethesda had been badgering him on the phone all night long, pressuring him to change his opinion about the throat wound from one of entry to one of exit.[533]

• A Letter of Silence was issued to all Navy participants in the autopsy immediately after the funeral. They were threatened with court martial if they even discussed the events of the autopsy with anyone. The letter was delivered to each of them in a threatening manner by Captain Stover.[534] According to Larry Hancock, Capt. Stover received the autopsy gag order from Admiral Burkley, on orders from the White House.[535]

• Wilma Tice said she saw Jack Ruby at Parkland Hospital; he was standing three feet to her side. Apparently in order to conceal the fact that Ruby was a key player in the murder plot, the commissioners wanted to quash the idea that Ruby was at Parkland, so the Warren Report stated that Ms. Tice had only "an obstructed view" of the man she later identified as Ruby; but in her commission testimony she said that at one point Ruby "was facing toward me."[536] In an FBI interview with Ms. Tice on July 22, 1964, she stated that two days previously, she had received an anonymous phone call warning her to keep her mouth shut.[537] How could the caller possibly have known that she was about to be interviewed by the FBI unless he was tied in with the commission – or the FBI? Seth Kantor was also adamant that he saw Ruby at Parkland. The commission as a whole decided not to believe Kantor, but in a statement dated May 2, 1977, commission assistant counsel Burt Griffin, who had interviewed Ms. Tice in Dallas two days after her FBI interview, informed Kantor that he believed Kantor's story that he saw Ruby at the hospital.[538]

• Two FBI agents came to the home of Dealey Plaza witness Richard Carr and told him that he wasn't a witness to the assassination unless he saw Lee Oswald at a window in the Book Depository; they also warned him to keep his mouth shut. A dozen Dallas policemen later came with a search warrant and ransacked his home while holding him and his wife at gunpoint. After moving to Montana he found three sticks of dynamite wired to his car, and was shot at on another occasion. He was attacked and stabbed after testifying at the Shaw trial in New Orleans.[539]

• As stated above, A.J. Millican signed an affidavit stating that he heard a total of nine shots, five of which were from the area of the colonnade. In late 1963 or early 1964, someone called him and threatened his life and those of his wife and sister.[540]

• Carl Renas, head of security for the Dearborn Division of the Ford Motor Company, drove the presidential limousine from Washington to Cincinnati. He noticed several bullet holes, including the one on the windshield's chrome molding strip, which he said was a "primary strike." The Secret Service told Renas to "Keep your mouth shut."[541]

• Mark Lane told the commission that he had spoken to a Dallas newspaper reporter who sought to question more than 150 people in the area, but "many of them told him that the FBI or the Secret Service ordered them not to talk." (It was "one of the reporters I referred to earlier.")[542] When Lane tried to interview Dean Andrews, a New Orleans attorney who had links to David Ferrie and Carlos Marcello, he told Lane that "Washington, D.C." had told him that he couldn't talk with Lane about "this." Andrews said that he was told that he would end up with a bullet in his head.[543]

• Helen Markham told Mark Lane that she had been told by the FBI, Secret Service agents and Dallas police not to discuss anything in relation to the case.[544]

• Bill Beckman, a Fort Worth photographer who went to Dallas to get a photograph of Billy Lovelady (to determine whether it was he or Oswald who was photographed in front of the Book Depository), was arrested by the Dallas police without other cause, questioned extensively and, according to the *Herald Tribune*, advised to leave the city. He left Dallas without the photograph.[545]

. Tippit murder eyewitness Acquilla Clemons was not asked to submit an affidavit or other statement to the commission, nor was she called to testify; according to Groden, men from the FBI and Dallas police came to her house and told her to keep her mouth shut.[546] In an interview with Dorothy Kilgallen, Ms. Clemons stated, "I'm not supposed to be talking to anybody, might get killed on the way to work."[547]

• Dealey Plaza eyewitness Jim Hicks told the Orleans Parish Grand Jury in 1968 that around 1:00 a.m. on the night before his Grand Jury testimony, he was awakened in his hotel room by two "colored" men who proceeded to push him through a plate glass window onto a patio on the sixth floor of the hotel. He also stated that he received eight or ten "crank calls" at his home, and someone told him that he had "better shut up or things will happen to your family."[548] (Hicks did not testify to the Warren Commission or its legal staff.)

This is also of interest here: Secret Service agent Roger Warner's November 24, 1963, interview of Karen Carlin, one of Jack Ruby's exotic dancers, included the following: "At the beginning of the interview Mrs. Carlin was highly agitated and was reluctant to make any statement to me. She stated to me that she was under the impression that Lee Harvey Oswald, Jack Ruby and other individuals unknown to her, were involved in a plot to assassinate President Kennedy and that she would be killed if she gave any information to the authorities."

It should be so obvious as to hardly need stating that all the bullying, threats, gag orders, etc., involving key witnesses in the case would not have been necessary if the assassination merely involved a single 'lone nut' assassin.

24. Alteration of Surveyor Figures

Both Robert Groden and Jim Marrs noted that two Texas surveyors, Bob West and Chester Breneman, hired by the Warren Commission to conduct a reenactment of the assassination in Dealey Plaza for the Secret Service and the FBI in 1964, and later to measure Dealey Plaza and the distances to the Book Depository, have said that their distance and elevation numbers were altered when published by the Warren Commission.[549] This seems to be another indication that the commission, or at least those who drafted its Report, were part of the conspiracy.

25. Treatment of Jean Hill

Shortly before Christmas 1963, the FBI started a 24-hour-a-day surveillance of Mrs. Hill, following her virtually each time she left her home. This surveillance, which the Bureau always claimed was for her protection, continued until the spring of 1965. On March 24, 1964, Arlen Specter interviewed Mrs. Hill, on behalf of the Warren Commission, at Parkland Memorial Hospital. But instead of simply asking her what she saw and heard, he bullied, threatened and insulted her. He taunted her about what she had reported seeing in Dealey Plaza, and warned her of "dire consequences" if she persisted in "this kind of behavior." She clearly recalls Specter telling her frostily that he knew all about her. She says that he accused her of "engaging in a 'shabby extramarital affair,' thirsting for publicity and notoriety, refusing to cooperate with federal authorities, and proving herself 'totally unreliable' as a witness." Unless the commission received her full cooperation from now on, she remembers him telling her, she would be "very, very sorry." Seized by repeated fits of anger, Specter at one point accused Mrs. Hill of "talking insanity." He told her that once the stenographer began to record the interview, she would be expected to give "proper answers."[550]

In early May of 1964, according to the Sloan and Hill book *JFK: The Last Dissenting Witness,* Mrs. Hill discovered that her three cameras had been taken from her bedroom closet; they mysteriously reappeared (sans film) a few days later. There were no signs of forced entry. Sometime between late 1964 and mid-1965, she was driving to a shopping center with her 11-year-old daughter in her nearly-new Plymouth Barracuda when she found that she couldn't steer the car. She crashed into a tree, but neither lady was injured. A subsequent inspection of the car indicated that someone had removed the nuts on the car's tie-rods, so that the bolts would fall out at some unknown point. In late fall of 1965, her friend "J.B. Marshall" found a clean, fresh cut in a line carrying brake fluid from the master cylinder to one of the front wheel cylinders in Mrs. Hill's car.[551]

26. Treatment of James Tague

James Tague went back to Dealey Plaza in May 1964 and took some pictures, with a motion picture camera, of the area where he had been standing at the time of the shooting. When Tague testified to the commission on July 23, 1964, commission assistant counsel Wesley Liebeler stated, "I understand that you went back subsequently and took some pictures of the area [Dealey Plaza]."

Tague: Yes; about a month ago.

Liebeler: With a motion picture camera?

Tague: Yes; I didn't know anybody knew about that.[552]

Tague had made his return visit alone and hadn't announced anything about it beforehand. He quickly drew the conclusion that the FBI must have been following him, otherwise Liebeler could not have known about this. Either the commission (or its agents) had Dealey Plaza under surveillance or they had Mr. Tague under surveillance. Tague says that he learned later that he was followed by the FBI for about eight months. In his memoir *Truth Withheld,* Tague noted that a piece of film he took in Dealey Plaza disappeared from his home.[553]

27. The Phony Warren Report

The clearest indication that the Warren Report is phony is, of course, that it concluded that Lee Oswald, from his perch in the "sniper's nest" on the sixth floor of the Book Depository, shot and killed President Kennedy. Nevertheless, Mr. Bugliosi tells us that the official investigations of the assassination were "well done."[554] The many shortcomings of the Warren Commission and its Report have been discussed in the present work and in numerous books by people like Harold Weisberg, Mark Lane, Sylvia Meagher, Robert Groden, Jim Marrs, Harrison Livingstone, Walt Brown, and several others. Mr. Bugliosi gives scant mention to Ms. Meagher's book, *Accessories After the Fact,* which systematically enumerates many of the shortcomings not only of the Warren Report but of the Dallas police and other authorities in the drama – the distortions, twisted logic, omissions, altered witness testimony, witnesses being verbally bullied into changing their testimony, generation of the ridiculous single-bullet theory, the failure even to consider other suspects in the shooting the failure to call important Dealey Plaza, Parkland Hospital, Bethesda Naval Hospital and other key witnesses (many of which have been noted in the present work) to testify, and so forth. Among other appalling omissions, the fact that Douglas Jackson and James Chaney, the two motorcycle policeman who were riding at the right rear of the presidential limousine, were not interviewed was inexcusable.

Mr. Bugliosi stresses that the esteemed commissioners and their staff counsel listened patiently and attentively to those who testified before them. Yes, they did – and then they *changed the testimony* of several people who testified, and occasionally cut people off when their testimony was heading into uncomfortable areas. Mr. Bugliosi doesn't mention this. Harold Norman disavowed some of the reports in his commission testimony.[555] When Norman started to testify about people he saw running toward the railroad tracks, Joseph Ball cut him off.[556] Lee Bowers was cut off mid-sentence by Ball when he started talking about "something out of the ordinary" that occurred behind the stockade fence during the shooting.[557] Sam Holland told Mark Lane that the commission changed his testimony. Lane told the commission that bus driver Cecil McWatters had indicated that the story in his affidavit was not true.[558] The commission omitted paragraphs of an FBI report that described Jack Ruby's connection to Dallas Mafia boss Joseph Civello. The three paragraphs were omitted from CE1536 (23H27; it contains no mention of Civello). The Warren Report states that Tippit murder scene witness Domingo Benavides was about 25 feet away from the Tippit murder scene; according to his testimony, he was only 15 feet away.[559] Roger Craig, Jean Hill, L.J. Lewis, and Abraham Zapruder also told researchers that their recorded testimony didn't match what they actually said when they testified. The commission's scribes deleted Jacqueline Kennedy's detailed description of her husband's fatal head wound. The deleted words were: "I was trying to hold his hair on. But from the front there was nothing. I suppose there must have been, but from the back you could see, you know, you were trying to hold his hair on, and his skull on."[560]

One of a number of absurdities in the Report: It tells us that Oswald "purchased his weapons under the name of Hidell in attempt to prevent their ownership from being traced."[561] Why, then, would he (supposedly) have his picture taken displaying those weapons? And why did he supposedly have them shipped to his own post office box?

Bugliosi says that the test conducted in a re-enactment of the assassination "confirmed the theory of Specter, Redlich, and other assistant counsels that the alignment of Kennedy's and Connally's bodies to each other in the presidential limousine was such that the bullet that struck Kennedy in his upper right back and exited his throat would have had to go on to hit Connally." And yet Bugliosi acknowledges that Connally had already testified in April 1964 that he was sure that he was *not* struck by the same bullet that struck Kennedy.[562] And did the Magic Bullet not enter the base of the back of the neck, rather than the upper right back?

As Harold Weisberg noted, the Warren Commission and Warren Report "both ignored or suppressed what was opposed to the predetermined conclusion that Oswald alone was the assassin." Sylvia Meagher, in her chapter on the Tippit murder, noted the propensity of the commission "first, to discount information inimical to the thesis that Oswald was the lone assassin, and, second, to proclaim that such information does not even exist."[563] The commission ignored all witnesses who heard shots from the right front, and ignored the testimony of people, including the Parkland doctors, who told them that President Kennedy had a single, massive wound at the back of his head and concluded that he was instead hit by a bullet that made a small entry in the upper back of his head (and another bullet whose entry point moved among the base of his neck, his upper right back and his lower right back). The commission had to produce a motive for Oswald to have killed Kennedy, and decided that Oswald "sought for himself a place in history…"[564] That being the case, one wonders why he emphatically and continuously denied the charges against him when he was in police custody.

Shenon and others have pointed out that the Warren Commission's findings were ultimately rejected by President Johnson himself. Interviewed by Leo Janos near the end of Johnson's life, the former president stated, "I never believed that Oswald acted alone, although I can accept that he pulled the trigger."[565] So there's one more person who doesn't believe the Warren Commission's conclusion of no conspiracy – the man who created that commission!

In commission assistant counsel Wesley Liebeler's introduction to the testimony of Philip Vinson, a high-school chum of Oswald's, he tells Vinson that "one of the purposes of the Commission is to try to determine, assuming Oswald's guilt, his motive."[566] Assuming Oswald's guilt? The task of commission assistant counsel Liebeler, himself an attorney, is supposed to find out who is guilty, and not to assume anything. Liebeler's statement is another indication that Oswald's "guilt" was a predetermined conclusion.

The Warren Report states, on page 49: "Unable to see the President as he turned to the right, the Governor started to look back over his left shoulder, but he never completed the turn…" That statement contains two falsehoods. On page 112, the Report states that Connally "never saw the President during the shooting sequence." The Zapruder film shows Connally turning around nearly 180 degrees to his right, and apparently looking *directly at* President Kennedy shortly after the shot to the latter's throat. The film shows that at no time did Connally look over his left shoulder. Also on page 112, the Report provides a somewhat more accurate picture of the situation, which also contradicts its earlier statement. It states there that Governor Connally "stated that he heard a shot, turned slightly to his right, and, as he started to turn back toward his left, was struck by the second bullet." The commission slightly misquoted Gov. Connally; they added the word *slightly*. What Connally actually said was, "I instinctively turned to my right because the sound appeared to come from over my right shoulder, so I turned to look back over my right shoulder..."[564] As he began to turn back to his left, he reacted to being hit by a bullet.

28. The Suspicious Deaths

As others have pointed out, the large number of suspicious deaths that occurred in the months and years after the assassination of President Kennedy seems to indicate conspiratorial activity. In fact, it seems to indicate that a "terror squad" was in operation during this time, taking care of loose ends, so to speak. I have found that some deaths are more suspicious than others, but the following deaths appear to be the most suspicious (the following list is in chronological order and is based on Jim Marrs' chapter "Convenient Deaths," Robert J. Groden's *The Killing of a President*, Chapter 16 of Sylvia Meagher's *Accessories After the Fact*, and Richard Belzer's book *Hit List*):

Officer J.D. Tippit; Lee Harvey Oswald; Jack Zangretti; Eddy Benavides; Betty McDonald; Grant Stockdale; Hank Killam; Bill Hunter; Betty McDonald; John G. "Gary" Underhill Jr.; Hugh Ward; Delesseps Morrison; Jim Koethe; Mary Pinchot Meyer; Maurice Gatlin; Mona B. Saenz; Rose Cheramie (aka Melba Marcades); Dorothy Kilgallen and her friend Mrs. Earl Smith; Albert "Guy" Bogard; Lee Bowers Jr.; Lt. Cmdr. William Bruce Pitzer; James Worrell Jr.; Jack Ruby; Harold Russell; David Ferrie; Eladio del Valle; Dr. Mary Sherman; John Crawford; Rev. Clyde Johnson; FBI man William C. Sullivan; mobsters Sam Giancana, Johnny Rosselli and Charles Nicoletti; George de Mohrenschildt; Carlos Prío Socarrás; Lou Staples; John A. Paisley; Congressman Hale Boggs, and possibly David Morales. Dates and details on these deaths can be found in publications such as those mentioned above.

Bugliosi says that stories about mysterious deaths are "myths" and "nonsensical," mainly, he says, because the people who died had already told their stories. That line of reasoning does not seem to apply to the following cases (apparently it never occurred to Mr. Bugliosi that the deaths could have been punishment for telling their stories, to stop them from saying more, or as a warning to others to keep quiet).

Mary Pinchot Meyer, JFK's last mistress, had confronted her ex-husband Cord Meyer with her suspicions about a cover-up and CIA involvement in the president's assassination; Cord reported these concerns to

James Angleton, and Angleton evidently took it from there. In September, Ms. Meyer met with LSD guru Timothy Leary in New York in a somewhat panicked state, telling him, among other things, "I may be in real trouble… I've gotten mixed up in some dangerous matters. It's real."[565] Angleton had bugged the rooms and telephones of Ms. Meyer in her Georgetown home.[566] She was murdered on October 12, 1964, with two shots to the head as she was taking her morning walk on the Chesapeake and Ohio Canal towpath along the Potomac in Georgetown, a neighborhood of Washington, D.C., in what appears to have been a CIA/Special Forces operation; see below. Ray Crump Jr., who was fishing further down the towpath at the time, was set up to take the blame for the hit on Ms. Meyer; he was arrested and put on trial, but acquitted.

Dorothy Kilgallen was in touch with Jack Ruby and was planning an exposé of the Warren Report and its conclusions. Ms. Kilgallen had written a number of stories challenging the Official Story. She had told Mark Lane, "I'm going to break this case … I'm going to do everything I can to find out how it happened." She secured the transcript of Jack Ruby's testimony before the Warren Commission while it was a classified document, and persuaded her newspaper, the now-defunct New York *Journal-American*, to publish the transcript. The transcript was published in serial form, and "within three hours after the first article was available at the newsstands, two FBI agents were at Miss Kilgallen's home," asking whence she obtained the transcript.[566] On November 8, 1965, her body was found in her bed in an obviously staged scene. Marc Sinclaire, Ms. Kilgallen's hairdresser, told Marlin Swing, a close friend to Kilgallen, that the book lying nearby was one that she had already read. Ms. Kilgallen needed eyeglasses to read all but the boldest print, but there was no mention of eyeglasses found on or around the bed. A death certificate issued on November 15 gave the cause of death as "acute ethanol and barbiturate intoxication - circumstances undetermined." The autopsy report said she had enough drugs in her system to kill at least ten men.[567] An exchange student who lived in Ms. Kilgallen's home at the time stated that he didn't believe she had taken her own life, saying that she was "very cheerful about life" and working on a book that she was "very enthusiastically finishing."[568]

Lt. Cmdr. William Pitzer was assistant head of the audio-visual unit at Bethesda. Pitzer died of a gunshot wound to the right temple in Bethesda Hospital. Pitzer was left-handed. Pitzer was found dead on October 29, 1966, in the TV production studio at the National Naval Medical Center at Bethesda. It was reported that Pitzer's left hand had been so mangled, as if "tortured," that his wedding ring couldn't be removed and given to his widow. The official cause of death was suicide, but Pitzer had told Dennis David that he was looking forward to retiring and had received several lucrative job offers.

Mr. Bugliosi stressed that David Ferrie's death on February 22, 1967, was due to natural causes. But if there was nothing suspicious about Ferrie's death, one wonders why two unsigned, undated letters were found in his apartment that suggested suicide. Dr. Nicholas Chetta and pathologist Ronald A. Welsh performed the autopsy on Ferrie. They concluded that he died from a massive cerebral hemorrhage due to a congenital intracranial berry aneurism that had ruptured at the base of his brain. Both Dr. Cyril Wecht and a fifth-degree black belt karate expert consulted by one researcher stated that a karate expert could inflict a blow to the back of the head causing a blood vessel to rupture at the base of the brain, resulting in death and leaving little or no external evidence of the assault.

Chicago Mob boss Sam Giancana was hit on June 19, 1975, five days before his scheduled appearance before the Church Committee. The dismembered body of Johnny Rosselli was found in a weighted oil drum in Biscayne Bay on August 7, 1976. He was killed before he could testify a second time to the Church Committee. Bugliosi doesn't even mention the possibility that Giancana and Rosselli could have been killed to prevent their telling what they knew about the Kennedy assassination. Testifying before the HSCA, John Whitten (testifying under the name "John Scelso"), a former intelligence officer in the CIA's office of clandestine operations, wondered aloud "if the government has ever looked into the possibility that [William] Harvey did not knock off Giancomo [*sic* – most probably Sam Giancana]."[569] William Harvey was operational head of Operation Mongoose, the plan to remove Castro from power. Richard Case Nagell told Dick Russell that Giancana and Rosselli were eliminated by the CIA. He said, "Somebody has been tying up loose ends over the years."[570] Church Committee staff investigators concluded that the murders of Rosselli and Giancana had been ordered by Florida Mafia boss Santos Trafficante, but Robert McNamara told Noel Twyman that the CIA "may have knocked off a few gangsters."[571] Since the CIA would probably not bother with murdering low-level gangsters, McNamara was surely referring to Giancana, Rosselli, and possibly Nicoletti.

George de Mohrenschildt "committed suicide" on March 29, 1977, and Charles Nicoletti was hit on the same day; Nicoletti was being sought for questioning before the HSCA at the time of his death. Both were scheduled to testify to the Church Committee. One week later, on April 5, 1977, Carlos Prío Socarrás, president of Cuba from 1948 to 1952, was another "suicide" by gunshot wound while being wanted for questioning by the HSCA. At the time of his death, Socarrás was a property developer and businessman in Miami.

J. Edgar Hoover moved against William C. Sullivan by placing W. Mark Felt into a new post above him on July 24, 1971, forcing Sullivan to resign on October 4. Sullivan had criticized Hoover for diverting so many Bureau resources to the nationwide hunt for communists. On November 9, 1977, Sullivan was fatally shot (in the neck) with a 30.06 rifle with a telescopic sight, while hunting in northern New Hampshire. The man who shot him, 22-yearold Robert Daniels, the son of a New Hampshire state policeman, claimed he thought Sullivan was a deer.[572] Sullivan, according to his attorney (Joseph Casey), had been called to testify to the HSCA; he was shot a few days before his scheduled appearance.[573]

Talbot referred to CIA assassin David Morales as a key link between the CIA and the criminal underworld, and says that Morales met with mobster Johnny Rosselli on a daily basis at JM/WAVE headquarters in Miami, where Morales was Theodore Shackley's paramilitary chief.[574] Morales slaughtered members of the Tupamaros, a leftist urban guerrilla group, in Uruguay and was involved in the infamous Phoenix program in Vietnam, where he acknowledged being involved in more assassinations. Gaeton Fonzi also described Morales as a CIA hit man.[575] Morales and the CIA may also have been involved in the assassination of Robert Kennedy. Morales told Robert Walton, his attorney, that he was in Los Angeles "when we got Bobby."[576] Morales, who hated JFK with a passion, "died mysteriously just before he was to testify before the House Select Committee on Assassinations in 1978."[577] Ruben "Rocky" Carbajal, a close friend of Morales', told Fonzi in an interview that he was convinced that Morales was killed by the CIA, to keep him from talking too much, but officially, his death on May 8, 1978, was due to a heart attack.

29. The Six Kennedys

The fact that there were so many different versions of the president's wounds seems to indicate confusion, obfuscation and conspiracy. Let us recap:

1. The real Kennedy: This is the Kennedy that the Parkland doctors and nurses saw, with a baseball-size wound at the lower right rear of the head, and no other head wound.

2. The Kennedy of the Warren Report and the Bethesda autopsy report prepared by doctors Humes, Boswell and Finck: a small wound slightly

above the external occipital protuberance (EOP) one inch to right of center, and an oval wound, high on the right side of the head, measuring 5.1 inches in greatest (presumably horizontal) dimension. The Report states, "After a bullet penetrated President Kennedy's neck, a subsequent shot entered the back of his head and exited through the upper right portion of his skull...That impact was evident from the explosion of the President's brain tissues from the right side of the head."[578] This is obviously inconsistent with the autopsy photographs and the Zapruder film.

3. The Zapruder film Kennedy: entry point unclear; an exit wound in the temporal and sphenoid regions, about the size of a small banana, in front of the right ear.

4. The Kennedy of the official autopsy photos: no large, gaping wounds in the rear or side of the head, and no bullet hole at the base of the back of the neck; the area in front of the right ear (the Zapruder "wound") is intact.

5. The Kennedy of the Autopsy Descriptive Sheet, prepared by Dr. Boswell, and reproduced herein as Figure 2 (page 229): a small bullet hole near the EOP, no bullet hole in the back of the neck, and no large wound in side or back of the head. In his HSCA interview on August 16, 1977, Dr. Boswell made it clear that there was essentially one enormous wound in the rear of the president's head, which is true, but it is completely inconsistent with his autopsy descriptive sheet, the official autopsy report and the official autopsy photos!

6. The Clark Panel Kennedy: In February 1968, four medical experts appointed by US Attorney General Ramsey Clark re-examined the photos and x-rays from the autopsy. They reported a small bullet hole in the back of the head, 10 centimeters (four inches) higher than was reported by Dr. Humes et al. in the autopsy report. Bugliosi assures us that even though the Clark Panel put the official small wound in the back of Kennedy's head four inches above where Dr. Humes placed it, "we have to be talking about the same wound."[579] Bugliosi apparently has no problem with the fact that there was a four-inch discrepancy between the Humes observations and the Clark Panel. Questioned by HSCA counsel about the 10 cm figure, Humes replied, "Well, I have a little trouble with that..."[580] The HSCA's Forensic Pathology noted that the photograph of the back of the president's head shows the wound in the cowlick area considerably above the external occipital protuberance, but the "photograph" provided (at 7HSCA104) is actually a drawing. In his May 1992 *JAMA* interview, Dr. Humes firmly rejected the HSCA conclusion the head wound was four inches above the external occipital

protuberance, repeating that it was *slightly* above the EOP. At the Shaw trial, Dr. Finck stated that the "entry" hole in the back of the head "was definitely not 4 inches or 100 millimeters above" the external occipital protuberance.[581] The HSCA consultants nevertheless accepted the 10 cm figure put forth by the Clark Panel. The problem with all of this is, of course, that the people on the Clark Panel were looking at a phony drawing and phony x-rays and photos from a phony autopsy report, and there was no tiny entrance wound from a bullet in the back of President Kennedy's head.

30. Wrong Body in the Kennedy Coffin

John Kennedy was not the person in the official autopsy photos and x-rays, and is not the person on whom the autopsy was performed, and it appears that he was not the person in Kennedy's coffin. Around 4:00 a.m. on Saturday, November 23, Bobby Kennedy viewed his brother in the official casket and hardly recognized him. "The morticians had made the slain president appear plastic. 'It doesn't look like him at all,' Bobby Kennedy said."[582] At 12:34 p.m., when the casket was in the East Room of the White House, Jacqueline Kennedy took one last look at what was supposed to be her husband. She later stated, "It wasn't Jack. It was like something you would see at Madame Tussaud's." This is acknowledged by Bugliosi himself, and is in line with the comparison shown in Figure 3 (page 230), which shows the left profile of the real John Kennedy at the top, with the official autopsy photo below. The lower photo is obviously not JFK. It appears to be a composite; everything from just in front of the sideburns to the back of the head being Kennedy, and the rest being someone else. Kennedy aide Arthur Schlesinger Jr. wrote in his journal that day, "When I came closer it looked less and less like him. It was not a good job, probably it could not have been with half his head blasted away. It was too waxen, too made up. It did not really look like him."[583] White House social secretary Nancy Tuckerman said, "It really is not like him." Charles Spalding, a writer and investment banker who helped in JFK's presidential campaign, said that the face resembled "the rubber masks stores sell as novelties."[584]

31. Statements of Jack Ruby

Interviewed in prison on June 7, 1964, Ruby told Earl Warren, "My life is in danger here ... I may not live tomorrow to give any further testimony." And "my brothers Sam, Earl, Hyman and my in-laws ... they are in jeopardy of loss of their lives ... right at the moment I am being victimized as part of a plot ... Lee Harvey Oswald isn't guilty of committing the crime of assassinating President Kennedy." Jack Ruby told the commission, "I have been used for a purpose," and "I am used as a scapegoat."[585] This is hardly the statement of someone who shot Oswald on the spur of the moment. Bugliosi chalks this all up to Ruby's being paranoid, mentally unbalanced, etc.

While in prison, Ruby gave Dallas County deputy sheriff Alvin Maddox Jr. a note saying it was a conspiracy and his motive was to silence Oswald. Ruby told journalist Tom Johnson that the plot was "the most bizarre conspiracy in the history of the world."[586] Bugliosi nevertheless tells us that there is "*no evidence* to show that Ruby was part of any conspiracy to murder President Kennedy."[587] At a sort of press conference during his 1964 trial (Bugliosi says the "press conference" was to a reporter from Fort Worth television station KTVT), the following exchange occurred:

> Ruby: Everything pertaining to what's happening has never come to the surface. The world will never know the true facts of what occurred, my motives. In other words, I'm the only person in the background that knows the truth pertaining to my testimony.
>
> Reporter (off camera): Do you think it will ever come out?
>
> Ruby: No, because unfortunately the people who have so much to gain and have such an ulterior motive for putting me in the position I am in will never let the true facts come above board to the world.
>
> Reporter: Are these people in very high positions, Jack?
>
> Ruby: Yes.

Bugliosi hides these statements by Ruby in his endnotes,[588] no doubt because they conflict so blatantly with Bugliosi's insistence in the main book that there was no conspiracy and Ruby was not part of one.

When asked by a reporter if President Kennedy would have been assassinated if Adlai Stevenson had been vice president, Ruby replied, "The answer is the man in office now." Not long before Ruby died, according to an article in the London *Sunday Times*, he told psychiatrist Werner Teuter that the assassination was "an act of overthrowing the government," and that he knew who had had President Kennedy killed. He also stated, "I was framed to kill Oswald."

Mr. Bugliosi nevertheless refuses to believe there was a conspiracy, even though he knew that Jack Ruby had stated quite unequivocally that it *was* a conspiracy!

32. Statements of E. Howard Hunt

During his last days (in 2003), E. Howard Hunt provided his son, Howard St. John Hunt, with a diagram of the assassination. He put "LBJ" at the top of the paper, and from that point there was a line to the name Cord Meyer, and two lines going from Cord Meyer – one to William Harvey and one to David Morales. At the time of the assassination, Cord Meyer headed the Covert Action Staff of the Directorate of Plans ("dirty tricks"), "responsible both for international operations and for guiding the area divisions of the Clandestine Service [Plans Directorate] in the conduct of covert action."[589] In 1968, Meyer was Richard Helms' deputy in the Directorate of Plans. From the name David Morales, the senior Hunt drew a line to the framed words "French Gunman Grassy Knoll." Later that week, Howard Hunt gave his son a fuller written account that mentioned discussions of assassination between Cord Meyer and CIA agent David Phillips, with Phillips recruiting William Harvey and Antonio Veciana. Veciana was the founder and leader of Alpha 66, one of the most violent of the anti-Castro groups. The senior Hunt also mentioned Veciana meeting with Frank Sturgis in Miami and enlisting David Morales in anticipation of killing President Kennedy there, and another meeting in that city involving Hunt, Morales and Frank Sturgis, on the subject of killing the president. But Hunt said that Morales had no direct role in the assassination.[590]

John McCloy told the Washington *Observer-Reporter* in 1975 (July 21 issue) that writings that propagated assassination conspiracy theories were "just nonsense."

Chapter 4

The Plot

A Word on Motives

I believe, and I think simple logic suggests, that the primary motives behind the assassination were those that have been noted by other writers and researchers, namely:

- To clear the way for a war in Vietnam in order to contain "communism." President Kennedy had issued National Security Action Memorandum 263 in October 1963, ordering a thousand military advisers back home from Vietnam, with the idea of withdrawing "the bulk of US personnel" by the end of 1965 and avoiding a US war in Vietnam completely. Prouty wrote that Kennedy "was getting out and he wanted that on the record. *That is why he was shot.*"[1] There was also the possibility that a unified Vietnam under "communist" rule would disrupt the CIA's drug smuggling activities in Southeast Asia. Federal Bureau of Narcotics agent Bowman Taylor discovered in 1963 that the CIA "was not only protecting the opium growers in Laos, it was facilitating the drug trade in Vietnam." The Agency was also managing the caravan that delivered raw opium to the world's biggest opium market in Houei Sai, Laos.[2] By the early 1960s, according to Robert Sam Anson, "CIA money was indirectly financing a vast opium industry. CIA-employed troops grew it, harvested it, and shipped it to Vientiane and Saigon aboard planes of Air America, the CIA airline."[3]

- To put a stop to ideas about "not merely peace in our time, but peace for all time," and easing Cold War tensions, as put forth in Kennedy's famous June 10, 1963, commencement speech at the American University. In the wake of that speech, it was stated that senior military officers "insist the present policies are weakening the US position relative to Russia and will go on weakening it until a shift in the balance of power will threaten."[6]

- To put a stop to the (back-channel) detente that President Kennedy was pursuing with Fidel Castro's Cuba in September 1963, with US Ambassador to Guinea William Attwood, ABC-TV newswoman Lisa Howard, Jean Daniel (a French journalist with L'Express) and Castro aide Dr. Rene Vallejo acting as intermediaries. Arthur Schlesinger Jr. told Anthony Summers, "I think the CIA must have known about this initiative."[5] This attempt at detente with the island nation may have been seen by the plotters as further "evidence" that the president was "soft on communism," this alleged softness having previously manifested itself when Kennedy refused to authorize a second air strike on Cuba during the Bay of Pigs invasion in 1961, allegedly causing the invasion to fail.

Ramon Sanchez had been part of a 1963 attempt by Frank Sturgis to sink a Soviet tanker and thus frustrate the entente established between JFK and Krushchev after the Cuban Missile Crisis.[6] Interviewed by Gaeton Fonzi of the HSCA in 1976, Antonio Veciana admitted that it was his CIA case officer, "Maurice Bishop," who had the idea to attack Soviet ships docked in Cuba in 1963. "The intention," said Veciana, "was to cause trouble between Kennedy and Russia. Bishop believed that President Kennedy and Soviet premier Nikita Krushchev had made a secret agreement that the USA would do nothing more to help in the fight against Castro. Bishop felt - he told me many times – that President Kennedy was a man without experience surrounded by a group of young men who were also inexperienced with mistaken ideas on how to manage this country. He said you had to put Kennedy against the wall in order to force him to make decisions that would remove Castro's regime."[7] (It is now widely believed, as Gaeton Fonzi came to believe, that "Maurice Bishop" was CIA agent David Atlee Phillips.) The Agency's provocative action in sending a U-2 spy plane over Soviet territory on May 1, 1960, effectively wrecking the May 16 summit conference between President Eisenhower and Nikita Krushchev, is a manifestation of the same mentality. It seems clear that the power elite that controls the CIA did not want peace.

• To put a stop to President Kennedy's proposed funding cuts to the CIA. According to Arthur Schlesinger, Kennedy "moved quietly to cut the CIA budget in 1962 and again in 1963, aiming at a 20 per cent reduction by 1966."[8]

• To ensure that Lyndon Johnson and J. Edgar Hoover would not be booted out of government. There were rumors that Johnson was going to be dropped from the Democratic presidential ticket for the 1965 election cycle. Hoover was nearly the mandatory retirement age of 70 for his position; when Johnson became president, he waived Hoover's mandatory retirement, extending his tenure "for an indefinite period of time." Hoover remained FBI head until his death in 1972 at age 77; he had been director of the Bureau for 48 years.

In addition to the above, I believe there may have been another motive for the assassination, one that is mentioned less often than the above: To get rid of a president who was unhealthy, heavily reliant on drugs, and obsessed with extramarital sex (with multiple partners). A.J. Langguth mentions weekly amphetamine injections during the 1960 presidential campaign, but a Secret Service agent told Seymour Hersh that during Kennedy's presidency, the shots were administered every six hours.[9] JFK also had Addison's disease, a disorder of the adrenal glands. Schlesinger stated that Kennedy didn't have Addison's "in the classical sense," but he took corticosteroid tablets from time to time; the treatment for Addison's evidently included injected corticosteroids and pellets implanted in Kennedy's thighs.[10] According to Richard Reeves, Dr. Janet Travell, one of JFK's White House physicians, injected Novocain into the president's muscles regularly, sometimes several times a day, and he also had venereal disease.[11] Robert Dallek tells us that the JFK's medications included Phenobarbital (a barbiturate), testosterone, penicillin and other antibiotics, and Tuinal (also a barbiturate) "to help him sleep."[12] The plotters may have believed that a heavily medicated Kennedy might not be able to be trusted to make key decisions in a crisis involving national security. And Kennedy, while president, reportedly had affairs with actresses, socialites, prostitutes, a stripper or two, Jacqueline Kennedy's press secretary, Mob party girl Judith Campbell, and two or three White House interns, as well as the aforementioned Mary Pinchot Meyer – the list was long. In his HSCA testimony, John Whitten, who had been CIA chief of covert operations for Mexico and Central America, made reference to the Secret Service "smuggling girls up and down the back steps" (of the White House, presumably).[13] All of the above points taken together were probably enough to lead the plotters to decide that John Kennedy was socially, politically, and medically unfit to be president and had to be terminated.

Speaking of motives, it is difficult to understand what would motivate Mr. Bugliosi to churn out his unfortunate attempt to resurrect the badly decomposed corpse of the Warren Report, filling his tome with twisted logic, false statements, made-up dialogue, and so forth. One cannot help but wonder if he was paid by some agency of the US government to do so. Mark Lane wrote in *Last Word*, "It would be interesting ... to learn where the funding for a massive book that few would read and for twenty years of work had originated."[14]

The Players

As is evident from the information provided in the previous chapters, several people played key roles in the effort to strip the president of security in Dealey Plaza, create and/or ensure the survival of the Official Story, ensure that Lee Oswald never came to trial, and otherwise facilitate the assassination and cover-up. Based on the preceding narrative, the list would include the president's Secret Service detail, Warren Commissioners Earl Warren, Allen Dulles and Gerald Ford (and the people who drafted the Warren Report), Arlen Specter, Jack Ruby, FBI director J. Edgar Hoover and certain of his agents, Dallas DA Henry Wade, Dallas police, Bethesda doctors Humes, Boswell and Finck, Pentagon generals and admirals, the operatives who generated the phony Oswald backyard photos and the phony autopsy photos and x-rays, and CIA employees Richard Helms and E. Howard Hunt. They were all in it together; but then, they had to be in order for the plot (and cover-up) to succeed.

The list of players would also include Lyndon Johnson aide Clifton "Cliff" Carter; Leonidas "Leon" Jaworski, a sometime lawyer for LBJ; and Henry Luce's *Life* magazine, though it is not clear whether decisions regarding the assassination-related content in 1963-64 were made by Luce or the magazine's publisher, C.D. Jackson. Cliff Carter sent Secret Service agents to retrieve and launder Gov. Connally's bloody clothing before it could be forensically examined. On the evening of November 22, Carter called Dallas DA Henry Wade repeatedly *from the White House* and ordered Wade not to allege a conspiracy. "Look no further [than Oswald]," he told Wade. A similar call was made to Texas attorney general Waggoner Carr. Leon Jaworski was special counsel to the Warren Commission and successfully blocked local investigations of the JFK assassination.[15] The November 29, 1963, and December 6, 1963, issues of *Life* magazine assured us that Oswald was the lone nut assassin. The cover of the February 21, 1964, issue of *Life,* appearing nearly eight months *before* the Warren Commission had published their report concluding that Oswald was the lone nut assassin, featured one of the phony backyard photos of "Oswald" holding the alleged assassination rifle. The only problem is that it is not the same rifle displayed to reporters in the Dallas police offices shortly after the assassination. That rifle has a notch for the shooter's hand on the shooter's side of the trigger and scope. The rifle in the *Life* photograph has no such notch. The accompanying article was entitled, "The Evolution of an Assassin," and it featured another of the backyard photos (on page 80).

Life also reversed certain Zapruder frames so that it looked like the president's head was moving forward at the moment of the fatal shot, among other efforts to support the Official Story. In a *Rolling Stone* article (October 20, 1977), Carl Bernstein reported that there was a close relationship between the CIA and Henry Luce's Time-Life organization.

Arlen Specter is the one Warren Commission assistant counsel who seems to have been under the most direct control or influence of the conspirators, the one who was the most diligent in trying to get the witnesses he interviewed to say what he wanted them to say, and the one who was the chief architect of the nonsensical single-bullet theory – the willing idiot, if you will, of the conspirators. Harrison Livingstone correctly noted that when Specter interviewed witnesses, he "repeatedly ignored, twisted, or distorted statements when they tended to conflict with the conclusion he wanted."[16] The *Saturday Evening Post* wrote, "Over the weekend of May 23-24, 1964, the [Warren] commission staged, at [Specter's] insistence, an elaborate reenactment of the assassination in Dallas. Specter's sole concern was to gain support for the single-bullet theory."[17] Specter falsely told author Epstein that the doctors found the magic bullet's path through JFK's body. FBI ballistics expert Robert Frazier testified in June 1964 that is was *possible* that both men were hit by the same bullet; but in the chapter on the basic facts of the assassination, written mainly by Specter, the Warren Report states: "Frazier testified that it [the bullet that first hit JFK] *probably* struck Governor Connally."[18] (Emphasis added.) According to Dr. David Mantik, FBI man Francis O'Neill regarded Specter as a flunky for the commission.[19] Specter's approach is typified by his interaction with Jean Hill, as described above. From 1964 on, Specter refused to debate with Mark Lane or any other critic of the Warren Commission.[20] In Dallas, Lyndon Johnson demanded that his belongings be transferred to *Air Force One* from the plane on which Johnson had flown to Dallas. He later stated in his affidavit for the commission that Kennedy aide Kenny O'Donnell had specifically told him to take "the President's plane" (*Air Force One*) back to Washington.[21] But O'Donnell told the commission that when he and Johnson talked at the hospital, there was no mention of which plane Johnson should use.[22] When Specter discovered the discrepancy, he approached O'Donnell and tried to persuade him to change his testimony retroactively so that it matched Johnson's. This was obviously done to protect Johnson and his version of events. O'Donnell, noting that his testimony had been given under oath, refused.[23]

Earl Warren denied key evidence and witnesses to the commission's staff, and refused to allow the other commission members to review Kennedy's autopsy photos and x-rays. He decided that Gov. Connally was mistaken in believing he was hit by a separate bullet from the one that supposedly entered the base of President Kennedy's neck. When interviewed by Warren and Gerald Ford in Dallas, Jack Ruby repeatedly asked to be taken to Washington so that he could tell the whole truth, but Warren denied Ruby's request.[24] Warren also blocked the commission staff from interviewing Silvia Durán, the woman who supposedly attended to Oswald when he supposedly approached the Cuban consulate in Mexico City in September 1963. Commission assistant counsel David Slawson told author Shenon that he wanted to bring Sra. Durán to the US to testify, but Earl Warren said no. Slawson recalled Warren saying, "We don't talk to communists."[25] In Israel, confronted by a reporter about questions regarding author Edward J. Epstein's *Inquest*, Earl Warren told the reporter that "it was the best we could do after ten months of intensive research… It was unanimous." But it wasn't unanimous. Commissioner Russell wanted Warren to add a footnote to the Report stating that the senator didn't agree with the single-bullet theory, but Warren refused.[26] In the commission's final executive session on September 18, 1964, Senator Russell said he wouldn't sign the report if it said that the same bullet passed through Kennedy and Connally. Senator Cooper agreed with Russell's dissent, and Congressman Boggs also had strong doubts about the single-bullet theory, and felt that the question was never resolved.[27] But Warren would not allow dissent from the single-bullet theory.

Congressman Ford served on two of the House Appropriations Committee's Subcommittees - the Subcommittee on the CIA, which authorized the Agency's secret budget, and the Department of Defense Subcommittee. Ford changed the commission staff's draft of its report from the language that the bullet had entered Kennedy's *back* "to a point slightly above the shoulder, to the right of the spine," to its entering "the base of the back of his neck at a point slightly to the right of the spine," which is the wording in the final Warren Report.[28] Ford didn't deny this, but said it was only an attempt to be more precise. More precise? Ford had no medical training, nor was he present during the autopsy. When the establishment of a House committee to re-investigate the assassination was being discussed in 1975, Ford warned against reopening the case, saying it would be "unwise."[29] It is now evident that Ford was on the commission mainly to look after the interests of the FBI. A memo from FBI deputy director Cartha DeLoach indicates that on December 12, 1963, Ford agreed to keep DeLoach "thoroughly advised as to the activities of the Commission ... on a confidential basis."[30] Ford also told FBI officials which commission members required additional FBI "efforts" in order to bring them into line with the FBI view of the assassination.[31] FBI documents obtained under the Freedom of Information Act years after the commission disbanded showed that unbeknownst to the other members, Ford had fed top secret information to the FBI while he was a member of the commission. According to Marrs, Canfield and Weberman, President Johnson placed Ford on the commission at the request of Richard Nixon.[32]

The Central Intelligence Agency (and the Mob)

Given the involvement of the CIA in the cover-up, one must naturally consider what involvement, if any, the then-director of the Agency, John McCone, may have had. I consider it unlikely that he was involved, for the following reasons: First, he was, like John Kennedy, a devout Catholic, and by all accounts liked and respected JFK. He also abhorred the idea of political assassination. When the question of murdering Fidel Castro came up once in a meeting in August 1962, Secretary of State Dean Rusk's secretary noted that McCone made it clear that they should not countenance talking or even thinking about that.[33] Second, McCone may not have been in full control of his organization. John Seigenthaler, Robert Kennedy's right-hand man at the Justice Department, told author Talbot that McCone was out of the loop and that Richard Helms was running the CIA.[34] According to Gaeton Fonzi, "the fraternity never accepted [McCone] ... the brotherhood of insiders who actually ran the Agency kept McCone in the dark about the CIA's most sensitive operations."[35] Helms told the Senate Intelligence Committee (the Church Committee) in 1975 that he had not told McCone about the Castro assassination plots. Given that fact, he probably would not have told McCone about the JFK assassination plot.

Toni Shimon, daughter of Joseph W. "Joe" Shimon, who in 1963 was officially "Washington Police Inspector" and a special White House aide, as well as a liaison to the CIA and to the Mafia's Johnny Rosselli, told Peter Janney that her father told her that James Angleton "ran everything, controlled everything in the CIA."[36] In early 1975, following statements that Warren Commission assistant counsel David Slawson had made recently to the *New York Times,* Slawson got a call from Angleton, who, in a sinister tone, asked Slawson if it was true that he wanted a new investigation of elements of the JFK assassination. "Slawson was convinced that Angleton was giving him a warning: 'Keep your mouth shut.'"[37] According to secret government documents that were declassified in 2017, Angleton was in charge of the operation to sabotage Jim Garrison's prosecution of Clay Shaw.

In his testimony to the HSCA, John Whitten stated that Angleton had "enormously influential contacts" with J. Edgar Hoover; he also stated that Army Col. J.C. King once told him that Angleton had ties to the Mafia and "he would not want to double-cross them."[38] It certainly is reassuring to know that the CIA's top counterintelligence person had a sense of loyalty to the Mafia! Michael Piper says that Angleton was a "prime mover behind the CIA operations utilizing the Corsican and Sicilian organized crime elements in Angleton's 'anti-communist' ventures."[39] In 1973, "during a drinking session in which President Kennedy was discussed, Morales said – according to his attorney, Robert Walton – 'We took care of that son of a bitch, didn't we?'"[40] William Harvey, according to his notes, was seeking a principal agent ("QJ/WIN") whose task would be to recruit underworld assassins and burglars; he wrote "Corsicans were recommended, as Sicilians could lead to the Mafia." So "the CIA hired Corsican drug smugglers as assassins, in order to protect certain Mafiosi in its employ."[41]

In the Church Committee Interim Final Report (p. 50), in the context of a discussion of the ZR/RIFLE (Executive Action) program, Richard Helms was quoted as saying, regarding CIA "asset" QJ/WIN: "If you needed somebody to carry out murder, I guess you had a man who might be prepared to carry it out." The CIA's *Clandestine Operations Manual for Latin America* recommends finding professional criminals, if possible, who will be hired to carry out specific selected jobs (i.e., murders). It is not clear that a high official of the US government should be looking for "somebody to carry out murder." On the "smoking gun" tape of June 23, 1972, a few days after the burglars were caught in the Watergate office complex, President Nixon told his aide H.R. Haldeman, "we protected Helms from one hell of a lot of things..." This was in the context of a discussion of how to get the FBI to stop investigating the Watergate break-in.

Jules "Ricco" Kimbel said he worked as an FBI/CIA asset and for organized crime, and implied that he did strong-arm work, including murder. He said that the Mob and the CIA worked together like one organization. "The mob," Kimbel said, "would handle contract work for the Agency, which could then plausibly deny any connection or knowledge of events should they become public."[42] A former New York City-based undercover agent for the CIA who was responsible for monitoring the activities of dissidents in the late 1960s and early 1970s told Seymour Hersh in a 1974 interview that "the Mafia was relied upon for the exchanges of information and also to assault targets selected by the CIA."[43] Federal sources reported that Jack Ruby met secretly with Johnny Rosselli in Miami during the two months preceding the assassination. The FBI had Rosselli under surveillance and monitored these meetings, but there is no record of the meetings having been disclosed to the Warren Commission. Jimmy Starr, the Hollywood gossip columnist and friend of Rosselli's, mentioned to one of the authors of *All American Mafioso*, "What I heard about the [John] Kennedy assassination was that Johnny [Rosselli] was the guy who got the team together to do the hit."[44] I nevertheless believe that government agents got the team together.

Jesse Ventura et al. note that CIA man David Phillips stated near the end of his life, "My final take on the assassination is there was a conspiracy, likely including American intelligence officers."[45] Antonio Veciana also said that he believed that "certain renegade members" of the CIA were involved in the assassination. "There are plenty of thugs on the [CIA] payroll, foreign and native born, but the management is genteel, rather scholarly, and reads the *New Republic*," writes Richard J. Barnet, to whom a disgruntled former CIA employee described the Agency as "the most dangerous organization in the world."[46] James Wilcott worked in the Finance Branch at the Tokyo CIA station. In the context of HSCA Classified Testimony, the following typed document was submitted to the committee as part of Wilcott's testimony, which I have edited somewhat in the interests of space and relevance:

> The Kennedy assassination came as no great shock to most of the people at Tokyo station in Japan, a class A Station of the CIA. It seemed a logical culmination of the steadily building anguish and discontent over the Bay of Pigs fiasco and Commie sell out [*sic*] of the Kennedy Administration; that was the prevailing sentiment. This was particularly true of the higher echelon people…"Treason" and "dupe of the USSR" were commonly employed during the heated political conversations concerning the September, 1963, Nuclear Test Ban Treaty. Administration support of integration, and "Kennedy's personal crusade" against the oil depletion allowance were also seen as an attack on free enterprise. Greatly feared, also, was a winding down and eventual pull-out in Viet Nam, with a political settlement, rather than an all-out military onslaught to win.… Based solely on what I heard at Tokyo Station, I became convinced that the following

> scenario is true ... CIA people killed Kennedy. Either it was an outright project of Headquarters with the approval of [John] McCone or it was done outside, perhaps under the direction of [Allen] Dulles or [Richard] Bissell. It was done in retaliation to Kennedy's reneging on a secret agreement with Dulles to support the invasion of Cuba... It was believed that unless Cuba was seized by military force all of Latin America would eventually go communist and the US would lose face and could not be relied upon as the bulwark against communist encroachment...There was no doubt that CIA was in 'as thick as thieves' with the Dallas Police ... Kennedy was not killed by the lone assassin Oswald as the Warren Commission concluded. He was killed with the criminal involvement of CIA! Further criminal implication of other government persons and private individuals is certain to be shown when all the facts are known.[47]

Wilcott indicated that he resigned from the CIA because he had come to believe that what the Agency was doing could not be reconciled with basic principles of democracy or basic principles of humanism. (Richard Bissell Jr. had been head of the CIA's Plans ["dirty tricks"] Department until he was dismissed by JFK in the wake of the Bay of Pigs fiasco. He departed in February 1962, and was replaced by Richard Helms. At the time of the assassination, Bissell was head of the Institute for Defense Analysis, a Pentagon think tank set up to evaluate weapons systems. Bissell was the man who in August 1960 asked Col. Sheffield Edwards, chief of the CIA's Office of Security, to contact the Mafia regarding their possible help in the assassination of Fidel Castro.) In the second Liberty Lobby trial, the jury found that CIA man Victor Marchetti had not been guilty of libel when he suggested in a magazine article that President Kennedy had been assassinated by people working for the CIA. Ruben "Rocky" Carbajal told Talbot flat out that the CIA killed President Kennedy.[48]

Chuck Giancana claims that his brother Sam told him in 1966 that the Outfit (the Chicago Mob) and the CIA took care of President Kennedy together. The conspiracy to assassinate JFK, Sam said, "went right to the top of the CIA," and involved current and former CIA directors, "some of the top people on the Dallas police force," Lyndon Johnson, Richard Nixon, and "a half dozen fanatical rightwing Texans."[49] It is worth noting here that during the HSCA investigation, FBI agents made determined efforts to conceal any possible links between the Mafia and the assassination.

The HSCA "believed that [William] Harvey, due to his contacts with La Cosa Nostra and the anti-Castro Cubans, and his known hatred of the

Kennedys coupled with his position as the head of the CIA's executive action project made him a possible suspect in the [John F.] Kennedy assassination."[50] Harvey's bosses were James Angleton and Richard Helms. But even with all this, it seems unlikely that President Kennedy was assassinated simply because Richard Helms and/or James Angleton wanted it done. To believe this is to believe that one or two CIA people took over significant parts of the government – the Pentagon, the FBI, the Secret Service, etc. It is much more likely, in my view, that the killing was perpetrated by a small group of people working *through* the CIA and military personnel such as doctors Humes, Boswell and Finck, and Army Special Forces. Dick Russell described the CIA as "merely a part of a much larger interdepartmental federation dominated by the Pentagon."[51]

The Pentagon (and the Mob)

Given the involvement of Pentagon elements and agencies of US intelligence in the events of Dallas and their aftermath, one must conclude that we experienced a right-wing coup d'état on November 22, 1963, and history shows that such coups are usually carried out by the military. Examples where a country's military determined that it should be running the country (rather than merely protecting the country from outside attack, which is what they should be doing) include Greece and Brazil in the sixties and seventies, Chile and Argentina in the seventies, Ethiopia in 1974-75, Libya from 1969 to 2011, and Myanmar today. Many of us are familiar with President Dwight Eisenhower's parting warning regarding the influence of the military-industrial complex. I believe a key element of that speech, particularly as it may relate to the JFK assassination, was the following: "The potential for the disastrous rise of misplaced power exists and will persist." In late summer 1963, Private Eugene B. Dinkin, an Army cryptographer stationed in Metz, France, heard of a conspiracy to assassinate President Kennedy that was being engineered by elements of the US military, possibly combined with an "ultra-right economic group." After being sent for psychological examinations to Landstuhl Army Hospital in Germany and Walter Reed Army Hospital, Dinkin was discharged from the Army.

In his memoirs, Nikita Krushchev recounts a key meeting in the midst of the Cuban Missile Crisis between Bobby Kennedy and Soviet ambassador Anatoly Dobrynin. According to Krushchev, RFK stated, "We are under severe stress. In fact we are under pressure from our military to use force against Cuba...If the situation continues much longer, the President is not sure that the military will not overthrow him and seize power."[52] According to Walt Brown, "The military chieftains looked on in horror as our Jupiter missile bases in Turkey and Italy were dismantled, giving rise to the suspicion that perhaps a trade had been agreed to between Kennedy and Krushchev..."[53]

Both Richard Nagell and Joseph B. Smith, "a twenty-two-year veteran of CIA clandestine work in the Far East and Latin America," stated that there was a right-wing clique in the Pentagon.[54] Near the end of his life, Arthur Schlesinger Jr. told Talbot, "Certainly we did not control the Joint Chiefs of Staff."[55] This is a poignant observation, and a disturbing one; if true, it means that President Kennedy was not the commander-in-chief of the US military! The Pentagon may have been beyond civilian control as early as 1961. In that year, a Pentagon analyst named Daniel Ellsberg discovered that the Joint Chiefs had a War Plan, "which told how they would go to war, and...that they had carefully hidden this fact from civilians, including among others the Secretary of Defense..."[56] More recently, Ellsberg stated, "There was virtually a coup atmosphere in Pentagon circles ... it was a mood of hatred and rage."[57] In January 1967, Senator Allen J. Ellender, a conservative Democrat from Louisiana, stated, "The truth of the matter is that in many important respects, the Congress and the nation are in the hands of the military. Add to this group the Department of State and you have a combination that calls the shots."[58] Gerry Hemming spoke of being approached from 1962 on by "some very serious people" from the Pentagon, of General rank, to go for terminating the leadership in Washington. "Now we're talking about the military and civilian people – we're talking about people who wore civilian clothes but were from the Pentagon or reservists, or what have you, of General rank..."[59]

The shenanigans at the (military) autopsy and the fact that high-ranking Navy people generated a phony autopsy report and issued gag orders to the autopsy participants clearly show military involvement in the overall conspiracy. Harold Weisberg pointed out that "top military brass immediately took over the autopsy, severely limiting what the surgeons could do and ordering them not to do...what had to be done ... and the autopsy surgeons were threatened with retaliation if they opened their mouths."[60] Bethesda was a Naval hospital, and the autopsists were Navy personnel. It is difficult to believe that all of this occurred without the knowledge and approval of the Chief of Naval Operations, Admiral David L. McDonald.

There were other Pentagon connections. Lt. Col. George Whitmeyer, the East Texas Section Commander of the Army Intelligence Reserve, was in the pilot car that preceded the Dallas motorcade. James Powell, who was a member of the Army's 112th Military Intelligence Group (MIG), was on the sixth floor of the Book Depository within minutes after the assassination.[61] Powell was found trapped inside the Depository after it had been sealed. It may be a coincidence, but according to Dick Russell, the 112th MIG maintained an "Oswald/Hidell" file.[62] Richard Case Nagell was a veteran of Army Intelligence. Marina Oswald's translator, Ilya Mamantov, a research geologist for Sun Oil, was chosen by John "Jack" Crichton and Dallas deputy police chief George Lumpkin. Crichton and Lumpkin were members of the Army's 488th Intelligence Reserve Unit; Crichton was head of that unit.[63] HSCA investigator Edwin Lopez said that Army Intelligence refused to cooperate with his investigation.[64]

Lt. Col. Daniel Marvin, an ex-Green Beret, stated in an interview that when he was a specialist in guerrilla training at the Fort Bragg, North Carolina, Army base, the JFK situation "was brought to us as a classic example of the way to organize a complete program to eliminate the nation's leader while pointing the finger at a lone assassin; it involved also the cover-up of the assassination itself. We had considerable detail; they had a mock layout of the plaza and that area, and showed where the shooters were and where the routes were to the hospital.... They told us that Oswald was not involved in the shooting at all; he was the patsy, the one that was set up. We did, myself and a friend of mine, form a very distinct impression that the CIA was involved in the Kennedy assassination." Lt. Col. Marvin also stated that during a coffee break one day, an instructor casually remarked on the "success of the conspiracy in Dallas." Marvin also said that "the Mafia was supposed to supply the resources they needed for killing someone here in the United States." In August 1965, fifteen months after his guerrilla training, Lt. Col. Marvin relates that he was summoned to a meeting with a CIA man who asked him if he would be willing to kill Lt. Cmdr. William Pitzer (see The Suspicious Deaths, above).[65] The Green Berets were part of the US Army, and the Army chief-of-staff at the time was General Earle Wheeler, a Vietnam hawk. In July 1964, President Johnson promoted Wheeler to be chairman of the Joint Chiefs of Staff.

There is also an apparent connection between Army Special Forces and the murder of Mary Pinchot Meyer. In his book *Mary's Mosaic,* Peter Janney says that author H.P. Albarelli was told by a source whom he had known for many years that William L. Mitchell (apparently an alias), a member of "Army Special Forces kill teams that operated domestically for the CIA and NSA," perpetrated the murder of Ms. Meyer at the request of the CIA's Domestic K [contracts] Office in Washington. According to L. Fletcher Prouty, the Army Special Forces (the Green Berets) "have long been the uniformed mercenaries of the CIA." It was apparently at the beginning of the 1960s that the Agency "realized that it could best achieve its aims by 'adopting' the Special Forces." Prouty tells us that the Special Forces fell under the operational direction of the CIA from 1961 through 1963.[66] Dr. Mantik recounts the story of a Special Forces captain, John McCarthy, who was convicted of murder in South Vietnam in January 1968. Jim DiEugenio interviewed Capt. McCarthy in August 1995, and implied "that the Pentagon was eager to convict a Special Forces man because they (the Pentagon) were not in charge of Special Forces operations."[67] If the Pentagon was not in charge of Special Forces operations, one wonders who was.

William Pepper, an attorney for the family of Dr. Martin Luther King Jr., developed information from two informants, "Staff Sergeant Warren" and "Staff Sergeant Murphy" (and an article by Steve Tomkins in the Memphis *Commercial Appeal*), indicating that there was a Special Forces Operation Detachment Alpha 184 sniper team (consisting of either six or eight men), selected from the 20th Special Forces Group (aka the Green Berets), commanded by Col. Henry H. Cobb Jr., in Memphis when Dr. King was shot. Special Forces Operational Detachment Alpha is the fundamental fighting unit of Army Special Forces. The team members were told that on the order, they were to assassinate Dr. King and Andrew Young (at the time a community organizer and mediator), who was to be Warren's target.[68] Loyd Jowers was the owner of Jim's Grill, near the Lorraine Motel in Memphis. In 1999, he was a defendant in a lawsuit brought by Martin Luther King Jr.'s widow Coretta Scott King against those who allegedly conspired to kill her husband. Jack Terrell, a former CIA covert operative, testified by videotape at the Jowers trial on February 7, 1999, that his friend 20th Special Forces Group Green Beret John D. Hill "had confessed to him that he had been a member of an Army sniper team in Memphis to shoot 'an unknown target'" on or around April 4, 1968. As in Dallas, there would be a triangulation of fire; Hill identified the Memphis sniper sites as a rooftop, a water tower, and a third-story window.[69] (In the event, a shooter in the bushes across from that Lorraine Motel balcony beat the Green Berets to the punch, so to speak; Loyd Jowers told Dr. King's son Dexter that the shooter was Memphis police lieutenant Earl Clark.)

The shooters in the Dal-Tex and Dallas County Records buildings in Dealey Plaza, based on the revelations of Lt. Col. Marvin, would probably have been Green Beret snipers, and Howard Hunt indicated that there was a French gunman on the grassy knoll. Alternatively, the shooters could have been people chosen from the CIA's stable of assassins. Among the people named in various sources as CIA hit men (in addition to David Morales) are Hugh Huggins (aka Hugh Howell);[70] Col. Jack Y. Canon;[71] Col. Ishmael Rodrigo, who became one of CIA agent Ed Lansdale's top Huk (Hukbalahap) killers in the Philippines and worked for the CIA in Manila and Saigon;[72] Col. Napoleón Valeriano, an ultra-right-wing Filipino Constabulary officer who became Ed Lansdale's "chief peasant killer" during the Huk rebellion and was a hit man in William Colby's Operation Phoenix in Vietnam;[73] the CIA's unnamed QJ/WIN, a foreign national with a criminal background;[74] and WI/ROGUE, a French Corsican criminal. Jim Marrs was told by ex-Army intelligence officer William Spector that WI/ROGUE was Christian Jacques David, a convicted French drug smuggler.[75] Piper also reported that Christian David was WI/ROGUE.[76]

The Star Chamber

My main purpose in writing this book was to refute Vincent Bugliosi's book on this subject (and, by extension, to refute the Warren Report), but I had a secondary purpose, which was to try to identify the members of the cabal that plotted the assassination of President Kennedy and other political figures in our country.

Whoever plotted the assassination of President Kennedy:

- induced the President's Secret Service contingent to ignore most of their standard security measures for Presidential motorcades and to seize the President's body at Parkland Hospital, forcibly and illegally, so that the autopsy could be controlled in Washington, and probably ordered the President's Secret Service contingent to go out drinking the night before the motorcade;
- had control of high-level CIA operatives and induced them to frame Oswald, line up assassins, etc.;
- induced FBI agents and other thugs to confiscate film in Dealey Plaza;
- knew that Jack Ruby had relatively unfettered access to the Dallas police offices, and forced him to murder the "patsy," at the cost of life in prison or possibly his own life, to prevent a trial wherein Oswald might have been acquitted (prompting a search for the real assassins);

• ensured that the official autopsy was botched, and caused a phony autopsy report and fake autopsy photographs and x-rays to be generated;

• had access to the sophisticated photographic equipment and techniques that were used to alter the Zapruder film;

• caused the intimidation, and even murder, of key witnesses in the murders of both President Kennedy and Officer J.D. Tippit;

• caused key evidence, such as the discovery of a Mauser rifle in the Book Depository and the photograph of the automobile parked in General Walker's driveway, to be altered;

• ensured that key testimony to the Warren Commission was altered to fit in with the Official Story;

• caused the disappearance of key pieces of forensic evidence from the National Archives;

• managed to prevent four successive inquiries into the assassination from arriving at the truth about it;

• given Earl Warren's insistence on an unanimous report and other strange comments and behaviors, was apparently able even to exert influence over the Chief Justice of the United States; and

• was obsessed with "communism" and its "containment," and was determined to use American combat troops to confront the "communists" in Vietnam. I have placed the term "communism" in quotes throughout the present work because the system of government that our policymakers so feared and loathed was not communism at all, but Stalinism, which is characterized by personalized one-man dictatorship; suppression of social and political dissent, independent thought and traditional religious beliefs, usually in conjunction with the creation of a secret police to locate and throttle dissenters; press censorship; centralized economic planning; nationalization of the means of production; and collectivization of agriculture and major industries. Under communism, the system dreamed up by Karl Marx and Friedrich Engels, society passes from capitalism to socialism and the dictatorship of the proletariat, and from there to communism, a classless society wherein the state "withers away." Anyone who is aware of the power and excesses of a Mao Zedong, a Kim Il Sung, or the system's namesake Josef Stalin can see that under those national leaders, the state did not "wither away." Those US policymakers who were so obsessed with "communism" probably never read a word that Marx or Engels wrote. And

> our willingness to lose 58,000 American lives in Vietnam to show the world that we hated "communism" is a good definition of "obsession."

All of this rules out the Mafia, the KGB, pro- and anti-Castro Cubans, and Lee Harvey Oswald; rather, it points instead to a ruthless, ultra-powerful, ultra-right-wing cabal working at the highest level of our own government. Organized crime may have played a part in lining up triggermen, but the idea that Jack Ruby was acting as an agent of the Mafia when he killed Oswald in Dallas seems unlikely; Bugliosi tells us that Bert Shipp, assistant news director for WFAA-TV in Dallas around the time of the assassination, knew Ruby well, and said, "The Mafia wouldn't have trusted Jack Ruby to take change to the bank."[77] After resigning from the HSCA, of which he was the original chairman, Congressman Henry Gonzalez told newsmen that he was forced out of the investigation by "vast and powerful forces, including the country's most sophisticated criminal element." The Soviets knew right away; TASS, the official Soviet press agency, in its first announcement about the assassination on November 23, declared that President Kennedy had been killed by "extreme right-wing elements" in the US.[78] David Rothkopf quotes a "senior defense contractor" as saying, "Look, there's a lot of talk about a shadow government, and I am here to tell you it's real. On every level the connections between our company and the government are amazingly deep."[79] The findings of Sterling Seagrave are of interest in this context. Tracing Philippine president Ferdinand Marcos' involvement with wartime Japanese General Tomoyuki Yamashita's legendary treasure, Seagrave "was led eventually to a group of American generals, admirals, and former CIA officials operating as a shadow force of Paladins in world affairs – some of the same superpatriots identified with the Iran-Contra arms scandal, the Nugan-Hand Bank scandal, and other CIA misadventures."[80]

There was in England from 1487 to 1641 an English law court that operated outside the Common Law, with no jury; it became known as the Star Chamber. It was made up of Privy Counsellors and common-law judges; it was "speedy and efficient, but also arbitrary and cruel," in the words of *The New American Desk Encyclopedia*. It became a political weapon for bringing actions against opponents to the policies of King Henry VIII, his ministers and Parliament. In the 1960s and 1970s, whether we feel comfortable in acknowledging it or not, there was in our wonderful democracy, the land of the free and the home of the brave, a killer elite, reminiscent of the English Star Chamber, clearly aloof from and contemptuous of all of our nice ideas about democracy and the rule of law, that ordered the elimination of John and Robert Kennedy, Lee Harvey Oswald, Dr. Martin Luther King Jr., Mary Pinchot Meyer, Dorothy Kilgallen, William Bruce Pitzer, Sam Giancana, Johnny Rosselli and apparently several others. This cabal operated at the highest levels of our own government, and was just as vicious and deadly as any "communist" regime that the cabal so feared and loathed. Their message was both clear and very disturbing: "Forget your democracy and your laws. We are in charge." Jack Ruby told us that people in very high positions were behind this assassination. Following is a list of people who 1) were in very high positions; 2) were Cold War "hawks;" and 3) were emotionally committed to fighting and winning a war in Vietnam to prevent a "communist takeover" there.

Lyndon Johnson started to duck just before the bullets started flying in Dealey Plaza. Phillip Nelson says Johnson's absence in the Altgens photo shows that he knew that Dealey Plaza was to be the killing zone. Immediately after taking the oath of office, Johnson turned to his right and got a wink and a grin from Texas Democratic Congressman Albert Thomas, "the pork barrel king of the Texas delegation" and chairman of the House Appropriations Subcommittee's subcommittee on defense, as if to say, "We did it!"[81] The wink and grin can be seen in a photograph on page 71 of Groden's book and on the internet. When I became aware of this wink and grin, which seemed to indicate that Congressman Thomas was somehow involved in the plot (with Johnson), I knew that it was necessary to learn how these two men were linked. They were both Texas politicians who were part of the federal government, of course, but that they were also members of the Suite 8F Group in Houston, which also included George and Herman Brown of the contracting firm of Brown and Root, Governor John Connally, Hugh Roy Cullen of Quintana Petroleum, Morgan J. Davis of Humble Oil, real estate developer and banker Walter M. Mischer (who also supported LBJ's political activities), Gus Wortham, Robert and Oveta Culp Hobby (Ms. Hobby was secretary of health, education and welfare in the Eisenhower administration and in 1963 was the editor and president of the Houston *Post*), and Sam Rayburn, Speaker of the US House of Representatives, among others. Congressman Thomas was Brown and Root's representative in the House of Representatives, according to Johnson biographer Robert Caro.[82] Gus Wortham's American General Insurance Company handled most of Brown & Root's insurance, and was a significant source of money for LBJ "through both the purchase of advertising time on KTBC and campaign contributions..."[83] The Suite 8F group may have been our Star Chamber, but one must ask whether this group had the motivation to plan and execute the assassination and the ability to control power centers in the CIA and the Pentagon.

Following Oswald's arrest, Lyndon Johnson himself called Will Fritz and told him, "You have your man."[84] Dr. Crenshaw told Harrison Livingstone that Johnson told Fritz not to say a thing.[85] Before President Kennedy was buried, Johnson ordered the death car (which had quickly been shipped from Dallas to Washington, D.C.) to be shipped to Detroit for complete refurbishing; all physical evidence of bullet marks, blood patterns, trajectories, etc., was thus destroyed. J. Edgar Hoover reported in a memo to Bureau staff that Johnson told him, "I want to get by with your report." It was Johnson who appointed the Warren Commission, and subsequently issued Executive Order No. 11652, which required that the assassination evidence be locked away from the American public until 2039. According to Johnson's account, Robert Kennedy told him over the telephone that the oath of office should be administered to him immediately.[86] But in "a later conversation Bobby taped for posterity, he said he had never told Johnson that the oath should be administered immediately."[87] As noted above, Johnson also lied about Kenny O'Donnell advising him to take *Air Force One* back to Washington.

Midway through the effort to save Lee Oswald, Dr. Crenshaw got a phone call from President Johnson, who told the doctor that he wanted a deathbed confession from the accused assassin. "There's a man in the operating room who will take the statement," Johnson said. Crenshaw had indeed noticed someone in the operating room whom Crenshaw didn't recognize; he was "a large man...[who] resembled Oliver Hardy." The man had a pistol in his back pocket and was wearing a doctor's gown, but no cap or mask. According to Harrison Livingstone, Dr. Crenshaw was pressured by his publisher to change his original manuscript, which had Johnson *ordering* Crenshaw to *kill* Oswald. Word came down *from the White House* that the Kennedy autopsy findings were to be kept secret. Former FBI assistant director Cartha DeLoach testified that the Bureau was asked *by the White House* to issue a statement saying that Oswald acted alone, without any plot involved.[88] The person in charge at the White House at that point was Lyndon Johnson.

When William Manchester was writing *The Death of a President*, Johnson refused to let him hear recordings between *Air Force One* and Andrews AFB and denied him access to notes from November 22 written by Cliff

Carter and Congressman Homer Thornberry.[89] Thornberry (Texas Democrat) was at Parkland while Kennedy's and Connally's wound were being seen to, and he accompanied Johnson to Love Field after he, Johnson and others left Parkland; he was also a member of the Suite 8F Group. In early November 1966, President Johnson requested, via Cartha DeLoach, background memoranda on eight Warren Commission critics (Edward Epstein, Sylvan Fox, Joachim Joesten, Penn Jones Jr., Mark Lane, Richard Popkin, Leo Sauvage and Harold Weisberg) whose books and articles had dominated the controversy.[90] Jack Ruby wrote notes from jail saying that Lyndon Johnson was behind the events of November 22, 1963. When Ruby was visited in jail by Clayton Fowler, Ruby reportedly took his long yellow pad and scribbled, "Johnson is behind them all the way." In a letter (in the fall of 1964) to a fellow prisoner who was leaving the jail, Ruby wrote that "Johnson is going to try to have an all-out war with Russia..." Another such note said, "They alone had planned the killing, by they I mean Johnson and others ... read the [J. Evetts Haley] book *A Texan Looks at Lyndon* and you may learn quite a bit about Johnson and how he has fooled everyone.... Believe me, compared to him I am a Saint..."

On August 9, 1984, attorney Douglas Caddy wrote to the Department of Justice to report that his client, Billie Sol Estes, had authorized him to tell Justice that he, Estes, was part of a four-person group headed by Lyndon Johnson that committed criminal acts in Texas in the 1960s (the other two were Cliff Carter and Mac Wallace). The letter also stated that Estes was willing to testify that Johnson ordered the murders of nine people, including President Kennedy.[91] Estes, who also had ties to the 8F Group, told several people that he sat in on one of the planning sessions for the JFK assassination, and that Johnson was present.

Dr. Crenshaw opined that only a "sovereign figure" – Lyndon Johnson – had the influence, power and knowledge to carry out the operations of murder and coverup. The statements of E. Howard Hunt, as reported by his son St. John Hunt, inculpating Johnson in the plot have been mentioned above. But I see a couple of problems with this idea that Johnson was the mastermind of the JFK assassination. First, notwithstanding Dr. Crenshaw's statement, Johnson was the vice president at the time of the assassination, and vice presidents don't really have that much power in our system. Nor was Johnson greatly respected or even well-liked in Washington. Second, given the participation of the FBI, Secret Service and other elements in the events of Dallas and their aftermath, we would have to envision something like the following scenario: a member of the

Joint Chiefs approaching, say, Richard Helms, with, "Johnson wants very badly to be president. We have to arrange the assassination of President Kennedy." This seems an unlikely scenario. Third, I believe that the same right-wing cabal that had President Kennedy eliminated was also responsible for the murders of Mary Pinchot Meyer, Dr. Martin Luther King Jr. and Robert Kennedy. It is difficult to conjure up a motive for Johnson to have Mary Meyer rubbed out, and likewise difficult to find a motive for Johnson, who was shepherding a civil rights bill through Congress, to have Dr. King killed. Johnson would scarcely have a motive to have Robert Kennedy killed in June 1968 to eliminate the competition for the presidency, since Johnson, earlier that year, had announced that he would not be seeking, and would not accept, the nomination of his party for a second term as president.

The behavior of the Secret Service in stripping the limousine of security and driving President Kennedy into an ambush in Dealey Plaza, among other things, have been detailed in Chapter 3, above. These agents must have been instructed to behave as he did, and from whom would they take instructions other than Secret Service chief James Rowley? Vincent Palamara says Rowley was a good friend of Lyndon Johnson and J. Edgar Hoover.[92] Rowley was also a former FBI agent. And did Rowley's boss, C. Douglas Dillon, not know anything about this? As Secretary of the Treasury, Dillon was in overall charge of Kennedy's Secret Service protection. Though appointed by President Kennedy, Dillon had supported Richard Nixon in the 1960 presidential campaign. In 1962, Dillon joined with David Rockefeller in pressing Kennedy to reduce government spending, except for defense, and in 1965, the two men joined with fellow Chase Manhattan directors, such as John McCloy, to create a formal group to promote the Vietnam War.[93] Dillon made sure he was out of the country during the assassination; he informed JFK that he planned to fly to Tokyo with other cabinet members on an official visit that would keep him out of the country from November 21 through 27.[94] Talbot describes Dillon as part of the Republican Party's ruling clique, and closely associated with the Dulles brothers, and notes that Dillon stonewalled Warren Commission assistant counsel Howard Willens' efforts to pry loose Secret Service records.[95] "Soon after the assassination," says Talbot, "Dillon and others began circulating the false rumor that Kennedy preferred his Secret Service guards to ride behind him in the motorcade."[96] Dillon was also a member of the "ExComm" (the Executive Committee of the National Security Council) set up to deal with the Cuban Missile Crisis, and was, along with John McCone, Gen. Maxwell Taylor and Paul Nitze, pressing for air strikes during the Missile Crisis.[97]

The comments and behavior of Richard Nixon during and after the assassination are suspicious. Nixon told the Warren Commission that he thought he was in New York the morning of November 22. He told the FBI's John Malone in February of 1964 that the only time he was in Dallas in 1963 was two days *before* the assassination.[98] But three years later, he told journalist Charles Witcover that he had flown to Dallas the day before the assassination and had returned to New York the following morning.[99] Nixon gave four different versions of how he first heard about the shooting in Dallas. Version 1: He was told by a man on a street corner. Version 2: He was told by a woman who had come out of her house screaming and crying.[100] Version 3: He heard about it while leaving Idlewild (now John F. Kennedy) Airport; a man ran up to his cab and told him that shots had been fired at the President.[101] Version 4: Nixon told an interviewer in 1967 that he was in a Dallas taxicab when he got the news. When *Esquire* magazine questioned Nixon on his whereabouts on the day of the assassination, he finally admitted to being in Dallas, but said that he left before noon. In fact he was in Dallas at the time Kennedy was shot. This was confirmed by the man Nixon was with in Dallas, Pepsico general counsel Harvey Russell.[102]

On a White House tape of June 23, 1972, speaking with his chief of staff H.R. Haldeman, Nixon mentions E. Howard Hunt. Nixon is heard to say, "...this Hunt, that will uncover a lot of things.... You open that scab there's a hell of a lot of things and we just feel that it would be very detrimental to have this thing go any further. This involves these Cubans, Hunt and a lot of hankypanky.... Your major guy to keep under control is Hunt..." Later the same day, Nixon told Haldeman, "...very bad to have this fellow Hunt, ah, he knows too damned much ... if it gets out that this is all involved.... It would make the CIA look bad, it's going to make Hunt look bad, and it's likely to blow the whole Bay of Pigs thing, which we think would be very unfortunate – both for CIA, and for the country, at this time..." The Bay of Pigs matter had ended in 1961. Haldeman stated that after he read Daniel Schorr's book *Clearing the Air*, "I put Schorr's facts together with mine. It seems that in all of those Nixon references to the Bay of Pigs, he was actually referring to the Kennedy assassination."[103]

There is moreover a connection between Nixon and Jack Ruby. In the mid-1940s, Ruby reportedly performed "information functions" for Congressman Nixon's staff, according to a government panel investigating organized-crime activities in 1947. The memo was discovered among FBI documents by political scientist Trowbridge Ford in 1975.[104] The Committee to Investigate Assassinations, headed by Washington attorney Bernard Fensterwald Jr., determined that in November, 1970, Nixon's attorney general and fellow Watergate conspirator John Mitchell had ordered the Justice Department to block the release of important ballistic evidence pertaining to the JFK assassination – evidence that, on the grounds of "national security," had never been turned over to the Warren Commission by the FBI.[105]

General Maxwell Taylor was chairman of the Joint Chiefs of Staff at the time. It seems likely that if the other members of the Joint Chiefs were involved, he would also be involved. Author Trumbull Higgins described Maxwell Taylor as "an intimate of Allen Dulles in the White House."[106] In a 1956 article, Gen. Taylor discussed the "international Communist movement" and stated that the central aim of US national security policy should be "the deterrence of Communist expansion in whatever form it may take." "In 1961," says Daniel Ellsberg, "the group most in favor of an enlarged intervention [in Vietnam], including the sending of ground troops, was headed by Maxwell Taylor and Walt Rostow."[107] Rostow was head of the State Department's Policy Planning Council at the time of the assassination. In the many meetings in 1961, according to Langguth, Rostow "had argued long and genially for bombing Vietcong sanctuaries within both Laos and North Vietnam."[108] Gen. Taylor was a hard-core "hawk" on Vietnam and wrote numerous memos to President Kennedy regarding the need for military intervention there. In an "Eyes Only" message to JFK, Gen. Taylor described the sending of US ground combat troops to Vietnam as "an essential action if we are to reverse the downward turn of events."[109] Taylor interfered with and watered down JFK's order to bring 1,000 US military personnel home from Vietnam by the end of 1963. Press accounts and official statements had given the impression, which persisted for years, that after Taylor's trip to Vietnam, he and his team had concluded that JFK's plan of sending only advisers and helicopters to Vietnam would be adequate to forestall a "communist" takeover, and had advised the president of this; but Daniel Ellsberg, while working on the research project that became the Pentagon Papers, eventually learned that the opposite was true. Taylor's secret cables to JFK in late October 1961, revealed in the Pentagon Papers, "not only recommended the introduction of a US military force into South Vietnam 'without delay' but also said that he had 'reached the conclusion that this is an *essential* action if we are to reverse the present downward trend of events.... In fact, I do not believe that our program to save South Vietnam will succeed without it.'"[110] L. Fletcher Prouty named Gen. Taylor as a member of the policymaking cabal that Prouty called the Secret Team, but David Halberstam wrote in *The Best and the Brightest* that the other members of the Joint Chiefs did not necessarily trust Taylor, so it is not clear that they would enter into a murder conspiracy with him. Furthermore, Gen. Taylor owed his position to President Kennedy and was known to have had a close personal relationship with him, so his membership in the killer elite remains an open question.

During the Cuban Missile Crisis in October 1962, Air Force General Curtis LeMay clashed repeatedly with President Kennedy, Robert McNamara, Air Force Secretary Eugene Zuckert and Gen. Taylor, arguing that he should be allowed to bomb nuclear missile sites in Cuba. In an October 19 exchange with JFK, Gen. LeMay said that the president's proposed naval blockade of Cuba "and political action, I see leading into war...This is almost as bad as the appeasement of Munich...I just don't see any other solution except direct military action *right now*."[111] According to Talbot, LeMay complained "off the record" to Fletcher Knebel, co-author of *Seven Days in May*, about Kennedy's "cowardice" at the Bay of Pigs, and told JFK himself that the BOP was "the greatest defeat in our history." Talbot notes that LeMay had close ties to militaristic congressional leaders and the far right, and that he made no secret of his loathing for the Kennedy administration.[112]

I consider it unlikely that David Shoup, commandant of the Marine Corps, would have been a member of our Star Chamber. He opposed plans for the commitment of US troops for combat in Vietnam, as well as the strategic hamlet program and efforts to train the South Vietnamese army. In an interview with ABC News, Shoup said the Vietnam War was "not worth the life or limb of a single American."[113] Arthur Schlesinger wrote, "Except for Shoup, the military leaders were Cold War zealots. They had sedulously cultivated relations with powerful conservative legislators – John Stennis, Mendel Rivers, Strom Thurmond, Barry Goldwater."[114] According to wikipedia.com, Shoup "became increasingly wary of what he felt was undue influence by the CIA and big business on foreign policy." Thus it seems doubtful that Shoup would be involved in the JFK murder conspiracy, least of all with the CIA, in order to clear the way for a war in Vietnam.

In trying to identify the members of the killer elite – our own Star Chamber – one cannot help but notice how often the names Johnson,

Hoover, McCloy, Dulles, Nixon, Rowley, Angleton and Helms appear in the narrative. These people, along with Pentagon elements as described above, presumably acting under the direction of certain members of the Joint Chiefs such as General Earle G. Wheeler (Army), Admiral David L. McDonald (Navy), and possibly Curtis E. LeMay (Air Force), may have been responsible for the Dallas conspiracy and cover-up. With regard to the Dallas assassination, there are, it seems to me, only two possibilities: Either the people named in this paragraph constituted the Star Chamber or they were acting under the orders of a higher, even more powerful cabal. But if one believes that the same people were involved in the 1963 assassination of President Kennedy, the 1964 murder of Mary Pinchot Meyer, and the 1968 assassinations of Robert Kennedy and Dr. King, then one must question the identification of the Joint Chiefs as part of the Star Chamber, which in turn would tend to favor the second option, above – that these killings were perpetrated by a higher cabal that continued to influence events through 1968, and possibly through 1975, which saw another series of suspicious deaths. The idea that the same cabal was involved in all four of the 1960s assassinations is based on the following: 1) each target was fatally shot in the head (indicating the work of professionals); 2) each target was agitating for social change and/or was openly critical of the conclusions of the Warren Report, 3) except for the Mary Meyer case (her attitude toward the Vietnam situation is unclear), each target was opposed to the commitment of US soldiers to a ground war in Vietnam; 4) in each case, an unwitting "patsy" (Lee Oswald, Ray Crump Jr., James Earl Ray, Sirhan Sirhan) was set up to give the impression that the killer had been caught, thus deflecting culpability from the true perpetrators; 5) US government agents and/or local police personnel on-site promptly engaged in numerous activities to suppress the truth and ensure the survival of the Official Story that was being created for each murder, and to quash efforts to demonstrate a conspiracy. By 1968, however, the personnel at the top of the Pentagon and elsewhere had changed.

At the time of the Robert Kennedy and Dr. King assassinations, General Harold K. Johnson had replaced General Wheeler as Army chief-of-staff, General John P. McConnell had replaced General LeMay as Air Force chief-of-staff, General Leonard F. Chapman Jr. had replaced General Wallace Greene as Marine Corps chief-of-staff, and Admiral Thomas H. Moorer had replaced Admiral McDonald as chief of naval operations. If the Star Chamber was based in the Pentagon at the Joint Chiefs level, that would mean that people like those three generals and Admiral Moorer had joined in the assassination frenzy, and had reconstituted the Star Chamber to include themselves, along with the nonmilitary actors listed at the beginning of this paragraph. In 1968, Henry H. Fowler was Treasury secretary, though James Rowley was still head of the Secret Service, J. Edgar Hoover was still head of the FBI, and Dean Rusk was still secretary of state. Lyndon Johnson was, of course, still the president, but as noted above, he would seem to have no reason to have Dr. King and Robert Kennedy killed. The killing of RFK did, however, benefit Richard Nixon, by eliminating a competitor in the 1968 presidential race. Recent comments by Cord Meyer seem to lend support to my theory of a 'continuity of assassination planners' independent of the people occupying the Joint Chiefs positions and/or the White House. In an interview with the writer C. David Heymann in 2001, Cord was asked who killed his ex-wife Mary. He replied, "The same sons of bitches that killed John F. Kennedy."[115]

It is also interesting to note how often the name Rockefeller continues to appear in discussions of corporate power and influence. The international banking czar David Rockefeller was a member of the corporate elite, according to various sources, and had been a director of the Council on Foreign Relations since 1949. He was vice president of the CFR and president of Chase Manhattan Bank in 1963. He knew and associated with Allen Dulles, Richard Helms and William Bundy. Warren Commissioner John McCloy handled the Rockefeller account at the law firm of Milbank, Tweed, Hadley and McCloy. Warren Commission assistant counsel Wesley Liebeler was a member of the Wall Street law firm of Carter, Ledyard & Milburn, which represented various Rockefeller, Standard Oil and Whitney interests.

Peter Dale Scott notes "the sustained if subtle campaign for Vietnam involvement, dating back to the first years of the Diem regime, waged by individuals connected to the Rockefeller-linked Socony Mobil Corporation and Chase Manhattan Bank."[116] According to Gibson, Allen Dulles used the Ford and Rockefeller Foundations to secretly finance CIA activities, and was associated with both the Rockefeller and Morgan groups.[117] John McCloy, the Nazi sympathizer, was tied in with David Rockefeller through the former's sometime chairmanship of Chase Manhattan. Dean Rusk was president of the Rockefeller Foundation immediately before becoming JFK's secretary of state. Douglas Dillon has been described as "a close associate of David Rockefeller's and a director of the Chase Manhattan Bank."[118] Dillon became chairman of the Rockefeller Foundation for three years starting in 1972, and was a member of the Rockefeller Commission of 1975 (the Commission on CIA Activities within the United States).

Henry Luce was connected to the Rockefellers by way of his membership on a panel of the Rockefeller Brothers Fund on *International Security: The Military Aspect*, headed by Nelson Rockefeller, calling for heavier military spending, in the "America at Mid-Century" studies (1958).[119] Gibson notes "the conflict between Kennedy and Morgan-Rockefeller interests over foreign policy," and adds, "The economic development Kennedy was supporting threatened Establishment control of Third World economies."[120] President Kennedy's domestic and foreign policies "posed a direct threat to the Rockefeller dynasty on multiple fronts..."[121] In an open letter to Kennedy in the July 6, 1962, issue of *Life* magazine, David Rockefeller demanded a "material reduction in the corporate income tax rate," and urged a "more effective control of expenditures and a determined and vigorous effort to balance the budget."[122] After being stabbed 22 times in prison, James Earl Ray, the patsy in the Martin Luther King case, appeared in court as a witness in 1982 (as part of the trial of the convicts who had attacked him). On the witness stand, he commented on the difficulty he had had in Tennessee courts establishing facts in any matter related directly or indirectly to the Martin King murder – that it was "due to the prevailing winds that blow from the *Tennessean*, the state's political establishment and the Rockefeller contingent." He was not given time to say any more. On hearing the Rockefeller name, "a dozen or so sheriff's deputies rushed me, rousted me out of the witness stand, and, aided by prison officials, hustled me down the back way into a squad car."[123]

Evelyn Lincoln, President Kennedy's private secretary, confidently told Harrison Livingstone in 1991 that J. Edgar Hoover, the CIA and the Mafia were involved in the conspiracy to kill President Kennedy.[124] On October 7, 1994, Ms. Lincoln wrote a letter to a Virginia schoolteacher in which she stated that she thought there were five people and groups involved in JFK's death: Lyndon Johnson, J. Edgar Hoover, the Mafia, the CIA and "the Cubans in Florida."[125] Marty Underwood, Secret Service advance man for JFK's stops in Houston and Austin, told researcher Vincent Palamara in 1991 that the CIA, the FBI and the Mafia all had foreknowledge of the assassination, and Underwood said that he got this information from Winston M. Scott, CIA station chief in Mexico City between 1956 and 1969.[126] Dr. McClelland told Bugliosi that he believed that "the CIA and FBI, mostly the CIA, were behind the conspiracy to kill Kennedy, and they brought in the Mafia, who carried out the killing."[127] Dr. Cyril Wecht believed that four or five people plotted the hit, and that Allen Dulles was one of them. Penn Jones Jr., who met with Robert Kennedy in the latter's Senate office to share his views, was convinced that the assassination was a coup d'état involving the CIA and the Joint Chiefs. In fact, Bobby Kennedy himself asked press secretary Frank Mankiewicz to find out all he could about JFK's assassination, and after doing some investigating, Mankiewicz concluded that the perpetrators were probably the Mob, anti-Castro Cuban exiles, and maybe rogue CIA agents.[128] Richard Goodwin, who was a White House aide and was briefly JFK's chief adviser on Cuba, told Talbot, "We know the CIA was involved, and the Mafia. We all know that."[129] But Billie Sol Estes said that the Mafia did not participate in the JFK assassination, and Jimmy "the Weasel" Fratianno once quoted Johnny Rosselli as telling him, "You know, we're supposed to be idiots, right? We hire a psycho like Oswald to kill the president, and then we get a blabbermouth two-bit punk like Ruby to shut him up. We wouldn't trust those two jerks to hit a f---ing dog." Walt Brown wrote that "the conglomerates" – the CIA, the corporations, Big Oil – were behind the assassination, though he was unable to name names.[130] These statements, coming from so many different sources, definitely have a ring of truth, and are supported by the various disclosures in the present work. But if Walt Brown is right, the questions remain: Which corporations? Which members of Big Oil?

The cabal could have been a high-powered committee of the Council on Foreign Relations, and it just so happens that the Bundy brothers, Douglas Dillon, Gerald Ford, Henry Luce, John McCloy, Richard Nixon, Walt Rostow, Dean Rusk, George Ball (who was acting secretary of state when Dean Rusk was on his way to a conference in Honolulu on November 22, 1963) and Nicholas Katzenbach were all CFR members, and Allen Dulles was president of the CFR in 1963. McGeorge Bundy was JFK's national security advisor; his brother William was assistant secretary of state for international security affairs at the time of the assassination of President Kennedy, and served as assistant secretary of state for Far Eastern and Pacific affairs under President Johnson (and at the time of the Robert Kennedy and Dr. King assassinations). The CIA's Richard Bissell Jr. told Senate investigators and a presidential commission in 1975 that the directive to create an assassination squad came from McGeorge Bundy and Walt Rostow.[131] Rostow and Dean Rusk were Vietnam hawks. Rusk "consistently favored strong American involvement [in Vietnam], arguing that 'aggression' had to be stopped."[132] At a meeting at the State Department on August 31, 1963, to discuss Vietnam, Rusk recommended that we "start on the firm basis of two things – that we will not pull out of Vietnam until the war is won, and that we will not run a coup."[133] Rusk "had argued since 1961 for the legitimacy and necessity of American bombing of North Vietnam."[134] Rostow was one of the chief engineers of our involvement in Vietnam, according to James Perloff.[135] Peter Dale Scott called Rostow "the leading civilian hawk and advocate for the US bombing of North Vietnam."[136] Admiral Arleigh Burke, moved to the ambassadorship of Portugal after talking back to Robert McNamara at the Pentagon, and General Lyman Lemnitzer, who was JCS chairman until reassigned by JFK in 1962 to be European chief of NATO, were CFR members. CIA heavies Richard Bissell Jr., Ray Cline, William Colby, Richard Helms, John McCone, and Frank Wisner were also CFR members. Colby was head of the Far East Division of the CIA at the time of the assassination.

The "investigations" of the CIA have been dominated by CFR members.[137] Even if the people in this paragraph constituted the Star Chamber, it would be difficult to ascertain whether or not they were acting in the context of the CFR or independently of that organization. Admiral Chester Ward, retired judge advocate general of the US Navy and longtime CFR member, has been quoted as saying that although the CFR, as such, does not control US defense and foreign policies, "CFR members, as individuals, acting in concert with other individual CFR members, do."[138]

The Council is supported by foundations that are in turn have been directed by men from the Bechtel Corporation, Chase Manhattan Bank, Cummins Engine, Corning Glass, Kimberly-Clark, Monsanto Chemical, and dozens of others.[139] Gulf, Ford Motor Company and Brown Brothers, Harriman are also involved. The major contributors over the years have been the Ford and Rockefeller foundations and the Carnegie Corporation.[140] Donald Gibson wrote that by the early 1960s, "the Council on Foreign Relations, Morgan and Rockefeller interests, and the intelligence community were so extensively inbred as to be virtually a single entity."[141] The political scientist Lester Milbraith once noted that the CFR "while not financed by government, works so closely with it that it is difficult to distinguish Council actions stimulated by government from autonomous actions."[142]

The Bilderberg Group, another elite policymaking group that meets behind closed doors, may have been behind the assassination. According to various sources, David Rockefeller, John McCloy, Allen Dulles, Douglas Dillon, Dean Rusk, Walt Rostow and McGeorge Bundy, among other key US political figures, were all tied in with the Bilderbergers. *Life* magazine's C.D. Jackson played a major role in creating the group, and David Rockefeller provided funding for it. Andreas von Rétyi wrote, "Numerous crucial events in politics and economics can be traced back to subtle manipulation by Bilderberg. Their goal: total global control... What is discussed there behind locked doors remains strictly secret, but we have no choice. Whatever the Bilderberger decides will shape our future. They rank among the central organs of a world-wide shadow government."[143]

The cabal may have included top executives from, for example, arms and explosives maker Du Pont; Dow Chemical, manufacturer of Agent Orange (widely used in Vietnam); Bell Helicopter (whose HU-1 "Huey" was also widely used in Vietnam) and other defense contractors and multinational corporations. Gerry Hemming stated that the "Hanford and Rocky Flats" (Dow Chemical) people provided funding for the hit on President Kennedy. Dow made napalm for the Vietnam conflict, and throughout the sixties, Dow's earnings increased about ten percent a year. Fletcher Prouty told Twyman in 1995 that such a power elite – he mentioned banking, finance, steel, defense, and oil – really runs our country.[144] As an outsider writing many years after the fact, I can only offer informed speculation.

The elimination of President Kennedy and later of Robert Kennedy and Dr. Martin Luther King Jr. were all of a piece with CIA projects such as Operation Mockingbird, the program to give articles in the national communications media a right-wing slant. According to the aforementioned article by Carl Bernstein in *Rolling Stone* magazine, the program had major influence over 25 newspapers and wire agencies, and was overseen by Allen Dulles from 1953, with Frank Wisner and Cord Meyer playing major roles. Henry Luce and C.D. Jackson were also involved. Other journalists reportedly willing to promote the views of the CIA included Joseph and Stewart Alsop (both of the *New York Herald Tribune*), Ben Bradlee (*Newsweek*), James Reston (*New York Times*), Walter Pincus (*Washington Post*), Walter Winchell (*New York Daily Mirror*), and the columnists Drew Pearson and Walter Lippmann. The Associated Press and United Press International were also cooperating with the CIA, according to Bernstein. Operation Mockingbird included the wiretapping of two US journalists (Robert Allen and Paul Scott). The "family jewels" CIA document reveals that this wiretapping was authorized by John McCone. The CIA also was connected with the publication of Walt Rostow's book *The Dynamics of Soviet Society* as well as Frank Trager's *Why Vietnam?*[145] The Church Committee found that approximately fifty of the CIA's assets were individual

American journalists or employees of US media organizations. That committee also found that approximately 250 books written in English were produced, subsidized, or sponsored by the CIA before the end of 1967.[146] The Star Chamber considered the United States a right-wing nation, and that included employing the Thought Police – the CIA and compliant national journalists - to enforce this concept. But domestic covert, police or intelligence activities on the part of the CIA are strictly prohibited by that agency's charter, and are thus illegal.

At the end of the day, the membership of the Star Chamber – and at this point they are all surely deceased - may not be as important as knowing that there *was* such a powerful, murderous cabal at work in our country in the sixties (and seventies, apparently) who took it upon themselves to eliminate national figures they considered to be politically incorrect, along with a number of other people who had the audacity to question the official version of events, or simply "knew too much." The idea – and the reality – of a handful of powerful people at the top of our government running our country the way some Mafia crime family would (and working with the Mafia) was, and remains, a national disgrace and a betrayal of the principles on which our country was founded and for which it stands. Our national leaders were meant to be chosen by a vote of the people, and not from among the right-wing slimeballs who remain alive after the CIA and Green Berets, on orders from a killer elite, have eliminated the competition by means of bullets to the head.

In the 1961 Supreme Court case of *Mapp v. Ohio*, Justice Tom Clark wrote, "Nothing can destroy a government more quickly than its failure to observe its own laws, or worse, its disregard of the charter of its own existence.... Our Government is the potent, the omnipresent teacher. For good or ill, it teaches the whole people by its example.... If the Government becomes a lawbreaker, it breeds contempt for law; it invites every man to become a law unto himself; it invites anarchy."[147]

Diagrams

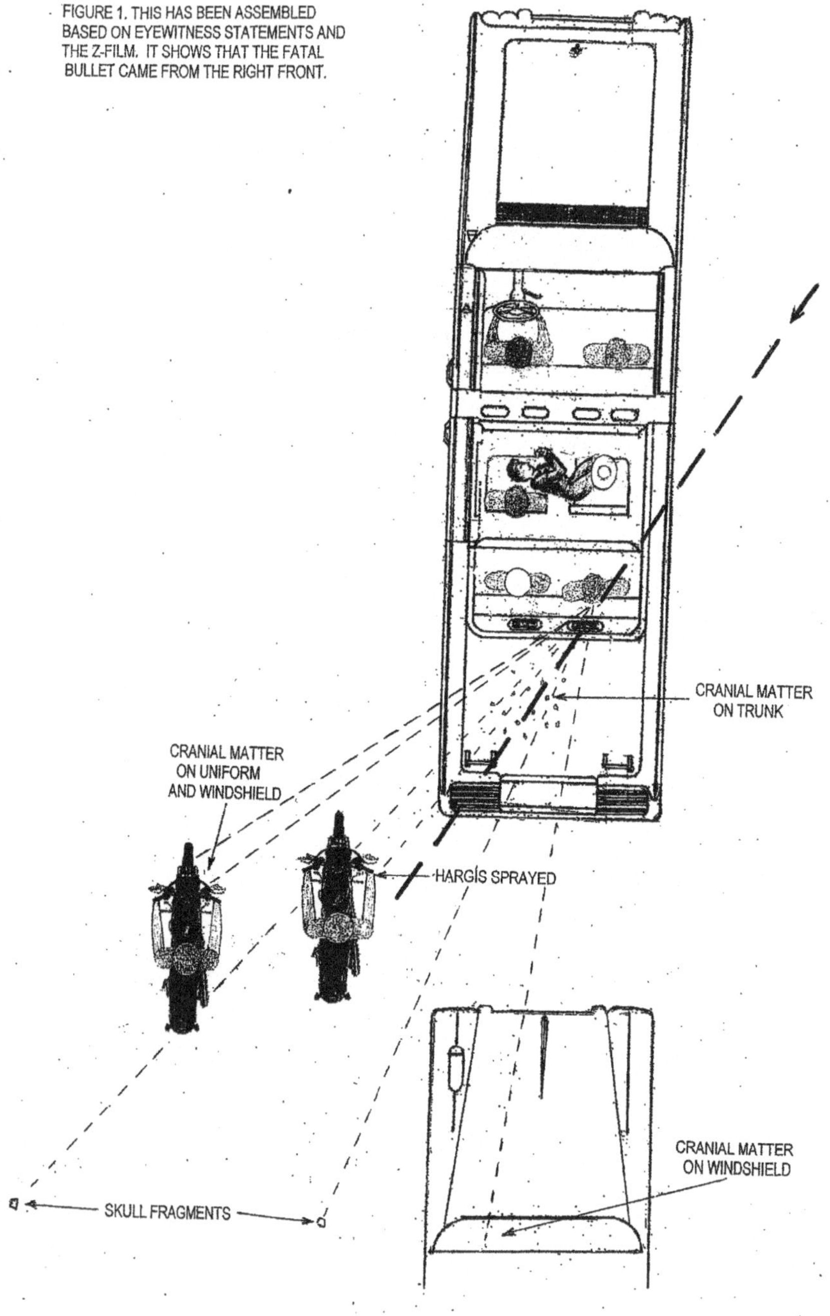

FIGURE 1. THIS HAS BEEN ASSEMBLED BASED ON EYEWITNESS STATEMENTS AND THE Z-FILM. IT SHOWS THAT THE FATAL BULLET CAME FROM THE RIGHT FRONT.

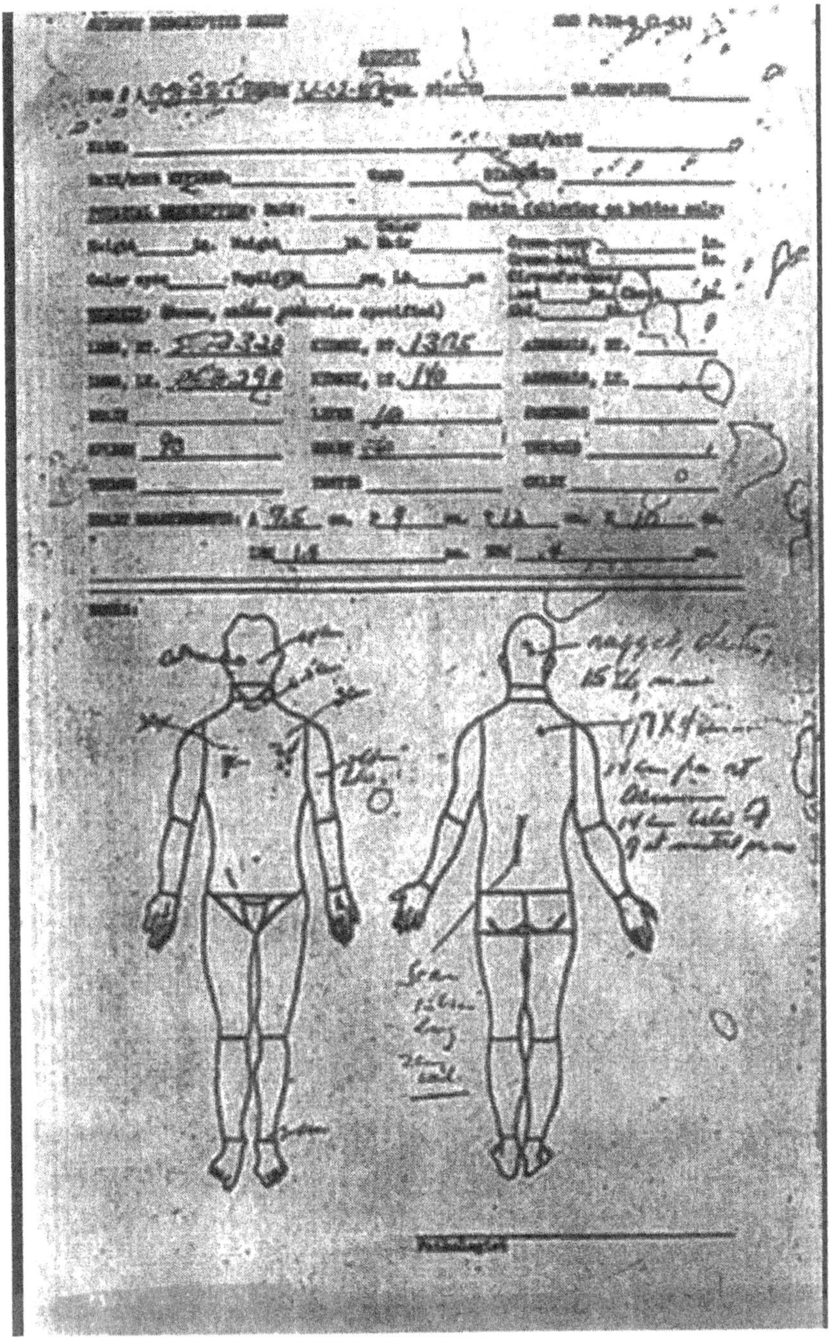

FIGURE 2. THIS IS THE AUTOPSY DESCRIPTIVE SHEET PREPARED BY DR. BOSWELL. IT SHOWS NO BULLET ENTRY WOUND IN THE BASE OF THE BACK OF THE NECK (FOR THE MAGIC BULLET), IN CONTRADISTINCTION TO WHAT THE WARREN REPORT TELLS US.

FIGURE 3. These two photographs are at the same scale (both ears are the same length). The top one is obviously John Kennedy; the bottom one is the stand-in, as depicted on an official autopsy photo. The noses and jaw lines don't match, and if you measure the depths of the two crania, front to back (at the foreheads), you will find that the fake Kennedy's skull is barely 90% the depth of that of the real Kennedy. The ears and sideburns seem to match, so the lower photo appears to be some kind of composite.

Endnotes

Notes to Introduction

1. James H. Fetzer, PhD, "Could Oswald Have Been Convicted?," in Fetzer (ed.), *Murder in Dealey Plaza: What We Know Now that We Didn't Know Then about the Death of JFK* (Chicago: Catfeet Press, 2000), p. 370. **2**. Vincent Bugliosi, *Reclaiming History: The Assassination of President John F. Kennedy* (New York: W.W. Norton, 2007), p. xiv. **3**. Id., pp. 990-91. **4**. Id. p. 969n. **5**. Id., p. 362. **6**. Id., p. xix. 7. David Talbot, *The Devil's Chessboard: Allen Dulles, the CIA, and the Rise of America's Secret Government* (New York: HarperCollins, 2015), p. 69. **8**. Tim Weiner, *Legacy of Ashes: The History of the CIA* (New York: Doubleday, 2007), pp. 24, 77. **9**. Talbot, *The Devil's Chessboard*, p. 261. **10**. William Corson, *The Armies of Ignorance: The Rise of the American Intelligence Empire* (New York: Dial Press, 1977), pp. 365-66; Darrell Garwood, *Under Cover: Thirty-five Years of CIA Deception* (New York: Grove Press, 1985), pp. 61-2; also John Discoe Smith, *I Was a CIA Agent in India*, published by the Communist Party of India, 1967. **11**. William Blum, *The CIA: A Forgotten History* (New Jersey: Zed Books, 1986), pp. 92-3, and Noam Chomsky, *Towards a New Cold War* (New York: Pantheon Books, 1982), p. 396, note 192, based on Wilbur Eveland. **12**. Weiner, op. cit., pp. 138-39. **13**. Blum, op. cit., pp. 100-01. **14**. Douglas Valentine, *The Strength of the Wolf: The Secret History of America's War on Drugs* (New York: Verso, 2004), p. 171. 15. Weiner, op. cit., pp. 576-77, notes to p. 141. 16. Blum, op. cit., p. 171. 17. Scott Shane, "Memories of a C.I.A. Officer Resonate in a New Era," nytimes.com, February 24, 2008. **18**. Ralph McGehee, *Deadly Deceits: My 25 Years in the CIA* (Melbourne: Ocean Press, 1999), p. 60; also John Stockwell, *In Search of Enemies: A CIA Story* (New York: W.W. Norton, 1978). **19**. Talbot, *The Devil's Chessboard*, p. 405; cf. McGehee, op. cit., p. 54. **20**. Talbot, *The Devil's Chessboard*, p. 199. **21**. Weiner, op. cit., p. 10. **22**. Linda Hunt, *Secret Agenda* (New York: St. Martin's Press, 1991), p. 132; Kai Bird, *The Chairman: John McCloy and the Making of the American Establishment* (New York: Simon & Schuster, 1992), pp. 362, 364, 370; John Loftus, *The Belarus Secret* (New York: Alfred A. Knopf, 1982), pp. 18, 20, 78. **23**. Alexander Cockburn and Jeffrey St. Clair, *Whiteout: The CIA, Drugs and the Press* (New York: Verso, 1998), pp. 167-70. **24**. Bertrand Russell, "16 Questions on the Assassination," in Fetzer, *Murder in Dealey Plaza*, p. 414. **25**. Bugliosi, main book, p. xiv. **26**. Id., p. xv. **27**. William Turner and Jonn Christian, *The Assassination of Robert F. Kennedy: A Searching Look at the*

Conspiracy and Cover-up 1968-78 (New York: Random House, 1978), p. 184. **28**. Id., pp. xxvi-xxvii. 29. Id., p. xxvii.

Notes to Chapter 1

1. Bugliosi, main book, p. xi. **2**. Bugliosi, main book, pp. xviii, xxvi. **3**. Id., p. 479n. **4**. Sarah Ellison, "Whose N.R.A. Is It?," *Vanity Fair*, August 2016, p. 106. **5**. Alexandra Zapruder, *Twenty-Six Seconds: A Personal History of the Zapruder Film* (New York: Twelve, 2016), p. 415. **6**. Bill Muntaglio and Steven L. Davis, *Dallas 1963: Patriots, Traitors, and the Assassination of JFK* (New York: Twelve, 2013), pp. 316-17. **7**. Jim Marrs, *Crossfire: The Plot That Killed Kennedy* (New York: Carroll & Graf, 1989), p. 439. **8**. 3H295; 19H508. **9**. Bugliosi, main book, p. 87. **10**. 2H46. **11**. CD1418, Mark Lane interview on the Barry Gray show over WMCA in New York City, 7/29/64, and Lane, *Last Word: My Indictment of the CIA in the Murder of JFK* (New York: Skyhorse Publishing, 2011), p. 16. **12**. 4H281. **13**. 2H35-6. **14**. WR, p. 120. **15**. Bugliosi endnotes, p. 397, and Bugliosi, main book, p. 792. **16**. 4H205-6. **17**. 4H258. **18**. 24H264; 4H205. *19*. 24H320. **20**. Bugliosi, main book, p. 170. **21**. Affidavit of J. Philip Lux, 11H216. **22**. Yeargan affidavit, 11H217. **23**. Bugliosi, main book, p. 170. **24**. WR, p. 118. Bugliosi acknowledges that the "discovery" that rifle number C2766 had been shipped to A. Hidell in Dallas was not until 4:00 a.m. on November 23 (main book, p. 790). **25**. Bugliosi, main book, p. 53; 6H170. **26**. 24H4, 24H207. **27**. 6H313. **28**. 24H4 and 19H474; these affidavits are identical. **29**. 2H204; FBI report, CD205, p. 13. **30**. Bugliosi, main book, p. 159n. **31**. Affidavit, 24H231. **32**. 2H159, 162. **33**. 6H157. **34**. 7H486. **35**. 2H138. **36**. 6H169. **37**. 6H164, 167. **38**. Bugliosi endnotes, p. 421n. **39**. 24H534 (FBI affidavit, January 10, 1964). **40**. 7H542. **41**. 7H34, 344. **42**. 7H523. **43**. 6H291. **44**. 15H525-26. **45**. WR, p. 644; FBI report, CD205, p. 158. **46**. Bugliosi endnotes, pp. 467-68; HSCA Final Report, p. 86. **47**. 4HSCA406. **48**. Bugliosi, main book, p. 854. **49**. 6H202-4; FBI report, December 2, 1963, CD205, p. 21. **50**. Bugliosi, main book, p. 806. **51**. 7H354-55. **52**. 24H406. **53**. 3H148-49; affidavit, 11H216-17; 7H355. **54**. 3H145. **55**. WR, p. 144. **56**. 19H470. **57**. Jesse Curry, *Retired Dallas Police Chief Jesse Curry Reveals His Personal JFK Assassination File* (Dallas: self-published, printed by American Poster and Publishing Company, 1969), p. 62. **58**. 5H134. **59**. Bugliosi, main book, p. 468. **60**. 2H193-94, 198. **61**. 19H486. **62**. 6H243-44. **63**. Shaw trial testimony, No. 24, pp. 30-1. **64**. Marrs, op. cit., p. 29. **65**. Sheriff's Dept. affidavit, November 22, 1963, 19H492. **66**. Bugliosi, main book, p. 1389. **67**. 6H207. **68**. CD711, letter from Hoover to Rankin, April 2, 1964. **69**. James H. Fetzer, PhD, "Smoking Guns' in the Death of JFK," in Fetzer, *Murder in Dealey Plaza*, p. 10. **70**. Bugliosi, main book, p. 463. **71**. Id., p. 464. **72**. Id., p. 806. **73**. Bugliosi endnotes, p. 332. **74**. 4H133, 79. **75**. Douglas Weldon, J.D., "The Kennedy Limousine: Dallas 1963," in Fetzer, *Murder in Dealey Plaza*, p. 147. **76**. 2H43. **77**. 7H508-10, 514; 12HSCA20. **78**. Philip Shenon, *A Cruel and Shocking*

Act: The Secret History of the Kennedy Assassination (New York: Henry Holt, 2013), p. 261. **79.** 5H59; 7HSCA81. **80.** 5H59-60. **81.** 2H365. **82.** WR, p. 92. **83.** Affidavit, 18H760. **84.** 2H143. **85.** Sylvia Meagher, *Accessories After The Fact: The Warren Commission, The Authorities, and The Report* (Indianapolis: Bobbs-Merrill, 1967), pp. 157-58, 90. **86.** CD 107, pp. 2-3, January 13, 1964; Bugliosi endnotes, p. 298. **87.** 2H73. **88.** Orleans Parish Grand Jury testimony, No. 25, pp. 20-21. **89.** Gary Aguilar, M.D., "The Converging Medical Case for Conspiracy in the Death of JFK," in Fetzer, *Murder in Dealey Plaza,* p. 195. **90.** Douglas P. Horne, *Inside the Assassination Records Review Board: The U.S. Government's Final Attempt to Reconcile the Conflicting Medical Evidence in the Assassination of JFK* (self-published, 2009), Vol. I, Appendix 9. **91.** 6H9. **92.** 17H29; 7HSCA292. **93.** 6H53. **94.** 6H71. **95.** 6H41. **96.** 6H42. **97.** Id. **98.** Harrison Edward Livingstone, *Killing the Truth: Deceit and Deception in the JFK Case* (New York: Carroll & Graf, 1993), p. 718. **99.** 6H36-37; 6H65, 67. **100.** 2H39, WCT Mark Lane. **101.** 17H2; WR, p. 520. **102.** 3H361-62. **103.** *Journal of the American Medical Association,* May 24/31, 1995, vol. 273, No. 20. **104.** "The Men Who Killed Kennedy," Part 7. **105.** 6H33. **106.** 6H141. **107.** Michael Benson, *Encyclopedia of the JFK Assassination* (New York: Checkmark Books, 2002), p. 482. **108.** Livingstone, *Killing the Truth,* p. 718. **109.** WR, p. 18. **110.** David Lifton, *Best Evidence: Conspiracy and Cover-Up in the Assassination of John F. Kennedy* (New York: MacMillan, 1980), p. 370n; Bugliosi endnotes, pp. 300-301. **111.** *Post-Dispatch,* December 1, 1963. **112.** Richard Dudman, "Commentary of an Eyewitness," *New Republic,* December 21, 1963, p. 18. **113.** Weldon, op. cit., in Fetzer, *Murder in Dealey Plaza,* pp. 139-140. **114.** Id., p. 141. **115.** Id., pp. 134, 136; the report is reproduced in Fetzer, *Murder in Dealey Plaza* , p. 430. **116.** Id., p. 147. **117.** 5H155. **118.** Bugliosi, main book, p. 500; 6HSCA55. **119.** J. Gary Shaw and Larry R. Harris. *Cover-Up: The Government Conspiracy to Conceal the Facts about the Public Execution of John Kennedy* (Cleburne, Texas: Self-published, 1976), p. 145. **120.** Horne, *Inside the Assassination Records Review Board,* Vol. I, p. 342; Ron Hepler, "The Wounding of Governor John Connally," in James H. Fetzer, PhD (ed.), *Assassination Science: Experts Speak Out on the Death of JFK* (Chicago: Catfeet Press, 1998), pp. 208, 241-43, 245. **121.** Bugliosi, main book, p. 471. **122.** Sheriff's Dept. affidavit, November 22, 1963, 19H518. **123.** Bugliosi endnotes, p. 316. **124.** 5H68-70. **125.** The report is reproduced in Fetzer, *Murder in Dealey Plaza,* p. 430. **126.** CD80, p. 2. **127.** David W. Mantik, MD, PhD, "Paradoxes of the JFK Assassination: The Medical Evidence Decoded," in Fetzer, *Murder in Dealey Plaza,* pp. 250, 291. **128.** Id., pp. 250, 284. **129.** 6H238. **130.** CD205, p. 27, FBI interview of Miller, December 18, 1963. **131.** Sheriff's Dept. affidavit, November 22, 1963, 24H217, 227. **132.** 6H252. **133.** Bugliosi endnotes, p. 494. **134.** 2H74. **135.** WR, p. 51. **136.** 2H166, 169, 171-72, 182. **137.** 6H181-3, WCT Barbara Rowland. **138.** 6H272; 7H220. **139.** 2H159. **140.** Bugliosi, main book, p. 416. **141.** 6H14. **142.** Bugliosi endnotes, pp. 498-9. **143.** 6H233. **144.**

7H512. **145.** Supplementary Investigation Report, November 22, 1963, 19H514. **146.** Sheriff's Dept. affidavit, 19H485, 24H217. **147.** Stewart Galanor, *Cover-Up* (New York: Kestrel Books, 1998), pp. 59-60; cf. 22H833. **148.** 22H833. **149.** Simmons testimony at Shaw trial, No. 19, p. 8. **150.** 19H480. **151.** 6H243-45. **152.** History Video, "Three Shots That Changed the World." **153.** FBI report, March 19, 1964, 22H834. **154.** FBI report, March 18, 1964, 22H836. **155.** 12HSCA23-24. **156.** Bugliosi endnotes, p. 303. **157.** Bugliosi, main book, p. xxix; Warren Report, pp. 91, 105; 2HSCA192. **158.** Bugliosi, main book, p. 476, citing 5H167, 174, WCT Robert Frazier, and 5H162-3, but the latter is Lyndal Shaneyfelt's testimony. **159.** Bugliosi, main book, p. 355. **160.** Id., pp. 207, 451, 461. **161.** WR, p. 573. **162.** Bugliosi, main book, p. 854. **163.** Bugliosi endnotes, p. 258. **164.** WR, p. 60. **165.** Bugliosi endnotes, p. 431. **166.** Id., pp. 436, 431. **167.** 6H130. **168.** 3H435. **169.** 6HSCA35. **170.** Bugliosi, main book, pp. 501n, 449. **171.** WR, p. 3. **172.** See, for example, Galanor, op. cit., and the CAT scan diagram in Fetzer, "'Smoking Guns' in the Death of JFK," in Fetzer, *Murder in Dealey Plaza*, p. 3. **173.** WR, p. 107. **174.** Bugliosi, main book, p. 448; CD827, p. 2, Letter, J. Edgar Hoover to J. Lee Rankin, April 16, 1964; FBI Laboratory Report, p. 3; CD1066, p. 283, FBI report, May 28, 1964. **175.** 2H143. **176.** James Sibert's ARRB testimony, pp. 110-11. **177.** Mantik, op. cit., in Fetzer, *Murder in Dealey Plaza*, p. 270. **178.** Robert J. Groden, *The Killing of a President: The Complete Photographic Record of the JFK Assassination, the Conspiracy, and the Coverup* (Viking Penguin/Penguin Books USA Inc., 1994), p. 79. **179.** 5H133-34. **180.** 5H59. **181.** WR, p. 92. **182.** Josiah Thompson, *Six Seconds in Dallas: A Micro-Study of the Kennedy Assassination* (New York: Bernard Geis Associates, 1967), p. 78. **183.** 4H136. **184.** 3H266, WCT Marrion L. Baker. **185.** Bugliosi endnotes, p. 343. **186.** Bugliosi, main book, p. 412n, citing 16H983. **187.** 2H380. **188.** P. 47 of Dr. Finck's testimony. **189.** Id., p. 171. **190.** Bugliosi, main book, p. 192. **191.** WR, p. 105. **192.** 2H376, 382. **193.** Richard J. Whalen, "The Kennedy Assassination," January 14, 1967, p. 24. **194.** 2H374-75. **195.** 4H114. **196.** WR, p. 95. **197.** 3H428-29. **198.** Bugliosi, main book, p. 479, and Thompson, op. cit. p. 71. **199.** Bugliosi, main book, ibid. **200.** Bugliosi, main book, p. 480; *Life*, "Matter of Reasonable Doubt," p. 48. **201.** Dissenting View Part VI: Addendum to the Forensic Pathology Panel Report, Submitted by Cyril H. Wecht, MD, JD; 7HSCA199, 200. **202.** Horne, *Inside the Assassination Records Review Board*, Vol. I, p. 394. **203.** Bugliosi, main book, p. 1390. **204.** WR, p. 60. **205.** Id., p. 90. **206.** 6H11, 6H42, 6H66, 6H35, 6H71, 6H136, respectively. **207.** WR, p. 90. **208.** Id., pp. 91-2. **209.** 17H15. **210.** 6H48; 7HSCA287. **211.** 7HSCA302. **212.** Bugliosi, main book, p. 405.

Notes to Chapter 2

1. For example, Bugliosi, main book, p. 65. **2.** WR, p. 731. **3.** Id., p. 734. **4.** Id., p.

245. **5.** Id., p. 9. **6.** Id., p. 85. **7.** Bugliosi, main book, pp. 807-8. **8.** WR, p. 117. **9.** Prouty to Lane: Lane, *Plausible Denial: Was the CIA Involved in the Assassination of JFK?* (New York: Thunder's Mouth Press, 1991) p. 138. James Wilcott, a former CIA finance officer who had served with the Agency in Tokyo, told the HSCA in 1978 that he had learned from a CIA case officer (shortly after the assassination) that Oswald had indeed been "recruited from the military for the express purpose of becoming a double agent assignment [*sic*] to the USSR," and received financial disbursements under an assigned cryptonym. (Summers, 2013, p. 486, notes to p. 145; HSCA Final Report, p. 198) Jim Garrison noted that Oswald's examination in Russian at El Toro indicated that he had been receiving intelligence training; and "Marine intelligence activity was guided by the Office of Naval Intelligence." See Jim Garrison, *On the Trail of the Assassins: My Investigation and Prosecution of the Murder of President Kennedy* (New York: Warner Books, 1988), p. 23. **10.** WR, Appendix XII, p. 644; FBI report dated June 3, 1964, at CD1036, p. 4. **11.** 6H426. **12.** WR, pp. 125, 15; 2H507-08. **13.** Anthony Summers, *Not in Your Lifetime: The Assassination of JFK* (London: Headline Publishing Group, 2013), p. 508, note 11 to p. 194. **14.** See Summers, op. cit., p. 72, and Meagher, op. cit., p. 50. **15.** Marrs, op. cit., p. 441. **16.** Harrison Edward Livingstone, *High Treason 2: The Great Cover-Up; The Assassination of President John F. Kennedy* (New York: Carroll & Graf, 1992), p. 454. **17.** Bugliosi, main book, p. 692. **18.** WR, pp. 110, 585. **19.** Id., p. 186. **20.** 1H36; 22H756. **21.** Shenon, op. cit., p. 172. **22.** Reports of interviews, December 5, 1963, 22H757, 23H393. **23.** Report of interview, December 5, 1963, 22H756. **24.** FBI report, December 13, 1963, 22H777. **25.** FBI interview with Coleman on June 3, 1964, 26H437-38. **26.** Report of FBI agent Vincent Drain, December 7, 1963, 26H753. **27.** 26H438. **28.** 11H416-17. **29.** Report of FBI agent Vincent Drain, December 7, 1963, 26H753. **30.** WR, p. 300; Bugliosi, main book, p. 1304n. **31.** CD2134. **32.** Meagher, op. cit., p. 381. **33.** 24H727. **34.** Bugliosi, main book, p. 1312. **35.** Id., p. 1304n; 25H8. **36.** WR, p. 732; 25H4-6. **37.** 24H727. **38.** 24H717. **39.** WR, pp. 305, 751-52; 25H25-74; 24H574-76, 578; 25H71-75. **40.** Bugliosi, main book, p. 1045. **41.** 3HSCA69. **42.** Summers, op. cit., p. 322. **43.** 3HSCA103. **44.** 3HSCA136. **45.** 3HSCA138. **46.** 3HSCA152. **47.** Summers, op. cit., p. 324. **48.** Lane, *Last Word*, p. 205. **49.** Jim Garrison, *On The Trail of the Assassins*, p. 64. CD776 refers to a sworn statement that Sra. Durán supposedly gave to the deputy director of Mexican Federal Security on November 23, 1963, stating that Oswald *was* the man who visited the Cuban Embassy in late September to apply for a visa to visit Cuba. **50.** Dick Russell, *The Man Who Knew Too Much* (New York: Carroll & Graf, 1992), p. 494; State Dept. airgram, December 2, 1963. **51.** Document 22, JFK documents, National Archives. **52.** Bugliosi, main book, pp. 1048-49. **53.** David Talbot, *Brothers: The Hidden History of the Kennedy Years* (New York: Simon & Schuster, 2007), p. 285, but without supporting references. **54.** LBJ Tapes, LBJ Library, 1993-94 releases, cited in Summers, op. cit, p. 336. **55.**

Summers, op. cit., p. 337. **56.** Bugliosi, main book, p. 1056. **57.** Shenon's interview with Slawson; see Shenon, op. cit., p. 295. **58.** E. Howard Hunt, Part 2, p. 8, HSCA Security Classified Testimony. **59.** Summers, op. cit., p. 332. **60.** Warren Hinckle and William W. Turner, *Deadly Secrets: The CIA-Mafia War Against Castro and the Assassination of JFK* (New York: Thunder's Mouth Press, 1992), p. xix. **61.** 4H210, WCT Will Fritz. **62.** Noel Twyman, *Bloody Treason: The Assassination of John F. Kennedy* (Rancho Santa Fe, CA: Laurel, 1997), p. 748. **63.** Lopez speaking as a sworn witness for the program *On Trial: Lee Harvey Oswald*, Showtime, 1986, quoted in Summers, op. cit., p. 540, note 15 to page 327. **64.** Bugliosi, main book, p. 1052n. **65.** Bugliosi endnotes, p. 388; 24H601-2. **66.** WR, p. 322. **67.** Id., pp. 129-30. **68.** 2H249-50; Bugliosi, main book, p. 956. **69.** 24H209; 26H384. **70.** 2H228. **71.** 2H249-50. **72.** 24H407. **73.** WR, p. 133. **74.** Id., p. 134. **75.** Id., p.133. **76.** 6H377. **77.** WR, p. 133. **78.** 3H178. **79.** Bugliosi, main book, p. 786. **80.** Id., p. 1385. **81.** 6H388. **82.** FBI report, 22H632. **83.** 6H387-89, 392. **84.** 6H388. **85.** 7H386. **86.** WR, p. 154. **87.** Ibid. **88.** 6H338-39. **89.** 6H329-31. **90.** 6H339. **91.** 3H182; affidavit, March 19, 1964, 22H681. **92.** Affidavit, March 19, 1964, 22H681. **93.** 3H173. **94.** 7H389. **95.** 7H382. **96.** 22H677. **97.** 3H229-30. **98.** 7H382. **99.** 3H208. **100.** 23H873, p. 83 of police transcript. **101.** Bugliosi, main book, pp. 109, 94; Bugliosi endnotes, p. 475. **102.** Bugliosi, main book, pp. 1439-40. **103.** Id., pp. 93-4. **104.** 2H236. **105.** 7H389. **106.** 22H661. **107.** 7H390. **108.** George J.A. O'Toole, *The Assassination Tapes: An Electronic Probe Into the Murder of John F. Kennedy and the Dallas Coverup* (New York: Penthouse, 1975), p. 135. **109.** Bugliosi, main book, p. 959. **110.** 22H652, 22H637. **111.** Bugliosi, id., p. 959. **112.** 24H412. **113.** Stanley J. Marks, *Coup D'Etat: Three Murders that Changed the Course of History* (San Marino, CA: Bureau of International Affairs, 1970), p. 19. **114.** Thompson, op. cit., p. 175. **115.** 4H260-61. **116.** Bugliosi, main book, p. 802. **117.** Id., p. 800. **118.** 26H829. **119.** 4H48. **120.** 4H23-4. **121.** Meagher, op. cit., p. 126. **122.** Summers, op. cit., p. 84. **123.** Bugliosi, main book, p. 799. **124.** Bugliosi endnotes, p. 427; 7HSCA369; Bugliosi, main book, pp. 803-4. **125.** 4H21. **126.** Marrs, op. cit., p. 444. **127.** Bugliosi, main book, p. xliv. **128.** 24H213. **129.** 6H383. **130.** 24H214. **131.** 22H682. **132.** 3H169-173. **133.** 3H169-170. **134.** 3H179. **135.** 3H175. **136.** Bugliosi, main book, p. 30. **137.** 6H351-53; WR, p. 143. **138.** 22H210. **139.** Meagher, op. cit., p. 66. **140.** Summers, op. cit., p. 92. **141.** CD5, p. 41. **142.** 4H213, WCT J.W. Fritz. **143.** 3H273. **144.** 3H273-74. **145.** WR, p. 154. **146.** Bugliosi, main book, p. 49. **147.** 3H275. **148.** Bugliosi, id., p. 890. **149.** 6H397. **150.** 3H249-50. **151.** 3H252, 263. **152.** 3H239. **153.** Bugliosi, id., p. 839. **154.** Id., p. 838. **155.** 3H225; WR, p. 141. **156.** 3H263. **157.** 26H679. **158.** CD1036, p. 4. **159.** WR, p. 155. **160.** Id., p. 152. **161.** 3H252 **162.** 6H329. **163.** HSCA Final Report, p. 235. **164.** 6HSCA109. **165.** 4HSCA401. **166.** WR, Appendix XI, p. 550, "Report of Capt. J.W. Fritz, Dallas Police Department, Interrogation of Lee Harvey Oswald." **167.** Bugliosi, id., pp. 823, 827. **168.** Id., p. 167. **169.**

Bugliosi endnotes, p. 505. **170.** WR, pp. 19, 61, 71, and Appendix XII, "Speculations and Rumors," pp. 639-40. **171.** Bugliosi, main book, p. 484. **172.** Id., p. 852. **173.** Bill Sloan, *JFK: Breaking the Silence* (Dallas: Taylor Publishing, 1993), pp. 16-19; Marrs, op. cit., p. 82. **174.** Bugliosi endnotes, p. 331; CD5, FBI memorandum, November 26, 1963, p. 150; CD1395, p. 50-1. **175.** Bugliosi endnotes, p. 237; CD1395, p. 50, FBI interview of Dr. A.B. Cairns on July 10, 1964. **176.** HSCA interview with Drs. Harper and Cairns, August 17, 1977, pp. 1-2, cited in Harrison Edward Livingstone, *Killing Kennedy and the Hoax of the Century* (New York: Carroll & Graf, 1995), p. 261. **177.** Horne, *Inside the Assassination Records Review Board*, Vol. I, Appendix 57. **178.** Bugliosi endnotes, p. 237. **179.** Mantik, op. cit., in Fetzer, *Murder in Dealey Plaza*, p. 279-80. Dr. Angel's memo can be found at 7HSCA228-30. **180.** Bugliosi endnotes, p. 237n. **181.** 6H290, 292. **182.** Bugliosi endnotes, p. 169. **183.** 6H294-95. **184.** 6H292. **185.** No. 14, p. 11 of his testimony. **186.** Charles A. Crenshaw, MD, with Jens Hansen and J. Gary Shaw, *JFK: Conspiracy of Silence* (New York: Signet, 1992), p. 5. **187.** 6H80. **188.** 6H40. **189.** Anthony Summers, *Conspiracy* (New York: Paragon House, 1989), p. 486. **190.** 5HSCA556. **191.** Bugliosi, main book, p. 165n. **192.** Id., p. 965. **193.** 4H276, 7H283. **194.** 3H406. **195.** 3H443. **196.** 26H104. **197.** Bugliosi, main book, p. 491. **198.** Bugliosi endnotes, p. 338. **199.** Bugliosi, main book, p. 493n; 3H394; WR, p. 195. **200.** WR, p. 195; Bugliosi, main book, p. 493. **201.** WR, p. 81. **202.** 25H808. **203.** 2H52. **204.** "How Five Investigations into JFK's Medical/Autopsy Evidence Got It Wrong," May 2003, note 9; essay at maryferrell.org. **205.** WR, p. 165. **206.** Ibid. **207.** 6H438, 440. **208.** Earlene Roberts affidavit, December 5, 1963, 7H439. **209.** 6H443, 450, 453-54. **210.** Earlene Roberts affidavit, December 5, 1963, 7H439. **211.** Ira David Wood III, "22 November 1963: A Chronology," in Fetzer, *Murder in Dealey Plaza*, p.88. **212.** 4H184. **213.** 3H306. **214.** 4H215. **215.** CD1418, p. 15, FBI letter, August 21, 1964. **216.** WR, Appendix XII, p. 581. **217.** 4H202. **218.** Garrison, op. cit., p. 194. **219.** 3H324. **220.** Bugliosi, main book, p. 74n. **221.** CD1107, p. 583. **222.** Meagher, op. cit., p. 255. **223.** Bugliosi, main book, p. 113. **224.** 7H502. **225.** 7H47. **226.** 7H84. **227.** 6H451, 461. **228.** 6H451. **229.** 7H69. **230.** 7H69. **231.** WR, p. 175. **232.** 23H861, p. 59 of police transcript. **233.** 23H868, p. 74 of police transcript. **234.** 4H185. **235.** 24H311. **236.** WR, p. 175. **237.** WR, ibid.; FBI report of interview, January 1, 1964, 19H181. **238.** 3H349. **239.** 3H311-12. **240.** 3H328, 334. **241.** 7H400. **242.** 6H450. **243.** 7H14. **244.** 7H7. **245.** 7H127. **246.** WR, p. 175; 23H521-23; the tag is mentioned in FBI agent Vincent Drain's affidavit at 24H253. **247.** 23H521-23. **248.** 7H439; 6H449. **249.** 7H30. **250.** 7H85. **251.** 3H312. **252.** 3H311. **253.** CD1418, p. 15, FBI letter, August 21, 1964. **254.** 6H450. **255.** 2H238. **256.** 7H69. **257.** 3H328. **258.** 3H347, 349. **259.** 6H457. **260.** WR, pp. 171, 653; 21H383-84. **261.** Bugliosi, main book, pp.135, 151. **262.** 3H310-11. **263.** WR, pp. 167-68. **264.** Groden, op. cit., p. 100. **265.** 23H870, p. 78 of police transcript. **266.** Marrs, op.

cit., p. 343. **267.** Bugliosi endnotes, p. 451. **268.** 3H482-83; WR, p. 171. **269.** WR, pp. 160-61; 3H476. **270.** 1HSCA486; 7HSCA377. **271.** Bugliosi, main book, p. 818. **272.** Garrison, op. cit., p. 199; Crenshaw, *JFK: Conspiracy of Silence,* p. 101. **273.** 6H439-40. **274.** Cited at Bugliosi, main book, p. 859n. **275.** Marrs, op. cit., pp. 347-48; Meagher, op. cit., p. 255. **276.** WR, Appendix XII, p. 582. **277.** See, for example, Groden, op. cit., p. 97. **278.** WR, p. 166. **279.** 24H225. **280.** 7H84. **281.** 3H349; 6H457. **282.** WR, p. 171. **283.** Translation of an article by Joachim Joesten from French, CD1107, pp. 583-4, FBI report May 15, 1964, p. 565. **284.** Bugliosi, main book, p. 816. **283.** Livingstone, *High Treason 2,* pp. 77, 463-69. **285.** Ralph D. Thomas, *Missing Links in the JFK Assassination Conspiracy* (Austin, TX: Thomas Investigative Publications, 1992), pp. 147-8; see *Texas Monthly,* December 1990.

Notes to Chapter 3

1. Bugliosi, main book, pp. 1437, 1439. **2.** Id., p. 967. **3.** Id., p. 433. **4.** Hinckle and Turner, op. cit., p. 266. **5.** Dick Russell, op. cit., p. 288. **6.** Hinckle and Turner, op. cit., pp. 266-67. **7.** Twyman, op. cit., p. 645. **8.** James H. Fetzer, "Prologue: 'Smoking Guns' in the Death of JFK," in Fetzer, *Murder in Dealey Plaza,* p. 12. **9.** 6H155; 6H168. **10.** Vincent Palamara, "The Secret Service: On the Job in Dallas," in Fetzer, *Murder in Dealey Plaza,* p. 161. **11.** *Gallery,* October 1975. **12.** HSCA Final Report, p. 233. **13.** Bugliosi, main book, p. 1246.

14. WR, p. 450. **15.** Gerald Blaine, with Lisa McCubbin, *The Kennedy Detail: JFK's Secret Service Agents Break Their Silence* (New York: Gallery Books, 2010), p. 177. **16.** Harrison Edward Livingstone, *The Radical Right and the Murder of John F. Kennedy: Stunning Evidence in the Assassination of the President* (Baltimore: Conservatory Press, 2004), note 150 to page 95. **17.** 2H216. **18.** 6H293. **19.** 4H171. **20.** 4H338. **21.** TheSecretServiceBlogspot.com. **22.** Report of Assistant Chief Charles Batchelor and Deputy Chiefs George Lumpkin and M.E. Stevenson, 21H571. **23.** 4H349. **24.** WR, p. 452. **25.** Blaine and McCubbin, op. cit., pp. 203-4. **26.** Prouty essay, "The Guns of Dallas," at maryferrell.org. **27.** V. Palamara's interviews with Kinney, 1992-94, cited in Palamara, op. cit. **28.** 6H290. **29.** WR, p. 48. **30.** 5H161. **31.** Affidavit, July 10, 1964, 7H440. **32.** WR, p. 51. **33.** 18H749. **34.** 18H734. **35.** *The Men Who Killed Kennedy,* Part 7; Palamara in Fetzer, *Murder in Dealey Plaza,* p. 168. **36.** VincePalamara.com, from an article in the Idaho *State Journal,* November 24, 2013. **37.** Philip Melanson, *The Secret Service: The Hidden History of an Enigmatic Agency* (New York: Basic Books, 2002). **38.** WR, Appendix XII, p. 641. **39.** 2H117, 119. **40.** 7H450. **41.** Larry A. Sneed, *No More Silence: An Oral History of the Assassination of President Kennedy* (Dallas: Three Forks Press, 1998), p. 96. **42.** Bugliosi main book, p. 506, and endnotes, p. 30. **43.** Bugliosi, main book, p. 34, and endnotes, p. 350. **44.** Statement of Emory P. Roberts, memorandum to Secret Service Chief Rowley,

November 29, 1963, 18H735, 739. **45.** November 29, 1963, 18H746. **46.** 7H344. **47.** 2H116; 18H723. **48.** 2H137. **49.** 2H73. **50.** 4H132. **51.** 5H180. **52.** "Notes taken during interview with Mrs. Johnson," June 15, 1964, Box 1, "Manchester," SFA-LBJL; quoted in Steven M. Gillon, *The Kennedy Assassination – 24 Hours After: Lyndon B. Johnson's Pivotal First Day as President* (New York: Basic Books, 2009), p. 46. **53.** 2H164. **54.** WR, p. 48. **55.** Blaine and McCubbin, op. cit., p. 212. **56.** HSCA interview with Gochenaur, June 1, 1977, RIF #180-10109-10310, quoted in Vincent Palamara, "The Secret Service: On the Job in Dallas," in Fetzer, *Murder in Dealey Plaza*, p. 165. **57.** Ira David Wood, "22 November 1963: A Chronology," in Fetzer, *Murder in Dealey Plaza*, pp. 115-16; see also the Church Committee testimony of James Gochenaur. **58.** 2H41. **59.** Bertrand Russell, op. cit., in Fetzer, *Murder in Dealey Plaza*, p. 416. **60.** Bugliosi, main book, p. 46. **61.** 3H194. **62.** Weldon, op. cit., in Fetzer, *Murder in Dealey Plaza*, p. 140. **63.** Mantik, "The Medical Evidence Decoded," in Fetzer, *Murder in Dealey Plaza*, p. 260. **64.** Id., pp. 242, 276; see also Livingstone, *High Treason 2*, p. 245. **65.** 7H469. **66.** Bugliosi, main book, p. 110; Ira David Wood III, "22 November 1963: A Chronology," in Fetzer, *Murder in Dealey Plaza*, p. 96. **67.** 18H742. **68.** Bugliosi endnotes, p. 330. **69.** 2H138, 141. **70.** 2H144. **71.** 25H721. **72.** Bugliosi, main book, pp. 1245, 1241. **73.** 5H454, 458, 462. **74.** 5H452-53. **75.** HSCA Final Report, p. 184. **76.** 18H760. **77.** 2H118. **78.** 18H762. **79.** 2H144. **80.** 4H353. **81.** 6H172. **82.** 6H263; Shaw trial transcript, No. 18, p. 84. **83.** Benson, op. cit., p. 13. **84.** This is from a National Geographic video. **85.** Benson, op. cit., p. 76. **86.** 6H297. **87.** 6H244. **88.** 2H160. **89.** 3H204. **90.** 24H214. **91.** 3H282. **92.** Report of Interview, January 10, 1964, 24H531. **93.** 6H328-29. **94.** FBI report, CD206, p. 9. **95.** Report of FBI interview, January 8, 1964, 24H535. **96.** FBI affidavit, 24H523. **97.** Garrison, op. cit., p. 18. **98.** 7H106. **99.** 3H175, 79. **100.** 6H371. **101.** 7H498. **102.** Walt Brown, *Treachery in Dallas* (New York: Carroll & Graf, 1995), p. 33. **103.** 7H394. **104.** 7H478. **105.** 5H56. **106.** Affidavit, 7H440. **107.** WR, p. 115. **108.** FBI affidavit, March 25, 1964, 22H685. **109.** Wood in Fetzer, *Murder in Dealey Plaza*, p. 68. **110.** Id., pp. 68, 82. **111.** 5HSCA582. **112.** 6H312. The HSCA states that it was "immediately after the assassination" that "approximately six to eight persons who appeared to be derelicts were taken either to the nearby Dallas County Sheriff's Office, or to the Dallas Police Department for questioning." (6HSCA257) The famous three tramps were among these "derelicts;" apparently the others were not photographed. **113.** Bugliosi, main book, p. 933; Ray LaFontaine and Mary LaFontaine, *Oswald Talked: The New Evidence in the JFK Assassination* (Gretna, LA: Pelican Publishing, 1996), pp. 24-27. **114.** Marrs, op. cit., p. 335. **115.** Michael Canfield and Alan J. Weberman, *Coup d'Etat in America: The CIA and the Assassination of John F. Kennedy* (New York: The Third Press, 1975), pp. 351-52. **116.** Janney, op. cit., p. 299. **117.** 6HSCA258-59. **118.** Bugliosi, main book, p. 932; Robert Blair Kaiser, "Mystery Tramps in Disguise?", *Rolling Stone*, April 24,

1975, p. 33. **119.** 6H312. **120.** 7H535. **121.** Meagher, op. cit., p. 25. **122.** 7H107. **123.** 6H312. **124.** Bugliosi, main book, p. 866; interview of D.V. Harkness by HSCA investigator Harold Rose on February 7, 1978, p. 1. **125.** 7H535. **126.** Bugliosi, loc. cit. **127.** Bugliosi endnotes, p. 485. **128.** Bugliosi main book, pp. 865-66. **129.** Marrs, op. cit., p. 78. **130.** Bugliosi, main book, p. 867; HSCA Final Report, p. 184. **131.** HSCA Final Report, p. 184. **132.** *The Men Who Killed Kennedy*, Part 7. **133.** Marrs, op. cit., p. 459; Bugliosi, main book, p. 321. **134.** Bugliosi, loc. cit. **135.** Bugliosi, loc. cit.; 11HSCA4. **136.** *Newsweek*, November 22, 1993. **137.** Bugliosi, main book, p. 364. **138.** Cited in Seth Kantor, *The Ruby Cover-Up* (New York: Zebra Books/Kensington Publishing Company, 1992), pp.178-79; Sullivan testified thus before the Senate Intelligence Committee. **139.** Shenon, op. cit., p. 143. **140.** Shenon, op. cit., pp. 71-2. **141.** Summers, *Not in Your Lifetime*, p. 117. **142.** Bernard Fensterwald Jr. and Michael Ewing, *Assassination of JFK: Coincidence or Conspiracy?* (New York: Kensington Publishing Corp., 1977). **143.** 5H105. **144.** James T. Tague, *Truth Withheld: A Survivor's Story* (Dallas: Excel Digital Press, 2003), pp. 86, 89-90, 113-18, 164. **145.** Mark Lane, *Rush to Judgment* (New York: Holt, Rinehart & Winston, 1966), p. 149. **146.** WR, p. 560. **147.** Bill Sloan, with Jean Hill, *JFK: The Last Dissenting Witness* (Gretna, LA: Pelican, 1992), p. 123. **148.** Peter Dale Scott, *Deep Politics and the Death of JFK* (Berkeley and Los Angeles: University of California Press, 1993), p. 45. **149.** 25H721. **150.** 5H550-51. **151.** Shenon, op. cit., p. 193. **152.** Bugliosi, main book, p. 1000, and endnotes, p. 116n; Shenon, op. cit., p. 439. **153.** 6H218. **154.** Bugliosi, main book, loc. cit.; letter from J. Edgar Hoover to J. Lee Rankin on June 5, 1964. Bugliosi cites the FBI report of April 24, 1964, on Lane's speech at the Ohio Museum of Natural History in Columbus on April 22, 1964. **155.** Orleans Parish Grand Jury testimony of Mark Lane, No. 25, p. 36. **156.** Sheriff's Department affidavit, November 22, 1963, 24H224; also 2H175. **157.** 2H183, WCT Arnold L. Rowland; Robert Sam Anson, *"They've Killed the President!" The Search for the Murderers of John F. Kennedy* (New York: Bantam Books, 1975), p. 183. **158.** 2H49, WCT Mark Lane. **159.** V.J. Brian letter to Capt. W.P. Gannaway, April 20, 1964, 17H495-96. **160.** 5H34. **161.** Penn Jones, *Forgive My Grief: A Critical Review of the Warren Commission Report on the Assassination of President John F. Kennedy*, Vol. 1, p. 137; cited in Russell, op. cit., p. 579. **162.** Lane, *Plausible Denial*, p. 344. **163.** 2H42, WCT Mark Lane. **164.** 22H839. **165.** 6HSCA296. **166.** Marrs, p. 82-4. **167.** Robert J. Groden and Harrison Edward Livingstone, *High Treason* (New York and Baltimore: Conservatory Press, 1989), p. 400. **168.** Marrs, op. cit., p. 574; Carr testimony at Shaw trial, No. 24, p. 20. **169.** Marrs, op. cit., p. 405. **170.** Benson, op. cit., p. 291. **171.** YouTube video. **172.** Phillip F. Nelson, *LBJ: The Mastermind of the JFK Assassination* (New York: Skyhorse Publishing, 2011, 2013), p. 504; Garrison, op. cit., p. 229. **173.** Summers, op. cit., p. 106. **174.** Id., p. 92. **175.** 8H239. **176.** 8H246. **177.** 11H362-63. **178.** 11H363. **179.** 3H196. **180.** 6H380. **181.** Tip O'Neill, with William Novak, *Man of the*

House: The Life and Political Memoirs of Speaker Tip O'Neill (Boston: G.K. Hall, 1988), p. 178. **182.** Peter Janney, *Mary's Mosaic* (New York: Skyhorse Publishing, 2016), pp. 284-85; from Woody Woodland's interview with Douglas P. Horne, November 19, 2009. **183.** Garrison, op. cit., pp. 65-67. **184.** Bugliosi endnotes, p. 395. **185.** Bugliosi, main book, p. 345. **186.** Shenon, op. cit., p. 148. **187.** Twyman, op. cit., p. 667. **188.** 24H247. **189.** Groden, op. cit., p. 67. **190.** WR, p. 178. **191.** 4H215. **192.** 4H216, 225. **193.** 7H285. **194.** Garrison, op. cit., pp. 217-18; 12HSCA16. **195.** FBI letter, May 22, 1964, 22H583; the photo is reproduced at Groden, op. cit., p. 124. **196.** 22H583. **197.** Bugliosi endnotes, p. 377. **198.** 15H641. **199.** Pp. 24-5 of Lane's testimony. **200.** 4H181. **201.** 24H287, 289. **202.** 4H233, WCT J.W. Fritz. **203.** Bugliosi, main book, p. 257. **204.** 12H54, WCT Capt. W.B. Frazier. **205.** Shenon, op. cit., p. 423. **206.** 12H36-39. **207.** 22H370. **208.** 13H17. **209.** CD84, p. 88. **210.** Shenon, op. cit., p. 477, without references. **211.** Essay at maryferrell.org. **212.** 12H31. **213.** Wesley Frazier provided this information in a talk he gave on September 26, 2014, and in an interview on the National Geographic Channel program, "This is the House." **214.** Bugliosi, main book, p. 180. **215.** Id., p. 200, and WR, p. 118. **216.** 24H829-30. **217.** 24H839-42. **218.** WR, pp. 238-39; 24H821, 823-24. **219.** Transcript of Lane interview on the Barry Gray radio program, July 29, 1964, over WMCA in New York City, CD1418, p. 12. **220.** Noted by Joachim Joesten, CD1107, p. 582. **221.** Pointed out by Mark Lane during interview on the Barry Gray radio program, CD1418, pp. 25-6. **222.** William Manchester, *The Death of a President: November 20 - November 25, 1963* (New York: Harper & Row, 1967), p. 300; see also Kenneth P. O'Donnell and David F. Powers, with Joe McCarthy, *Johnny, We Hardly Knew Ye* (Boston: Little, Brown, 1972), p. 41. **223.** 6H216. **224.** Lane, *Rush to Judgment,* p. 345; Groden and Livingstone, op. cit. p. 123; Sheriff's Dept. affidavit, November 23, 1963, 19H535. **225.** Groden, op. cit., p. 32. **226.** Bugliosi endnotes, p. 358. **227.** Twyman, op. cit., p. 150. **228.** Marrs, op. cit., p. 78. **229.** Meagher, op. cit., p. 23; 19H467-68, 508. **230.** Weldon, op. cit., in Fetzer, *Murder in Dealey Plaza,* p. 140. **231.** Mantik, op. cit., in Fetzer, *Murder in Dealey Plaza,* p. 260. **232.** HSCA Final Report, p. 128. **233.** Mark Lane and Dick Gregory, *Murder in Memphis: The FBI and the Assassination of Martin Luther King* (New York: Thunder's Mouth Press, 1993, 1997), p. 303. **234.** Gaeton Fonzi, *The Last Investigation* (New York: Thunder's Mouth Press, 1993), p. 234. **235.** Mark Lane, "The Right to Know," Appendix Four, in Lane and Gregory, *Murder in Memphis,* pp. 303-4. **236.** Mark Lane and Dick Gregory, *Code Name "Zorro": The Murder of Martin Luther King, Jr.* (Englewood Cliffs, NJ: Prentice Hall, 1977), pp. 303-4. **237.** Fensterwald and Ewing, op. cit., pp. 298-99, 452-53, 464. **238.** From Marchetti's April 1975 article in *True* magazine, cited in Garrison, op. cit., p. 234. **239.** Patrick Nolan, *CIA Rogues and the Killing of the Kennedys* (New York: Skyhorse Publishing, 2013), p. 33. **240.** Lane, *Plausible Denial,* p. 222. **241.** The entire document is reproduced in Fetzer, *Assassination Science,* pp. 445-47, and in

Lane, *Last Word*, pp. 114-18. **242.** Bugliosi, main book, p. 1440. **243.** Id., p. 1446. **244.** Fensterwald and Ewing, op. cit., p. 184. **245.** Philip Melanson, "The CIA's Secret Ties to Local Police," *The Nation*, March 26, 1983, p. 367. **246.** Summers, op. cit., pp. 117, 442; HSCA Final Report, p. 410. **247.** Lane, *Last Word*, p. 49. **248.** Talbot, *Brothers*, pp. 386-87. **249.** "JFK Assassination: The Definitive Guide," History Channel video. **250.** Summers, op. cit., p. 458, note 6 to p. 23. **251.** Bugliosi endnotes, p. 275n. **252.** Summers, loc. cit. **253.** 10HSCA93, note 67; Lane, *Last Word*, pp. 57-63, 65. **254.** Lane, *Plausible Denial*, pp. 75-6. **255.** 7H30. **256.** 7H19. **257.** 7H79. **258.** WR, p. 178. **259.** 6H443-44. **260.** 7H111. **261.** 3H299. **262.** N.M. McDonald, "Officer Recalls Oswald Capture," *Dallas Morning News*, November 24, 1963, p. 13. **263.** Marks, op. cit., pp. 6, 73. **264.** 7H12. **265.** 7H17. **266.** 7H21. **267.** 24H243. **268.** 7H51, 54. **269.** 7H40. **270.** Bugliosi, main book, p. 1072. **271.** Id., pp. 1075-76. **272.** Marrs, op. cit., pp. 419-20. OK **273.** 15H491-92. **274.** 15H356-57. **275.** 13H257-8. **276.** 13H278. **277.** Bugliosi, main book, p. 1110. **278.** *The Washington Post*, September 7, 1976. Many publications spell the mobster's name 'Roselli,' but he took his name from an Italian painter named Rosselli, and his business card also said 'Rosselli.' His given name was Filippo Sacco. **279.** Bugliosi, main book, p. 1078. **280.** Id., p. 1129. **281.** HSCA Final Report, p. 157. **282.** Quoted in Marrs, op. cit., p. 419. **283.** Bugliosi main book, p. 299. **284.** Id., pp. 1458-59. **285.** HSCA Security Classified Testimony, James B. Wilcott, No. 29, p. 25. **286.** Report of Capt. J.W. Fritz, Dallas Police Department. **287.** Galanor, op. cit., p. 81, and Document 35 in his photo section. **288.** Bugliosi endnotes, p. 393; 4H289. **289.** Interview, December 17, 1963, 22H778. **290.** Marrs, op. cit., pp. 451-52. **291.** 6HSCA140, 221-23. **292.** 6HSCA335. **293.** 6HSCA140. **294.** 2HSCA322; 6HSCA40. **295.** 6HSCA146, HSCA Final Report, p. 56. **296.** Bugliosi endnotes, p. 401. **297.** Id., p. 403; 6HSCA177. **298.** 2HSCA322-24, 335. **299.** 2HSCA322, 344. **300.** 2H36. **301.** WR, p. 647. **302.** Bugliosi, main book, p. 966. **303.** 4H288. **304.** 6HSCA140. **305.** Livingstone, *High Treason 2*, p. 454. **306.** 3H284-85. **307.** WR, p. 134. **308.** Bugliosi endnotes, p. 405; CD897, p. 150; FBI interview of R.L. Studebaker, March 10, 1964. **309.** 5H48. **310.** 6H268. **311.** 3H288. **312.** 24H320. **313.** 7H289. **314.** CD5, p. 129. **315.** 4H266. **316.** CD897, p. 158; 7H143-44, 148-49. **317.** 6H307. **318.** 7H97-8. **319.** 24H314. **320.** 7H103. **321.** 24H307. **322.** FBI interview, December 3, 1963, 22H751. **323.** WR, p. 248. **324.** Bugliosi endnotes, p. 536. **325.** WR, p. 135. **326.** 4H3, 5. **327.** 4H267. **328.** 7HSCA15. **329.** Bugliosi main book, p. 1069. **330.** William Matson Law, with Allan Eaglesham, *In the Eye of History: Disclosures in the JFK Assassination Medical Evidence* (Southlake, Texas: JFK Lancer Publications, 2005), pp. 69-70, 9. **331.** Sloan, *The Last Dissenting Witness*, p. 182. **332.** Horne, *Inside the Assassination Records Review Board*, Vol. I, Appendix 61; ARRB interview, February 14, 1997. **333.** Horne, *Inside the Assassination Records Review Board*, Vol. IV, p. 988. **334.** Summers, *Conspiracy*, p. 483; Livingstone, *High Treason 2*, p. 256. **335.** Livingstone, *High Treason 2*, p. 239. **336.** Horne, *Inside the Assassination Records Review Board*, Vol. I, Appendix 38. **337.** Id. **338.** Lifton, op. cit., p. 630; Livingstone, *High Treason 2*, p. 309; Summers, *Conspiracy*, p. 482. **339.** Livingstone, *High Treason 2*, p. 165. **340.** 7HSCA15. **341.** Livingstone, *High Treason 2*, p. 89. **342.** Bugliosi, main book, p. 1070. **343.** 2H366. **344.** Livingstone, *High Treason 2*, p. 246. **345.** Id., p. 277. **346.** 2H349-50. **347.** Shenon, op. cit., pp. 19-20. **348.** Dr. Michael Baden, with Judith Adler Hennessee, *Unnatural Death: Confessions of a Medical Examiner* (New York: Ivy Books, 1989), p. 5. **349.** Clay Shaw trial transcript, Part 2, February 24, 1969, p. 199. **350.** Id., p. 100. **351.** Horne, *Inside the Assassination Records Review Board*, Vol. I, p. 358. **352.** Bugliosi, main book, p. 433; 7HSCA137. **353.** Bugliosi, main book, p. 449. **354.** Id., pp. 382-83. **355.** 7HSCA17. **356.** Bugliosi, main book, p. 382. **357.** Id., p. 393. **358.** Horne, *Inside the Assassination Records Review Board*, Vol. I, Appendix 68; 7HSCA10. **359.** Livingstone, *High Treason 2*, pp. 132-33. **360.** 7HSCA261. **361.** Clay Shaw trial transcript, testimony of Dr. Pierre A. Finck, Part 1, p. 48 of his testimony; he didn't say anything about being out on the loading dock when this question was asked. **362.** Bugliosi, main book, p. 386. **363.** 7HSCA261; also Dennis L. Breo, "JFK's Death - The Plain Truth from the MDs Who Did the Autopsy," *Journal of the American Medical Association*, vol. 267, no. 20, May 27, 1992, p. 2799. **364.** Horne, *Inside the Assassination Records Review Board*, Vol. III, p. 668, note 1. **365.** Id., Vol. 1, Appendices 56 and 69; 7HSCA9. **366.** 7HSCA9, 10. **367.** Mantik, op. cit., in Fetzer, *Murder in Dealey Plaza*, p. 279. **368.** Id., p. 286. **369.** Shaw trial testimony, Part 2, pp.116-17. **370.** 6H33. **371.** Lifton, op. cit, pp. 601-2 and Lifton video; Livingstone, *High Treason 2*, pp. 211, 269. **372.** *The Washington Post*, November 10, 1998, p. A-3, quoted by Aguilar, op. cit., in Fetzer, *Murder in Dealey Plaza*, p. 212. **373.** ARRB testimony, May 7, 1997, pp. 43-4. **374.** Livingstone, *High Treason 2*, p. 237. **375.** Dennis L. Breo, *JAMA*, vol. 267, no. 20, May 27, 1992, p. 2798; Douglas Horne, "Evidence of a Government Cover-up: Two Different Brain Specimens in President Kennedy's Autopsy," in Fetzer, *Murder in Dealey Plaza*, p. 306. **376.** See Livingstone, *High Treason 2*, pp. 183-287. **377.** Douglas P. Horne, "Evidence of a Government Cover-Up: Two Different Brain Specimens at President Kennedy's autopsy," in Fetzer, *Murder in Dealey Plaza*, pp. 306-8. **378.** Groden, op. cit., p. 87. **379.** 6H136. **380.** Statement of November 22, 1963, 21H216. **381.** 18H744-45. **382.** 18H734. **383.** 2H81. **384.** "The Secret Service Interviews, Kennedy Assassination Chronicles," Summer 1997, p. 20. **385.** Blaine and McCubbin, op. cit., pp. 216-17. **386.** HSCA interview with Ebersole, March 11, 1978, p. 3. **387.** JFK Records, File No. 014463, Record No. 180-10105-10399, National Archives, cited in Galanor, op. cit., p. 33. **388.** Lifton, op. cit., pp. 631-33. **389.** Aguilar, op. cit., in Fetzer, *Murder in Dealey Plaza*, p. 198. **390.** Livingstone, *Killing the Truth*, Appendix J, p. 705. **391.** ARRB interview of Joe O'Donnell, February 28, 1997, p. 2. **392 .** Bugliosi, main book, p. 1005. **393.** 6H33. **394.** Bugliosi, main book, p. 406. **395.** Bugliosi, main book, pp.

405-6. **396.** 6H20. **397.** Bugliosi, main book, p. 404. **398.** 2H377. **399.** 2H380. **400.** Clay Shaw trial, p. 31 of Dr. Finck's testimony. **401.** 2H352. **402.** 7HSCA16. **403.** 2H356. **404.** 2H365. **405.** Aguilar, op. cit., in Fetzer, *Murder in Dealey Plaza*, p. 186. **406.** Bugliosi, main book, pp. 427-28. **407.** 6H6. **408.** ARRB MD 86, Interview Report of Francis X. O'Neill, January 10, 1978, pp. 10-11. **409.** Bugliosi, main book, p. 403n. **410.** Aguilar, op. cit., in Fetzer, *Murder in Dealey Plaza*, p. 201. **411.** Bugliosi, loc. cit. **412.** 6H48. **413.** 7HSCA286-87. **414.** 6H81. **415.** Aguilar, op. cit., in Fetzer, *Murder in Dealey Plaza*, p. 216, note 113. **416.** Bugliosi, loc. cit. **417.** Bugliosi, id., p. 256. **418.** 2H361. **419.** 2H351. **420.** 2H366, 368, 369. **421.** WR, p. 89. **422.** 2H349. **423.** 2H351. **424.** 16H980. **425.** Bugliosi endnotes, p. 245. **426.** Dr. Finck testimony, February 25, 1969, pp. 8, 15. **427.** Id., p. 23. **428.** Bugliosi, main book, pp. 390, 428; Bugliosi endnotes, p. 224. **429.** Bugliosi, main book, p. 396. **430.** Id., p. 157. **431.** Id., p. 397; 7HSCA176, 125-26. **432.** Bugliosi, main book, p. 157. **433.** Horne, *Inside the Assassination Records Review Board*, Vol. I, Appendix 19. **434.** See Dr. Charles A. Crenshaw, with J. Gary Shaw, D. Bradley Kizzia, JD, Gary Aguilar, MD, and Cyril Wecht, MD, JD, *Trauma Room One: The JFK Medical Coverup Exposed* (New York: Paraview Press, 2001). **435.** Summers, *Not in Your Lifetime*, p. 23. **436.** ARRB testimony, p. 126. **437.** spartacus-educational.com. **438.** Livingstone, *Killing the Truth*, p. 42, and photo section. **439.** Livingstone, *High Treason 2*, p. 326. **440.** Mantik, op. cit., in Fetzer, *Murder in Dealey Plaza*, pp. 244-46. **441.** ARRB deposition of James Sibert, pp. 67-68, and ARRB deposition of Earl McDonald, May 14, 1996, and Contact Profile, written by Douglas Horne, MB 28, p. 3; Mantik, op. cit., in Fetzer, *Murder in Dealey Plaza*, p. 246. **442.** Livingstone, *High Treason 2*, p. 306. **443.** Bugliosi, main book, p. 424. **444.** Id., p. 408. **445.** Horne, *Inside the Assassination Records Review Board*, Vol. I, Appendix 32; Dr. Humes' ARRB testimony, February 13, 1996, p. 72. **446.** Horne, *Inside the Assassination Records Review Board*, Vol. I, Appendix 57; Lifton, op. cit., p. 660. **447.** ARRB interview, May 10, 1996. **448.** Horne, *Inside the Assassination Records Review Board*, Vol. I, Appendix 71. **449.** ARRB interview, September 12, 1997. **450.** 7HSCA37-9. **451.** Bugliosi, main book, p. 407. **452.** Bugliosi endnotes, p. 613; Billie Sol Estes, *Billie Sol Estes: A Texas Legend* (Texas: BS Productions, 2005). **453.** Horne, *Inside the Assassination Records Review Board*, Vol. I, Appendix 70. **454.** Ms. Spencer's June 5, 1997, ARRB deposition, pp. 33, 37, 50, 52-4, and 60. **455.** Bugliosi endnotes, pp. 264-65; see also ARRB deposition of Saundra Kay Spencer, June 7, 1997, p. 50. **456.** Bugliosi endnotes, p. 268. **457.** 6H6. **458.** 7HSCA37. **459.** ARRB testimony of James Sibert, p. 65. **460.** Bugliosi endnotes, p. 283; cf. 7HSCA104. **461.** Mantik, op. cit., in Fetzer, op. cit., p. 240. **462.** O'Neill's ARRB testimony, September 12, 1997, pp. 161-62; Sibert's ARRB testimony, September 11, 1997, p. 128, cited by Aguilar, op. cit., in Fetzer, op. cit., p. 208. **463.** Fetzer, "'Smoking Guns' in the Death of JFK," in Fetzer, op. cit, p. 9; Aguilar, op. cit., in Fetzer, op. cit., pp. 189, 212; O'Neill's testimony, September 12, 1997, pp. 161-62; Sibert's testimony, September 11, 1997, p. 128; ARRB testimony of John Stringer, July 16, 1996, pp. 136-37. **464.** Mantik, op. cit., in Fetzer, op. cit., p. 286. **465.** 7HSCA37. **466.** Cf. Mantik, op. cit., in Fetzer, *Murder in Dealey Plaza*, p. 247. **467.** Bugliosi, main book, pp. 1059-61, 435. **468.** Wood, op. cit., in Fetzer, op. cit., pp. 63-4. **469.** Mantik, "Paradoxes of the JFK Assassination: The Silence of the Historians," in Fetzer, op. cit., p. 400, from a December 13, 1998, letter to *The Nation*. **470.** Mantik, "The Medical Evidence Decoded," in Fetzer, op. cit, p. 290. **471.** Id., pp. 267, also Mantik, "Paradoxes of the JFK Assassination: The Silence of the Historians," in Fetzer, op. cit, p. 400, from a December 13, 1998, letter to *The Nation*. **472.** Fetzer, op. cit, Appendix F, p. 442, "Deposition of J. Thornton Boswell, M.D., before the ARRB on 26 February 1996." **473.** Fetzer, "'Smoking Guns' in the Death of JFK," in Fetzer, op. cit, p. 8. **474.** Fetzer, op. cit, Appendix E, p. 437; see also Fetzer, *Assassination Science*. Further details on the phony nature of the autopsy photos and x-rays can be found in Aguilar, op. cit., in Fetzer, *Murder in Dealey Plaza*, p. 200ff. **475.** Call Report (ARRB), June 12, 1997, in Fetzer, *Murder in Dealey Plaza*, p. 312. **476.** Bugliosi endnotes, p. 354. **477.** ARRB Meeting Report, June 18, 1997, Call Report, June 26, 1997; ARRB Meeting Report, August 14, 1997, in Fetzer, op. cit, pp. 315, 318, 321-22, respectively. **478.** Call Report, reproduced in Horne, "Interviews with Former NPIC Employees: The Zapruder Film in November 1963," in Fetzer, op. cit, p. 318. **479.** ARRB Meeting Report, August 14, 1997, in Fetzer, *Murder in Dealey Plaza*, p. 322. **480.** Meeting Report of ARRB interview with Homer McMahon, July 14, 1997; see Fetzer, op. cit, p. 319. **481.** Janney, op. cit., p. 292. **482.** ARRB Meeting Report, 6/18/97, in Fetzer, op. cit, p. 315. **483.** Bugliosi endnotes, p. 353. **484.** Mike Pincher, JD, and Roy L. Schaeffer, "The Case for Zapruder Film Tampering: The Blink Pattern." in Fetzer, *Assassination Science*, p. 221, and Lifton, op. cit., pp. 555-57. **485.** Marrs, op. cit., p. 69. **486.** Bugliosi, main book, p. 506. **487.** 4H148. **488.** Bugliosi, id., p. 410. **489.** Bugliosi endnotes, pp. 331-32; HSCA record 180-10001-10396, p. 50. **490.** Fetzer, *Murder in Dealey Plaza*, Appendix A, p. 422. **491.** Newcomb and Adams, p. 122; cited in Livingstone, *Killing Kennedy*, p. 145; report of FBI interview with Abraham Zapruder; see Fetzer, *Assassination Science*, p. 233. **492.** Mantik, "Special Effects in the Zapruder Film: How the Film of the Century was Edited," in Fetzer, *Assassination Science*, p. 315. **493.** Daryll Weatherly, "A New Look at the 'Film of the Century,'" Appendix in Livingstone, *Killing Kennedy*, pp. 376-77. **494.** See also Peter F. Model and Robert J. Groden, *JFK: The Case for Conspiracy* (New York: Manor Books, 1977), p. 143, and Livingstone, *High Treason 2*, p. 367. **495.** Mark North, *Act of Treason: The Role of J. Edgar Hoover in the Assassination of President Kennedy* (New York: Carroll & Graf, 1991), pp. 639-40. **496.** 2HSCA143. **497.** Model and Groden, op. cit., p. 143. **498.** Weatherly in Livingstone, *Killing Kennedy*, Appendix, p. 379. **499.** Mantik, "The Zapruder Film Controversy," in Fetzer, *Murder in Dealey Plaza* , p. 352. **500.** See *The Fourth Decade*, March 1995, and Jack White, "Evidence...or

Not? The Zapruder Film: Can It Be Trusted?" in Fetzer, *Assassination Science*, p. 215. **501.** Bugliosi, main book, p. 506. **502.** Groden and Livingstone, op. cit., pp. 416-17, from ARRB testimony. **503.** Bugliosi endnotes, p. 351. **504.** Fetzer, "'Smoking Guns' in the Death of JFK," in Fetzer, *Murder in Dealey Plaza*, p. 10, quoting Twyman, op. cit., p. 151. **505.** Michael T. Griffith, "Evidence of Alteration in the Zapruder Film," 1998, essay at miketgriffith.com. **506.** White, op. cit., in Fetzer, *Assassination Science*, p. 217. **507.** Fort Worth *Star Telegram*, April 14, 1978; cited in Chuck Marler, "The JFK Assassination Re-enactment: Questioning the Warren Commission's Evidence," in Fetzer, *Assassination Science*, p. 250. **508.** Jack White, "Evidence...or Not? The Zapruder Film: Can It Be Trusted?" in Fetzer, *Assassination Science*, p. 219; emphasis in original; see also Livingstone, *Killing Kennedy*, p. 69. **509.** Fred T. Newcomb and Perry Adams, *Murder from Within* (Santa Barbara, CA: Probe, 1974), p. 117. **510.** Twyman, op. cit., p. 127, and his notes to Z-303 photo. **511.** White, op. cit., in Fetzer, *Assassination Science*, p. 217. **512.** Livingstone, *Killing Kennedy*, p. 140. **513.** Fetzer, *Murder in Dealey Plaza*, Appendix B, p. 426. **514.** Mantik, " The Medical Evidence Decoded," in Fetzer, *Murder in Dealey Plaza*, p. 243. **515.** White, op. cit., in Fetzer, *Assassination Science*, p. 218; see also Twyman, op. cit., and as summarized by Michael T. Griffith on his internet homepage. Griffith published *Compelling Evidence: A New Look at the Assassination of President Kennedy* (Grand Prairie, TX: JFK Lancer Productions, 1996). Further observations on the anomalies in the Z-film are brought together in Harrison Livingstone, *Killing Kennedy*. See also Jack White, "The Great Zapruder Film Hoax," and David W. Mantik, MD, PhD, "Paradoxes of the JFK Assassination: The Zapruder Film Controversy," in Fetzer, *Murder in Dealey Plaza*. **516.** Mantik, "The Zapruder Film Controversy," in Fetzer, op. cit., pp. 332, 337, 354. **517.** Bugliosi, main book, p. 508. **518.** Bugliosi, main book, p. 508; endnotes, p. 291. **519.** 6H158. **520.** 6H168-70. **521.** 6H164-65. **522.** Bugliosi, main book, pp. 504-5. **523.** Livingstone, *Killing Kennedy*, pp. 61-2; Groden op. cit., pp. 37, 162; Livingstone, *High Treason 2*, p. 416. **524.** Bugliosi endnotes, p. 90. **525.** Interview of Dino Brugioni with Len Osanic on YouTube.com. **526.** 6H211, 221. **527.** 11H416-7, WCT Edwin Walker. **528.** Marrs, op. cit., p. 319. **529.** Meagher, op. cit., p. 136 and p. 139, note 23; see also *New York Times*, December 17, 1963, p. 31. **530.** Part 1, p. 52, of his testimony, February 24, 1969. **531.** Finck testimony, part 3, pp. 5-6. **532.**Transcript of Lane interview on the Barry Gray radio program, July 29, 1964, over WMCA in New York City, CD1418, p. 30. **533.** Horne, *Inside the Assassination Records Review Board*, Vol. III, p. 672, note 5. **534.** Horne, op. cit., Vol. I, Appendix 26. **535.** Larry Hancock, *Someone Would Have Talked: The Assassination of President John F. Kennedy and the Conspiracy to Mislead History* (JFK Lancer, 2006), p. 307. **536.** WR, p. 336. **537.** 25H225. **538.** Bugliosi endnotes, p. 449n, May 2, 1977, statement to Kantor. **539.** Marrs, op. cit., pp. 318-19; Groden and Livingstone, op. cit., p. 121. **540.** Marrs, op. cit., p. 574. **541.** Crenshaw, *JFK: Conspiracy of Silence*, p. 106. **542.** 2H59. **543.** Mark Lane

Orleans Parish Grand Jury testimony, No. 25, p. 28. **544.** 2H51, WCT Mark Lane. **545.** Lane, *Rush to Judgment*, pp. 274, 355; cf. 22H794. **546.** Groden, op. cit., p. 97; Twyman, op. cit., p. 282. **547.** Lee Israel, *Kilgallen (*New York: Delacorte Press, 1979), p. 395. **548.** James Hicks Orleans Parish Grand Jury testimony, No. 14, pp. 3, 4, 8, 17 and 19 of his testimony. **549.** Groden, op. cit., p. 34, and Marrs, op. cit., p. 458. **550.** Sloan, *The Last Dissenting Witness*, p. 72, 101; Marrs, op. cit., p. 483. **551.** Sloan, op. cit., pp. 151-54, 162; Sloan, *Breaking the Silence*, p. 139. **552.** 7H555. **553.** James T. Tague, *Truth Withheld: A Survivor's Story* (Dallas: Excel Digital Press, 2003), pp. 86-90, 113-18, 164. **554.** Bugliosi endnotes, p. 131; *New York Times*, June 12, 1975, p. 23. **555.** Wood, op. cit., in Fetzer, *Murder in Dealey Plaza*, p. 37. **556.** 3H192. **557.** 6H288. **558.** 2H53-4. **559.** WR, p. 166. **560.** Groden, op. cit., p. 38 **561.** WR, p. 315. **562.** Bugliosi, main book, pp. 353, 355; WR, pp. 97, 105. **563.** Meagher, op. cit., p. 270. **564.** WR, p. 423. **565.** Leo Janos, "The Last Days of the President: LBJ in Retirement," *The Atlantic*, July 1973, p. 39. **566.** 8H75. **564.** 4H132. **565.** Janney, p. 271, from Timothy Leary, *Flashbacks* (Los Angeles: J.P. Tarcher, 1983), pp. 190-91. **566.** See, for example, Nina Burleigh's biography of Ms. Meyer, *A Very Private Woman: The Unsolved Murder of Presidential Mistress Mary Meyer* (New York: Bantam Books, 1998), p. 204. **567.** Groden, op. cit., p. 111; Marrs, op. cit., p. 426; Israel, op. cit., p. 410. **568.** There were more anomalies in the case; see, for example, Ventura, op. cit., pp. 203-6, and Sara Jordan, "Who Killed Dorothy Kilgallen," *Midwest Today*, October 21, 2007. **569.** HSCA Security Classified Testimony, No. 32, p. 148, May 16, 1978. **570.** Dick Russell, op. cit., p. 580. **571.** Twyman, op. cit., p. 643. **572.** See Jim Marrs, "Ex-Agent 6th to die in a 6-month span," Fort Worth *Star-Telegram*, November 10, 1977. **573.** Curt Gentry, *J. Edgar Hoover: The Man and the Secrets* (New York: W.W. Norton, 1991), p. 546n. **574.** Talbot, *Brothers*, pp. 109, 398. **575.** Twyman, op. cit., pp. 427, 454, 482; Fonzi, op. cit., p. 380. **576.** Twyman 1995 interview with Walton, in Twyman, op. cit., p. 471. **577.** E. Howard Hunt, *American Spy: My Secret History in the CIA, Watergate and Beyond* (Hoboken, NJ: John Wiley & Sons, 2007), pp. 126-147. **578.** WR, p. 109. **579.** Bugliosi, main book, p. 395. **580.** 1HSCA329. **581.** Finck testimony, Part 3, February 25, 1969, p. 23. **582.** *Newsweek*, November 22, 1993, p. 73. **583.** Arthur Schlesinger Jr. Journal, November 23, 1963 – 5:15 a.m., 363, Wesleyan University Special Collections and Archives [WM-WU], Middleton, CT, quoted in Gillon, op. cit., p. 214. **584.** Tuckerman, Spalding and Mrs. Kennedy's accounts of JFK's appearance in casket: Manchester, op. cit., p. 443; Bugliosi, main book, p. 199. **585.** 5H211. **586.** Dick Russell, op. cit., p. 684. **587.** Bugliosi endnotes, p. 447. **588.** Id., p. 644. **589.** G.J.A. O'Toole, *Encyclopedia of American Intelligence and Espionage: From the Revolutionary War to the Present* (New York: Facts of File, 1988), p. 298. **590.** Erik Hedegaard, "The Last Confessions of E. Howard Hunt," *Rolling Stone*, April 5, 2007.

Notes to Chapter 4

1. Quoted in Groden and Livingstone, op. cit., p. 405. **2.** Douglas Valentine, *The Strength of the Wolf: The Secret History of America's War on Drugs* (New York: Verso, 2004), p. 420. **3.** Anson, op. cit., p. 294. **4.** Summers, *Not in Your Lifetime,* p. 369. **5.** Summers, op. cit., p. 301-2. **6.** "High Officers in the Armed Forces Concerned Over U.S. Defense Policy," *U.S. News and World Report,* July 15, 1963. **7.** Peter Dale Scott and Jonathan Marshall, *Cocaine Politics: Drugs, Armies, and the CIA in Central America* (Berkeley: University of California Press, 1991), p. 121; see also Warren Hinckle and William W. Turner, *The Fish Is Red: The Story of the Secret War Against Castro* (New York: Harper & Row, 1981), p. 201. **8.** Arthur M. Schlesinger Jr., *A Thousand Days: John F. Kennedy in the White House* (Boston: Houghton Mifflin, 1965), p. 428. **9.** A.J. Langguth, *Hidden Terrors* (New York: Pantheon Books, 1978), p. 134; Seymour M. Hersh, *The Dark Side of Camelot* (Boston: Little, Brown, 1997), pp. 5, 234. Richard Reeves, *President Kennedy: Profile of Power* (New York: Simon & Schuster, 1993), p. 178, also mentions amphetamine injections "for energy." **10.** Schlesinger, *A Thousand Days,* p. 96; Richard Reeves, *President Kennedy: Profile of Power* (New York: Simon & Schuster, 1993), p. 42. **11.** Reeves, op. cit., pp. 146, 43. **12.** Robert Dallek, *Flawed Giant: Lyndon Johnson and His Times 1961-1973* (New York: Oxford University Press, 1998), p. 399. **13.** Scelso testimony, op. cit., p. 151. **14.** Lane, *Last Word,* p. 137. **15.** Talk given by John Judge at a one-day conference entitled *The Fourth Reich in America.* **16.** Livingstone, *High Treason 2,* p. 71. **17.** *Saturday Evening Post,* January 14, 1967, p. 69. **18.** Edward Jay Epstein, *Inquest: The Warren Commission and the Establishment of Truth* (New York: Viking, 1966), pp. 123, 125; WR, p. 105. **19.** Mantik, "The Medical Evidence Decoded," in Fetzer, *Murder in Dealey Plaza,* p. 245. **20.** For more on this, see Mark Lane, "Was the CIA Involved in Dallas?," in Frazier, *Assassination Science,* p. 218. **21.** 5H563. **22.** 7H451. **23.** Kenneth P. O'Donnell and David F. Powers, with Joseph McCarthy, *Johnny, We Hardly Knew Ye: Memories of John Fitzgerald Kennedy* (Boston: Little, Brown, 1972), p. 36. **24.** See, for example, 5H190. **25.** Quoted in Shenon, pp. 309-11, 549. **26.** Harold Weisberg, *Whitewash IV: Post Assassination Transcript* (Hyattstown, MD: self-published, 1966), p. 21. **27.** Shenon, op. cit., pp. 474, 502; Bugliosi, main book, p. 455. **28.** *USA Today,* July 3, 1997, and Mantik, "The Medical Evidence Decoded," in Fetzer, *Murder in Dealey Plaza,* p. 230; WR, p. 3. **29.** James M. Naughton, "Ford Vows Curb on Social Outlays," *New York Times,* September 14, 1975, p. 1. **30.** Marrs, op. cit., p. 466. **31.** Lane, *Plausible Denial,* p. 43. **32.** Marrs, op. cit., p. 466; Canfield and Weberman, op. cit., pp. 33-4. **33.** Summers, op. cit., p. 299. **34.** Talbot, *Brothers,* p. 87. **35.** Fonzi, op. cit., p. 334. **36.** Janney, op. cit, p. 312. **37.** Shenon, op. cit., p. 538. **38.** Scelso testimony, pp. 74, 168; Col. King was the original head of Operation Success, the CIA operation to overthrow Jacobo Árbenz in Guatemala in 1954. He was chief of the Western

Hemisphere Division of the CIA at the time of the assassination, and was involved in the CIA's Castro and Trujillo assassination plots; see Gerard Colby and Charlotte Dennett, *Thy Will Be Done* (New York: HarperCollins, 1995), pp. 325, 348, 354, 738-40. **39.** Michael C. Piper, *Final Judgment: The Missing Link in the JFK Assassination* (Liberty Lobby, 1998), p. 103. **40.** Fonzi, op. cit., p. 390; Talbot, *The Devil's Chessboard,* p. 501; Summers, op. cit., p. 593, note to page 438. **41.** "Notes in Draft re: ZR/RIFLE Project," cited in Valentine, op. cit., p. 226. **42.** William F. Pepper, *Orders to Kill: The Truth Behind the Murder of Martin Luther King* (New York: Carroll & Graf, 1995), p. 162. **43.** *New York Times,* March 10, 1975, p. 9; cited in Anson, op. cit., p. 300. **44.** Charles Rappleye and Ed Becker, *All American Mafioso: The Johnny Rosselli Story* (New York: Doubleday, 1991), p. 248. **45.** Hancock, op. cit., quoted in J. Ventura et al., op. cit., pp. 72, 260. **46.** Richard J. Barnet, *Roots of War* (New York: Atheneum, 1972), pp. 294-95. **47.** HSCA Security Classified Testimony, James B. Wilcott, No. 29, pp. 9-27, March 22, 1978. **48.** Talbot, *Brothers,* p. 400. **49.** Sam and Chuck Giancana, *Double Cross: The Explosive, Inside Story of the Mobster Who Controlled America* (New York: Warner Books, 1992), pp. 333-34. **50.** HSCA Record No. 180-10142-10383, HSCA Segregated CIA Collection, No. 757, repeated at No. 1928. **51.** Dick Russell, op. cit, p. 288. **52.** Nikita Krushchev, *Krushchev Remembers* (New York: Bantam Books, 1971), pp. 551-52; cited in Anson, op. cit., p. 266. **53.** Brown, op. cit., p. 317. **54.** Dick Russell, op. cit., pp. 236-37. **55.** Talbot, *Brothers,* p. 4. **56.** David Halberstam, *The Best and the Brightest* (New York: Random House, 1972), p. 45. **57.** Talbot, *Brothers,* p. 173. **58.** Quoted in Seymour Melman, *Our Depleted Society* (New York: Holt, Rinehart & Winston, 1965), p. 223. **59.** Twyman interview with Hemming in Twyman, op. cit., p. 661. **60.** Harold Weisberg, *Post Mortem: JFK Assassination Cover-Up Smashed!* (Frederick, MD: Self-published, 1975), p. 233. **61.** Wood in Fetzer, *Murder in Dealey Plaza,* p. 22; Dick Russell, op. cit., pp. 569-70; Twyman, op. cit., p. 533. **62.** Dick Russell, op. cit., p. 570. **63.** Peter Dale Scott, "The Hidden Government Group Linking JFK, Watergate, Iran-Contra and 9/11," essay at maryferrell.org. **64.** Dick Russell, op. cit., p. 708. **65.** *The Men Who Killed Kennedy,* Part 6; see also The Suspicious Deaths, above. According to mcadams.posc.mu.edu, R. Robin Palmer and Allan Eaglesham wrote to Dr. J. D. Rose, editor of *The Fourth Decade,* in 1997 casting doubts on Lt. Col. Marvin's credibility. **66.** L. Fletcher Prouty, "Green Berets And the CIA," *The New Republic,* August 30, 1969, pp. 9-10. **67.** Mantik, "The Medical Evidence Decoded," in Fetzer, *Murder in Dealey Plaza,* p. 286-87. **68.** Pepper, op. cit., p. 419. **69.** William F. Pepper, *An Act of State: The Execution of Martin Luther King* (New York: Verso, 2003), p. 207; Pepper, *Orders to Kill,* pp. 427,429; also Pepper's talk at the Modern Times Bookstore in San Francisco on February 4, 2003, reproduced at maryferrell.org. **70.** Sloan, *Breaking the Silence,* pp. 175-76. **71.** Dick Russell, op. cit., pp. 110,127, from Charles Willoughby papers, MacArthur Archives, Norfolk, VA. **72.** Sterling Seagrave, *The Marcos Dy-*

nasty (New York: Harper & Row, 1988), p. 250. **73.** Id., pp. 147, 152. **74.** *Assassination Plots*, pp. 37, 43-5; Dick Russell, op. cit., p. 559. **75.** Dick Russell, op. cit., p. 785, note 14; Marrs, op. cit., p. 206. **76.** Piper, op. cit., p. 234. **77.** Bugliosi, main book, p. 1131; Bert Shipp, Oral History Collection, Sixth Floor Museum at Dealey Plaza. **78.** Bugliosi, main book, p. 1256; Foreign Broadcast Information Service, *USSR and East Europe Review*, November 26, 1963. **79.** David Rothkopf, *Superclass: The Global Power Elite and the World They Are Making* (New York: Farrar, Straus & Giroux, 2009), p. 202. **80.** Seagrave, op. cit., p. 3. **81.** Alfred Steinberg, *Sam Johnson's Boy: A Close Up of the President from Texas* (New York: Macmillan, 1968), pp. 577, 601. **82.** Robert Caro, *The Years of Lyndon Johnson: The Passage of Power* (New York: Alfred A. Knopf, 2012), pp. 524-25. **83.** Id., p. 524. **84.** *The Men Who Killed Kennedy*, Part 1. **85.** Livingstone, *High Treason 2*, p. 115. **86.** Lyndon Johnson affidavit, 5H564. **87.** Caro, op. cit., p. 327. **88.** Cartha DeLoach's 1975 testimony to the Church Committee. **89.** Max Holland (ed.), *The Kennedy Assassination Tapes* (New York: Alfred A. Knopf, 2004), p. 309n. **90.** Lifton, op. cit., p. 306. **91.** Douglas Caddy, Esq., "Letter to Mr. Stephen S. Trott, Assistant Attorney General, Criminal Division, U.S. Department of Justice, August 8, 1984." **92.** Vince Palamara, *The Third Alternative – Survivor's Guilt: The Secret Service and the JFK Murder* (Pittsburgh: self-published, 1993), p. 53. **93.** Donald Gibson, *The Kennedy Assassination Cover-up* (New York: Nova Science Publications, Inc., 2000), p. 67, citing Peter Collier and David Horowitz, *The Rockefellers: An American Dynasty* (New York: Holt, Rinehart and Winston, 1976), pp. 410, 416. **94.** Talbot, *The Devil's Chessboard*, p. 560; Dillon memo to JFK, October 28, 1963, JFK Library. **95.** Talbot, *The Devil's Chessboard*, pp. 170, 199, 583-84. **96.** Talbot, op. cit., p. 584; no references. **97.** A.J. Langguth, *Our Vietnam: The War 1954-1975* (New York: Simon & Schuster, 2000), p. 188. **98.** 23H831, report of FBI interview with Nixon by John F. Malone, assistant director of the New York office. **99.** John H. Davis, *Mafia Kingfish: Carlos Marcello and the Assassination of John F. Kennedy* (New York: McGraw-Hill, 1989), pp. 413-14. **100.** *Esquire*, November 1973. **101.** Jules Witcover in *Saturday Evening Post*, February 25, 1967. **102.** L. Fletcher Prouty, *JFK: The CIA, Vietnam, and the Plot to Assassinate John F. Kennedy* (New York: Carol Publishing Group/Birch Lane Press, 1992), pp. 119, 350-51. **103.** H.R. Haldeman, with Joseph DiMona, *The Ends of Power* (New York: Times Books, 1978), pp. 38-9. **104.** Marrs, op. cit., p. 269. In his endnotes (pp. 547-48), Bugliosi says that a document stating that Ruby was performing certain functions for Nixon's staff in the 1940s was phony. **105.** Davis, op. cit., p. 410. **106.** Trumbull Higgins, *The Perfect Failure: Kennedy, Eisenhower and the CIA at the Bay of Pigs* (New York: W.W. Norton, 1987). **107.** Daniel Ellsberg, *Papers On the War* (New York: Simon & Schuster, 1972) p., 239. **108.** Langguth, *Our Vietnam*, p. 154. **109.** Ellsberg, op. cit., p. 56. **110.** Daniel Ellsberg, *Secrets: A Memoir of Vietnam and the Pentagon Papers* (New York: Viking Press, 2002), p. 397. **111.** Bugliosi, main book, p. 1328; *New York Times*, October

5, 1997, p. 16, quoting from Ernest R. May and Philip D. Zelikow (eds.), *The Kennedy Tapes: Inside the White House during the Cuban Missile Crisis* (Cambridge, MA: Harvard University Press, 1997); Dino Brugioni, *Eyeball to Eyeball: The Inside Story of the Cuban Missile Crisis* (New York: Random House, 1992), pp. 266-67; also *The New Yorker*, June 19, 1995. **112.** Talbot, *Brothers*, pp. 146, 172, 66, 165. **113.** Allen Mikaelin, *Medal of Honor: Profiles of America's Military Heroes From the Civil War to the Present* (New York: Hyperion Books, 2003), p. 131; H.R. McMaster, *Dereliction of Duty: Lyndon Johnson, Robert McNamara, the Joint Chiefs of Staff, and the Lies that Led to Vietnam* (New York: HarperCollins, 1997), p. 64. **114.** Arthur M. Schlesinger Jr., *Robert Kennedy and His Times* (Boston: Houghton Miflin, 1978), p. 450. **115.** *Life* magazine special issue, *The Greatest Unsolved Mysteries of All Time*, 2014, p. 91. **116.** Peter Dale Scott, "The Vietnam War and the CIA-Financial Establishment," in Mark Selden (ed.), *Re-making Asia: Essays on the American Uses of Power* (New York: Pantheon Books, 1974), p. 127. **117.** Gibson, op. cit., p. 72; cf. Collier and Horowitz, op. cit., p. 412. **118.** Gibson, op. cit., p. 74. **119.** Ferdinand Lundberg, *The Rockefeller Syndrome* (Secaucus, NJ: Lyle Stuart, 1975), p. 361. **120.** Gibson, op. cit., p. 87. **121.** Talbot, *The Devil's Chessboard*, pp. 555-56. **122.** *Life*, July 6, 1962, pp. 31-3. **123.** James Earl Ray, *Tennessee Waltz* (St. Andrews, Tennessee, 1987), pp. 232-33. **124.** Livingstone, *High Treason 2*, p. 437. **125.** Benson, op. cit., p. 139. **126.** Benson, op. cit., p. 235; Dick Russell, op. cit., p. 236; Palamara, *The Third Alternative*, p. 35, cited in Twyman, op. cit., pp. 768, 769n. **127.** Bugliosi, main book, p. 407. **128.** Lamar Waldron, with Thom Hartmann, *Legacy of Secrecy* (Berkeley, CA: Counterpoint, 2008), p. 462. **129.** Talbot, *Brothers*, p. 303. **130.** Walt Brown, *The Guns of Texas Are Upon You* (Williamsport, PA: Last Hurrah Press, 2005), p. 224. **131.** Weiner, op. cit., p. 186. **132.** Stanley Karnow, *Vietnam: A History* (New York: Viking/ Penguin, 1983), p. 702. **133.** Based on Krulak's memo as it appears in *The Pentagon Papers* (New York: Bantam Books, 1971), pp. 204-5. **134.** Ellsberg, *Secrets*, p. 53. **135.** James Perloff, *The Shadows of Power: The Council on Foreign Relations and the American Decline* (Appleton, WI: Western Islands, 1988, 1989), p. 127. **136.** Scott, *Deep Politics*, p. 338, note 29. **137.** See Lawrence H. Shoup and William Minter, *Imperial Brain Trust: The Council on Foreign Relations and United States Foreign Policy* (New York: Monthly Review Press, 1977), p. 61. **138.** Barry Goldwater, *With No Apologies* (New York: William Morrow, 1979), p. 278. **139.** L. Fletcher Prouty, *The Secret Team: The CIA and Its Allies in Control of the United States and the World* (Englewood Cliffs, NJ: Prentice-Hall, 1973), p. 195. **140.** David Horowitz (ed.), *Corporations and the Cold War* (New York and London: Bertrand Russell Peace Foundation, 1969), p. 30. **141.** Gibson, op. cit., p. 72. **142.** Quoted in Prouty, *The Secret Team*, p. 195. **143.** See, for example, Andreas von Rétyi, *Bilderberger: The Timetable of the New World Order*, 2006, quoted in Rothkopf, *Superclass*, pp. 276-7; David C. Korten, *When Corporations Rule the World*, (W. Hartford, CT: Kumarian Press, and San Francisco: Berrett-Koehler

Publishers 1995), p. 137; Peter Thompson, "Bilderberg and the West," in Holly Sklar (ed.), *Trilateralism: The Trilateral Commission and Elite Planning for World Management* (Boston: South End Press, 1980). **144.** Twyman interview with Prouty, in Twyman, op. cit., p. 536. **145.** Blum, op. cit., p. 128. **146.** *Final Report of the Select Committee to Study Governmental Operations with Respect to Intelligence Agencies* (Church Committee Report): *The Investigation of the Assassination of President Kennedy: Performance of the Intelligence Agencies,* 94th Congress, 2nd session, Washington, D.C., Government Printing Office, 1976, Book I, pp. 455, 193. **147.** 367 U.S. 643, 81 S.Ct. 1684, quoted in Melvin M. Belli, *The Belli Files: Reflections on the Wayward Law* (Englewood Cliffs, NJ: Prentice-Hall, 1982), pp. 170-71.

Suggestions for Further Reading

Benson, Michael. *Who's Who in the JFK Assassination: An A to Z Encyclopedia.* New York: Citadel Press/Carol Publishing Group, 1993.

Blum, William. *Rogue State: A Guide to the World's Only Superpower.* Monroe, ME: Common Courage Press, 2000, 2005.

-------, *Killing Hope: U.S. and C.I.A. Interventions Since World War II.* Monroe, ME: Common Courage Press, 1995, 2008.

Brown, Walt. *The Warren Omission: A Micro Study of the Methods and Failures of the Warren Commission.* Wilmington, DE: Delmax, 1996.

Evans, Rowland, and Robert Novak. *Lyndon B. Johnson: The Exercise of Power.* New York: The New American Library, 1966.

Garrison, Jim. *A Heritage of Stone.* New York: G.P. Putnam's Sons, 1970.

Grant, R.G. *Assassinations: History's Most Shocking Moments of Murder, Betrayal, and Madness.* Pleasantville, New York: Reader's Digest/Toucan Books, 2004.

Hinckle, Warren. *If You Have a Lemon, Make Lemonade.* New York: G.P. Putnam's Sons, 1973.

Kurtz, Michael. *The JFK Assassination Debates.* Lawrence, KS: University Press of Kansas, 2006.

Lundberg, Ferdinand. *The Rich and the Super-Rich: A Study in the Power of Money Today.* New York: Lyle Stuart, 1968.

Marchetti, Victor, and John D. Marks. *The CIA and the Cult of Intelligence.* New York: Alfred A. Knopf, 1974.

Marks, Stanley J., and Ethel M. Marks. *Yes, Americans, a Conspiracy Murdered JFK!* San Marino, CA: Bureau of International Affairs, 1992.

McCoy, Alfred. *The Politics of Heroin: CIA Complicity in the Global Drug* Trade. New York: Lawrence Hill Books, 1991.

McKnight, Gerald. *Breach of Trust: How the Warren Commission Failed the Nation and Why.* Lawrence: University of Kansas Press, 2005.

Morrow, Robert D. *First Hand Knowledge: How I Participated in the CIA-Mafia Murder of President Kennedy.* New York: S.P.I. Books, 1992.

Noguchi, Thomas T., M.D., with Joseph DiMona. *Coroner.* New York: Simon & Schuster, 1983.

Prados, John. *Presidents' Secret Wars: CIA and Pentagon Covert Operations Since World War II*. New York: William Morrow & Co., 1986.

Scheim, David E. *Contract on America: The Mafia Murder of President John F. Kennedy*. New York: Shapolsky Publishers, 1988 (originally published in 1983).

Smith, Joseph Burkholder. *Portrait of a Cold Warrior*. New York: G.P. Putnam's Sons, 1976.

Smith, Matthew. *Conspiracy: The Plot to Stop the Kennedys*. New York: Citadel Press/Kensington Publishing Corporation, 2005.

Trento, Joseph J. *The Secret History of the CIA*. Roseville, Calif.: Prima, 2001.

Turner, William, and Jonn Christian. *The Assassination of Robert F. Kennedy: A Searching Look at the Conspiracy and Cover-up 1968-78*. New York: Random House, 1978 (republished by Thunder's Mouth Press in 1993 as *The Assassination of Robert F. Kennedy: The Conspiracy and Coverup*).

Weisberg, Harold. *Never Again! The Government Conspiracy in the JFK Assassination*. New York: Carroll & Graf, 1995.

Wise, David. *The American Police State: The Government Against the People*. New York: Random House, 1976.

Index

C

E

F

G

N

S

T

Y

Z